Acknowledgmen

I wish to express my love and gratitude to my dearly departed friend Jean, who first introduced me to vegetarianism many years ago; to my partner Zach, for his love and support; to Josh Meckel, my computer technical expert, for his brilliant website construction and management skills; to Louise Gagnon, my sous chef and recipe tester; to my Gentle Chef Cooking Group administrators on Facebook, Kathryn Hill, Sandra Pope Hays, Martina Moore, Isabelle Nuenninghoff; and to all of my readers for their continuing support and encouragement.

Also by The Gentle Chef:

The Gentle Chef Cookbook
Vegan Cuisine for the Ethical Gourmet

The Non-Dairy Evolution Cookbook
A Modernist Culinary Approach to Plant-Based Dairy-Free Foods

Seitan and Beyond
Gluten and Soy-Based Meat Analogues for the Ethical Gourmet

The Vegan Eggz Cookbook
Plant-Based Egg Alternatives for the Ethical Gourmet
(Digital Only: www.thegentlechef.com)

Nuts About Almonds! - A Mini-Cookbook of Fresh and Cultured Almond Curd Cheeses
(Digital Only: www.thegentlechef.com)

The Gentle Sea Cookbook
Plant-Based Seafood Inspired Recipes for the Compassionate Soul
(Digital Only: www.thegentlechef.com)

Written and published by Skye Michael Conroy

Email: thegentlechef@gmail.com

Website: https://www.thegentlechef.com

"The word "veganism" denotes a philosophy and way of living which seeks to exclude - as far as is possible and practical - all forms of exploitation and cruelty to animals for food, clothing or any other purpose; and by extension, promotes the development and use of animal-free alternatives for the benefit of animals, humans and the environment. In dietary terms, it denotes the practice of dispensing with all products derived wholly or partly from animals." ...The Vegan Society

Compassion (derived from Latin and meaning: "to suffer together with") is a profound human virtue and emotion prompted by the pain of other living beings and is ranked as one of the greatest virtues in numerous philosophies and spiritual traditions. More vigorous than empathy, the feeling of compassion commonly gives rise to an active desire to alleviate another's suffering.

Sentience implies the ability to experience pleasure and pain. As vegans, we believe that all sentient beings are entitled, at the very least, to the right not to be subjected to unnecessary suffering.

This understanding of sentience and the desire to alleviate suffering is the primary motivator for embracing veganism and a strict plant-based diet.

Table of Contents

Soy-Based Meat Alternatives

More Sauces and Gravies

Gentle Seafoods

Breakfast and Brunch

Soups and Stews

Appetizers and Small Plates

Accompaniments

Foreword

Let me start off by saying that this is not a vegan health food cookbook. It was never intended to be. While I do enjoy the health benefits a plant-based diet offers, I became vegan for the benefit and well-being of the animals. Please don't misunderstand, human health is very important, and it inspires many people to embrace a plant-based diet, but that is not the primary goal of veganism. In order to win people over to vegan cuisine, I aim for the best flavors and textures and not always the healthiest options. As a chef, I love preparing rich, comforting and satisfying meals.

My journey as a vegan chef started as a non-professional hobby, from which my first Gentle Chef Cookbook was published in 2012, but then evolved as I began to study the culinary arts in depth. After receiving formal plant-based chef training and certification, I continued to experiment on my own with plant-based ingredients and ultimately organized my recipes into several more specialized cookbooks.

My cookbooks are dedicated to breaking the reliance on commercially prepared and processed vegan foods as much as possible by providing detailed instructions for preparing delicious meals that you and your whole family will enjoy. Detailed instructions are included in this cookbook for preparing many of the components of my recipes with unprocessed, wholesome ingredients. My philosophy is: "everything in moderation". Even plant-based foods can be unhealthy and fattening if not consumed sensibly.

You won't find nutrition information included with the recipes because the cookbook wasn't written for individuals monitoring calorie and nutrient intake. However, the recipes were created using wholesome ingredients as much as possible and refined ingredients were included only when absolutely necessary to achieve proper textures.

Regarding food allergies and sensitivities: This cookbook utilizes a wide variety of plant ingredients, including those that can provoke allergy or sensitivity in certain individuals. I rely heavily on gluten and soy as the foundation for many of the meat analogue recipes. Soy and tree nuts are used extensively in the non-dairy chapter. If you have sensitivity to either gluten, soy or tree nuts, obviously those specific recipes are not suitable for you. I recommend doing some research to find recipes that specifically benefit individuals with your particular ingredient allergy or sensitivity.

Vegan cooking is an adventure and I invite you to share the adventure with me. Peace begins on our plates... Chef Skye Michael Conroy

Glossary of Cooking Terms and Special Ingredients

Some cooking terms and ingredients in this cookbook may be very familiar while others may not be familiar at all. Before attempting the recipes, it's helpful to familiarize yourself with these terms and recipe ingredients and understand what they are and why they are being used. Some recipe ingredients can be prepared at home.

Agar powder is a tasteless seaweed derivative and a widely used plant-based replacement for gelatin. Only the powdered form is used in the recipes in this cookbook. Agar powder can be purchased in some health food and natural food stores or mail ordered through the internet.

All-purpose flour simply refers to common white flour. All-purpose flour is made from a blend of high-gluten hard wheat and low-gluten soft wheat. It differs from whole wheat flour in that the bran and germ have been removed from the wheat kernel (berry) prior to grinding into flour. Unbleached all-purpose flour undergoes less processing than bleached all-purpose flour (which is usually bleached chemically) and is thus a better choice. Unbleached flour bleaches naturally as it ages.

Browning liquid is used to create a rich brown color in soups, stews and gravies. In meat analogues, especially those approximating beef, it is used as a color enhancer to produce a more appetizing appearance. My own recipe for natural browning liquid made with organic sugar can be found on page 28. Commercial versions such as Gravy Master™ and Kitchen Bouquet™ can be found in most markets where jar gravy is located.

Coconut oil, refined provides the solid fat essential for thickening many of the non-dairy products in this book. In many respects, it shares striking similarities to dairy butterfat, but without the cholesterol (and animal exploitation). Coconut oil becomes semi-solid at room temperature and very solid when chilled; therefore, it must be melted for proper measurement in recipes. This can be done by removing the metal lid from the jar and placing the jar into a microwave to heat for 30 seconds to 1 minute (depending upon the solidity of the coconut oil). Avoid overheating the oil, especially when preparing cultured foods. Alternately, the jar can be placed in about an inch of simmering water and melted in the same manner. Repeated melting and re-hardening of the oil will not harm it.

The amount of coconut oil used in the recipes has been carefully calculated to produce the best results. Although it may be tempting to reduce or eliminate the oil for health and weight control purposes, this is not recommended. The non-dairy products will not thicken or set properly and this will adversely affect the finished texture. It is much better to moderate your consumption of non-dairy foods than to tamper with oil ratios in the recipes. The best creams and cheeses, whether dairy or non-dairy, must contain fat to carry flavor and provide texture.

Virgin coconut oil is not recommended for making non-dairy foods except for ice cream and other desserts. While in most cases I would always recommend less-refined or less-processed ingredients, this is not the case when it comes to coconut oil used in most non-dairy foods - unless you're okay with your butter, creams and cheeses having a distinct coconut undertaste. Refining removes the coconut flavor and aroma from coconut oil and therefore is a better option. Save the virgin coconut oil for sweets and treats.

De-scented food-grade cocoa butter has properties similar to coconut oil and could potentially be used as a replacement (which would be a good option for those allergic to coconuts). However, it is not available to me locally and is very expensive through the internet; therefore, I haven't had the opportunity to experiment with it at this time. Sustainably-sourced palm oil is another potential alternative but I have never worked with it.

Refined coconut oil can be found in many larger supermarket chains, health food stores and natural food stores or purchased online through food retail websites.

Cooking oil refers to vegetable/plant oils that can withstand high heat. The best oils for high temperature cooking are refined (mild) olive oil, safflower, sunflower, canola, peanut, corn and soybean.

Extra-Firm Tofu is made from soymilk that has been coagulated and pressed into blocks. It should not be confused with extra-firm silken tofu, which has a custard-like texture.

For the purposes of the meat and seafood analogue preparation in this cookbook, only extra-firm water-packed tofu is used. Extra-firm tofu is sold in plastic tub containers filled with water and will always be found in the refrigerated section of the market.

Before using extra-firm block tofu in the seafood analogue recipes in this cookbook, it will need to be pressed to remove the excess water. This can be done using the standard method of pressing between absorbent lint-free towels, such as paper towels, or by pressing using a tofu press (see *Preparing Tofu for the Recipes* on page 26). The tofu press is a spring-loaded device which effectively presses water from a U.S. standard-size block of commercial water-packed tofu.

Garbanzo bean flour (also known as chickpea flour, besan flour, ceci flour or gram flour) is a gluten-free flour produced by grinding dried garbanzo beans. It is very affordable and can be found in most health food stores or natural markets. Soy flour, fava bean flour or yellow pea flour can be substituted, if more convenient. Garbanzo bean flour can easily be prepared at home by grinding dry garbanzo beans in a high-powered blender and then sifting to remove any stray larger particles.

Glucomannan powder, also known as konjac root powder, is the special ingredient used in this cookbook for preparing seafood analogues. Glucomannan is a pure soluble fiber derived from konjac root. It has no protein, no fat, no carbohydrates, and is gluten-free. As a food additive, it is used as an emulsifier and thickener. As a food ingredient, it is used commercially and at home for preparing Japanese shirataki noodles.

The aroma of freshly prepared konjac has a distinct seafood-like aroma. Glucomannan can sometimes be found in health food stores (where it is often sold as a diet aid), but is most reliably purchased through online sources such as ModernistPantry.com and Amazon.com.

Guar gum, also called *guaran*, is a natural substance derived from the ground seeds of the guar plant which grows primarily in Pakistan and the northern regions of India. Food gums, such as guar, belong to a group of stabilizing compounds called polysaccharides. It is used as a thickener and stabilizer in making non-dairy butter and salad dressings; it adds viscosity and stretch to cheese melts; and it prevents ice crystallization in ice cream. Without guar gum as a stabilizer, non-dairy ice cream would become coarse, icy and hard due to the growth of ice crystals as the mixture freezes. Guar gum can be purchased in some supermarkets, in most health food and natural food stores, or purchased online through food retail websites such as ModernistPantry.com and Amazon.com. Guar gum can be replaced with an equal amount of sodium alginate or xanthan gum if desired.

High-powered blenders, such as the Vitamix® or Blendtec®, are required for processing cashews and other thick ingredients such as tofu. Standard blenders simply don't have the power to churn through the ingredients used to make cheeses and you can quickly burn out the motor.

A bonus feature of the Vitamix™ blenders is the "tamper tool" which can be inserted through the lid. This helps keep thick mixtures turning in the blades, without having to start and stop the blender as frequently to stir.

However, one drawback to the high-powered blenders is their exorbitant price, but as the old saying goes, "you get what you pay for". They're definitely worth the investment and will save you countless hours of time and frustration in the kitchen. I have heard that the Ninja® blender and Oster® Versa blender are affordable and effective alternatives; however, I haven't had the opportunity to work with these appliances.

Immersion blender, or stick blender, is a kitchen appliance that blend ingredients or purées food in the container in which they are being prepared. An immersion blender is recommended for preparing vegan mayonnaise and butter according the recipes in this cookbook. An immersion blender is distinguished from a standard/high-powered blender and food processor, as the latter two require that the food be placed in a special container for processing. It is also distinguished from a rotary hand mixer, which does not chop the food as it is blended.

Kala namak, also known as Himalayan black salt, is an Indian salt with a high mineral content, most notably sulfur, which gives it its characteristic and pungent "hard-boiled egg" smell. Oddly enough, it is pink in color when dry but turns black when moistened. It is used in eggless egg foods as it imparts a cooked egg flavor and aroma. Be advised, that if you detest the sulfurous odor of hard-boiled eggs, you probably will not care for this salt. Kala namak can be found in Indian food stores as well as online. Himalayan pink salt is not the same thing, so this can make purchasing rather confusing since kala namak is also pink when dry. Specifically look for the name kala namak or Himalayan black salt.

Kappa Carrageenan is a seaweed derivative that has been safely used in cooking for hundreds of years as a thickening, stabilizing and gelling agent. Kappa carrageenan, which is molecularly different from iota and lambda carrageenan, is used as a firming agent for the Melty Mozzarella cheese, Camembrie cheese and Crock Beer Cheese in this cookbook, due to its ability to melt when reheated. It is also used as a firming ingredient in some of my dessert recipes. Agar and food gums cannot be used as a substitute in these recipes. Kappa carrageenan is only available online through specialty food ingredient retailers such as Modernist Pantry and Amazon.com. For safety information regarding carrageenan, please visit my GentleChef.com website and click on the "Resources" section in the upper right hand corner.

Lactic Acid Powder is used as an alternative to lemon juice for adding flavor, acidity and tanginess to non-dairy foods. Lactic acid is sometimes referred to as "milk acid", since lactic acid is the compound responsible for causing milk to sour and since it was first isolated in a laboratory from sour milk in 1780. Lactic acid is a by-product of the fermentation of sugar by the lactobacillus bacteria.

Commercial lactic acid powder is usually produced by the fermentation of carbohydrates from plants (rather than being derived from milk), but always double-check your source before purchasing. It has advantages over lemon juice in many non-dairy applications since it is the precise flavor produced in cultured foods, whereas lemon juice yields a sour citrus flavor.

Liquid lactic acid is commonly used as a pH buffer for home brewing beer. Unless its source is indicated, it may be derived from dairy, which is unsuitable for vegans. Citric acid powder can be used as a substitute for lactic acid powder but will not provide the same cultured dairy flavor.

Lactic acid can be mail ordered through ModernistPantry.com and other online sources such as Amazon.com.

Lecithin, simply stated, is a natural, waxy substance derived from the processing of organic soybeans. It is an essential ingredient for promoting the emulsification of soymilk or nut milk with oil when making non-dairy butter; in other words, it binds the oil and milk together. Soy lecithin can be purchased in liquid, powder or granular forms and can be found in most health food and natural food stores, or online through food retail websites. Granular lecithin does not dissolve well, so I highly recommend grinding it into a fine powder before using. In my experience, liquid lecithin produces better results over its dry counterpart.

For those who are allergic to soy, sunflower lecithin, which is derived from sunflower seeds, can be substituted for soy lecithin. However, it does not possess the rich golden color of soy lecithin. In fact, liquid sunflower lecithin has the color of melted chocolate while the dry version has a soft beige tint, so expect a color variation in the butter when using sunflower lecithin. Unless you have an allergy to soy, I highly recommend the soy lecithin over the sunflower lecithin.

Liquid smoke is a water-based seasoning distilled from real wood smoke and is used in meat analogues to provide a "cold-smoked" flavor. Personally, I don't feel it quite captures the intensity of actual cold-smoking, so I tend to use it in generous amounts. Some people are sensitive to smoke flavors, or don't care for smoke flavors at all, so it can be reduced or replaced with equal amounts of water as desired, although this will significantly alter the intended flavor of the meat analogue or finished dish.

"Hickory" liquid smoke and "mesquite" liquid smoke are the most commonly available smoke flavors, but other wood flavors are available if you do a little searching. For most recipes, the "hickory" flavor is recommended and the "mesquite" flavor reserved for Southwestern/Tex-Mex and South American cuisine. Liquid smoke can be found in most major grocery stores, usually alongside other condiments and marinades. It can also be purchased through the internet. If you enjoy true smoked foods, as I do, and you have a cold-smoker at home, the meat analogues can be briefly smoked to add that much desired smoke intensity.

Mirin is an essential condiment used in Japanese cuisine and is an ingredient in a few of the sauces and marinades in this cookbook. It is a type of rice wine similar to sake, but with a lower alcohol content and higher sugar content (for this reason, it is sometimes referred to as "sweet mirin").

Mellow white miso paste is a seasoning which originated in Japan and is produced by the fermentation of soybeans (or chickpeas or barley) with salt and the fungus "kōji" (*Aspergillis oryzae*). Miso adds umami (a Japanese word used to describe a pleasant savory flavor) to foods. Mellow white miso paste is used as a seasoning in many of the meat analogues and non-dairy cheeses in this cookbook.

Mellow white miso paste can be found in natural food markets and health food stores in the refrigerator section. It has a very long refrigerator shelf life, usually about 2 years. If you're new to miso, be aware that mellow white miso paste is actually beige or light brown in color and not actually white.

Mise en place (pronounced *meez-ahn-plahs*) is a French term (literally translated as "put in place") and refers to assembly and preparation of all ingredients and tools before cooking begins. This means that all ingredients should be cleaned, peeled, chopped or measured beforehand. Although the term itself doesn't appear in the recipes, it is an important culinary technique and one of the most often ignored. Many people prepare and cook at the same time and this is a bad habit that often leads to mistakes and failures. Practice mise en place consistently and your cooking experience will be both a pleasure and success.

Mushroom powder is used to add umami (a complex savory flavor) to vegan beaf and porq and their simmering broths. It's also an instant way to add an incredible depth of earthy flavor to hearty soups and stews, and brown gravies and sauces. Mushroom powder can be found in many specialty and gourmet food markets; through the internet; or it can easily be prepared by grinding dried porcini, portabella or shiitake mushrooms in a dry blender, spice grinder or coffee grinder. I prefer porcini mushroom for the beaf and beaf simmering broth, since it is typically darker and adds the proper depth of color. For porq, portabella powder works well, since it is a bit lighter.

If you absolutely cannot access mushroom powder, add one teaspoon of browning liquid to enrich color in the beaf recipes and ½ teaspoon for the porq recipes. Please note that mushroom powder has a very concentrated pungent aroma which may not be pleasing to some noses; however, only the umami flavor, and not the mushroom aroma, will be perceptible in the finished meat analogues.

Neutral vegetable oil, as referenced in this cookbook, refers to any plant oil with a mild taste such as safflower, sunflower, soybean, extra-mild olive oil (refined), avocado, grapeseed, canola or soybean oil. This should not be confused with commercial labeling where "vegetable oil" often refers to soybean oil.

Non-stick cookware is mentioned frequently in this cookbook, so I felt it was worth mentioning here. I prefer and recommend the new non-stick cookware technology over the older Teflon™ cookware. The new non-stick cookware utilizes ceramic-based nanotechnology to create a non-stick surface that is said to be resistant to flaking and more stable upon exposure to high heat than older non-stick technology such as Teflon™. This new cookware is safer too because it's made without perfluorooctanoic acid, known as PFOA, the potentially toxic chemical used in the manufacture of Teflon™ non-stick pans.

While stainless steel cookware is the safest and most durable for most cooking applications, meat analogues (due to the nature of the protein and their lack of fat) tend to stick while pan-searing or sautéing unless substantial amounts of oil are used. With non-stick cookware, a light misting of cooking oil is all that is required for pan-searing and sautéing. A well-seasoned cast iron skillet is the next best option for cooking foods with a tendency to stick if non-stick cookware is not being used.

Nori, also known as sushi nori, is a dry, edible paper made from compressed bits of seaweed. It has a moderate ocean aroma and flavor and is most commonly known for preparing sushi. Nori will turn to mush and disintegrate when exposed to liquids. It is used in this cookbook as a flavoring and coloring agent for the Sweet Clamz recipe.

Nut milk bags are made from ultra-fine nylon mesh or cotton muslin. They are very effective for straining micro-fine solids from nut, seed and grain milks and for straining the okara (pulp) from soymilk. They are also economical as they can be washed and reused repeatedly (as opposed to cheesecloth). If you cannot locate a nut milk bag, try improvising with a ladies' knee-high nylon stocking.

To use the bag, hold it at the top and place it over a large container. Pour in the milk or cream and with your other hand gently massage and squeeze the bag to press the liquid through the mesh. Turn the bag inside out to rinse and discard or compost the solids. Wash with unscented natural dish soap in hot water, rinse well and lay flat on a clean dish towel to dry.

A strainer lined with 3 to 4-layers of cheesecloth will work in a similar manner, except the milk or cream will need to be stirred with a spoon to help the liquid pass though the cheesecloth. Nut milk bags can sometimes be found in health food or natural food stores but can easily be found and purchased through the internet.

Nutritional yeast flakes are used in this cookbook as a flavoring and coloring ingredient. Nutritional yeast is a non-active form of yeast and a source of complete protein and vitamins, especially the B-complex vitamins. It adds umami (a complex savory flavor) to foods. Some brands of nutritional yeast flakes are fortified with vitamin B12. The vitamin B12 is produced separately and then added to the yeast. It is naturally low in fat and sodium and is free of sugar and dairy. Nutritional yeast flakes can be found in most health and natural food stores or online through food retail websites such as Amazon.com. The conversion ratio for nutritional yeast flakes to powder is 2:1. In other words, if a recipe calls for 2 tablespoons nutritional yeast flakes, use 1 tablespoon nutritional yeast powder. Do not confuse nutritional yeast with brewer's yeast.

Olive oil is labeled by different names indicating the degree of processing the oil has undergone, as well as the quality of the oil itself. Extra-virgin olive oil is the highest grade available, followed by virgin olive oil. The word "virgin" indicates that the olives have been pressed to extract the oil; no heat or chemicals have been used during the extraction process, and the oil is pure and unrefined. Save the more expensive extra-virgin and virgin oils for dressings and vinaigrettes, dipping crusty bread or drizzling over bruschetta, since they do not perform well in moderate to high heat applications such as sautéing and frying. The flavor of the virgin oils can also be too strong for many dishes. Mild and extra-mild olive oil, on the other hand, are refined and filtered. They have a delicate, neutral flavor that is suitable for most cooking applications and have a higher smoke point (410° F) than virgin or extra-virgin oils, which makes them ideal for cooking over medium to high heat.

Store olive oil in its original container in a cool, dark place. If refrigerated, olive oil tends to solidify but will return to its original liquid state when warmed to room temperature. Refrigeration does not harm most grades of olive oil, but it is not recommended unless storing for longer periods of time. Refined olive oil should smell mild and have a delicate flavor; virgin olive oils should have a fresh, grassy aroma and flavor. If the oil smells acrid or tastes bitter, it has turned rancid and should be discarded.

Organic sugar is made from organic sugar cane and should not be confused with refined white sugar. The juice is pressed from organic raw sugar cane, evaporated and then crushed into crystals. In adherence with strict Organic Standards, the fields are green cut and not burned or treated with herbicides or synthetic fertilizers. No chemicals or animal by-products are used to decolorize the sugar. This makes it very different from refined white sugar, which has typically been decolorized by filtering through animal bone char. Organic sugar is my sweetener of choice for cooking because of its availability, cost and neutral flavor. Organic powdered sugar can be made from organic sugar. Organic light and dark brown sugar can also be made from organic sugar, with the inclusion of organic blackstrap molasses. Recipes for both light and dark brown sugar can be found in this cookbook.

Parchment paper, also known as bakery release paper, is a cellulose-based paper that is used in baking as a disposable non-stick surface. In this cookbook, it is used as an alternate to a silicone baking mat for lining baking sheets and pans when baking meat analogues. It can also be used as an option for wrapping meat analogues prior to wrapping in aluminum foil when contact with aluminum foil is undesirable. To do so, wrap the meat analogue first with the paper and then follow the directions for wrapping with the foil prior to steaming or baking.

Pickling Lime Powder (also known as "food-grade calcium hydroxide") is an alkaline powder most commonly used for preserving the crispness in pickles and for processing corn for hominy grits, tortillas and tortilla chips. It is also found in commercial shirataki noodles, commercial vegan "seafoods" and other commercial foods prepared with konjac. It is not an extract from the lime citrus fruit. In this cookbook, it is used in very small amounts to activate the glucomannan powder (konjac root powder) in the seafood analogue recipes. Without it, the glucomannan powder will not activate, so do not omit this ingredient!

Pickling lime powder can be found in most supermarkets where products for home canning are located, or mail ordered through the internet (e.g., Mrs. Wages™ Pickling Lime). Pickling lime powder is perfectly safe for human consumption when used as directed in this cookbook. It is strongly alkaline but it is not toxic in small amounts.

Probiotic capsules (vegan) contain strains of "friendly" bacteria which are beneficial to the human intestinal tract. They are usually taken as a dietary supplement for repopulating the intestinal flora, but for the purpose of this cookbook, they are used as an alternative to rejuvelac for culturing cashew milk (for buttermilk) and thicker cashew emulsions (for sour cream and a variety of cheeses). Be sure to check labels to ensure that these cultures are obtained from non-dairy sources (or certified vegan). The bacterial strains in probiotic capsules are pure since they are produced in a laboratory, as opposed to "wild" cultures found in rejuvelac and kombucha. This helps ensure that contamination by rogue bacteria or yeasts does not occur during culturing of non-dairy foods.

Probiotic capsules can contain one strain of bacteria, such as *Lactobacillus acidophilus*, or they can contain many strains of beneficial *Lactobacillus, Bifidobacterium and/or Streptococcus thermophilus* bacteria. When choosing probiotic capsules for culturing purposes, choose a product that contains a variety of these bacteria. This will create a more complex flavor in non-dairy foods than using a single strain alone. These products should be refrigerated and replaced regularly to ensure freshness and bioavailability. If the cashew milk or emulsion is not becoming tangy after 12 to 24 hours, the bacterial strains in the probiotic capsules are no longer active; purchase fresh product. They can be found in health food or natural food markets, or purchased online from retailers that offer fast shipping.

For non-dairy foods cultured with rejuvelac, please see my Non-Dairy Evolution Cookbook.

Poultry seasoning is a blend of aromatic herbs and spices and is commonly used, as the name implies, for seasoning poultry. For our purpose it used as a flavoring ingredient in chikun and turky and their respective simmering broths. It can also be used to season stuffing or dressing, broths, soups, stews, gravies and sauces. Obviously, the term "poultry" is not used or acceptable in the ethical plant-based diet but the seasoning blend itself is traditional and available commercially under this name. It typically does not and should not contain any animal products. Poultry seasoning can easily be prepared at home using my own seasoning blend called "Aromatica" (page 40).

Raw apple cider vinegar is vinegar produced from organic and unpasteurized apple cider. The "mother" is made up of the yeasts and fermentation by-products that are produced when the cider ferments to vinegar. These by-products settle as sediment at the bottom of the bottle, therefore the bottle should be shaken before use. Most commercial companies pasteurize their vinegar and filter out this sediment. I prefer it in recipes because I feel it has a more complex flavor than filtered apple cider vinegar; however, if you don't have any in your pantry, the common and more economical filtered version can be substituted.

Red miso paste is a seasoning which originated in Japan and is produced by the fermentation of soybeans with salt and the fungus "kōjikin" (aspergillis oryzae). Red miso adds umami (a Japanese word used to describe a pleasant savory flavor) to foods. Red miso paste, which has a stronger flavor than mellow white miso paste and a deep brick red color, is used as a seasoning and coloring ingredient in the Garden Ham and Spicy Italian Pancetta recipes in this cookbook. Red miso paste can be found in natural food markets and health food stores in the refrigerator section. It has a very long refrigerator shelf life, usually about 2 years.

Refined coconut oil; see **Coconut oil, refined**

Rice flour is an inexpensive, gluten-free, starchy flour with a subtle flavor. It can be used as an alternative to all-purpose flour for preparing roux and for dredging purposes when frying.

Roux (pronounced "roo") is a primary thickening agent for soups, gravies, sauces and stews with origins dating back more than 300 years in French cuisine. A roux is made by cooking equal parts of all-purpose flour and plant fat (mild olive oil; non-dairy butter or margarine; or a mixture of the two) until the raw flour flavor is eliminated and the mixture has achieved the desired color. When a dark roux is desired, non-dairy butter or margarine is recommended since it browns better than mild olive oil when heated.

Precooking the flour allows the starch granules to swell and absorb moisture from added liquids without the flour clumping or forming lumps. A well-prepared roux promotes silky smoothness and a nutty flavor as it thickens hot liquids. When cooked to a golden or brown stage, a roux takes on a rich, toasted flavor and adds color to the dish (non-dairy butter or margarine is better for creating a dark roux).

A roux forms the foundation of soups, sauces, gravies and stews, whereas a slurry (a mixture of starch and water) can be added later if necessary for additional thickening (you wouldn't want to add an uncooked roux later because of the raw flour flavor).

A roux is also more stable in heated liquids than a slurry (it doesn't break down and lose its thickening power as quickly) because it contains more solids than pure starch. Appearance is a factor too, as a roux remains opaque in heated liquids, while a slurry produces a glossy appearance, which is undesirable in many dishes such as gravies and stews.

When preparing soups and stews, vegetables are often cooked in the hot oil before the flour is added, or more accurately sprinkled over the cooked vegetables. This is a French culinary technique called *singer* (pronounced sin-jay), which means to "lightly coat, dust or sprinkle with flour". After the flour is cooked with the oil and vegetables to remove the raw flour flavor, the liquids in the recipe are incorporated in increments while stirring to prevent clumping of the flour.

Shelf life refers to the length of time that a food may be stored without becoming unfit for consumption. However, shelf life alone is not an accurate indicator of how long a food can safely be stored. Many foods can remain fresh for several days past their recommended shelf life if stored and refrigerated properly. In contrast, if these foods have already been contaminated with harmful bacteria, the guideline becomes irrelevant. Shelf life also depends on the degradation mechanism of a specific food. Most foods can be influenced by several factors such as acid and salt content; exposure to light, heat and moisture; transmission of gases; and contamination by micro-organisms.

The general guideline for refrigerator shelf life of any prepared food that does not contain preservatives, heavy salt content or vinegar is 7 to 10 days.

Silicone baking mat refers to a non-stick, flexible baking sheet produced by several manufacturers (i.e., Silpat™ and Silchef™). It's made of silicone with a reinforced glass weave and is effective at temperatures ranging from -40°F to 480°F. It does not require greasing and provide even heat transfer. As such, it can be used as an alternate to parchment paper for lining the metal baking sheet when baking meat analogues. It can be found in gourmet shops, department store kitchenware sections or purchased online.

Silken tofu is a variety of tofu commonly used in plant-based cooking to create sauces, thick creams and custard-like textures. It can also be used in combination with other ingredients to replicate eggs in a variety of egg-free dishes. It has a smooth and very delicate texture compared to the firmer water-packed block tofu.

Magnesium chloride and calcium chloride are the coagulants (called nigari in Japan) used to make silken tofu. These coagulants are added to soymilk and the mixture is then sealed in aseptic cartons. In other words, the resulting bean curd is produced inside its own package, rather than being drained and pressed into blocks. Silken tofu packaged in this manner needs no refrigeration until the carton is opened. This gives it an extended shelf life, compared to fresh water-packed tofu sold in tub containers. However, silken tofu can now often be found in tub containers in the refrigerated section next to the water-packed block tofu. This can be somewhat confusing if you're new to tofu, so it's important to read labels and be aware of what you're purchasing.

Sodium alginate is a flavorless food gum derived from brown seaweed. It is used in the food industry to add viscosity and stability to a wide range of food products. In molecular gastronomy, it is combined with calcium chloride or lactate or similar to create spheres of liquid surrounded by a thin jelly membrane. Sodium alginate is both food and skin safe and can be used as an alternate to guar gum and xanthan gum in this cookbook. Sodium alginate can be purchased from ModernistPantry.com or other online sources such as Amazon.com.

Soymilk, plain unsweetened refers to homemade or commercial soymilk that contains no sweeteners or flavors such as vanilla. Preferably, it should not contain any added thickeners. Plain unsweetened soymilk is specified for many of the recipes in this cookbook because of its natural stability and similarity to dairy milk in protein, carbohydrate and fat composition.

Slurry refers to a mixture of starch (usually cornstarch or unmodified potato starch) and cold water which is whisked together until smooth and then added to soups, stews and sauces as a thickener. If a dry starch is added directly to a hot liquid, the starch granules cannot disperse easily and lumps will form. Once mixed with water, the slurry can be added directly to the hot liquid. The liquid must be brought up to a simmer each time to ensure the starch reaches its full thickening potential before more is added. Stir in a little at a time until you reach the desired consistency. A roux (see "Roux") is usually the primary base thickener for a soup, sauce or gravy used at the beginning of the recipe, while a slurry can be added later if additional thickening in required. Starch slurries add gloss to liquids. A roux adds opaqueness and is thus preferred for gravies.

Stainless steel cooling rack is a flat rack made from an open mesh network of closely arranged stainless steel wires set on short legs to raise it above surface level. While it's typically used for cooling baked goods, it is used in this cookbook for lining baking sheets prior to baking some of the meat analogues. The raised surface provides air circulation so the meat analogue doesn't excessively brown from contact with the hot baking surface and the rack is lined with parchment paper or a silicone baking mat to prevent sticking. It's important that the rack have thick, strong wires so it won't sag in the center.

Cooling racks can be round, square or rectangular and can range from small to large; however, for the purpose of this cookbook, the cooling rack should be rectangular and should fit inside a standard-size baking sheet.

T is the abbreviation for "tablespoon" and "tsp" is the abbreviation for "teaspoon".

Tapioca flour, also known as tapioca starch, is a carbohydrate extracted from the cassava plant (Manihot esculenta). It is used worldwide as a thickening agent in foods. It differs from wheat flour, rice flour, cornstarch and unmodified potato starch in that it produces a gooey, stretchy texture when heated in liquids. This characteristic makes it an ideal thickener for non-dairy cheeses, cheese melts and cheese sauces. Tapioca flour can be purchased in some supermarkets, in most health food and natural food stores, or online through food retail websites such as Amazon.com. If you absolutely cannot obtain tapioca flour, use cornstarch or unmodified potato starch as a substitute (although the finished texture will be different).

Tamari, soy sauce or Bragg Liquid Aminos™ are liquid seasonings made from soybeans. Tamari and soy sauce can also include wheat. Reduced-sodium tamari and soy sauce is available for those wishing to lower their sodium intake. Although soy sauce (also known as shoyu) and tamari are both made from fermented soybeans, Japanese tamari has a smoother, more complex and well-balanced flavor compared to soy sauce (which is sharper due to the difference in raw materials and a stronger alcoholic fermentation).

Bragg Liquid Aminos™ are made from non-GMO soybeans and purified water. This product can be used as a replacement for tamari and soy sauce and contains 16 amino acids, including the nine essential amino acids. Bragg Liquid Aminos™ have not been fermented or heated and are alcohol and gluten-free. The packaging label states that the product has only a small amount of naturally occurring sodium, but I find it to be just as salty tasting as tamari and soy sauce, so use it in the same measurements as you would tamari or soy sauce.

Tempeh is a cultured food made by the controlled fermentation of cooked soybeans with the fungus *Rhizopus oligosporus* (aka tempeh "starter"). This fermentation binds the soybeans into a compact white cake. Tempeh is not related to TVP/TSP or tofu at all, other than the fact that all three are produced from soybeans. Tempeh has been a favorite food and staple source of protein in Indonesia for several hundred years. Many find it useful as a meat replacement, since it has a firm texture and a nutty mushroom flavor.

Typically, tempeh is sliced or cut into cubes and fried until the surface is crisp and golden brown. To mellow the flavor and make it better able to absorb marinades, cut the tempeh block in half and then simmer in water for about 10 minutes. Drain, blot dry and then slice or cube and place in the marinade. Chill for a minimum of one hour and even better overnight before frying.

It can also be crumbled or grated and used as a unique alternative to ground seitan and TVP/TSP in recipes such as Sloppy Joes, tacos, burritos or chili. Tempeh can also be used as an ingredient in soups, spreads, salads and sandwiches. Tempeh is now commonly available in many supermarkets, as well as in Asian markets and health food stores.

tsp is the abbreviation for "teaspoon" and "T" is the abbreviation for "tablespoon".

TVP (textured vegetable protein) and **TSP** (textured soy protein) are two abbreviations, often interchangeably used, to describe a commercially produced soy-based meat analogue. This processed protein is actually a by-product of soybean oil production. The soy protein is extracted, extruded (a manufacturing process that causes a change in the structure of the soy protein) and then dried into various shapes and sizes. This results in a fibrous material that is similar in texture to meat when rehydrated. This process is done using factory equipment and is not something that can be produced in a home kitchen. TVP/TSP cooks quickly, contains no fat and has a protein content equal to that of meat. It is a very economical and versatile source of protein for the plant-based diet.

Many TVP/TSP producers use hexane (a chemical solvent) to separate soy fat from soy protein. Although the FDA claims that hexane is safe to use in the processing of soy proteins, there is very little available data on how much of the chemical residue remains after processing and what the possible long-term effects of consumption may be. It has been argued that TVP/TSP has been safely used in the food industry for decades, primarily as a meat extender in restaurants, prison kitchens and school cafeterias.

If you are concerned about the possibility of trace amounts of hexane in TVP/TSP and/or the use of genetically modified soybeans in its production, there is a solution to this concern: Organic TSP. Organic TSP is made from water-extracted, defatted soy flour (produced from organic, non-GMO soybeans) that is cooked, extruded and then dried. It contains no possible trace of hexane because hexane is not used in the extraction process. However, be aware that organic TSP may cost more. TVP can be found in natural food stores, some larger supermarket chains and online (e.g., Amazon.com). Organic TSP may be a bit more difficult to locate but can be found in some natural food stores or purchased online.

Unmodified potato starch is one of the less familiar starches used as a food thickener. It can be used in equal amounts as an alternate to cornstarch. Do not confuse unmodified potato starch with potato flour, which is actually ground dehydrated potatoes and avoid modified potato starch (which has been physically, enzymatically, or chemically treated in such a manner that changes its properties).

Vegan Eggz Essentials is a commercial product used in several recipes in this cookbook to create remarkably realistic simulations of cooked eggs, and to function in a similar manner as eggs in some recipes.

Vegan Eggz Essentials is not an egg replacer or complete mix like other commercial egg replacer products on the market. The product consists of 2 special ingredients portioned and sealed in their own individual pouches (labeled "Essentials A" and "Essentials B") and sold in one convenient package. These two ingredients are then used in recipes with other ingredients to simulate eggs or function like eggs in cooking (a good analogy would be lactic acid and kappa carrageenan used in non-dairy cheesemaking; they're not a complete mix but rather two ingredients which make the cheese recipe work).

Vegan Eggz Essentials is 100% plant-based, egg-free, dairy-free, nut-free and gluten-free and contain no nutritional value of its own other than dietary fiber.

Vegan Eggz Essentials is my first product sold under The Gentle Chef label and is solely available by mail order through ModernistPantry.com. The product can be shipped worldwide.

Vegan probiotic capsules; see **Probiotic capsules, vegan**

Vital wheat gluten is the natural protein found in wheat. Vital wheat gluten is used in plant-based cooking to produce meat analogues. In baking, a small amount is often added to yeast bread recipes to improve the texture and elasticity of the dough.

In commercial vital wheat gluten production, a mixture of wheat flour and water is kneaded vigorously by machinery until the gluten forms into a mass. Approximately 65% of the water in the wet gluten is removed by means of a screw press; the remainder is sprayed through an atomizer nozzle into a drying chamber, where it remains at an elevated temperature a short time to evaporate the water without denaturing the gluten. The process yields a flour-like powder with a 7% moisture content, which is air cooled and transported to a receiving container. In the final step, the collected gluten is sifted and milled to produce a uniform product.

When preparing meat analogues, vital wheat gluten must be high-quality in order to develop the proper elasticity in the dough. Be sure it is labeled at a minimum of 75% protein. Bargain and bulk gluten are generally of lesser quality and may contain a significant amount of starch. Excess starch will yield a bread-like texture in the finished product.

Vital wheat gluten can be measured by volume, by scooping up the gluten with a measuring cup and leveling off the top with a table knife; or measured by weight (which is more accurate).

Wakame is a sea vegetable, or edible seaweed. It has a subtly sweet ocean flavor and sturdy texture that holds up well in cooking and is my favored ingredient for creating a seafood flavor in seafood analogues.

White Shoyu, or white soy sauce, is a condiment with a long tradition in Japan. Clearer and mellower than traditional dark soy sauce, it has a light amber color that infuses foods with umami flavor without darkening them. Tamari, soy sauce or Bragg Liquid Aminos™ can be used as a substitute but these products will impart a darker color. White shoyu can sometimes be found in gourmet or Asian markets, or mail ordered through the internet.

Preparing Tofu for Recipes

Extra-firm water-packed block tofu is used in many of the meat and seafood analogue recipes in this cookbook and can be found in the refrigerated section of the market. Do not confuse this with extra-firm silken tofu, which is a delicate, custard-like Japanese tofu. Silken tofu will not work in these applications.

Before using in the recipes, the extra-firm tofu will need to be pressed to remove as much water as possible. It may seem redundant to press the water from the tofu, only to add water back when preparing the recipes. However, the reason for this is very simple: Removing the soaking water removes any excess coagulant used in making the tofu. Also, water content in tofu varies from brand to brand and even from block to block. By removing the liquid from the tofu, weighing it, and then adding back a precise amount of water, recipe results remain consistent.

When weighing the tofu for the recipes, minor weight variations are acceptable and will not negatively affect the recipe results. Be sure to weigh the tofu after pressing, unless otherwise indicated. A precision digital ounce/gram scale is recommended for accuracy.

Pressing can be done ahead of time using a tofu press (allow several hours of pressing time); or the tofu can be wrapped in several layers of paper towels or a lint-free kitchen towel and pressed on a flat surface using the palms of your hands assisted by your upper body weight. The advantage of using a tofu press first, is that it will remove a substantial amount water, which then saves on paper towel usage.

When pressed sufficiently, the tofu should feel barely damp and have a crumbly texture. Some stores now offer pre-pressed extra-firm block tofu. To reiterate, whether home-pressed or commercially pre-pressed, the tofu should feel barely damp and crumble easily.

If pressed ahead of time, keep the pressed tofu refrigerated in an airtight container for up to 3 days until ready to use.

Recipe Incidentals

Worcestershire Sauce

This is my signature plant-based version of the classic condiment. It's an essential ingredient for preparing beaf and beaf simmering broth and was placed into this chapter for that reason. Traditional commercial Worcestershire sauce contains anchovy paste and is not suitable for those adhering to a plant-based diet. There are a few brands of vegan Worcestershire sauce on the market, and they are good, but they're not readily available to everyone. This recipe yields about 1 and ¼ cup. I use this condiment so frequently that I always double the recipe.

Ingredients

- 1 and ½ cup raw apple cider vinegar
- ½ cup dark balsamic vinegar
- ½ cup tamari, soy sauce or Bragg Liquid Aminos™
- 3 T dark brown sugar
- 1 medium onion, chopped
- 3 cloves garlic, crushed
- 1 and ½ inch piece ginger root, peeled and sliced
- 1 tsp lemon zest, loosely packed
- 1 tsp orange zest, loosely packed
- 1 tsp liquid smoke
- 1 tsp whole cloves
- 1 tsp whole black peppercorns
- 1 tsp prepared Dijon mustard or ½ tsp whole mustard seeds
- 1 bay leaf
- pinch dried wakame flakes (optional; replaces the anchovy flavor found in the non-vegan version)

Preparation

Place all of the ingredients in a medium saucepan and bring to a boil over medium-high heat. Reduce the heat to a rapid simmer and cook until the sauce is reduced by half volume, about 30 to 40 minutes.

Let cool and then press and strain through a fine mesh sieve or a double layer of cheesecloth into a jar with a lid. Store the sauce in the refrigerator for up to 3 months.

Browning Liquid

For purists like myself who prefer to make their own recipe components, I've developed what is to my knowledge the first and only browning liquid made with organic sugar. Browning liquid is useful for adding a rich brown color to meat analogues, sauces, gravies, soups and stews.

This browning liquid has no added caramel color, nor does it have the sweet undertaste of commercial browning liquids. As a general rule for soups, gravies and stews use 1 teaspoon per 4 cups of liquid. This recipe yields about ⅓ cup browning liquid. Gravy Master™ is a suitable commercial alternative to homemade browning liquid.

Warning: This recipe produces copious amounts of smoke. Do not attempt to prepare this recipe unless you have an overhead exhaust fan for your stove that vents outside!

Ingredients

- ¼ cup very hot water
- 2 T tamari, soy sauce or Bragg Liquid Aminos™
- 1 T dark balsamic vinegar
- ½ cup organic sugar

Preparation

In a small measuring cup, mix the very hot water, tamari and vinegar; set aside.

In a small saucepan, place the dry sugar over medium-low heat. The goal is to melt the dry sugar and bring it to a darkly caramelized stage (essentially burnt). Swirl or gently shake the saucepan back and forth occasionally as the sugar begins to melt but do not stir. Melting will take several minutes. Be sure to run an overhead stove exhaust fan as the sugar will produce smoke as it begins to burn.

As the sugar continues to melt and darken, it will begin to rise in the saucepan. At this point, begin stirring gently with a wire whisk. When the sugar reaches a very dark brown color, reduce the heat to low. Now, while whisking vigorously, add the broth mixture a little at a time to the melted sugar. The mixture will foam and sizzle, so don't be alarmed. Very hot steam will also be released, so try to keep your hands back as you stir with the whisk to avoid steam burns.

Continue to stir until the mixture is smooth and then remove the saucepan from the heat to cool. Once cooled, the browning liquid will have a syrupy consistency. The concentrated liquid will have a rather bitter, burnt flavor; however, when used in small amounts as recommended, it will add a beautiful brown color and enhance the flavor of your favorite recipes. Store the mixture in an airtight jar in your pantry; refrigeration is not necessary. Replace the mixture after 4 months.

Garbanzo Bean Flour

Garbanzo bean flour (also known as chickpea flour, besan flour, gram flour, chana flour or cici flour) is used a great deal in my recipes. However, if you have a difficult time finding it locally, a cost-effective option is to grind your own. This can be done simply with a high-powered blender. Dry garbanzo beans are readily available in most supermarkets, usually in the aisle where dried beans and peas are found. If they're not there, check the aisle where Mexican and other ethnic foods are located. One pound of dried beans (about 2 cups) will yield one pound of ground flour. Do not use canned garbanzo beans!

Preparation

To grind your own flour, work in one cup batches. Add one cup of dried beans to a dry, high-powered blender, cover and process until finely powdered. Place a fine mesh sieve over a large bowl, add the flour and shake gently to sift the flour through the fine mesh. Discard any remaining particles in the sieve. Transfer the flour to a sealable container and repeat the process with the remaining dried beans.

Old-Fashioned Brown Sugar (Organic)

Homemade brown sugar is very easy to make. It has a warmer color and richer flavor compared to its commercially-processed counterpart.

Ingredients

- 1 cup organic cane sugar
- ¼ cup organic unsulfured molasses (for dark brown sugar)
  or 1 T organic unsulfured molasses (for light brown sugar)

Preparation

Place the organic sugar in a food processor with a standard chopping blade. Begin processing and drizzle the molasses into the food processor through the food chute. Continue processing until evenly combined. Store the brown sugar in an airtight container at room temperature.

Instant Chikun Bouillon Powder

This convenient instant powder can be used to prepare a comforting and savory chikun bouillon by the cup; or the quart as a quick alternative for the chikun simmering broth (page 41). Bouillon is the French word for "broth".

Ingredients

- 1 cup nutritional yeast flakes
- 5 T fine sea salt or kosher salt
- ¼ cup onion powder
- 3 T organic sugar
- 1 T poultry seasoning
- 1 T garlic powder
- 1 T dried celery flakes
- 1 T dehydrated carrot flakes (optional)
- 2 tsp dried parsley flakes
- ½ tsp ground white pepper

Preparation

Process the ingredients in a dry blender until finely powdered; store in an airtight container for up to 6 months.

For a soothing mug of golden chikun broth, dissolve 1 level teaspoon bouillon powder, or more to taste, in 8 ounces of piping hot water. Stir well. A fine seasoning sediment will settle on the bottom of the mug, so stir occasionally while sipping or simply discard the sediment after consuming.

To prepare an instant chikun broth for soups and stews, use 1 level teaspoon of bouillon powder for each cup of simmering water, or more or less to taste. For chikun simmering broth, add 4 tablespoons (¼ cup) bouillon powder to 3 quarts (12 cups) simmering water. Add additional herbs and spices as desired to accommodate specific regional cuisines and season the prepared broth with salt to taste.

To clarify large quantities of broth, let the prepared broth cool to room temperature and pour into a sealable container, discarding any seasoning sediment that has settled on the bottom of the cooking pot. Refrigerate overnight, or for up to 10 days, which will allow any micro-fine seasoning sediment to further settle on the bottom of the container. Decant the clear portion of broth and use in recipes as needed.

Introduction to Meat and Seafood Analogues

Many people who embrace a plant-based diet do so for ethical reasons and not because they dislike the flavor and texture of meat and seafood. But finding satisfying meat and seafood alternatives is not always easy for individuals who once enjoyed the flavors and textures associated with these foods, or for individuals who grew up with meat and seafood-based dishes as a traditional part of their family or ethnic heritage.

Meat and seafood analogues (imitations) are generally understood within the vegan context to mean 100% plant-based foods that mimic or approximate certain aesthetic qualities, such as texture, flavor and appearance, of specific types of meat and seafood. This differs from meat and seafood substitutes or alternatives. For example, a grilled piece of tofu can serve as a substitute or alternative to meat or fish, but when it's used as ingredient and transformed in some way to replicate the texture of chicken or fish, it becomes a meat or seafood analogue.

This chapter focuses on approximating the appearance, flavors and textures of some of the meats and seafoods that many of us grew up with: foods that are familiar and represent tradition and foods that evoke a feeling of nostalgia.

Meat and seafood analogues provide the satisfaction of eating something we can sink our teeth into; of hearty foods that fill us up and stick to our ribs, and foods that remind us of holiday traditions, and cookouts and camping trips with friends and family in the summertime.

Some home cooks may think that preparing meat and seafood analogues is too complex and may feel intimidated by the process, but this concern is unfounded as long as one can follow a recipe. While having some plant-based cooking experience is helpful, I've put a lot of forethought into writing the recipes in order for even the novice cook to achieve success.

Please note that the basic meat analogues are neutrally and very lightly seasoned. This allows for additional seasoning or marinating before grilling, sautéing, frying or stewing according to the specific cuisine being prepared. In other words, don't expect the analogue itself to be bursting with flavor - it needs to be seasoned just like real meat when preparing dishes.

A complaint I receive occasionally is that all of the basic analogues are so much alike in flavor, with just minor variations in ingredients. That's true, but even real meat is rather bland and similar until it's seasoned. Since we're working with plant-based ingredients, and not real animal flesh, there's only so much we can do to create distinctly separate and unique flavor profiles in the analogue itself. In vegan cuisine, distinctly separate and unique flavor profiles really depend upon the seasoning of the dishes which incorporate the analogues.

So, if you're a former meat and seafood aficionado, remember that we can only approximate the aesthetic qualities of meat and seafood with plant-based ingredients and home kitchen equipment. If you curb your expectation of creating exact reproductions, then these recipes should sufficiently satisfy your desire for meat and seafood-like appearances, textures and flavors.

Seitan and Plant Protein Blends

Seitan (pronounced "say-tan"), or wheat meat, is an amazingly versatile, protein-rich meat analogue made from wheat gluten. The word seitan is of Japanese origin and was coined in 1961 by George Ohsawa, a Japanese advocate of the macrobiotic diet. Gluten (from the Latin *glutinum*, meaning "glue") is a protein complex that appears in foods processed from wheat and related species, including barley and rye. Wheat gluten is not a complete protein in itself (lysine is the missing amino acid) which means that additional ingredients must be added to complete its amino acid profile (miso, tamari, nutritional yeast or bean flour, for example). Lysine can also easily be obtained by consuming other plant protein sources in the daily diet (it doesn't have to be consumed at the same meal).

Unfortunately, some individuals cannot benefit from the nutrition and versatility of seitan due to gluten sensitivity or total intolerance (Celiac disease), and must obtain their protein from vegetables, soy and other legumes, and gluten-free grain sources such as quinoa, amaranth or buckwheat (which is actually not a grain but a seed).

Vital wheat gluten (sometimes labeled as "vital wheat gluten flour") is not the same as high-gluten wheat flour. High-gluten wheat flour is typically used in baking to give breads a chewy texture. It also contains a large proportion of starch, unlike isolated vital wheat gluten.

Vital wheat gluten must be high-quality in order to develop the proper texture for meat analogues. Be sure the packaging is labeled at a minimum of 75% protein. Bargain and bulk gluten may be of lesser quality and/or it may contain a significant amount of starch. Vital wheat gluten can be found in health food stores, and many supermarkets now carry it as well. It can also be purchased through the internet.

While some of the meat analogues in this cookbook are entirely gluten-based, some are entirely soy-based. Many others are prepared by combining gluten with tofu or textured vegetable/soy protein. While combining gluten and tofu together to create a meat analogue is not a new concept, the proportion of ingredients, seasonings and cooking methods are what make these meat analogues so unique. Many of my seafood analogues are prepared using tofu and konjac root powder (glucomannan), which is a dietary plant fiber.

Textured vegetable/soy protein (TVP/TSP) and Butler Soy Curls™ are commercial soy-based meat analogues which are ready to rehydrate, season and use in recipes. Textured vegetable/soy protein, a by-product of soybean oil production, is a processed protein. The soy protein is extracted, extruded (a manufacturing process that causes a change in the structure of the soy protein) and then dried into various shapes and sizes. This results in a fibrous material that is similar in texture to meat when rehydrated. Butler Soy Curls™ are made from the whole soybean using a proprietary production method.

Cooking methods vary depending upon the type of plant protein being used and the desired finished texture, flavor and appearance of the meat analogue. Each method was carefully determined to create the best texture, flavor and finished appearance.

Preparing meat analogues at home is an art and science unto itself, much like the art and science of baking. Whether the recipe calls for a teaspoon (tsp), a tablespoon (T) or a cup (and fractions thereof), always use level measurements.

Since volume measurements for dry ingredients can sometimes be unreliable, I have included metric weight measurements for primary recipe ingredients such as vital wheat gluten and tofu. Volume measurements for water used to prepare the meat analogues include both standard U.S. measurements and metric. And please, no "eye-balling" volume measurements - that may work for some cooking techniques but it doesn't work when preparing meat analogues.

The recipes provided in this cookbook were formulated to produce appetizing results, and have been tested many times in my own kitchen; therefore, experimenting with dry ingredient to liquid ingredient ratios is not recommended, as this can upset moisture balance and change textures significantly enough to negatively affect the finished product. While adjusting or substituting seasonings to suit your taste is to be expected, avoid substituting primary functional ingredients or adding large amounts of unspecified extra ingredients, as this can also upset moisture balance or change flavors and textures significantly enough to negatively affect results. In other words, be creative and have fun but don't make too many changes and then wonder why something didn't turn out properly.

Depending upon the desired texture of the finished product, hand-kneading is utilized in varying degrees to develop the gluten and create meat-like textures. Gluten strands form as the glutenin and gliadin molecules cross-link to create a sub-microscopic network. Kneading promotes this formation.

Meat analogues combining gluten and tofu require vigorous kneading for several minutes in order to sufficiently develop the gluten strands in the dough. This development is essential for producing the best texture in the finished product. A food processor, fitted with either a standard chopping blade or plastic dough blade, is therefore required for such a task.

Traditional Cooking Methods for Meat Analogues

Wheat gluten is not digestible in its raw state; therefore, it must be cooked. For seitan, the traditional method is simmering in a seasoned broth. A very gentle simmer is essential when cooking seitan using this method alone. This means that the cooking pot needs to be monitored closely and the heat regulated to maintain the gentle simmer. Rapid simmering or boiling will produce a spongy texture and no amount of pan frying will save your finished product. On the other hand, merely poaching seitan in hot broth without simmering will produce a tougher, rubbery texture, as not enough liquid will be absorbed.

Through a great deal of experimentation with cooking techniques using gluten, and blends of gluten and tofu, I discovered that better meat-like textures could be produced in some of the meat analogues by utilizing a combination cooking method that includes both baking and simmering. When using this combination method, pre-baking sets the texture of the dough and simmering completes the cooking process. Pre-baking also regulates the amount of liquid the dough will absorb, creating dense meaty textures while preventing spongy finished textures. While I still recommend a gentle (but active) simmer when using the combination cooking method, the temperature of the simmering broth is not as critical since pre-baking has already set the texture of the dough. However, merely poaching in hot broth should be avoided, since not enough liquid will be absorbed to complete the cooking process.

Meat analogues containing gluten will expand up to twice their size through absorption of the broth during simmering, therefore, the broth should be generously seasoned to enhance the flavor of the finished product. If the broth has little flavor, it will "leach" the seasonings from the dough.

Fresh homemade broths are always best and are recommended since the complex flavor of the broth is infused into the meat analogue as it simmers. They are also more wholesome since they don't contain corn syrup solids and hydrolyzed proteins, which are commonly found in commercial vegetarian broth cubes and bouillon paste. And nothing quite compares to the comforting aroma of a homemade broth filling the kitchen.

The recipes for these broths can be found with the recipes for the specific meat analogue being prepared. They're not difficult to make but they do involve some chopping of vegetables and about an hour of cooking time. I realize that busy schedules and time constraints don't always allow the home cook to prepare every component of a recipe from scratch, so quick options are also provided for preparing the simmering broths.

An important point I'd like to mention is the quality of water used for preparing meat analogues and simmering broths, or in any recipe for that matter. Avoid unfiltered tap water if at all possible, since tap water is full of impurities. Faucet mounted filters (PUR™, for example) are a godsend for ensuring clean water. They're also economical and kinder to the environment than disposable plastic water containers.

Oven-baking is used for some meat analogues with pressure-cooking offered as an alternative (additional information about pressure-cooking meat analogues can be found on page 36). Either method typically involves rolling or wrapping the dough in aluminum foil before placing in the oven or pressure cooker. This not only creates and holds the shape but seals in moisture.

It's very important that you use heavy-duty aluminum foil when oven-baking meat analogues. Regular foil can easily rupture from expansion of the dough as it cooks (especially with gluten and tofu blends), and from steam pressure which builds up inside the foil. Always err on using too much foil rather than not enough and when in doubt, rewrap with an additional sheet of foil. Pressure-cooking is a bit more forgiving, since the pressure inside the cooker prevents the foil from rupturing as easily. For this method, either standard or heavy-duty foil can be used.

Meat analogue recipes that offer oven-baking as an option have been tested in my own radiant heat oven which is calibrated to the correct temperature. I have placed 2 different brands of oven thermometers in my oven, one on the top shelf and the other on the bottom, to ensure accuracy of cooking temperatures when preparing my recipes. When my oven is preheated to 350°F, it reaches that temperature and the gas flame switches off. When my oven door is opened and a cold foil package is placed inside, the temperature immediately begins to drop by as much as 75 to 100 degrees Fahrenheit. The gas flame then switches back on to raise the temperature back to 350°F and the flame switches off again. This cycle repeats during the remaining cooking time. So, the package is not cooked consistently at 350°F.

Convection or fan-assisted ovens are more efficient at maintaining an even heat, so these cycles in temperature variations are not as dramatic. Convection ovens work by distributing heat evenly around the food by circulating hot air with a fan, removing the blanket of cooler air that surrounds food when it is first placed in an oven and allowing food to cook more evenly at a lower temperature than in a conventional oven (this is known as convective heat transfer). For this reason, convection-baking meat analogues at the same temperature as a radiant heat oven can lead to over-cooking and dry results. To avoid over-cooking, switch the fan off or adjust by lowering the oven temperature by 25°F/10°C.

Steam cooking is used for the individual hand-rolled sausages. You will need a large pot with a lid and a steamer insert for this method. The seasoned dough is either wrapped or rolled in aluminum foil before being steamed. They can also be steamed in pressure-cooker.

Standard or heavy-duty aluminum foil can be used for wrapping the sausages before steaming but pop-up aluminum foil is more convenient and easier to manage. Pop-up foil is commonly used in the restaurant industry for wrapping baked potatoes. It's very convenient because cutting foil to create wrappers is not required. While pop-up foil is not available in all supermarkets, it is commonly used in hair salons for hair coloring and can be found in beauty supply stores. It can also be purchased online. Pop-up foil is very thin and flimsy, so double wrapping the sausages is required so they do not burst open while steaming.

Some individuals may express concern about their food coming into contact with aluminum foil. If this is a personal concern or you have any doubt, there is a simple solution: cut a piece of parchment paper to line the foil before rolling or wrapping. This will keep the dough from coming into contact with the aluminum foil. However, the foil is still required for the outer layer.

All meat analogues containing gluten benefit from refrigeration after preparation and before finishing and serving. Chilling changes the structure of the cooked gluten in a beneficial way, which in turn enhances the texture of the meat analogue. So, don't rush or omit this step. Meat analogues simply require a little pre-planning, so prepare them a minimum of 8 hours before you plan to finish and serve. Meat analogues and simmering broths should be cooled to near room temperature before refrigerating.

For meat analogues that have been simmered in broth, include about ¼ cup of the broth in the food storage container or bag before refrigerating as this will keep the product moist. Products containing gluten/soy blends can be refrigerated in this manner for up to 1 week, and up to 10 days for strictly gluten-based analogues.

All meat analogues containing gluten or a combination of soy and gluten can be frozen for up to 3 months and then thawed and reheated or finished at your convenience. Simmering broths can be frozen for up to 3 months. Simmered meat analogues should be frozen without the broth.

Most prepared meat analogues benefit from finishing in some manner before serving. This can include pan-searing, pan-glazing, sautéing, frying, broiling, pan-grilling, or outdoor grilling. For pan-searing, pan-glazing, sautéing and pan-grilling, use a non-stick skillet or grill pan, or a well-seasoned cast iron skillet, since meat analogues are notorious for sticking to stainless steel (even with cooking oil present).

For outdoor grilling, season the grill grating with cooking oil to discourage sticking. Brush meat analogues with cooking oil before placing under the broiler or on the grill. This applies even if the meat analogue was marinated or a sauce is being used. There is very little fat content in meat analogues, other than the trivial amount of oil that was added during preparation, and plant fat (oil) is what will keep the "meat" tender, juicy and flavorful.

Pressure-Cooking Meat Analogues

Pressure Cookers - How They Work

Pressure cookers work on one basic principle: Steam pressure. A sealed pot, heated by an electrical heating element or on the stovetop, generates steam under pressure which helps food cook faster. The sealed pot is constructed with a safety valve that controls the steam pressure inside. Pressure-cooking can be used for quick simulation of the effects of long braising (which refers to oven cooking foods partially submerged in liquid). Almost any food which can be cooked in steam or water-based liquids can be cooked in a pressure cooker. Foil-wrapped meat analogues that are typically baked or steamed can also be cooked in a pressure cooker, but different rules apply.

My recipes recommend using an electric pressure cooker (for example, Instant Pot™, which is a popular cooker). Electric pressure cookers automatically regulate the internal steam pressure and are essentially a "set it and forget it" method of cooking. If you wish to use a stove-top pressure cooker, please refer to its manual for operating. All of the foil-wrapped meat analogues in this cookbook are cooked on the "high" pressure setting and you will need to set the timer on the cooker manually. If your cooker has pre-set cooking options, choose the "meat" or "chicken" option and manually override the cooking timer setting according to the recipe.

The high-pressure steam of pressure-cooking has two major effects:

1. It raises the boiling point of the water or other liquid in the pot from 212°F (100°C) to 250°F (121°C). Exposed foods are subjected to this higher boiling temperature and this causes the food to cook faster. Most pressure cookers have a cooking pressure setting between 0.8 – 1 bar (11.6 – 15 psi) above sea level pressure (sea level pressure is around 1.016 bar) so a pressure cooker operates at 1.816 to 2.016 bar. The standard cooking pressure of 15 psi (pounds per square inch) above sea level pressure was determined by the United States Department of Agriculture in 1917. At this pressure, water boils at 250°F (121°C). So there really is nothing special about pressure-cooking other than it raises the boiling point of water or liquids in order to steam/cook foods at a higher temperature than that of a conventional steamer.

2. This increased steam pressure forces liquid into foods which are exposed to the steam. This not only helps the food cook faster but it also tenderizes certain foods like grains, legumes and vegetables, much faster than by conventional steaming or simmering.

However, meat analogues sealed in foil packages respond differently than exposed foods. In a sealed package, the gluten dough (or gluten and tofu combination) is not exposed to the direct steam, since the foil serves as a moisture barrier. The water in the pressure cooker is not being forced into the dough. Therefore, the package is simply being steamed at a boiling temperature of 250°F (120°C), as opposed to being steamed in a conventional steamer at 212°F (100°C) or baked in an oven at a common temperature of 350°F/175°C.

While pressure-cooking may cook the dough faster than a conventional steamer, it will not necessarily cook the dough faster than in an oven set at a higher temperature. Therefore, the foil-wrapped dough still requires pressure-cooking for the suggested cooking time in order to cook all the way through properly. And while it may seem unusual to pressure cook foods for 2 hours (as an example), it is important to remember that we're not cooking exposed foods - we're cooking gluten dough sealed in a foil package.

Pressure-Cooking Meat Analogues versus Oven-Baking

Pressure-cooking foil-wrapped meat analogues has its own advantages and disadvantages over oven-baking. Based upon my own research and experimentation, I have found that pressure-cooking does not really save any more time over oven-baking when cooking foil-wrapped meat analogues (due to the reasons discussed previously). Also, many of the larger foil-wrapped roasts may not fit into the compact chamber of a pressure-cooking pot.

One advantage of pressure-cooking is for those who have trouble with foil-wrapped meat analogues bursting while oven-baking. Rupturing of the package is due to steam pressure which builds up inside the package. The pressure inside the package is greater than the surrounding pressure in the oven, so the package may burst if wrapped improperly or insufficiently in order to equalize the pressure. This can not only ruin the finished product but can create a big mess in the oven. With pressure-cooking, the pressure inside the cooking chamber is greater than that within the foil package, so bursting does not occur, even if the package is wrapped improperly or insufficiently.

Another advantage to pressure-cooking is for those who have inconsistent oven temperatures or ovens that run too hot, causing the final product to become dry and bread-like, rather than moist and shreddable. If lowering the oven temperature by 25°F/10°C has not resolved the issue, pressure-cooking may be the best option.

Another and very distinct advantage of pressure-cooking is that it does not overheat the kitchen during the warm summer months, as compared to an oven.

At this time, I don't recommend using parchment paper (or other plant substances) as the only wrapping barrier inside the chamber. The recipes contain a precise amount of water, and parchment paper, or other permeable plant substances, could allow excess moisture to be forced into the dough. However, feel free to experiment on your own and at your own risk.

Pressure-Cooking Seitan as an Alternative to Simmering

In my humble opinion, the joy of cooking not only involves eating and enjoying the food we create but experiencing the cooking process and being actively involved in it. There are some methods that I don't feel can be improved upon and this is one of them. If we're always looking to change the process for the sake of convenience and time management - or simply because it's the latest trend - we lose a great deal from the experience. There's nothing quite like the aroma of a fragrant vegetable broth that fills the kitchen while seitan gently simmers in the cooking pot.

Visually managing the cooking process is important too because we can see what's going on in the cooking pot, while in a closed cooking chamber we cannot. When simmering seitan, the broth is gradually absorbed by the dough in a controlled manner, whereas in a pressure cooker the broth is forced into the dough under pressure. For the sake of convenience, or for "set it and forget it" cooking, I think a slow-cooker would be a better option since it cooks gently. So, at this time I will not be exploring pressure-cooking as an alternative to simmering seitan.

As a chef, I'm a bit "old school" when it comes to "tried and true" methods. Don't get me wrong, the pressure cooker is excellent for certain cooking applications - but just not all applications. If you choose to experiment with this method as an alternative to simmering, that is entirely up to you and I wish you much success.

Meat Analogue Specialties
Chikun Cutlets, Tenders and Nuggets

Chikun is a versatile, plant-based meat created from a blend of wheat protein, soy protein from tofu and select seasonings. The dough is shaped into either cutlets, tenders or nuggets, pre-baked to seal in the ingredients and set the texture, and then simmered in a seasoned golden broth to complete the cooking process before finishing and serving or using in recipes.

Chikun is neutrally and very lightly seasoned which allows for additional seasoning or marinating before grilling, sautéing, frying or stewing according to the specific cuisine being prepared. A food processor is recommended for kneading the dough, but it can be kneaded by hand or in a stand mixer if preferred.

After pre-baking and simmering, the cutlets, tenders or nuggets require chilling for a minimum of 8 hours before finishing and serving. Refrigeration will firm and enhance texture, so this step should not be omitted or rushed. Chilling will also allow time for marinating if desired.

Dry Ingredients

- 1 cup (150 grams) vital wheat gluten
- 2 tsp onion powder
- 1 tsp garlic powder

Blender Ingredients

- 5 oz/142 grams **pressed** extra-firm tofu (not silken tofu)
- ⅔ cup (160 ml) water
- 1 T mellow white miso paste
- 1 T neutral vegetable oil
- ¾ tsp fine sea salt or kosher salt
- ¼ tsp poultry seasoning

Simmering Broth

- 3 quarts (12 cups) chikun simmering broth (page 41)

Additional Items Needed

- baking sheet
- stainless steel cooling rack (not required but recommended)
- parchment paper or silicone baking mat
- a food processor is recommended for kneading the dough but not required

Preparation

Prepare the simmering broth and bring to a simmer in a large covered cooking pot. If preparing the broth from scratch, prepare and bring to a simmer 30 minutes before preparing and pre-baking the dough. This will allow sufficient time to simmer the vegetables before adding the chikun.

Place a stainless-steel cooling rack on a baking sheet and line the rack with parchment paper or a silicone baking mat. The cooling rack is not required, but it is recommended, as it will prevent excessive browning which would occur from direct contact with the hot baking sheet.

Preheat the oven to 350°F/175°C.

Please note that the oven temperature recommended in the recipe was determined using a conventional home oven (radiant heat). If you have a convection oven (fan-assisted) and you cannot turn the fan off, reduce the recommended temperature by 25°F/10°C. All baking times should remain the same.

Combine the dry ingredients in a large mixing bowl. Crumble the pressed tofu into a blender and add the remaining blender ingredients. Process the contents until the tofu is completely liquefied and the mixture is smooth and creamy. This is essential! Stop the blender as necessary to scrape down the sides.

Scoop the tofu mixture into the dry ingredients (a small amount of the tofu mixture will remain in the blender; this is inconsequential). Combine with a sturdy silicone spatula until the tofu mixture is incorporated and a ball of dough begins to form. The mixture may seem a bit dry at first. Do not add more water; just keep mixing.

Place the dough into a food processor fitted with a standard chopping blade or plastic dough blade and process for 1 full minute. Do not over-process or the finished chikun may be tough.

If kneading by hand or in a stand mixer, knead the dough vigorously for 3 full minutes. This is very important in order to develop the gluten. Test the dough by stretching it. If it tears easily, more kneading is required. The dough needs to exhibit a moderate degree of elasticity in order to produce the proper finished texture.

For Cutlets: *With a sharp knife, divide the dough into 6 pieces. Flatten the pieces with the palm of your hand. Stretch the dough against your work surface with your fingers and form into cutlet shapes. Flatten the cutlets again with the palm of your hand. If the dough is resistant to shaping, let it rest a few minutes to relax the gluten. Place the cutlets on the parchment paper or baking mat.*

For Tenders: *Tenders are narrow strips of chikun. They're thicker than cutlets and longer than nuggets and are ideal for breading and frying. With a sharp knife, divide the dough into 6 pieces. Stretch a piece of dough until it begins to tear and then let it contract. Don't try to smooth the surface of the tender, as bumps and irregularities will yield a better finished texture and appearance. Place the tender on the parchment paper or baking mat and repeat with the other pieces.*

For Nuggets: *Nuggets are one or two-bite pieces of chikun. Like tenders, they're also ideal for breading and frying. With a sharp knife, divide the dough into 12 pieces. Stretch a piece of dough as far as it can be stretched without tearing completely and then twist and wind it around your index finger, pinching the dough so it doesn't unwind (if the dough tears too easily, it needs additional kneading). Place the nugget on the parchment paper or baking mat and repeat with the other pieces. While this may seem like tedious work, the nuggets can be formed quickly once the technique is mastered.*

Place the baking sheet on the middle rack of the oven. Bake uncovered for 20 minutes and then remove from the oven. The dough will puff a bit during baking but will return to normal upon cooling. If the dough puffs or inflates excessively, your oven is too hot, so reduce temperature by 25°F/10°C next time.

Bring the broth to a boil. If the broth was made from scratch, use a slotted spoon to remove and discard the larger solids. It's not necessary to strain the broth completely.

Lower the chikun pieces into the boiling broth and immediately reduce the heat to a gentle simmer. Leave the pot uncovered and set a timer for 20 minutes. Do not boil! Turn the pieces occasionally once they float to the top of the pot. After simmering, remove the cooking pot from the heat, cover and let the chikun cool in the broth for a few hours or until lukewarm.

Transfer the chikun to a food storage bag and add ¼ cup of broth, or a desired marinade. Handle the cutlets carefully as they can be fragile. Refrigerate for a minimum of 8 hours to firm and enhance the chikun texture before finishing and serving or using in recipes. Chilling is very important so do not omit this step. The cutlets, tenders and nuggets can be stored in the refrigerator for up to 1 week or frozen without the broth for up to 3 months and then thawed and finished at your convenience.

Strain the cooled broth into a sealable container and refrigerate. During this time, any seasoning sediment will settle on the bottom of the container. The broth can be refrigerated for up to 1 week or frozen for future use at your convenience. Decant the clear portion for preparing gravies or sauces that can be served with the finished chikun; or use for other recipes as desired. Discard the sediment.

After chilling, the cutlets, tenders or nuggets are ready to be marinated/seasoned and finished as desired (if frying, lightly blot them with a paper towel to remove excess moisture before breading and placing in the hot oil).

For outdoor grilling, season the grill grating with cooking oil to discourage sticking. Brush the chikun with cooking oil before placing under the broiler or on the grill. This applies even if the chikun was marinated or a sauce is being used.

Aromatica

A commercial poultry seasoning alternative.

Ingredients

- 2 T dry rubbed sage
- 2 T dried thyme leaves
- 2 T dried marjoram leaves
- 2 T dried rosemary leaves or 1 tsp ground rosemary
- 1 tsp celery seed
- 1 tsp ground white pepper

Preparation

Process the dried herbs and spices in a spice grinder or dry blender until finely powdered; store in an airtight container for up to 6 months

Chikun Simmering Broth

Chikun simmering broth is used for preparing Chikun cutlets, tenders and nuggets (page 38). It can also be used as a flavorful broth base for preparing golden sauces, gravies, soups and stews, or used in any recipe calling for seasoned chicken broth. Additional herbs or spices can be added to accommodate specific regional cuisines. This recipe yields about 3 quarts of prepared broth.

Ingredients

- 3 quarts (12 cups) water
- 3 large onions, peeled and chopped
- 3 ribs celery, chopped
- 1 large carrot, unpeeled and chopped
- small handful parsley stems
- 6 cloves garlic, crushed
- ¼ cup nutritional yeast flakes
- 4 tsp fine sea salt or kosher salt, or more to taste
- 1 T organic sugar
- 1 tsp whole black peppercorns
- 1 tsp dry rubbed sage
- 3 sprigs fresh thyme or ½ tsp dried thyme leaves
- 1 small sprig fresh rosemary

The sage, thyme and rosemary can be replaced with ¾ tsp Aromatica (page 40) or commercial poultry seasoning if desired.

Preparation

Combine all ingredients in a large cooking pot, cover and simmer for a minimum of 1 hour. Strain and discard the larger solids from the broth with a slotted spoon before simmering chikun. After simmering, let the broth cool and then strain into a sealable container to remove any remaining solids and refrigerate. During this time, any seasoning sediment will settle on the bottom of the container.

The broth can be refrigerated for up to 1 week or frozen for future use at your convenience. To use, simply decant the clear portion and discard the fine sediment. Be sure to add back a little water as necessary before using, since the broth will have become concentrated from evaporation during simmering.

If using the broth immediately for other purposes, strain through a fine sieve into another cooking pot and discard the solids.

Quick Broth Options

Fresh homemade broth is always best and is recommended. However, for the sake of convenience and expediency, a quick chikun simmering broth can be made with Better Than Bouillon™ Vegetarian No Chicken Base (1 tsp for each cup water) or other commercial no-chicken broth cubes (½ cube for each cup water), or more or less to taste.

For a superb instant and homemade chikun broth, try my Instant Chikun Bouillon Powder (page 30). Add additional herbs and spices as desired to accommodate specific regional cuisines and season the prepared broth with salt to taste.

Coq au Vin, Vegan-Style

Coq au Vin consists of tender chikun simmered in a luscious red wine sauce with mushrooms and pearl onions and garnished with parsley. Serve over cooked eggless noodles or cooked long-grain rice. This recipe yields about 4 servings.

Ingredients

- 10 oz Chikun cutlets or tenders (page 38)
- 6 T Bacun Grease (page 232)
- 8 oz cremini or white mushrooms, quartered
- 1 and ½ cup pearl onions, thawed from frozen
- ¼ cup all-purpose flour
- 2 cups dry red wine (e.g. Cabernet Sauvignon; Merlot)
- 2 cup chikun simmering broth (page 41)
- 6 sprigs fresh thyme or 1 tsp dried thyme leaves
- 1 bay leaf
- ½ tsp fine sea salt or kosher salt, or more to taste
- coarse ground black pepper to taste
- chopped fresh parsley for garnish

Preparation

Add the bacun grease to a deep non-stick skillet and place over medium heat to melt. Brown the chikun in the hot grease and transfer to a plate.

In the same skillet, sauté the pearl onions and mushrooms until the onions are translucent and golden and the mushrooms have rendered their liquid. Sprinkle in the flour and mix well. Continue to cook for about 2 minutes to eliminate the raw flour taste.

Incorporate the wine in increments while stirring. Stir in the broth and add the chikun, thyme, bay leaf and salt; season with black pepper. Bring the mixture to a simmer and cook uncovered for 20 minutes, stirring occasionally, to reduce and thicken the sauce. Season the stew with additional salt to taste and remove the thyme stems and bay leaf before serving. Garnish with chopped parsley after plating.

Kung Pao Chikun

Diced chikun, sliced garlic, grated ginger and green onions are stir-fried in a spicy Szechuan sauce with dry roasted peanuts. Serve with steamed jasmine rice.

Ingredients

- 1 recipe Chikun cutlets, tenders or nuggets (page 38), diced into ½-inch pieces
- ¼ cup cornstarch or unmodified potato starch for dusting the chikun
- 2 T cooking oil plus 1 tsp sesame oil for frying
- 5 scallions including green tops, chopped
- 4 cloves garlic, thinly sliced
- 1 T freshly grated ginger
- 1 to 2 tsp crushed red pepper flakes
- 1 tsp coarse ground black pepper
- ⅓ cup unsalted dry-roasted peanuts

For the Sauce

- ¼ cup water
- 1 T dark brown sugar
- 1 T rice vinegar
- 1 T dry sherry or Shaoxing rice wine (substitute with water if necessary)
- 1 T tamari, soy sauce or Bragg Liquid Aminos™
- 1 tsp sesame oil
- 1 tsp cornstarch or unmodified potato starch

Preparation

Toss the diced chikun with the starch in a deep bowl or food storage bag until evenly dusted.

Combine the ingredients for the sauce in a small dish, whisking well to ensure the starch is fully dissolved. Set aside.

Thinly slice the garlic and set aside in a bowl with the grated ginger and chopped scallions.

In a wok or deep skillet, add the cooking oil and 1 tsp sesame oil and place over medium heat. When hot, add the red pepper and black pepper and cook about 30 seconds.

Add the chikun and stir-fry until the chikun is lightly browned.

Add the ginger, garlic and scallions and stir-fry an additional minute or two. Add the sauce, toss well, and cook until the sauce begins to thicken. Fold in the peanuts. Serve immediately with jasmine rice.

Chikun Yakitori

Japanese-style marinated, skewered and grilled chikun.

Ingredients

- 1 recipe Chikun nuggets (page 38)
- chopped scallions for garnish
- sesame seeds for garnish
- cooking oil for grilling or broiling

Marinade Ingredients

- ¼ cup
- ¼ cup tamari, soy sauce or Bragg Liquid Aminos™
- ¼ cup mirin (Japanese sweet rice wine) - or additional broth
- 1 T dark brown sugar
- 2 T sake or dry sherry (optional)
- 2 cloves garlic
- 2 tsp cornstarch or unmodified potato starch
- 1 tsp fresh grated ginger
- 1 tsp sambal oelek or Sriracha™

Preparation

Soak bamboo skewers in water for several hours prior to grilling. This will discourage the wood from burning. For mini appetizers, use 6-inch bamboo skewers and tear the chikun into smaller pieces before skewering.

Process the marinade ingredients in a blender until smooth. Pour the marinade into a small saucepan and place over medium heat. Bring to simmer and cook for a few minutes until slightly thickened. Let cool.

Pour the cooled marinade into a food storage bag and add the chikun. Press the air out of the bag, seal and refrigerate for several hours before grilling or broiling.

Skewer the chikun nuggets.

For Pan-Grilling: Reserve the marinade to be used as a dipping sauce. Oil a non-stick grill pan for pan-grilling. Garnish with chopped scallions and sesame seeds and serve with the dipping sauce.

For Oven-Broiling: Reserve the marinade to be used as a dipping sauce. Brush the skewered chikun with oil before broiling to keep the chikun moist. Garnish with chopped scallions and sesame seeds and serve with the dipping sauce.

For Outdoor Grilling: Reserve the marinade to be used as a dipping sauce. Brush the skewered chikun with oil before outdoor grilling to keep the chikun moist and from sticking to the grill. Garnish with chopped scallions and sesame seeds and serve with the dipping sauce.

Mediterranean Chikun

Tender morsels of chikun are sautéed in white wine, lemon juice and Mediterranean seasonings and then garnished with Kalamata olives and parsley for a light and refreshing flavor.

Ingredients

- 10 oz Chikun cutlets (page 38), sliced into strips
- 1 tsp dried basil leaves
- 1 tsp dried oregano leaves
- ½ tsp ground cumin
- ¼ tsp crushed red pepper
- 2 T dry white wine, such as Chardonnay or Sauvignon Blanc (substitute with lemon juice if desired)
- 1 T fresh lemon juice
- 1 medium onion, halved and thinly sliced
- 3 cloves garlic, minced (1 T)
- 2 T olive oil
- 2 T chopped parsley for garnish
- pitted Kalamata olives for garnish
- sea salt or kosher salt and coarse ground black pepper to taste

Preparation

Combine the basil, oregano, cumin and red pepper in a small dish; set aside. Combine the wine and lemon juice in separate small dish; set aside. Add the oil to a large non-stick skillet or wok and place over medium heat; sauté the onion until tender and translucent. Add the garlic and sauté 30 seconds.

Add the sliced chikun and sauté, tossing frequently, until lightly browned. Add the wine/lemon juice mixture and the seasonings and toss well to distribute. Continue to sauté until most of the liquid has evaporated but the chikun is still moist; season with salt and pepper to taste.

Serve on top of orzo, couscous or rice and garnish with the parsley and optional Kalamata olives. The seasoned chikun can also be served hot or cold in a flat-bread wrap or pita pocket with your favorite grilled or fresh vegetables and optional sauce (such as Tahini sauce, page 106; or Greek Tzatziki, page 197).

Chikun and Vegetable Stir-Fry

Flash-cooked vegetables and tender morsels of chikun are tossed together with an Asian-inspired sauce.

Ingredients

- 8 oz Chikun cutlets (page 38) sliced into strips; or Soy Chikun Strips (page 94)
- 2 T tamari, soy sauce or Bragg Liquid Aminos™
- 1 T mirin (Japanese sweet rice wine)
- 2 T peanut oil (or other high-heat cooking oil)
- 2 tsp sesame oil
- 6 cups stir-fry vegetables of your choice, chopped, julienned or shredded (separate the cruciferous or crunchy vegetables from the tender, quick-cooking vegetables and place into separate bowls)
- 1 T fresh grated ginger
- 3 cloves garlic, minced (3 T) minced
- 1 to 2 T Sriracha™ or sambal oelek

Preparation

Combine the tamari and mirin in a small bowl; set aside. Combine the oils in a small dish; set aside.

Heat a wok until very hot. Swirl the oils around the sides of the wok. Add any cruciferous or crunchy vegetables and stir-fry until the colors are bright. Add the ginger and garlic and stir-fry for 30 seconds.

Add the chikun and swirl the tamari/mirin mixture around the sides of the wok. Continue to stir-fry, tossing frequently, until the cruciferous vegetables are tender crisp.

Add any quick-cooking vegetables (such as pea pods and bean sprouts) and toss for 30 seconds. Add the chili sauce and toss well just before removing from the heat. Serve immediately over jasmine rice, sticky rice or Asian noodles.

Shredded Chikun

Shredded chikun amazingly resembles baked, shredded chicken in flavor, aroma and texture. It is prepared from a blend of wheat protein from gluten, soy protein from tofu and select seasonings. Shredded chikun is ideal for use in recipes where a shredded texture is desired, such as chilled chikun salad, hot or cold wraps or sandwiches, stir-fries, flash sautés, Mexican cuisine (tamales, enchiladas, taquitos, flautas and burritos). The chikun can also be torn into meaty tenders or nuggets and battered and fried. For soups and stews, shredded chikun should be added just before serving to retain its texture.

Shredded chikun is minimally and neutrally seasoned which allows for additional seasoning when using in recipes; or try using a dry seasoning rub prior to wrapping and baking (such as Jamaican Jerk dry rub or Cajun dry rub on page 50). Several quick and easy seasoning and finishing suggestions follow the recipe. This recipe yields about 1 and ½ lb. or 24 oz.

For this recipe, an Instant Pot™ or other electric pressure cooker is recommended for cooking the chikun. It can also be oven-baked if preferred. Pressure-cooking discourages the foil package from rupturing under internal steam pressure, which can sometimes occur during oven-baking if there is a weak point in the foil wrap. Pressure-cooking also offers more uniform and consistent temperature control, whereas ovens can vary. This ensures consistently moist results. When oven-baking, be sure to wrap with additional heavy-duty foil to ensure that the package does not rupture from steam pressure which builds up inside the package during baking.

A food processor with a standard chopping blade or plastic dough blade is required for processing the sticky dough, which in turn will provide sufficient gluten development essential for the desired finished texture. Kneading by hand, or with a stand mixer, will most likely not develop the gluten sufficiently to provide the desired finished texture.

Chef's Note: Pulled porq can be created by making some minor adjustments to this recipe. Simply add 1 tablespoon mushroom powder and 1 teaspoon liquid smoke to the blender ingredients. Substitute ½ teaspoon cumin for the Aromatica (aka poultry seasoning). Follow the recipe in exactly the same manner.

Dry Ingredients

- 1 and ½ cup (225 grams) vital wheat gluten
- 4 tsp onion powder
- 2 tsp garlic powder

Blender Ingredients

- 10 oz/284 grams **pressed** extra-firm tofu (not silken tofu)
- 1 cup plus 2 T (270 ml) water*
- 2 T mellow white miso paste
- 2 T neutral vegetable oil
- 1 tsp fine sea salt or kosher salt
- ½ tsp Aromatica (page 40) or commercial poultry seasoning (optional)

Additional Item Needed

- 18-inch wide heavy-duty aluminum foil

The moisture content of tofu can vary, even after pressing. If the pressed tofu being used is extremely dry, try adding an additional 2 tablespoons water to the blended tofu mixture. If the pressed tofu being used is still quite damp, reduce the water by 2 tablespoons (an overly wet dough can cause the dough to creep onto the motor shaft of the food processor when processing).

Preparing the Dough

Fill the pressure cooker with 2 to 3 cups of water and put the trivet in place. If using an oven, preheat the oven to 350°F/175°C.

Please note that the oven temperature recommended in the recipe was determined using a conventional home oven (radiant heat). If you have a convection oven (fan-assisted) and you cannot turn the fan off, reduce the temperature by 25°F/10°C. The baking time should remain the same.

Combine the dry ingredients in a large mixing bowl.

Crumble the pressed tofu into a blender and add the remaining blender ingredients. Process the contents until the tofu is completely liquefied and the mixture is smooth and creamy. This is essential! Stop the blender as necessary to scrape down the sides.

Scoop the tofu mixture into the dry ingredients and combine with a sturdy silicone spatula until the tofu mixture is incorporated and a sticky ball of dough begins to form. Let the dough rest 10 minutes. This will give the gluten a chance to absorb the liquid and help reduce stickiness.

Place the dough into a food processor fitted with a standard chopping blade or plastic dough blade and process for 90 seconds to 2 full minutes. If you have a smaller capacity food processor, you may want to divide the dough in half and process separately. This will reduce wear and tear on the motor.

The processor will bounce and rock on the counter during processing, especially as the dough reaches its desired elasticity, so you will need to hold it in place. The dough, when sufficiently processed, should be sticky, somewhat glossy and resemble warm, stretchy taffy. If not, the quality of your gluten may be in question; try processing a bit longer. Occasionally, the sticky dough may creep up onto the motor shaft of the processor during processing. Simply, clean up with a dampened paper towel.

Quick Dough Mixing for Large Capacity Food Processers

If you have a large capacity food processor, the dough can be mixed entirely in the food processor; no blender needed. To do this, crumble the pressed tofu into the food processor and process into a coarse paste. Add the onion and garlic powder, white miso, Aromatica (poultry seasoning), salt and oil. Process as smooth as possible. Scrape down the processor bowl as needed. Add the gluten to the tofu mixture and pour in the water. Process for 2 full minutes. Proceed with the recipe as instructed.

Foil-Wrapping the Dough

Warning! It is very important to use only heavy-duty aluminum foil for this recipe. Regular foil is not sturdy enough and can easily rupture from steam pressure which builds up inside the sealed package.

Tear off a sheet of foil (about 18-inches) and place it on your work surface. Transfer the dough to the foil and shape into a compact mass. If you are using a dry rub seasoning, rub 2 to 3 teaspoons of the mixture over the dough. Fold the slab of dough in the foil (don't roll), creating a semi-flat package.

When oven-baking, fold in the ends but leave a little room (about 1-inch on each side) to allow the dough to expand as it bakes. This is very important! When pressure-cooking, leaving additional room in the foil is unnecessary. Now crimp the folded ends to seal the package. Rewrap the package in the same manner in a second sheet of foil. For oven-baking, rewrap in a third sheet of foil.

Pressure Cooking

Cook on high (or the setting for cooking chicken) for 1 hour and 30 minutes (with most programmable cookers, you will need to manually override the preset cooking time). After cooking, turn the cooker off and let the steam naturally release for 30 minutes. Do not release the steam valve until the 30 minutes is completed. Remove from the cooker to cool until the package can be handled comfortably.

Oven Baking

Place the foil package directly on the middle rack of the oven and set a timer for 2 hours. Remove from the oven to cool until the package can be handled comfortably.

Shredding the Chikun

Remove the foil and recycle. While the roast is still warm, use your hands to bend the roast in half to split it lengthwise; this will reveal the "grain". Tear the roast in half following where it has been split. Bend and tear those pieces in half lengthwise. Now, with your fingers, pull the chikun into long strings or shreds, following the grain as much as possible. Tear those pieces into smaller bite-size shreds, once again, following the grain as much as possible. Use in your favorite recipes as desired. Store airtight in the refrigerator and use within one week. You can also store the chikun in the freezer for up to 3 months.

Troubleshooting

If the finished product is yielding a bread-like texture, check your gluten. A bread-like texture may indicate poor quality gluten that contains too much starch. The gluten must be guaranteed a minimum of 75% protein. Also, be sure to process the tofu mixture until completely liquefied before adding to the dry ingredients. If your gluten quality is not in question, try changing the brand of tofu.

A bread-like texture may also indicate that the dough was not kneaded sufficiently to develop the gluten strands. For this reason, a food processor is required for sufficient gluten development.

Also check your oven temperature. If the oven is running too hot, it can overcook the chikun; manually adjust the temperature as needed. Be sure to triple-wrap the dough with the foil and seal securely to prevent moisture loss while baking. If you have consistent problems when oven-baking this recipe, try using the electric pressure cooker method instead.

Jamaican Jerk Spice Rub

For spicy Jamaican Jerk Shredded Chikun, rub the chikun dough (page 47) with 2 to 3 teaspoons of the mixture prior to wrapping and foil and cooking. The dry rub can also be used for grilling Chikun cutlets, tenders or nuggets (page 38). Simply rub the chikun with cooking oil and then generously rub with the mixture prior to grilling.

Ingredients

- 2 T onion powder
- 1 T dried thyme
- 1 T ground allspice
- 1 T sea salt or kosher salt
- 1 T organic sugar
- 2 tsp coarse ground black pepper
- 2 tsp cayenne pepper
- 2 tsp garlic powder
- ½ tsp grated nutmeg
- ½ tsp ground cinnamon

Preparation

Combine the ingredients in a bowl. Store the mixture in an airtight container for up to 6 months until ready to use.

Cajun Spice Rub

For spicy Cajun Shredded Chikun, rub the chikun dough (page 47) with 2 to 3 teaspoons of the mixture prior to wrapping and foil and cooking. The dry rub can also be used for grilling Chikun cutlets, tenders or nuggets (page 38). Simply rub the cutlets with cooking oil and then generously rub with the mixture prior to grilling.

Ingredients

- 3 T coarse sea salt or kosher salt
- 3 T sweet paprika
- 1 T onion powder
- 1 T garlic powder
- 1 T dried thyme leaves
- 1 T dried oregano leaves
- 2 tsp coarse ground black pepper
- 2 tsp cayenne pepper
- 1 bay leaf, crumbled

Preparation

Process the ingredients in a dry blender until the bay leaf is completely powdered. Store the mixture in an airtight container for up to 6 months until ready to use.

Chef's Favorite Fried Chikun

This is my "go-to" recipe for crispy and delicious vegan fried chikun. The dipping and dredging ingredients also work great for battering/breading assorted vegetables (such as zucchini, mushrooms, eggplant, green tomato slices, etc.) and sticks of non-dairy cheese for deep-frying.

Ingredients

- 1 recipe Shredded Chikun (page 47), torn into meaty tenders or large nuggets
- cooking oil for frying

Dipping Ingredients

- 1 cup plain unsweetened soymilk or almond milk
- 1 and ½ tsp Gentle Chef Vegan Eggz Essentials A
- ½ tsp Gentle Chef Vegan Eggz Essentials B

If you don't have the Gentle Chef Vegan Eggz Essentials on hand, whisk together these alternate dipping ingredients: ½ cup plain unsweetened soymilk or almond milk and ½ cup No-Eggy Mayo (page 263) or commercial vegan equivalent.

Dredging Ingredients

- 1 cup panko-style bread crumbs
- 1 cup all-purpose flour
- 2 T nutritional yeast
- 1 and ½ tsp sea salt or kosher salt
- 1 tsp Aromatica (page 40) or commercial poultry seasoning
- ½ tsp ground black pepper
- ½ tsp sweet paprika or smoked paprika

Preparation

Place the chikun pieces into a sealable food storage bag.

Process the dipping ingredients in a mini-blender for 20 seconds. If using the alternate dipping ingredients, whisk them in a bowl until smooth. Pour the mixture into the bag, seal and turn the bag to coat the chikun pieces thoroughly.

Combine the dredging ingredients in a roomy food storage container. Add the dipped chikun pieces, seal the container and shake until the pieces are well coated. Open the container to allow the breading to dry while the cooking oil is heating.

In a deep skillet or wok, add about 2-inches of oil and place over medium-high heat. To test the oil for the proper frying temperature, drop a few breadcrumbs into the hot oil. If they begin to sizzle and brown, the oil is ready. Carefully place the coated pieces into the hot oil; avoid over-crowding. Fry until golden brown, turning occasionally with a wire spider or slotted spoon and place on a plate lined with paper towels to drain. Repeat with any remaining pieces. If the oil gets too hot, simply reduce the heat to medium. Serve with vegan ranch dressing or BBQ sauce for dipping if desired.

Crispy Coconut Curry Chikun

Tender chikun breaded with panko and coconut and fried until crisp and golden. Served with a spicy sweet tropical sauce. This recipe can also be made with Shrymp (page 151).

Ingredients

- 1 recipe Shredded Chikun (page 47), torn into meaty tenders or nuggets
- 1 cup plain soymilk or almond milk
- ⅔ cup rice flour or all-purpose flour
- 1 tsp fine sea salt or kosher salt
- 2 cups shredded coconut, sweetened or unsweetened (your choice)
- 1 and ½ cup panko crumbs
- 1 and ½ tsp curry powder
- ½ tsp coarse ground black pepper
- finely chopped That basil or cilantro for garnish (optional)
- cooking oil for deep frying

Dipping Sauce Ingredients

- ½ cup pineapple mango jam or orange marmalade
- 1 T Asian chili garlic sauce or sambal oelek, or more to taste

Preparation

Stir together the sauce ingredients and set aside; or chill until ready to serve.

In a bowl, whisk together the flour, milk and salt to create a smooth batter. Set aside.

Add the shredded coconut, panko crumbs, curry powder and black pepper to a food processor and process into a very coarse flour. Be sure to leave plenty of texture. Transfer to a bowl and set aside.

Dredge the tenders or nuggets in the batter and then in the coconut crumb mixture until thoroughly coated. Set aside on a plate to dry for about 20 minutes.

Heat a sufficient amount of oil for deep-frying in a deep skillet, wok or deep fryer over medium-high heat.

When the oil begins to shimmer, fry the battered chikun until golden brown. Remove with a spider or slotted spoon to avoid dislodging the crumb coating. Transfer to a plate lined with paper towels to drain briefly.

Garnish with the optional Thai basil or cilantro and serve hot with the dipping sauce.

Steak Bites

Steak bites are tender chunks of beaf seitan. "Beaf" is a hybrid word derived from the consonants of the word "beef" and the vowels of the word "wheat". To create the steak bites, the seasoned gluten dough is torn into small chunks. The chunks are pre-baked to set their texture and then simmered in a hearty broth to complete the cooking process before finishing. Steak bites are neutrally seasoned, which allows for additional seasoning or marinating according to the specific cuisine being prepared. Steak bites can be finished by pan-glazing and browning in a skillet or they can be marinated and threaded onto skewers for the grill.

Steak bites require chilling for a minimum of 8 hours after simmering to firm and enhance their texture before finishing, so plan accordingly. For gluten-free, soy-based steak strips, please see page 100.

Dry Ingredients

- 1 and ½ cup (225 grams) vital wheat gluten
- 2 T porcini mushroom powder
- 4 tsp onion powder
- 2 tsp garlic powder
- ½ tsp ground white pepper

Liquid Ingredients

- 1 cup (240 ml) water
- 3 T tamari, soy sauce or Bragg Liquid Aminos™
- 2 T neutral vegetable oil
- 2 tsp Worcestershire Sauce (page 27) or commercial vegan equivalent

Simmering Broth

- 3 quarts (12 cups) beaf simmering broth (page 56)

Additional Items Needed

- baking sheet
- stainless steel cooling rack (not required but recommended)
- parchment paper or silicone baking mat

Optional Pan-Glaze Ingredients for Finishing

- 2 T non-dairy butter or margarine
- 2 T dry red wine or reserved simmering broth
- 2 tsp Worcestershire Sauce (page 27) or commercial vegan equivalent
- a few pinches coarse ground black pepper
- ground spices and/or fresh or dried herbs of your choice (optional)

Preparation

Prepare the simmering broth and bring to a simmer in a large covered cooking pot. If preparing the broth from scratch, prepare and bring to a simmer 30 minutes before preparing and pre-baking the dough. This will allow sufficient time to simmer the ingredients before adding the beaf.

Place a stainless-steel cooling rack on a baking sheet and line the rack with parchment paper or a silicone baking mat. The cooling rack is not required, but it is recommended, as it will prevent excessive browning which would occur from direct contact with the hot baking sheet.

Preheat the oven to 350°F/175°C.

Please note that the oven temperature recommended in the recipe was determined using a conventional home oven (radiant heat). If you have a convection oven (fan-assisted) and you cannot turn the fan off, reduce the temperature by 25°F/10°C. The baking time should remain the same.

Combine the dry ingredients in a large mixing bowl. Stir together the liquid ingredients in a separate bowl or measuring cup.

Pour the liquid mixture (not the simmering broth) into the dry ingredients and combine thoroughly with a sturdy silicone spatula to form the dough and begin developing the gluten.

Transfer the dough to a work surface and knead vigorously until very elastic. Pick up the dough and stretch it into a long strand until it begins to tear. Place it on your work surface and then loosely roll it up into a lumpy mass. Knead a few strokes. Repeat the stretching, rolling and kneading technique until the dough is separating into stringy strands when stretched, finishing by loosely rolling it into a lumpy mass on your work surface. The goal of this technique is to isolate the strands of gluten, which in turn will create the proper beaf texture in the finished steak bites.

Now, tear the dough into bite-size chunks and place them on the parchment paper or baking mat. Place the baking sheet on the middle rack of the oven. Bake uncovered for 25 minutes and then remove from the oven. The steak bites will form a dry crust while baking. This is normal and will disappear when the steak bites are simmered.

Bring the broth to a boil. If the broth was made from scratch, use a slotted spoon to remove and discard the larger solids. It's not necessary to strain the broth completely.

Lower the pre-baked steak bites into the boiling broth and immediately reduce the heat to a gentle simmer. Leave the pot uncovered and set a timer for 20 minutes. Monitor the pot frequently to make sure the broth is maintained at a simmer. Do not boil the steak bites but don't let them merely poach in hot broth either. Move the steak bites occasionally in the broth once they float to the top of the pot. After simmering, remove the cooking pot from the heat, cover and let the steak bites cool in the broth for a few hours or until lukewarm.

Transfer the steak bites to a food storage bag and add ¼ cup broth, or a desired marinade. Refrigerate for a minimum of 8 hours to firm and enhance the beaf texture before finishing. Chilling is very important so do not omit this step. The steak bites can be stored in the refrigerator for up to 10 days or frozen without the broth for up to 3 months and then thawed and finished at your convenience.

Strain the cooled broth into a sealable container and refrigerate. During this time, any seasoning sediment will settle on the bottom of the container. The broth can be refrigerated for up to 1 week or frozen for future use at your convenience. Decant the clear portion for preparing gravies or sauces that can be served with the finished steak bites; or use for other recipes as desired. Discard the sediment.

Finishing the Steak Bites

Combine the wine or reserved broth with the Worcestershire in a small dish. Stir in any desired optional seasonings. In a large non-stick skillet or well-seasoned cast iron skillet, melt the butter or margarine over medium heat. Sauté the steak bites, moving them frequently until lightly browned on all sides. Add the wine/broth mixture. Continue to sauté the steak bites in the mixture, turning frequently until most of the liquid has evaporated and the steak bites are nicely glazed; season with black pepper to taste. Arrange the steak bites on a serving platter, insert toothpicks and serve immediately.

Grilling Steak Bites for Brochette, Kebab, Satay and Kushiyaki

"En brochette" is the French term and "shish kebab or shish kabob" is the Middle Eastern term for skewered and grilled chunks of meat with or without vegetables. "Satay" is the Indonesian term for seasoned, skewered and grilled meat, typically served with a dipping sauce. In Japanese cuisine, "kushiyaki " typically refers to beef that is skewered and grilled. Steak bites have a high moisture content and tender texture which makes them ideal for skewering and grilling.

Before grilling, marinate the steak bites in your favorite marinade and chill them for 8 hours or overnight. For mini appetizer skewers, use 6-inch bamboo skewers and you may want to cut or tear the steak bites into smaller pieces before skewering. When using bamboo skewers, soak them in water for several hours before skewering and grilling to prevent the wood from burning.

For beaf en brochette and shish kebab, skewer the steak bites with any vegetables of your choice, such as thickly sliced zucchini, eggplant, cherry tomatoes, mushrooms and chunks of onion and bell pepper (pineapple is ideal for skewering and grilling too). Satay is not typically skewered with vegetables. Season or brush the skewers with a favorite grilling sauce. For Japanese beaf kushiyaki, refer to the recipe on page 57.

Brush or spray a non-stick grill pan or outdoor grill grating with cooking oil before grilling to keep the beaf and vegetables from sticking. Brush the beaf with cooking oil before broiling or outdoor grilling, and then generously and frequently with the marinade or sauce of your choice while broiling or grilling to keep the beaf moist and tender.

Beaf Simmering Broth

Beaf simmering broth is used for simmering Steak Bites (page 53) and Prime Cut Roast Beaf (page 58). It can also be used as a savory broth base for preparing brown sauces, gravies, 'jus', hearty soups and stews, or used in any recipe calling for seasoned beef broth. Additional herbs or spices can be added to accommodate specific regional cuisines. This recipe yields about 3 quarts of prepared broth.

Ingredients

- 3 quarts water (12 cups)
- 3 large onions, peeled and quartered
- 3 ribs celery, chopped
- 1 large carrot, unpeeled and chopped
- small handful parsley stems
- 6 cloves garlic, crushed
- ½ cup tamari, soy sauce or Bragg Liquid Aminos™*
- 2 T mushroom powder
- 2 T nutritional yeast flakes
- 1 T dark brown sugar
- 1 T Worcestershire Sauce (page 27) or commercial vegan equivalent
- 1 tsp fine sea salt or kosher salt, or more to taste
- 1 tsp whole black peppercorns

Preparation

Combine all ingredients in a large cooking pot, cover and simmer for a minimum of 1 hour. Strain and discard the larger solids from the broth with a slotted spoon before simmering beaf.

After simmering, let the broth cool and then strain into a sealable container to remove any remaining solids and refrigerate. During this time, any seasoning sediment will settle on the bottom of the container.

The broth can be refrigerated for up to 1 week or frozen for future use at your convenience. To use, simply decant the clear portion and discard the fine sediment. Be sure to add back a little water as necessary before using, since the broth will have become concentrated from evaporation during simmering.

If using the broth immediately for other purposes, strain through a fine sieve into another cooking pot and discard the solids.

Quick Broth Options

Fresh homemade broth is always best and is recommended. However, for the sake of convenience and expediency, a quick beaf simmering broth can be made with any commercially prepared low-sodium vegetable stock or broth, plus 2 tsp tamari, soy sauce or Bragg Liquid Aminos™ for each cup, or more or less to taste. Add additional herbs and spices as desired to accommodate specific regional cuisines and season the prepared broth with salt to taste.

Beaf Kushiyaki
(Japanese Skewered Grilled Beaf)

Tender beaf steak bites are marinated in a savory and sweet tamari-based sauce before skewering and grilling.

Ingredient

- 1 recipe Steak Bites (page 53)
- chopped scallions for garnish

Marinade Ingredients

- ½ cup Japanese sake or mirin (or water with 1 tablespoon rice vinegar)
- ¼ cup tamari, soy sauce or Bragg Liquid Aminos™
- ¼ cup dark brown sugar
- 1 T cooking oil, plus additional for grilling
- 2 tsp Worcestershire Sauce (page 27) or commercial vegan equivalent
- 5 cloves garlic
- 1 tsp toasted sesame oil
- 1 tsp sambal oelek or Sriracha™, or ½ tsp crushed red pepper flakes (or more to taste)

Preparation

Soak bamboo skewers in water for several hours prior to grilling. This will discourage the wood from burning. For mini appetizers, use 6-inch bamboo skewers and tear the steak bites into smaller pieces before skewering.

Process all marinade ingredients in a blender until smooth. Pour into a food storage bag and add the steak bites. Press the air out of the bag, seal and refrigerate for several hours before grilling or broiling.

Skewer the marinated beaf.

Brush or spray a non-stick grill pan or outdoor grill grating with cooking oil before grilling to keep the beaf from sticking. Brush the beaf with cooking oil before broiling or outdoor grilling, and then generously and frequently with the marinade while broiling or grilling to keep the beaf moist and tender.

Garnish with the chopped scallions before serving.

Prime Cut Roast Beaf

Succulent and tender prime cut roast beaf slices are delicious served 'au jus' or with your favorite gravy or sauce. Leftovers are superb for hot or cold deli-style sandwiches too. A recipe for "Yorkies" (individual Yorkshire puddings), a classic holiday accompaniment with roast beaf, follows this recipe on page 60. A recipe for quick pan gravy is also included on page 60.

This recipe yields about 1 and ½ lb. Prime cut roast beaf requires chilling for a minimum of 8 hours after simmering to firm and enhance its texture before pan-glazing, so plan accordingly.

Dry Ingredients

- 1 and ½ cup (225 grams) vital wheat gluten
- 2 T porcini mushroom powder
- 4 tsp onion powder
- 2 tsp garlic powder
- ½ tsp ground white pepper

Liquid Ingredients

- 1 cup (240 ml) water
- 3 T tamari, soy sauce or Bragg Liquid Aminos™
- 2 T neutral vegetable oil
- 2 tsp Worcestershire Sauce (page 27) or commercial vegan equivalent
- 1 tsp Browning Liquid (page 28) or commercial equivalent

Pan-Glaze Ingredients

- 2 T non-dairy butter or margarine
- 2 T dry red wine or dry sherry (optional)
- 2 tsp Worcestershire Sauce (page 27) or commercial vegan equivalent
- a few pinches coarse ground black pepper
- optional: ground spices and/or fresh or dried herbs of your choice

Simmering Broth

- 3 quarts (12 cups) beaf simmering broth (page 56)

Additional Items Needed

- baking sheet
- stainless steel cooling rack (not required but recommended)
- parchment paper or silicone baking mat

Preparation

Prepare the simmering broth and bring to a simmer in a large covered cooking pot. If preparing the broth from scratch, prepare and bring to a simmer 30 minutes before preparing and pre-baking the dough. This will allow sufficient time to simmer the ingredients before adding the beaf.

Preheat the oven to 350°F/175°C.

Place a stainless-steel cooling rack on a baking sheet and line the rack with parchment paper or a silicone baking mat. The cooling rack is not required, but it is recommended, as it will prevent excessive browning which would occur from direct contact with the hot baking sheet.

Combine the dry ingredients in a large mixing bowl. Stir together the liquid ingredients in a separate bowl or measuring cup.

Pour the liquid mixture (not the simmering broth) into the dry ingredients and combine thoroughly with a sturdy silicone spatula to form the dough and begin developing the gluten.

Transfer the dough to a work surface and knead vigorously until very elastic. Test the dough by stretching. If it tears easily, knead a little longer and test again. The dough should be able to stretch considerably without tearing.

Now, form the dough into a thick, compact slab. Don't worry about smoothing the surface too much, as some bumps and irregularities will yield a more natural finished appearance. Transfer the dough to the parchment paper or baking mat.

Place the baking sheet on the middle rack of the oven. Bake uncovered for 45 minutes and then remove from the oven. The roast will form a dry crust while baking. This is normal and will disappear when the roast is simmered.

Bring the broth to a boil. If the broth was made from scratch, use a spider or slotted spoon to remove and discard the larger solids. It's not necessary to strain the broth completely.

Lower the roast into the boiling broth and immediately reduce the heat to a gentle simmer. Leave the pot uncovered and set a timer for 45 minutes. Monitor the pot frequently to make sure the broth is maintained at a simmer. Do not boil the roast but don't let it merely poach in hot broth either. Turn the roast occasionally in the broth as it simmers to ensure even cooking. After simmering, remove the cooking pot from the heat, cover and let the roast cool in the broth for a few hours or until lukewarm.

Transfer the roast to a food storage bag and add ¼cup of broth, or a desired marinade. Refrigerate for a minimum of 8 hours to firm and enhance the beaf texture before finishing. Chilling is very important so do not omit this step. The roast can be refrigerated for up to 10 days before finishing or frozen without the broth for up to 3 months and then thawed and finished at your convenience.

Strain the cooled broth into a sealable container and refrigerate. During this time, any seasoning sediment will settle on the bottom of the container. The broth can be refrigerated for up to 1 week or frozen for future use at your convenience. Decant the clear portion for preparing 'au jus', gravy or sauce that can be served with the sliced roast; or use for other recipes as desired. Discard the sediment.

Finishing the Roast

Bring the roast to room temperature for about 1 hour before finishing.

Combine the wine or broth and tamari in a small dish; set aside. In a large, deep non-stick skillet, melt the butter or margarine over medium heat. Add the roast and turn it to coat with the butter or margarine. Lightly brown the roast, turning frequently. Add the liquid seasonings. The mixture will sizzle and begin to caramelize, turning the roast a beautiful deep brown color. Add the pepper and optional spices and herbs and continue to turn in the mixture to form a crust. Transfer to a serving platter and slice.

Note: If pan-glazing has not sufficiently reheated the roast, place it in a shallow baking dish, cover securely with foil and reheat in a 350°F/175°C oven for 15 to 20 minutes. The roast can also be covered and briefly heated in the microwave before slicing and serving.

Quick Pan Gravy for Roast Beaf

To make a quick pan gravy for sliced roast beaf, add 4 tablespoons non-dairy butter or margarine to the same non-stick skillet used for pan-glazing the roast and heat on a medium setting until the butter or margarine melts.

Sprinkle in ¼ cup all-purpose flour or rice flour and stir to form a thick, smooth paste (roux). Cook the roux until it emits a nutty aroma, about 1 to 2 minutes.

Incorporate 2 cups of reserved beaf simmering broth in small increments, whisking vigorously until smooth after each addition of broth. Continue to whisk, loosening any caramelized bits of glaze stuck to the skillet as you stir. To enrich the brown color, add ½ teaspoon to 1 teaspoon browning liquid (Gravy Master™ or Kitchen Bouquet™).

Increase the heat to medium-high and stir frequently until the mixture is bubbling and begins to thicken; season with salt and pepper to taste. Reduce the heat to low to keep warm until ready to serve, stirring occasionally.

"Yorkies"
(Individual Yorkshire Puddings)

Yorkshire Pudding is an English dish traditionally made from a batter consisting of eggs, flour and milk and then baked in hot pan drippings. It's not a pudding in the American sense of the word but rather a cross between a popover and a soufflé. The dish is usually served with roast meat and gravy and is a staple of British cuisine.

Creating a vegan version without eggs posed a fundamental problem, since the eggs are necessary to inflate the batter as the pudding cooks. However, with a few adjustments and substitutions, a satisfying - albeit less inflated version - can be made. Be sure to read though the directions first and then follow them carefully for success. Serve the "Yorkies" with sliced Prime Cut Roast Beaf and plenty of savory pan gravy.

Ingredients

- 1 cup all-purpose flour
- 2 tsp baking powder
- ½ tsp fine sea salt or kosher salt
- 2 T non-dairy butter or margarine, melted
- 1 T olive oil
- 1 tsp Worcestershire Sauce (page 27) or commercial vegan equivalent
- 1 and ¼ cup plain unsweetened soymilk or almond milk, room temperature

Special Item Needed

- 6-cup muffin tin

Preparation

Prepare, pan-glaze and reheat the Prime Cut Roast Beaf as directed on page 58.

Assemble the ingredients for the pudding while the roast is in the oven. If you plan to serve the roast and puddings with gravy, prepare the gravy at this time and set aside over low heat to stay hot, stirring occasionally.

When the roast is done heating, remove and cover with foil to keep warm. Increase the oven to 425°F/220°C.

Combine the flour, baking powder and salt into a mixing bowl.

In a small dish, mix together one tablespoon of the melted butter or margarine with the Worcestershire sauce and 1 tablespoon olive oil to create the "pan drippings". Divide evenly into the bottoms of the 6-cup muffin tin.

Place the muffin tin in the oven and set a timer for 3 minutes to heat the "pan drippings".

Meanwhile, add the milk and the remaining tablespoon of melted butter or margarine to the flour and whisk to create a batter. Small lumps are okay.

After 3 minutes, remove the muffin tin from the oven and immediately pour the batter, dividing evenly in each cup (about ⅓ of the way full). Place in the oven on a middle rack and set a timer for 35 minutes. Keep in mind that the puddings will only inflate slightly and not in a dramatic fashion as their traditional egg-based counterparts.

10 minutes before the puddings are done, slice the roast and arrange on a serving platter.

Remove the muffin tin from the oven and let cool for about 5 minutes. Serve hot with the roast beaf and plenty of hot gravy.

Stewing Beaf

Stewing Beaf, as the name implies, is ideal for pot roast, stews, soups and pot pies or any recipe that involves simmering in hot liquids. It was formulated differently to produce a shredded texture when simmered and is remarkably similar to beef that has been slow-simmered for hours. Stewing beaf is neutrally seasoned which allows it to absorb additional herb and spice flavors from simmering liquids.

While stewing beaf can be pre-cooked in the oven, pre-cooking in an electric pressure cooker, such as an Instant Pot™, is recommended. Pressure-cooking discourages the foil package from rupturing under internal steam pressure, which can sometimes occur during oven-baking if there is a weak point in the foil wrap.

A food processor with a standard chopping blade or plastic dough blade is required for processing the dough, which in turn will provide sufficient gluten development essential for the desired finished "shredded" texture. Kneading by hand, or with a stand mixer, will most likely not sufficiently develop the gluten to provide the desired finished texture.

This recipe yields about 1lb., after simmering, which should be ample for most recipes.

Dry Ingredients

- 1 cup (150 grams) vital wheat gluten
- 1 T porcini mushroom powder
- 2 tsp onion powder
- 1 tsp garlic powder
- ¼ tsp ground white pepper

Blender Ingredients

- 2.5 oz (71 grams) **pressed** extra-firm tofu (not silken)
- ⅔ cup (160 ml) water
- 2 T mellow white miso paste
- 1 T neutral vegetable oil
- 2 tsp Worcestershire Sauce (page 27) or commercial vegan equivalent
- 1 and ½ tsp Browning Liquid (page 28) or commercial equivalent
- ½ tsp fine sea salt or kosher salt

Additional Item Needed

- 18-inch-wide heavy-duty aluminum foil

Preparation

Fill the pressure cooker with 2 to 3 cups of water and put the trivet in place. If using an oven, preheat the oven to 350°F/175°C.

Please note that the oven temperature recommended in the recipe was determined using a conventional home oven (radiant heat). If you have a convection oven (fan-assisted) and you cannot turn the fan off, reduce the temperature by 25°F/10°C. The baking time should remain the same.

Combine the dry ingredients in a large mixing bowl.

Crumble the pressed tofu into a blender and add the remaining blender ingredients. Process the contents until the tofu is completely liquefied and the mixture is smooth and creamy. This is essential! Stop the blender as necessary to scrape down the sides.

Scoop the tofu mixture into the dry ingredients (a small amount of the tofu mixture will remain in the blender; this is inconsequential) and stir with a sturdy silicone spatula until the tofu mixture is incorporated and a sticky ball of dough begins to form.

Place the dough into a food processor fitted with a standard chopping blade or plastic dough blade and process for 90 seconds.

Foil-Wrapping the Dough

Warning! It is very important to use only heavy-duty aluminum foil for this recipe. Regular foil is not sturdy enough and can easily rupture from steam pressure which builds up inside the sealed package.

Tear off a sheet of foil (about 18-inches) and place it on your work surface. Transfer the dough to the foil and shape into a compact slab. Shaping perfection is unnecessary. If you are using a dry rub seasoning, rub about 2 teaspoons of the mixture over the dough. Fold the slab of dough in the foil (don't roll), creating a semi-flat package. Fold in the ends but leave a little room (about 1-inch on each side) to allow the dough to expand as it bakes. This is very important! Crimp the folded ends to seal the package.

For Pressure Cooking

Place the foil package on the trivet, seal the lid, close the steam valve and set the cooker on high (or the setting for cooking meat) for 1 hour and 15 minutes (with most programmable cookers, you will need to manually override the preset cooking time). After cooking, turn the cooker off and let the steam naturally release for 30 minutes. Do not release the steam valve until the 30 minutes is completed. Remove from the cooker to cool until the package can be handled comfortably. The foil package can also be chilled for up to one week or frozen for up to 3 months before stewing.

For Oven Baking

Place the foil package directly on the middle rack of the oven and set a timer for 1 hour and 30 minutes. Remove from the oven to cool until the package can be handled comfortably. The foil package can also be chilled for up to one week or frozen for up to 3 months before stewing.

Preparing the Beaf for Stewing

Remove the foil and recycle. The exterior of the beaf will be hard and shriveled; this is normal and will resolve once the beaf is stewed. Using your hands, bend the roast in half to split it lengthwise; this will reveal the "grain". Tear the roast in half following where it has been split. Bend and tear those pieces in half lengthwise. Now, with your fingers, pull the beaf into long strips, following the grain as much as possible. Tear those pieces into smaller bite-size pieces. The pieces can also be cubed or diced. For pot pies and saucy casseroles, mix the diced beaf with the other ingredients before baking. For soups and stews, add the beaf the last 20 minutes of cooking time before serving.

For pot roasts or slow cooker recipes, leave the entire piece of beaf intact. After simmering, transfer to a serving platter and shred with a fork into chunks.

Beer-Braised Shredded Beaf

Stewing beaf, when shredded, amazingly resembles slow-cooked shredded beef in texture. The shredded beaf is superb for hot sandwiches when finished by skillet braising in a mixture of beer and savory seasonings.

Ingredients

- 1 recipe Stewing Beaf (page 62)
- 2 T tamari, soy sauce or Bragg Liquid Aminos™
- 1 T Dijon or spicy mustard
- 1 tsp Worcestershire Sauce (page 27) or commercial vegan equivalent
- ¼ tsp coarse ground black pepper, or more to taste
- ¼ tsp dried thyme leaves
- 2 T cooking oil
- 1 medium onion, halved and thinly sliced
- 4 cloves garlic, minced
- 1 bottle or can (12 oz) beer of your choice

Preparation

Prepare and then chill the Stewing Beaf according to the cookbook directions.

Remove the foil and recycle. Using your hands, bend the roast in half to split it lengthwise; this will reveal the "grain". Tear the roast in half following where it has been split. Bend and tear those pieces in half lengthwise. Now, with your fingers, pull the beaf into long strings or shreds, following the grain as much as possible. Tear those pieces into smaller bite-size shreds.

In a small dish, combine the tamari, mustard, Worcestershire, black pepper and thyme; set aside.

Add the oil to a large non-stick skillet or wok and place over medium heat; sauté the onion until tender and translucent. Add the garlic and sauté 30 seconds.

Add the shredded beaf and sauté, tossing frequently, until lightly browned. Add the tamari seasoning mixture and the beer and stir well to combine. Simmer uncovered, stirring frequently, until almost all the liquid has evaporated but the beaf is still moist. Serve hot as a filling for sandwiches.

Spicy Beef Barbacoa

Barbacoa is a spicy Tex-Mex barbecue sauce that is superb when tossed with shreds of Stewing Beaf and served with tortillas, fresh salsa and guacamole. This recipe yields about 2 cups.

Ingredients

- 1 recipe Stewing Beaf (page 62)
- 2 cups beaf simmering broth (page 56)
- ¼ cup apple cider vinegar
- ¼ cup fresh lime juice
- 1 can (7 oz) chipotle peppers in adobo sauce
  (this ingredient packs a fiery heat, so reduce the amount for a milder sauce)
- 8 cloves garlic
- 2 tsp ground cumin
- 2 tsp dried oregano
- ½ tsp ground cloves
- sea salt or kosher salt, to taste

Preparation

Prepare and then chill the stewing beaf according to the cookbook directions.

Remove the foil and recycle. Using your hands, bend the roast in half to split it lengthwise; this will reveal the "grain". Tear the roast in half following where it has been split. Bend and tear those pieces in half lengthwise. Now, with your fingers, pull the beaf into long strings or shreds, following the grain as much as possible. Tear those pieces into smaller bite-size shreds.

Process all sauce ingredients in a blender until smooth. Transfer the mixture to a medium saucepan and bring to a gentle simmer.

Cook uncovered for 45 minutes to reduce the mixture to about 2 cups. Add the shreds of beaf and toss well. Serve with tortillas, fresh salsa and guacamole.

Salisbury Steak
with Savory Onion Mushroom Gravy

Salisbury steak consists of seasoned and pan-grilled meatless burger patties topped with a savory onion and mushroom gravy (recipe for the gravy follows this recipe).

For meatless hamburger patties, divide the dough into 6 portions and shape into round patties. Omit the gravy. Pan-grill or outdoor grill as desired. For outdoor grilling, brush the hamburger patties with cooking oil to prevent them from sticking and drying out on the grill.

Dry Ingredients

- 1 cup (150 grams) vital wheat gluten
- 1 T porcini mushroom powder
- 1 T dried minced onion
- 2 tsp onion powder
- 1 and ½ tsp garlic powder
- ½ tsp coarse ground black pepper
- ¼ tsp ground dried rosemary

Wet Ingredients

- ¼ cup dry TVP/TSP granules (textured vegetable/soy protein)
- ¼ cup boiling water (to reconstitute the TVP/TSP granules)
- ¾ cup (180 ml) water
- 2 T tamari, soy sauce or Bragg Liquid Aminos™
- 2 tsp Worcestershire Sauce (page 27) or commercial vegan equivalent
- 1 T olive oil

Finishing Marinade

- ¼ cup water
- 1 tsp Worcestershire Sauce (page 27) or commercial vegan equivalent

Additional Items Needed

- baking sheet
- stainless steel cooling rack (not required but recommended)
- parchment paper or silicone baking mat

Preparation

In a small bowl, add the ¼ cup boiling water to the TVP/TSP granules and let reconstitute for 10 minutes.

In another bowl, combine ¾ cup cool water with the remaining wet ingredients. Stir the reconstituted TVP/TSP granules into the wet mixture. Set aside.

Place a stainless-steel cooling rack on a baking sheet and line the rack with parchment paper or a silicone baking mat. The cooling rack is not required, but it is recommended, as it will prevent excessive browning which would occur from direct contact with the hot baking sheet.

Preheat the oven to 350°F/175°C.

Please note that the oven temperature recommended in the recipe was determined using a conventional home oven (radiant heat). If you have a convection oven (fan-assisted) and you cannot turn the fan off, reduce the temperature by 25°F/10°C. The baking time should remain the same.

Thoroughly stir together the dry ingredients in a large mixing bowl. Give the wet ingredients a quick stir and then pour all at once into the dry ingredients.

Fold the mixture together with a silicone spatula just until all ingredients are incorporated and a soft dough begins to form. Do not knead the dough as this will make the dough elastic and difficult to shape into patties.

Flatten the dough evenly in the bottom of the mixing bowl and divide into 4 roughly equal portions with the edge of the spatula.

Pick up a piece of dough, form into a ball and then press flat in the palm of your hand. Now press flat on the baking sheet and then continue to press and shape the dough into oval-shaped patties with your fingers.

Drape a large sheet of foil over the baking sheet and crimp the edges to seal the foil. Place on the middle rack of the oven and bake for 50 minutes.

Remove the baking sheet and let the steaks cool for about 30 minutes with the foil cover in place. When cool enough to handle, but still warm, remove the foil and carefully transfer the steaks to a food storage bag. Add the finishing marinade, press out as much air as possible and seal the bag. Refrigerate until well-chilled and most of the marinade has been absorbed before grilling (the steaks can remain stored in this bag in the refrigerator for up to 10 days before grilling). Once the steaks have absorbed the marinade, they can also be frozen for up to 3 months. Simply wrap them between layers of wax paper or parchment paper and place them in a freezer storage bag. Be sure to thaw them completely before grilling.

Finishing and Serving the Steaks

Prepare the gravy (the recipe follows on page 68) and set aside over low heat to keep warm.

Oil a large non-stick skillet or grill pan and place over medium heat. Pan-sear the steaks until nicely browned on both sides. Arrange on serving plates, top with the gravy and garnish with the chopped parsley and snipped chives.

Savory Onion and Mushroom Gravy

Ingredients

- 2 T olive oil
- ½ medium onion, sliced thin and then chopped
- 6 oz white mushrooms, sliced or chopped
- 2 T non-dairy butter or margarine
- ¼ cup all-purpose flour
- 2 cups beaf simmering broth (page 56) or similar
- ½ tsp dried thyme leaves
- 1 tsp Browning Liquid (page 28) or commercial equivalent, or more as needed for color
- sea salt or kosher salt and coarse ground black pepper, to taste

Preparation

Add the olive oil to a large saucepan and place over medium heat. Add the mushrooms and onion and sauté until the liquid has evaporated and the mushrooms begin to brown. Stir in the butter until melted.

Sprinkle in the flour and stir until a thick paste forms (roux). Cook the mixture until the flour is golden and emits a nutty aroma, about 2 minutes. The flour will stick to the bottom of the saucepan, but don't worry, as it will release when the broth is incorporated.

Incorporate the broth in increments, stirring well after each addition. Add the thyme and bring the mixture to a boil, stirring frequently. Reduce the heat and simmer, about 10 minutes.

Season the gravy with salt and pepper to taste. Add enough browning liquid to achieve a rich brown color. Keep warm over low heat until ready to serve.

Meatless Meatballs

These tender and delicious meatless meatballs are perfect for using in your favorite pasta sauce, soup, stew or for meatball sandwiches. They hold up very well to prolonged simmering in sauces, soups and stews, unlike many commercial plant-based meatballs which tend to break down. The prepared meatballs require several hours of refrigeration before using in recipes to firm and enhance their texture, so plan accordingly. This recipe yields approximately 10 large meatballs, 20 medium meatballs or 25 small meatballs.

Dry Ingredients

- 1 cup vital wheat gluten (150 grams)
- 1 T garbanzo bean flour
- 1 T mushroom powder
- 1 T dried minced onion
- 2 tsp onion powder
- 2 tsp dried parsley
- 1 and ½ tsp garlic powder
- ½ tsp coarse ground black pepper

Wet Ingredients

- 2 T dry TVP/TSP granules (textured vegetable/soy protein)
- 2 T boiling water (to reconstitute the TVP/TSP granules)
- ½ cup water
- 3 T tamari, soy sauce or Bragg Liquid Aminos™
- 1 T olive oil

Simmering Broth

- 3 quarts (12 cups) beaf simmering broth (page 56) or porq simmering broth (page 77), or any seasoned vegetable broth

Seasoning Variations

• For Italian meatballs omit the dried parsley from the dry ingredients and add 1 tsp dried basil leaves, 1 tsp dried oregano leaves and ¼ tsp crushed red pepper.

• For Swedish meatballs omit the dried parsley from the dry ingredients and add ½ tsp ground nutmeg and ½ tsp ground allspice.

• For Mexican meatballs omit the dried parsley from the dry ingredients and add 1 tsp dried oregano leaves, ½ tsp ground cumin, ½ tsp ground coriander and ¼ tsp ground red pepper.

• For Mediterranean meatballs add 1 tsp dried oregano leaves and ½ tsp ground cumin to the dry ingredients.

• For Moroccan meatballs add ½ tsp ground cumin, ½ tsp ground allspice and ¼ tsp ground red pepper to the dry ingredients.

Preparation

Prepare the simmering broth in a large cooking pot prior to preparing the meatballs. If the broth was made from scratch, cover and allow it to simmer for one hour.

Stir together the dry ingredients in a large mixing bowl. Set aside.

In a small bowl, add 2 tablespoons boiling water to the TVP/TSP granules to reconstitute. In a standard or mini-blender, add the ½ cup water with the remaining liquid ingredients. Add the reconstituted TVP/TSP granules to the liquid ingredients in the blender and pulse the blender a few times to coarsely grind the granules. The goal is to leave some texture but reduce the size of the granules.

Pour the blender ingredients into the dry ingredients. Mix just until the liquid is incorporated and the dry ingredients are moistened; the mixture may seem a bit dry. Do not knead the dough or the meatballs will be difficult to roll.

Pinch off a piece of dough and compress the dough in your hands. Roll the dough into a round meatball shape between your palms, about ¾-inch diameter for small meatballs, 1-inch diameter for medium meatballs or 1 and ½-inch diameter for large meatballs and set aside on your work surface. Repeat with the remaining dough. Try to work quickly when rolling; the gluten in the dough becomes more elastic the longer the dough sits, and this will make rolling more difficult.

Bring the broth to a boil. If the broth was made from scratch, use a slotted spoon to remove and discard the larger solids. It's not necessary to strain the broth completely.

Add the meatballs to the boiling broth and immediately reduce the heat to a gentle simmer. Cook uncovered 25 minutes for large meatballs, 20 minutes for medium meatballs and 15 minutes for small meatballs.

Check frequently to maintain the broth at a very gentle simmer. Do not boil! Turn occasionally once the meatballs float to the top of the pot. When simmering is complete, remove the pot from the heat and let the meatballs cool in the broth for several hours or until lukewarm. Transfer the meatballs to a food storage bag with ¼ cup of broth and refrigerate for a minimum of 8 hours before browning in the skillet. This will firm and enhance their texture, so do not omit this step. The meatballs can be stored in the refrigerator for up to 10 days before browning and serving or frozen without the broth for up to 3 months and then thawed and finished at your convenience.

Be sure to reserve the simmering broth. The broth can be strained and used immediately for soups, stews, sauces or gravies. Be sure to add back a little water as necessary before using, since the seasoning will have become concentrated from evaporation during simmering.

If the broth won't be used immediately, strain into a sealable container and refrigerate. During this time, any seasoning sediment will settle on the bottom of the container. Simply decant the clear portion for use in other recipes. The broth can be refrigerated for up to 10 days or frozen for future use at your convenience.

Browning the Meatballs

Brown the meatballs in a non-stick skillet with 2 tablespoons of cooking oil over medium heat. Add them to your favorite sauce, soup or stew the last 15 minutes of cooking time before serving.

Succulent Roast Turky

Succulent Roast Turky is created from a special blend of wheat protein, soy protein from tofu and select seasonings. The roast is pre-baked until partially cooked, which seals in the ingredients and sets the texture. The roast will also create its own "skin" while pre-baking.

The partially cooked roast is then simmered in a seasoned broth to complete the cooking process, infuse the roast with additional flavor and ensure that the roast remains moist and tender. After simmering the roast, the ample amount of remaining seasoned broth can be used for sauces, gravies, soups and stews.

The roast is finished by pan-glazing until golden brown before slicing and serving. This combination cooking method produces a tender, succulent, "white meat" roast with a superb texture that cannot be achieved by baking or simmering alone.

A food processor is recommended for efficient kneading of the dough in order to produce the best finished texture; however, processing in a stand mixer or hand-kneading is acceptable. The roast requires a substantial amount of preparation time before finishing (including refrigeration in order to optimize its texture), so prepare at least the night before or up to 1 week ahead and then pan-glaze and reheat when ready to serve. This recipe yields an extra-large roast, about 2.5 lbs.

Please note: This roast is very large and the foil package may not fit inside some pressure cooker chambers. Therefore, oven-baking is standard for pre-cooking the roast prior to simmering. However, if you can manage it, pressure cook on high for 1 hour and 30 minutes with 30 minutes natural release of steam. Then simmer as directed to finish the cooking process.

Dry Ingredients

- 2 cups (300 grams) vital wheat gluten
- ¼ cup all-purpose flour
- 4 tsp onion powder
- 2 tsp garlic powder

Blender Ingredients

- 10 oz/284 grams **pressed** extra-firm tofu (not silken)
- 1 and ½ cup (360 ml) water
- 2 T neutral vegetable oil
- 2 T mellow white miso paste
- 2 tsp fine sea salt or kosher salt
- 2 tsp nutritional yeast flakes
- 1 tsp poultry seasoning

Turky Simmering Broth

- 16 cups (4 quarts/1 gallon) water
- 4 large onions, peeled and quartered
- 4 ribs celery, chopped
- 2 carrots, unpeeled and chopped
- 1 handful parsley stems (leaves removed and saved for the pan-glaze and garnish)
- 8 cloves garlic, crushed

- ⅓ cup nutritional yeast flakes
- 2 T tamari, soy sauce or Bragg Liquid Aminos™
- 4 tsp fine sea salt or kosher salt
- 2 tsp organic sugar
- 8 sprigs fresh thyme or 2 tsp dried thyme leaves
- 2 tsp dry rubbed sage
- 1 sprig fresh rosemary
- 2 bay leaves
- 1 and ½ tsp whole peppercorns

Chef's Notes: The fresh thyme, sage and rosemary can be replaced with 1 teaspoon Aromatica (page 40) or commercial poultry seasoning, if desired. Fresh homemade broth is always best and is recommended for this recipe; however, for the sake of convenience the simmering broth can be made using commercial "no-chicken" broth cubes or bouillon paste.

Pan-Glaze Ingredients

- 3 T non-dairy butter or margarine
- 1 T tamari, soy sauce or Bragg Liquid Aminos™
- ¼ cup dry white wine or reserved simmering broth
- 1 tsp each minced fresh rosemary, sage and thyme - or ¼ tsp poultry seasoning
- coarse ground black pepper, to taste

Additional Item Needed

- 18-inch-wide heavy-duty aluminum foil

Preparation

Preheat the oven to 350°F/175°C.

Please note that the oven temperature recommended in the recipe was determined using a conventional home oven (radiant heat). If you have a convection oven (fan-assisted) and you cannot turn the fan off, reduce the temperature by 25°F/10°C. The baking time should remain the same.

Combine the dry ingredients in a large mixing bowl; set aside.

Crumble the pressed tofu into a blender and add the remaining blender ingredients. Process the contents until the tofu is completely liquefied and the mixture is smooth and creamy. This is essential! Stop the blender as necessary to scrape down the sides.

Scoop the tofu mixture into the dry ingredients (a small amount of the tofu mixture will remain in the blender; this is inconsequential) and combine with a sturdy silicone spatula until the tofu mixture is incorporated and a sticky ball of dough begins to form.

Place the dough into a food processor fitted with a standard chopping blade or plastic dough blade and process for 1 full minute. If you have a smaller capacity processor, process in two batches.

If using a stand mixer or kneading by hand, knead the dough vigorously for 3 full minutes. This is very important in order to develop the gluten. Test the dough by stretching it. If it tears easily, more kneading is required. The dough needs to exhibit a moderate degree of elasticity in order to produce the proper finished texture.

Foil-Wrapping the Dough

Warning! It is very important to use only heavy-duty aluminum foil for this recipe. Regular foil is not sturdy enough and can easily rupture from steam pressure which builds up inside the sealed package.

Tear off a large sheet of foil (about 24-inches) and place it on your work surface. Place the dough onto the foil and shape it into a rounded ball. Now, lift the edge of the foil over the dough and begin rolling into a cylinder, pinching the ends closed simultaneously while rolling. The goal is to create a thick, compact cylindrical package. Twist the ends tightly to seal, being careful not to tear the foil. Bend the twisted ends in half to lock them tight.

Tip: While the ends need to be twisted tightly to seal the package, avoid twisting inwards so far as to tightly compress the dough. The dough will expand significantly as it bakes. Leaving room on each end for expansion will relieve pressure on the foil and thus discourage rupturing during baking.

Wrap with a second and third sheet of foil and twist the ends tightly to completely seal the package. Place the package directly on the middle rack of the oven and bake for 1 hour and 30 minutes.

While the roast is pre-baking, prepare the simmering broth. Add all of the broth ingredients to a large cooking pot and bring to a boil. Cover with a lid and reduce the heat to a gentle simmer. For quick broths, bring the water and bouillon paste, cubes or powder to a simmer in a large covered cooking pot after the roast has been removed from the oven.

Remove the roast from the oven and let cool for about 30 minutes. Unwrap the roast and with a fork, pierce the roast 4 times on the top and 4 times on the bottom.

If the broth was made from scratch, use a slotted spoon to remove and discard the large solid ingredients. It's not necessary to strain the broth completely. Bring the broth to a boil and carefully lower the roast into the broth. Reduce the heat to a simmer and cook for 1 hour. Turn the roast occasionally as it simmers. Monitor the pot frequently and adjust the heat as necessary to maintain the simmer. The broth should be gently bubbling. Do not boil, but do not let the roast merely poach in hot liquid either, as a gentle simmer is necessary to penetrate the roast and finish the cooking process.

Remove the pot from the heat, cover and let cool for several hours or until lukewarm. Remove the roast, seal in a food storage bag with ¼ cup broth and refrigerate for a minimum of 8 hours before finishing. The roast can be refrigerated for up to 1 week before finishing or frozen without the broth for up to 3 months and then thawed and finished at your convenience. If the roast was frozen, thaw for several days in the refrigerator before finishing.

Finishing the Roast

Bring the roast to room temperature for about 2 hours before finishing. Preheat the oven to 350°F/175°C. Lightly blot the roast with a paper towel.

In a large, deep non-stick skillet or wok, melt the butter or margarine over medium heat. Add the roast and turn with 2 large spoons to coat the roast in the butter or margarine (wooden spoons are ideal, as they won't mar the surface of the roast). Continue to turn the roast occasionally until lightly browned. Add the tamari and continue to turn about 1 minute. Now add the wine or reserved broth, the herbs and a few pinches of black pepper. Continue to pan-glaze until the liquid has evaporated and the roast achieves a beautiful golden-brown color.

Transfer to a shallow baking dish, cover with foil and bake for 30 minutes to heat through. Transfer the roast to a serving platter, slice and serve immediately. Store any leftover roast in a food storage bag or sealable container in the refrigerator. Consume within 5 days or freeze.

Tip: Thinly sliced cold leftover roast makes superb hot or cold sandwiches. For hot sandwiches, slice the cold roast and then wrap the slices securely in foil. Place the foil package in a hot oven or in a steamer until heated through. The slices can also be gently reheated in the microwave.

Amber Gravy

This recipe produces a velvety smooth and savory gravy that is superb for serving over slices of Succulent Roast Turk'y and/or mashed potatoes and dressing.

Ingredients

- 4 cups reserved turky simmering broth (page 71), or vegetable broth
- 2 T olive oil
- 2 T non-dairy butter or margarine
- ¼ cup all-purpose flour or rice flour
- 1 tsp Worcestershire Sauce (page 27) or commercial vegan equivalent
- ½ tsp Browning Liquid (page 28) or commercial equivalent
- ¼ tsp Aromatica (page 40) or commercial poultry seasoning
- coarse ground black pepper, to taste
- sea salt or kosher salt, to taste (as needed)

Preparation

In a large saucepan, melt the butter or margarine in the oil over medium-low heat. Add the flour and whisk vigorously to create a roux (a smooth paste used for thickening). Cook until the roux emits a nutty aroma, about 2 minutes.

Slowly incorporate the broth, a little at a time, while whisking vigorously to eliminate lumps. Initially the mixture will be very thick and pasty and some of the flour may begin to brown and stick to the bottom of the saucepan. This is normal and will resolve as the stock continues to be added. When the mixture has thinned a bit and becomes very smooth, it's safe to pour in the remaining stock.

Add the Worcestershire, browning liquid and poultry seasoning. Continue to cook and stir until the mixture just begins to come to a boil. Reduce the heat to a gentle simmer and cook uncovered, stirring frequently, until the gravy is slightly thickened. For a thicker gravy simply simmer until the liquid reduces a bit. Season the gravy with pepper to taste and add salt as needed. Keep covered and warm over low heat until ready to serve. Stir occasionally.

Porq Chunks

To create porq chunks, seasoned gluten dough is torn into small chunks. The chunks are pre-baked to set their texture and then simmered in a seasoned vegetable broth to complete the cooking process before finishing. Porq chunks can be seasoned or marinated as desired and then browned in a skillet for use in your favorite recipes calling for pork.

Porq chunks require chilling for a minimum of 8 hours after simmering to firm and enhance their texture before browning in the skillet, so plan accordingly.

Dry Ingredients

- 1 and ½ cup (225 grams) vital wheat gluten
- 2 T onion powder
- 1 T garlic powder
- ½ tsp ground white pepper

Blender Ingredients

- 5 oz (142 grams) pressed extra-firm tofu (not silken)
- ¾ cup (180 ml) water
- 2 T tamari, soy sauce or Bragg Liquid Aminos™
- 2 T mellow white miso paste
- 2 T cooking oil

Simmering Broth

- 3 quarts (12 cups) porq simmering broth (page 77) or any seasoned vegetable broth

Preparation

Prepare the simmering broth and bring to a simmer in a large covered cooking pot. If preparing the broth from scratch, prepare and bring to a simmer 30 minutes before preparing and pre-baking the dough. This will allow sufficient time to simmer the ingredients before adding the porq.

Place a stainless-steel cooling rack on a baking sheet and line the rack with parchment paper or a silicone baking mat. The cooling rack is not required, but it is recommended, as it will prevent excessive browning which would occur from direct contact with the hot baking sheet.

Preheat the oven to 350°F/175°C.

Please note that the oven temperature recommended in the recipe was determined using a conventional home oven (radiant heat). If you have a convection oven (fan-assisted) and you cannot turn the fan off, reduce the temperature by 25°F/10°C. The baking time should remain the same.

Crumble the pressed tofu into a blender and add the remaining blender ingredients. Process the contents until the tofu is completely liquefied and the mixture is smooth and creamy. This is essential! Stop the blender as necessary to scrape down the sides.

Scoop the tofu mixture into the dry ingredients and combine with a sturdy silicone spatula until the tofu mixture is incorporated and a stiff dough begins to form. The mixture may seem a bit dry at first; just keep mixing. Transfer the dough to a clean work surface (do not flour the work surface) and knead vigorously until it is springy and elastic.

Pick up the dough and stretch it into a long strand until it begins to tear. Place it on your work surface and then loosely roll it up into a lumpy mass. Knead a few strokes. Repeat the stretching, rolling and kneading technique until the dough is separating into stringy strands when stretched, finishing by loosely rolling it into a lumpy mass on your work surface. The goal of this technique is to isolate the strands of gluten, which in turn will create the proper texture in the finished chunks.

Tear the dough into bite-size chunks and place them on the parchment paper or baking mat. Place the baking sheet on the middle rack of the oven. Bake uncovered for 25 minutes and then remove from the oven. The chunks will form a dry crust while baking. This is normal and will disappear when the chunks are simmered.

Bring the broth to a boil. If the broth was made from scratch, use a slotted spoon to remove and discard the larger solids. It's not necessary to strain the broth completely.

Lower the pre-baked chunks into the boiling broth and immediately reduce the heat to a gentle simmer. Leave the pot uncovered and set a timer for 20 minutes. Monitor the pot frequently to make sure the broth is maintained at a simmer. Do not boil the chunks but don't let them merely poach in hot broth either. Move the chunks occasionally in the broth once they float to the top of the pot. After simmering, remove the cooking pot from the heat, cover and let the chunks cool in the broth for a few hours or until lukewarm.

Transfer the porq chunks to a food storage bag and add ¼ cup broth, or a desired marinade. Refrigerate for a minimum of 8 hours to firm and enhance the porq texture before finishing. Chilling is very important so do not omit this step. The chunks can be refrigerated for up to 1 week or frozen without the broth for up to 3 months and then thawed and finished at your convenience.

Strain the cooled broth into a sealable container and refrigerate. During this time, any seasoning sediment will settle on the bottom of the container. The broth can be refrigerated for up to 1 week or frozen for future use at your convenience. Decant the clear portion for preparing gravies or sauces that can be served with the finished porq chunks; or use for other recipes as desired. Discard the sediment.

Finishing the Porq Chunks

Season or marinate the porq chunks as desired. Brown them in an oiled non-stick skillet over medium-high heat.

Pulled Porq

Pulled porq can be created by making some minor adjustments to the Shredded Chikun recipe on page 47. Simply add 1 tablespoon mushroom powder and 1 teaspoon liquid smoke to the blender ingredients. Substitute ½ teaspoon cumin for the Aromatica (aka poultry seasoning). Follow the recipe in exactly the same manner.

Porq Simmering Broth

Porq simmering broth is used for the Porq Chunks recipe (page 75) and the Medallions of Roast Porq (page 79). It can also be used as a savory, all-purpose vegetable broth base for preparing gravies, vegetable soups and stews, or used in any recipe calling for seasoned pork broth. Additional herbs or spices can be added to accommodate specific regional cuisines. This recipe yields about 3 quarts of prepared broth.

Ingredients

- 3 quarts (12 cups) water
- ¼ cup tamari, soy sauce or Bragg Liquid Aminos™
- 3 large onions, peeled and quartered
- 3 ribs celery, chopped
- 2 large carrots, unpeeled and chopped
- small handful parsley stems
- 6 cloves garlic, crushed
- 2 T nutritional yeast
- 2 tsp fine sea salt or kosher salt, or more to taste
- 1 tsp whole black peppercorns
- 1 bay leaf
- 3 sprigs fresh thyme or ½ tsp dried thyme

Preparation

Combine all ingredients in a large cooking pot, cover and simmer for a minimum of 1 hour. Strain and discard the larger solids from the broth with a slotted spoon before simmering porq. After simmering, let the broth cool and then strain into a sealable container to remove any remaining solids and refrigerate. During this time, any seasoning sediment will settle on the bottom of the container. The broth can be refrigerated for up to 1 week or frozen for future use at your convenience. To use, simply decant the clear portion and discard the fine sediment. Be sure to add back a little water as necessary before using, since the broth will have become concentrated from evaporation during simmering.

If using the broth immediately for other purposes, strain through a fine sieve into another cooking pot and discard the solids.

Quick Broth Options

Fresh homemade broth is always best and is recommended. However, for the sake of convenience and expediency, a quick porq simmering broth can be made with Better Than Bouillon™ Organic Vegetable Base (1 tsp for each cup water) or other commercial vegetable broth cubes (½ cube for each cup water), or more or less to taste. Pre-prepared commercial vegetable broths are also available in aseptic cartons from most markets. Add additional herbs and spices as desired to accommodate specific regional cuisines and season the prepared broth with salt to taste.

Sweet and Sour Porq

Chunks of tender vegan porq are browned in the skillet with onion, bell pepper and sweet pineapple and the tossed with a tangy sweet and sour sauce. Serve with steamed jasmine rice.

Primary Ingredients

- 12 oz Porq Chunks (page 75)
- ¼ cup cooking oil for frying
- 1 medium onion, cut into chunks
- 1 red bell pepper, cut into chunks
- 1 green bell pepper, cut into chunks
- 1 and ½ cup pineapple chunks
- 2 T sliced scallions for garnish
- ½ tsp sesame seeds for garnish

Sauce Ingredients

- 1 T cornstarch or unmodified potato starch
- 2 T water
- ½ cup raw agave syrup
- 6 T rice vinegar
- 4 tsp tamari, soy sauce or Bragg Liquid Aminos™
- 3 T tomato ketchup
- 2 tsp minced garlic

Preparation

Prepare the sauce first by mixing together the cornstarch and water in a small dish to make a slurry. In a small saucepan, whisk together the remaining sauce ingredients and place over medium heat to bring to a simmer. Whisk in the slurry and cook until the mixture thickens; reduce the heat to low to keep warm.

In a non-stick skillet, add 2 tablespoons cooking oil and place over medium-high heat. Brown the porq chunks in the hot oil and transfer to a paper-towel lined plate.

Add the remaining 2 tablespoons cooking oil to the skillet and stir-fry the vegetables until just tender. Add the porq chunks back to the skillet, add the sauce and toss well to coat and heat through.

Serve over steamed jasmine rice. Garnish with the scallions and sesame seeds.

Medallions of Roast Porq
with Peppercorn Herb Gravy

Tender slices of vegan roast porq are dressed with a savory amber gravy flavored with marjoram, thyme and whole peppercorns.

Dry Ingredients

- 1 and ½ cup (225 grams) vital wheat gluten
- 2 T onion powder
- 1 T garlic powder
- ¼ tsp ground white pepper
- ¼ tsp ground thyme

Blender Ingredients

- 2.5 oz/71 grams **pressed** extra-firm tofu (not silken tofu)
- 1 cup (240 ml) water
- 2 T mellow white miso paste
- 2 T cooking oil

Simmering Broth

- 3 quarts (12 cups) porq simmering broth (page 77) or any seasoned vegetable broth

Pan-Glaze Ingredients

- 2 T non-dairy butter or margarine
- 2 T dry sherry or dry white wine (optional)
- a few pinches coarse ground black pepper
- optional: ground spices and/or fresh or dried herbs of your choice

Preparation

Prepare the simmering broth and bring to a simmer in a large covered cooking pot. If preparing the broth from scratch, prepare and bring to a simmer 30 minutes before preparing and pre-baking the dough. This will allow sufficient time to simmer the ingredients before adding the chops/cutlets.

Place a stainless-steel cooling rack on a baking sheet and line the rack with parchment paper or a silicone baking mat. The cooling rack is not required, but it is recommended, as it will prevent excessive browning which would occur from direct contact with the hot baking sheet.

Preheat the oven to 350°F/175°C.

Please note that the oven temperature recommended in the recipe was determined using a conventional home oven (radiant heat). If you have a convection oven (fan-assisted) and you cannot turn the fan off, reduce the temperature by 25°F/10°C. The baking time should remain the same.

Combine the dry ingredients in a large mixing bowl.

Crumble the pressed tofu into a blender and add the remaining blender ingredients. Process the contents until the tofu is completely liquefied and the mixture is smooth and creamy. This is essential! Stop the blender as necessary to scrape down the sides.

Scoop the tofu mixture into the dry ingredients (a small amount of the tofu mixture will remain in the blender; this is inconsequential) and combine with a sturdy silicone spatula until the tofu mixture is incorporated and a stiff dough begins to form. The mixture may seem a bit dry at first; just keep mixing. Transfer the dough to a clean work surface (do not flour the work surface) and knead vigorously until it is springy and elastic, about 2 minutes.

Stretch the dough until it begins to tear and then roll it up into a mass. If it tears too easily, knead an additional minute or until it can be stretched a bit before tearing. Shape the mass into a log shape about 8-inches long.

Place the dough on the parchment paper or baking mat. Bake uncovered on the middle rack of the oven for 45 minutes and then remove from the oven.

Bring the broth to a boil. If the broth was made from scratch, use a slotted spoon to remove and discard the larger solids. It's not necessary to strain the broth completely.

Lower the roast into the boiling broth and immediately reduce the heat to a gentle simmer. Leave the pot uncovered and set a timer for 45 minutes. Monitor the pot frequently to make sure the broth is maintained at a simmer. Do not boil. Turn the roast occasionally as it simmers. After simmering, remove the cooking pot from the heat, cover and let the roast cool in the broth for a few hours or until lukewarm.

Transfer the roast to a food storage bag and add ¼ cup of broth, or a desired marinade. Refrigerate for a minimum of 8 hours to firm and enhance the porq texture before finishing and serving. Chilling is very important so do not omit this step. The roast can be refrigerated for up to 1 week or frozen without the broth for up to 3 months and then thawed and finished at your convenience.

Strain the cooled broth into a sealable container and refrigerate. During this time, any seasoning sediment will settle on the bottom of the container. The broth can be refrigerated for up to 1 week or frozen for future use at your convenience. Decant the clear portion for preparing gravies or sauces that can be served with the finished roast; or use for other recipes as desired. Discard the sediment.

Finishing the Roast

Bring the roast to room temperature for about 1 hour before finishing.

In a large, deep non-stick skillet, melt the butter or margarine over medium heat. Add the roast and turn it to coat with the butter or margarine. Lightly brown the roast, turning frequently. Add the sherry or wine

and continue to sauté until almost evaporated. Add the pepper and optional spices and herbs and continue to turn in the skillet until golden brown. Transfer to a serving platter and slice.

Note: If pan-glazing has not sufficiently reheated the roast, place it in a shallow baking dish, cover securely with foil and reheat in a 350°F/175°C oven for 15 to 20 minutes. The roast can also be briefly heated in the microwave before slicing and serving.

Peppercorn Herb Gravy

An elegantly smooth amber gravy flavored with marjoram, thyme and peppercorns. It's lovely for dressing tender medallions of vegan roast porq.

Ingredients

- 2 T olive oil
- 2 T non-dairy butter or margarine
- ¼ cup all-purpose flour or rice flour
- 2 cups reserved porq simmering broth
- 2 tsp whole peppercorns (green or black)
- 1 tsp dried marjoram leaves
- ¾ tsp Browning Liquid (page 28) or commercial equivalent
- ½ tsp dried thyme leaves
- sea salt or kosher salt and coarse ground black pepper, to taste
- 2 T chopped fresh parsley

Preparation

Add the olive oil to a small saucepan and place over medium heat. Add the butter or margarine and stir until melted.

Whisk in the flour to create a thick paste (roux) and cook until the flour is golden and emits a nutty aroma, about 2 minutes. The flour will stick to the bottom of the saucepan, but don't worry, as it will release when the broth is incorporated.

Incorporate the broth in increments while vigorously stirring.

Add the peppercorns, marjoram, browning liquid and thyme. Bring to a simmer and continue to stir until the mixture thickens. Add salt and pepper to taste. Reduce heat to low until ready to serve; stirring occasionally. Just before serving, stir in the parsley.

Garden Ham

Generously flavored with hickory smoke, brown sugar and warm spice, garden ham is reminiscent of a natural uncured ham and can be served hot or cold. The ham can be finished with a savory tamari-black pepper glaze or a sweet and spicy brown sugar-mustard glaze included with the recipe; however, any sweet, spicy or savory glaze can be used as desired. Spicy brown or Dijon mustard is the ideal condiment for enhancing the flavor of the sliced ham.

While the ham can be prepared in the oven, it is ideal for preparing in an Instant Pot™ or other electric pressure cooker (however, the oven should still be used for glazing and reheating the ham). Pressure-cooking discourages the foil package from rupturing under internal steam pressure, which can sometimes occur during oven-baking if there is a weak point in the foil wrap. This recipe yields about 2 lbs.

Aromatic Brine Ingredients

- 2 and ¼ cup (540 ml) water
- 2 T nutritional yeast flakes
- 2 T light brown sugar
- 2 T red miso paste*
- 2 T liquid hickory smoke
- 2 T neutral vegetable oil
- 2 and ¼ tsp fine sea salt or kosher salt
- 2 tsp whole cloves
  (or more if you prefer a stronger clove flavor reminiscent of holiday ham)
- ½ tsp ground ginger
- ½ tsp ground white pepper

*If you cannot obtain red miso paste, substitute with 1 tablespoon tamari, soy sauce or Bragg Liquid Aminos™ and 1 tablespoon tomato paste, although this will alter the finished flavor to a degree.

Dry Ingredients

- 2 cups (300 grams) vital wheat gluten
- ¼ cup all-purpose flour
- 2 T onion powder
- 1 T garlic powder

Pan-Browning Ingredient

- 2 T non-dairy butter or margarine

Additional Item Needed

- 18-inch wide heavy-duty aluminum foil

Optional Tamari-Black Pepper Glaze Ingredients

- 2 T tamari, soy sauce or Bragg Liquid Aminos™
- coarse ground smoked black pepper or coarse ground black pepper, to taste

Optional Brown Sugar-Mustard Glaze Ingredients

- 2 T dark brown sugar
- 1 T prepared Dijon or spicy mustard
- 1 tsp tamari, soy sauce or Bragg Liquid Aminos™
- 1 tsp liquid hickory smoke

Preparing the Aromatic Brine

In a saucepan, bring the water to a brief boil and then remove from the heat. Add the remaining aromatic brine ingredients and stir until the sugar, yeast, miso and salt dissolves. Let the mixture cool to near room temperature (the mixture must cool before proceeding; do not add hot brine to the dry ingredients!)

Meanwhile, thoroughly mix together the dry ingredients in large mixing bowl; set aside.

Preparing the Dough

Fill the pressure cooker with 2 to 3 cups of water and put the trivet in place. If using an oven, preheat the oven to 350°F/175°C.

Please note that the oven temperature recommended in the recipe was determined using a conventional home oven (radiant heat). If you have a convection oven (fan-assisted) and you cannot turn the fan off, reduce the temperature by 25°F/10°C. The baking time should remain the same.

Strain the aromatic brine through a fine sieve into the dry ingredients in the mixing bowl and discard the strained solids (straining will remove any whole and undissolved seasoning sediment).

Combine thoroughly with a silicone spatula to develop the gluten. Let the dough rest 10 minutes to allow the dry ingredients to absorb as much liquid as possible.

Foil-Wrapping the Dough

Warning! It is very important to use only heavy-duty aluminum foil for this recipe. Regular foil is not sturdy enough and can easily rupture from steam pressure which builds up inside the sealed package.

Tear off a sheet of foil (about 18-inches) and place it on your work surface. Place the dough directly on top.

Form the dough into a round mass. The dough will be soft and will tend to spread out, but try to keep it as compact as you can. Now, lift the edge of the foil over the dough and begin rolling into a cylinder, pinching the ends closed simultaneously while rolling. The goal is to create a thick, compact, cylindrical package. This may take practice, so be patient. Twist the ends tightly to seal, being careful not to tear the foil. Bend the twisted ends in half to lock them tight.

Rewrap with an additional large sheet of foil and twist the ends tightly to completely seal the package. For oven-baking, rewrap in a third sheet of foil.

Pressure-Cooking

Place the foil package on the trivet, seal the lid, close the steam valve and set the cooker on high (or the setting for cooking meat) for 2 hours (with most programmable cookers, you will need to manually override the preset cooking time). After cooking, turn the cooker off and let the steam naturally release for 30 minutes. Do not release the steam valve until the 30 minutes is completed. Remove from the cooker to cool. Refrigerate the ham in the foil wrapper for a minimum of 8 hours before finishing. This will firm and enhance the texture.

Oven-Baking

Place the foil package directly on the middle rack of the oven and set a timer for 2 hours. Remove from the oven to cool. Refrigerate the ham in the foil wrapper for a minimum of 8 hours before finishing. This will firm and enhance the texture.

Finishing the Ham

For deli-style luncheon slices, no further finishing is necessary. Simply slice and serve hot, cold or room temperature. An electric deli-slicer is recommended for uniform thin slicing. Serve with your favorite prepared mustard to complement the flavor of the ham. Thick ham slices are ideal for pan-grilling.

For finishing as a baked ham, try one of the following glaze options:

Tamari-Pepper Glaze Option

Let the wrapped ham come to room temperature for about 1 hour before finishing. Preheat the oven to 350°F/175°C.

In a skillet, lightly brown the ham on all sides in 2 tablespoons of non-dairy butter or margarine over medium heat. Add the tamari and continue to glaze the ham until nicely browned and then season with black pepper to taste. Transfer the ham to a baking dish, cover with foil and bake for 30 minutes. Transfer to a cutting board or serving platter for slicing.

Brown Sugar-Mustard Glaze Option

Let the wrapped ham come to room temperature for about 1 hour before finishing. Preheat the oven to 350°F/175°C.

Mix together the glaze ingredients in a small dish until the sugar dissolves; set aside.

In a skillet, brown the ham on all sides in 2 tablespoons of non-dairy butter or margarine over medium heat. Transfer the ham to baking dish and brush to coat evenly with the glaze. Cover with foil and bake for 30 minutes. Transfer to a cutting board or serving platter for slicing.

Chef's Premium Bacun

Over the years I have published several bacun recipes but I feel this recipe excels above the rest. It is prepared with a blend of wheat protein from gluten, soy protein from tofu and my own special blend of seasonings. This yields a finished product that is remarkably similar to real bacon in flavor, appearance and texture with a nice balance of salty, smoky and sweet. There are several steps to this recipe; however, don't be intimated because it's relatively easy to prepare when following the step-by-step directions and the results are well worth the effort.

For this recipe, two batches of dough will be mixed to create the bacun. Dough 1 is for the light marble layer and Dough 2 is for the dark marble layer.

Please note: A food processor is required for this recipe for creating the proper texture in the dough. Do not attempt to process the dough in a blender.

The bacun can baked in an oven or cooked in a large capacity electric pressure cooker (the foil package is rather large and may not fit into a small capacity pressure cooker). This recipe yields a large slab of bacun, about 1 and ½ lbs.

Required Equipment

- food processor with standard chopping blade or plastic dough blade
- 18-inch wide heavy-duty aluminum foil

Ingredients for Dough 1

- 5 oz/142 grams **pressed** extra-firm tofu (not silken tofu)
- 1 T olive oil
- 2 tsp garlic powder
- 1 tsp fine sea salt or kosher salt
- ½ cup vital wheat gluten
- ½ cup water

Ingredients for Dough 2

- 5 oz/142 grams **pressed** extra-firm tofu (not silken tofu)
- 6 T tamari, soy sauce or Bragg Liquid Aminos™
- 1 T liquid hickory smoke
- 1 T light brown sugar
- 1 T Worcestershire Sauce (page 27) or commercial vegan equivalent
- 1 T olive oil
- 4 tsp onion powder
- 1 T smoked paprika
- ¼ tsp ground white pepper
- 1 cup vital wheat gluten
- ¼ cup water

Optional Rub Ingredients

- 1 tsp smoked black pepper or coarse ground black pepper
- for sweeter bacun, real maple syrup or brown sugar

Preparing the Tofu for the Recipe

Press the tofu until it is not releasing any more water and then wrap the tofu in paper towels or a lint-free kitchen towel and squeeze as dry as possible. Removing as much moisture as possible is essential to this recipe. The tofu should be crumbly and barely moist. Weigh the recommended amounts after pressing and squeezing dry and set aside. Gather, measure and set aside the remaining ingredients.

Preparing Dough 1

Preheat the oven to 350°F/175°C. If using a pressure cooker, add a few cups of water to the cooker and insert the trivet stand.

Crumble the tofu into the food processor and add the olive oil, garlic powder and salt. Process as smooth as possible. Stop to scrape down the sides of the processor bowl as needed.

Add the gluten and the water and process for exactly 2 minutes. Towards the end of processing, the processor will bounce around so you will need to hold it in place.

Divide the dough into 2 pieces and set aside.

Preparing Dough 2

Crumble the tofu into the food processor and add the remaining ingredients except for the gluten and water. Process as smooth as possible. Stop to scrape down the sides of the processor bowl as needed.

Add the gluten and the water and process for exactly 2 minutes. Towards the end of processing, the processor may bounce around so you will need to hold it in place. Please note that the texture of Dough 2 will be slightly different and possibly less elastic than Dough 1. This is normal.

Divide the dough into 3 pieces and set aside.

Layering, Foil-Wrapping and Cooking the Dough

Warning! It is very important to use only heavy-duty aluminum foil for this recipe. Regular foil is not sturdy enough and can easily rupture from steam pressure which builds up inside the sealed package.

Tear off a large sheet of foil (about 18-inches) and place on your work surface.

Take a piece of Dough 2 and flatten into a disc. Place the flattened dough onto the foil. Next, repeat with a piece of Dough 1 and place on top of the first disc. Repeat with the remaining pieces of dough, alternating as you stack.

Firmly press down on the stack until it is about 1-inch thick. Now, use your fingers to press and shape the dough into a compact, square slab. Don't worry about being too precise; the dough will expand during baking to conform to the shape of the foil package.

If desired, season the surface of the dough with ½ teaspoon of the optional black pepper. Flip the slab over and repeat with the remaining pepper. For sweeter bacun, rub the exterior of the dough with maple syrup or pack with brown sugar.

Fold the slab of bacun over in the foil several times (don't roll) to create a flat package. Fold in the sides of the foil, crimping to seal the foil as you fold but leave about 1-inch of air space on each side to allow for expansion of the dough as it bakes.

Rewrap in a second sheet of foil in the same manner. Place the package directly on the middle oven rack and bake for 2 hours. For pressure-cooking, place the package on the trivet inside the pressure cooker. Cook on high for 90 minutes. Turn the unit off but do not release the steam. Set a timer for 30 minutes and allow the steam pressure to subside naturally.

Remove from the oven or pressure cooker. Let the bacun cool in the foil until it reaches near room temperature. It's helpful (but not essential) to place a heavy object, such as a cast iron skillet, on the foil package to compress it as it cools and keep the slab of bacun flat. This also helps condense the bacun and improves texture. Refrigerate the foil package for a minimum of 8 hours. Chilling will firm and enhance the texture and make slicing easier; this is important. The bacun can be stored in the refrigerator for up to 10 days before slicing and finishing or in the freezer for up to 3 months.

For the best finished texture, use an electric slicer or very sharp knife and slice the bacun as thinly as possible. Of course, if you prefer a thicker cut, that's entirely up to you. When sliced thin, the bacun may tatter a bit but this only adds to the authentic finished texture and appearance when fried.

Finishing the Bacun

Finishing the bacun in the oven is my preferred method since heating is controlled. To do this, preheat the oven to 375°F/190°C. Line a baking sheet with aluminum foil or parchment paper and lay the slices in a single layer on top. Generously mist or brush the slices on both sides with cooking oil. Bake for 15 to 20 minutes.

Transfer to a plate lined with paper towels to blot any excess oil. As the bacun cools it will crisp up a bit while still retaining a nice chewy texture. Serve warm; chop, dice or crumble in recipes; or layer on your favorite sandwich.

Optionally, the bacun slices can be fried in a skillet with a generous layer of cooking oil over medium heat. Avoid frying at a high temperature to prevent burning. Transfer to a plate lined with paper towels to blot any excess oil. Serve warm; chop, dice or crumble in recipes; or layer on your favorite sandwich.

Spicy Italian Pancetta

Pancetta is an un-smoked Italian bacon that is seasoned with black pepper and other spices and herbs before rolling and salt-curing. My meat-free version is seasoned with my own blend of spices and herbs to impart a distinctive Italian flavor. For this recipe, two batches of dough will be mixed to create the pancetta. Dough 1 is for the light marble layer and Dough 2 is for the dark marble layer. The pancetta can be baked in an oven, or an electric pressure cooker for convenience.

Aromatic Seasoning Ingredients

- 1 and ½ tsp finely ground black pepper
- 2 tsp dried basil leaves
- 2 tsp dried oregano leaves
- ¼ tsp ground fennel seed
- ¼ tsp ground red pepper (optional)

Dry Ingredients for Dough 1

- ½ cup (75 grams) vital wheat gluten
- 1 T garlic powder

Liquid Ingredients for Dough 1

- 6 T (90 ml) water
- 1 T olive oil
- ½ tsp fine sea salt or kosher salt

Dry Ingredients for Dough 2

- 1 cup (150 grams) vital wheat gluten
- 1 T onion powder
- 2 tsp sweet paprika

Liquid Ingredients for Dough 2

- ½ cup plus 2 T (150 ml) water
- 2 T tamari, soy sauce or Bragg Liquid Aminos™
- 2 T nutritional yeast flakes
- 2 T red miso paste
- 1 T olive oil

Additional Item Needed

- 18-inch wide heavy-duty aluminum foil

Combine the Aromatic Seasoning Ingredients

Combine the aromatic seasoning ingredients in a small dish and using the back of a spoon, grind the mixture until the oregano and basil are coarsely ground; set the mixture aside. This blend will not be added to the dough, but rather layered over the dough before rolling in the foil.

Preheat the oven to 325°F/170°F. For pressure-cooking, place the trivet stand inside your pressure cooker and add a few cups of water. The water level should not exceed the height of the trivet.

Preparing Dough 1

Combine the dry ingredients for Dough 1 in a medium mixing bowl.

Stir together the liquid ingredients for Dough 1 in a separate bowl or measuring cup until the salt dissolves.

Pour the liquid ingredients into the dry ingredients and mix well to incorporate. Knead the dough with a spoon or spatula in the bowl until the dough offers some resistance to mixing. Divide the dough into 2 pieces. Set aside.

Preparing Dough 2

Combine the dry ingredients for Dough 2 in a large mixing bowl.

Whisk together the liquid ingredients for Dough 2 in a separate bowl or measuring cup until the miso and yeast dissolves (the yeast will not dissolve completely).

Pour the liquid ingredients into the dry ingredients and mix well to incorporate. Knead the dough with a spoon or spatula in the bowl until the dough offers some resistance to mixing, about 2 minutes. Kneading can also be done in a food processor fitted with a dough blade attachment and processed for about 1 minute. Divide the dough in half.

Layering and Foil-Wrapping the Dough

Warning! It is very important to use only heavy-duty aluminum foil for this recipe. Regular foil is not sturdy enough and can easily rupture from steam pressure which builds up inside the sealed package.

Now you will begin the layering process which will create the marbling effect for the pancetta.

Tear off a sheet of foil (about 18-inches) and place on your work surface. Take a piece of Dough 1 (the light dough) and flatten into a disc. Place the flattened dough onto the foil. Sprinkle about ¼ of the aromatic seasonings over the disc of dough (don't worry if some of the seasonings scatter on the foil).

Next, repeat with a piece of Dough 2 (the dark dough) and place on top of the first disc. Scatter ¼ of the aromatic seasonings over the disc of dough. Repeat with the second piece of Dough 1, again scattering ¼ of the aromatic seasonings over the disc of dough.

Finish layering with the second piece of Dough 2 and scatter the remaining seasoning over the dough. Firmly press down and stretch the stack against the foil until it is about ¼-inch thick.

Now, roll the dough into a cylinder and then use your hands to compress the dough into a thick compact log. Press any seasoning mixture that has scattered on the foil into the log.

Roll the dough in the foil to create a cylindrical package and twist the ends tightly to seal. Bend the ends in half to lock them tight. Repeat this wrapping procedure with an additional sheet of foil. For oven-baking, rewrap with a third sheet of foil.

Pressure Cooker

Place the package on the trivet inside the pressure cooker. Cook on high for 1 hour and 15 minutes. Turn the unit off but do not release the steam. Set a timer for 30 minutes and allow the steam pressure to subside naturally.

Cool the pancetta in the foil and then refrigerate for a minimum of 8 hours. Chilling will firm and enhance the texture and make slicing easier; this is important. The pancetta can be stored in the refrigerator for up to 1 week before slicing and finishing or in the freezer for up to 3 months.

For the best finished texture, use a very sharp knife and slice the pancetta as thinly as possible. Of course, if you prefer a thicker cut, that's entirely up to you. The slices can also be cut into narrow strips if desired. Pancetta can also be small diced.

Oven-Baking

Place the package directly on the middle oven rack and bake for 90 minutes.

Cool the pancetta in the foil and then refrigerate for a minimum of 8 hours. Chilling will firm and enhance the texture and make slicing easier; this is important. The pancetta can be stored in the refrigerator for up to 1 week before slicing and finishing or in the freezer for up to 3 months.

For the best finished texture, use a very sharp knife and slice the pancetta as thinly as possible. Of course, if you prefer a thicker cut, that's entirely up to you. The slices can also be cut into narrow strips if desired. Pancetta can also be small diced.

Finishing the Pancetta

Finishing the pancetta in the oven is my preferred method since heating is controlled. To do this, preheat the oven to 350°F/175°C. Line a baking sheet with parchment paper and lay the slices (or diced pancetta) on the paper. Mist or brush the slices or dice with cooking oil. Bake for 20 minutes. Let the pancetta cool for about 5 minutes and then transfer to a paper towel-lined plate to blot any excess oil. If so inclined, scrunch the slices as you lay them on the plate to give the pancetta a textured, rippled appearance. As the slices cool, they should crisp up a bit and hold that shape.

Optionally, the pancetta slices or dice can be briefly fried in a non-stick skillet with a light layer of cooking oil over medium to medium-low heat. Frying "low and slow" is preferable to frying at a high temperature. The pancetta will brown (and burn) quickly and the texture will become hard if the temperature is too high. Transfer to a plate lined with paper towels to blot any excess oil.

Serve warm; chop, dice or crumble in recipes; or layer on your favorite sandwich. Use within 10 days or freeze for up to 3 months.

Roast Mock Lamb
with English Mint Sauce

Succulent and tender mock lamb is pan-glazed with white wine, rosemary and lemon zest and then sliced and served 'au jus' and with a garnish of tangy mint sauce. This recipe yields about 1 and ½ lb. Please note: Mock Lamb requires chilling for a minimum of 8 hours after simmering to firm and enhance its texture before pan-glazing, so plan accordingly.

Dry Ingredients for the Roast

- 1 and ½ cup (225 grams) vital wheat gluten
- 2 T portabella mushroom powder
- 4 tsp onion powder
- 2 tsp garlic powder
- ½ tsp ground white pepper

Liquid Ingredients for the Roast

- 1 and ¼ cup (300 ml) water
- 2 T extra-virgin olive oil
- 1 and ½ tsp fine sea salt or kosher salt

Simmering Broth Ingredients

- 3 quarts water (12 cups)
- 3 large onions, peeled and quartered
- 3 ribs celery, chopped
- 3 large carrots, unpeeled and chopped
- small handful parsley stems
- 6 large cloves garlic, crushed
- 1 T portabella mushroom powder
- 4 tsp fine sea salt or kosher salt, or more to taste
- 1 tsp whole black peppercorns
- 1 large sprig fresh rosemary
- 3 sprigs fresh thyme or ½ tsp dried thyme leaves
- 1 bay leaf

Jus Ingredients

- 1 cup reserved simmering broth
- optional: ½ tsp beet powder
- (crush the powder to eliminate hard lumps if necessary before mixing with the broth)

English Mint Sauce Ingredients

- ¼ packed cup fresh chopped mint leaves
- 3 T white wine vinegar
- 1 T hot water
- 1 tsp organic sugar
- 2 pinches sea salt or kosher salt

Pan-Glaze Ingredients

- 2 T non-dairy butter or margarine
- 2 T dry white wine or fresh lemon juice
- 1 T tamari, soy sauce or Bragg Liquid Aminos™
- 2 tsp minced fresh rosemary
- 1 tsp fresh lemon zest
- a few pinches coarse ground black pepper

Additional Items Needed

- baking sheet
- stainless steel cooling rack (not required but recommended)
- parchment paper or silicone baking mat

Preparation

Prepare the simmering broth and bring to a simmer in a large covered cooking pot at least 30 minutes before preparing and pre-baking the dough. This will allow sufficient time to simmer the ingredients before adding the roast.

Preheat the oven to 350°F/175°C.

Please note that the oven temperature recommended in the recipe was determined using a conventional home oven (radiant heat). If you have a convection oven (fan-assisted) and you cannot turn the fan off, reduce the temperature by 25°F/10°C. The baking time should remain the same.

Place a stainless-steel cooling rack on a baking sheet and line the rack with parchment paper or a silicone baking mat. The cooling rack is not required, but it is recommended, as it will prevent excessive browning which would occur from direct contact with the hot baking sheet.

Combine the dry ingredients for the roast in a large mixing bowl. Stir together the liquid ingredients for the roast in a separate bowl or measuring cup.

Pour the liquid mixture (not the simmering broth) into the dry ingredients and combine thoroughly with a sturdy silicone spatula to form the dough and begin developing the gluten.

Transfer the dough to a work surface and knead vigorously until very elastic. Test the dough by stretching. If it tears easily, knead a little longer and test again. The dough should be able to stretch considerably without tearing.

Now, form the dough into a thick, compact roast shape. Don't worry about smoothing the surface too much, as some bumps and irregularities will yield a more natural finished appearance. Transfer the dough to the parchment paper or baking mat.

Place the baking sheet on the middle rack of the oven. Bake uncovered for 45 minutes and then remove from the oven. The roast will form a dry crust while baking. This is normal and will disappear when the roast is simmered.

Bring the broth to a boil. It's not necessary to strain the vegetable solids; this can be done later after the broth has cooled.

Lower the roast into the boiling broth and immediately reduce the heat to a gentle simmer. Leave the pot uncovered and set a timer for 45 minutes. Monitor the pot frequently to make sure the broth is maintained at a simmer. Do not boil the roast but don't let it merely poach in hot broth either. Turn the roast occasionally in the broth as it simmers to ensure even cooking. After simmering, remove the cooking pot from the heat, cover and let the roast cool in the broth for a few hours or until lukewarm.

Transfer the roast to a work surface and pierce repeatedly on all sides with a fork. Place into a food storage bag and add the jus. The jus is intended to mimic the juices of medium-cooked roast lamb (the beet powder is optional and if you choose not to use it, simply add ¼ cup of the simmering broth to the storage bag to keep the roast moist).

Seal the bag and refrigerate for a minimum of 8 hours to firm and enhance the mock lamb texture before finishing. Chilling is very important so do not omit this step. The roast can be stored in the refrigerator for up to 10 days before finishing or frozen without the broth for up to 3 months and then thawed and finished at your convenience.

Strain the cooled simmering broth into a sealable container and refrigerate. During this time, any seasoning sediment will settle on the bottom of the container. The broth can be refrigerated for up to 10 days or frozen for future use at your convenience. Decant the clear portion for preparing jus, gravy or sauce that can be served with the sliced roast; or use for other recipes as desired. Discard the sediment.

Finishing the Roast

Bring the roast (sealed in the storage bag) to room temperature for about 1 hour before finishing. Set the roast on a plate and set aside. Pour the jus into a small saucepan and warm over low heat.

Add the mint sauce ingredients to a blender and process as smooth as possible. The sauce will be thin. Set aside until ready to serve the roast.

Create the pan-glaze by combining the wine or lemon juice with the tamari in a small dish; set aside.

In a large, deep non-stick skillet, melt the butter or margarine over medium heat. Add the roast and turn it to coat with the butter or margarine. Lightly brown the roast, turning frequently. Add the pan-glaze mixture. The mixture will sizzle and begin to caramelize, turning the roast a beautiful deep brown color. Add the rosemary, lemon zest and pepper and continue to turn in the mixture to form a crust. Transfer to a serving platter and slice. Drizzle the slices with the warmed jus and the mint sauce just before serving.

Note: If pan-glazing has not sufficiently reheated the roast, place it in a shallow baking dish, cover securely with foil and reheat in a 350°F/175°C oven for 15 to 20 minutes. The roast can also be briefly heated in the microwave before slicing and serving.

Soy-Based Meat Alternatives
Soy Chikun Strips

Soy chikun strips are incredibly easy to make and remarkably resemble grilled strips of lightly seasoned chicken. The ingredients are simple: tofu and a seasoning marinade. The secret is all in the preparation technique. A tofu press is recommended in order to compress the tofu properly and remove as much water as possible. However, the traditional plate and heavy weight method will work too, but the texture may not be as dense.

Each block of tofu will yield 8 ounces of prepared chikun. Most households do not possess more than one tofu press, so if you wish to prepare additional chikun strips, press the first block and then store in the refrigerator in an airtight container while additional blocks are pressed. For additional blocks, simply double or triple the water and seasonings in the recipe.

Important! Do not use a toaster oven for baking the tofu!

Ingredients

- 1 block (about 14 oz before pressing) extra-firm tofu (not silken tofu)
- ⅓ cup water
- 1 tsp nutritional yeast
- ½ tsp fine sea salt or kosher salt
- ½ tsp onion powder
- ¼ tsp poultry seasoning
- ¼ tsp garlic powder

Preparation

Press the tofu until thoroughly compressed and as much water has been removed as possible (keep stored in the refrigerator while pressing). This will take a minimum of several hours (overnight being ideal). Blot the tofu with a paper towel.

Preheat the oven to 350°F/175°C. Place a stainless-steel cooking rack on a baking sheet and line with parchment paper. Place the block of tofu on the parchment paper and bake for 1 hour and 30 minutes. The tofu will develop a firm golden crust while baking. Let the block cool completely after baking.

Trim the crust from the block of tofu since it will be rather tough. Small amounts of crust may remain, that's okay. For chikun strips, simply slice the tofu into strips. For shredded chikun, use the tines of a fork to tear off bite-size pieces. Place the strips or shreds into a food storage bag.

Now, in a small bowl, whisk together the remaining ingredients. The dry seasoning powders may take a moment to dissolve, so keep whisking until blended. Pour the seasoning marinade over the tofu in the bag. Press as much air out of the bag as possible; seal and refrigerate for several hours (overnight is best).

Note: Other herbs and spices can be added to the marinade to accommodate specific ethnic food flavors.

For a Tex-Mex variation, prepare the marinade with the basic recipe and add 1 tsp mild chili powder, an additional ½ tsp onion powder, ½ tsp ground cumin, an additional ¼ tsp garlic powder and ¼ tsp chipotle chili powder.

For an Asian Stir Fry variation, marinate and sauté the chikun as directed and add a dash or two of tamari while sautéing. Toss with a tablespoon of chili garlic sauce just before removing from the skillet.

For a Mediterranean variation, prepare the marinade with the basic recipe but reduce the water to ¼ cup. Add 1 T lemon juice, 1 tsp dried basil, 1 tsp dried oregano, an additional ½ tsp onion powder and an additional ¼ tsp garlic powder. Finish with fresh ground black pepper.

The strips or shreds are now ready to be pan-grilled or sautéed. This step is necessary to prepare the chikun for serving or using in recipes. Lightly oil a non-stick skillet with cooking oil and place over medium heat. Add the chikun including any residual marinade.

Sauté until the excess liquid has evaporated and the chikun is golden. Use a gentle touch while sautéing; the chikun is firm but can break apart excessively if stirred roughly. Use immediately in your favorite hot recipe or chill for use in cold recipes (wraps, salads, etc.) For soups and stews, add the chikun just before serving to avoid becoming too soft.

Store any leftovers in an airtight container in the refrigerator. Use within 5 days or freeze up to 1 month.

Indonesian Chikun Salad
with Spicy Peanut Sauce

The dressing for this salad is tangy, creamy and slightly spicy with bold Southeast Asian flavors. Peanut butter is rich in natural plant fat/oil, so additional oil isn't added to the dressing - it just doesn't need it. I chose crunchy peanut butter since many Indonesian and Southeast Asian dishes call for chopped or ground peanuts; however, smooth peanut butter can be used if this is your preference. Sambal oelek is a crushed chili paste commonly used in this regional cuisine, but Sriracha™ can be substituted if this is what you have on hand.

Dressing Ingredients

- ¼ cup warm water
- 2 tsp organic sugar
- 2 T rice vinegar
- 2 T fresh lime juice
- 2 T tamari, soy sauce or Bragg Liquid Aminos™
- 1 T sambal oelek or Sriracha™
- 1 T fresh grated ginger root
- ½ cup natural unsalted crunchy peanut butter
- 1 large scallion, white and green parts, finely chopped

Dressing Preparation

In a bowl or large cup, dissolve the sugar in the warm water. Stir in the remaining ingredients except for the scallion and whisk vigorously until creamy. Stir in the scallions and refrigerate in a covered container for several hours to blend the flavors before using.

Salad Ingredients

- 8 oz lightly pan-grilled Soy Chikun Strips (page 94)
  or Shredded Chikun (page 47)
- ½ English cucumber, seeded and julienned
- 2 average-size carrots, peeled and julienned or shredded
- ¼ cup chopped cilantro or mint leaves
- fresh lime wedges
- Butterhead lettuce leaves (Butter, Boston or Bibb lettuces all fall within this category)

Salad Preparation

Toss the chikun, cucumber and carrots with ¼ cup of the sauce and chill for about 30 minutes. Add the cilantro and toss to combine. Fill lettuce leaves with the salad and drizzle additional dressing over each lettuce cup. Serve with lime wedges.

Sweet and Smoky Tofu Bacun

Tofu bacun is so easy to prepare and yields excellent results. It just requires a little time for pressing the tofu (8 to 12 hours), marinating the tofu with the seasoning liquid (a minimum of 12 hours), and low-oven-baking or drying in a food dehydrator (about 2 hours). For this recipe I recommend using a tofu press, such as the TofuXpress®, that will hold the shape of the tofu while compressing the texture and removing the water prior to marinating. This recipe yields about 8 oz/½ lb of bacun.

Ingredients

- 1 block **pressed** extra-firm tofu (not silken tofu)
- high-temp cooking oil for frying

Marinade Ingredients

- ⅔ cup water
- ⅓ cup tamari, soy sauce or Bragg Liquid Aminos™
- ¼ cup dark brown sugar or real maple syrup
- 1 T Worcestershire Sauce (page 27) or commercial vegan equivalent
- 1 T liquid hickory smoke

Preparation

Press the tofu to remove as much water as possible. Blot the surface dry and then cut ⅛-inch thick slices lengthwise.

Combine the marinade ingredients and stir until the sugar dissolves. If you prefer a less salty bacun, opt for low-sodium tamari or soy sauce. Pour a small amount of the marinade into a small food storage container and begin layering the tofu strips into the container, overlapping the slices as you layer. Handle the slices carefully as they will be rather delicate.

Pour the remaining marinade over the slices and seal the container. There should be sufficient marinade to just about cover the slices completely. Seal the container and refrigerate for a minimum of 12 hours and up to 48 hours, with 24 hours being ideal.

Preheat the oven to 225°F/110°C. Place a non-stick baker's cooling rack on a baking sheet. If you don't have a cooling rack, line the baking sheet with parchment paper.

Place the slices in a single layer on the rack. Again, handle the slices carefully as they will be rather delicate. Place the sheet on the middle oven rack and low-bake for 2 hours.

Alternately, a food dehydrator can be used at the highest setting. Dry for 2 hours or until the slices are dry to the touch but not completely dehydrated.

Place the slices in a food storage container and refrigerate until ready to finish and serve.

Finishing the Bacun

Tofu bacun benefits from frying in oil to create the crispy texture. Pour enough high-temp cooking into a skillet to cover the bottom completely and place over medium-high heat. Add the strips to the skillet without overcrowding and fry until nicely browned, turning occasionally. Transfer to a plate lined with paper towels to drain. Try laying the bacun on the towel with an undulation to mimic a cooked bacon appearance. If desired, season with some coarse ground black pepper while still hot. The bacun will crisp further as it cools and will hold the undulated shape.

Serve immediately or store in a sealed container in the refrigerator until ready to use in recipes. Pre-fried bacun can be reheated in a low oven.

Mock Prosciutto Crudo

Prosciutto crudo is an Italian dry-cured ham that is usually thinly sliced and served uncooked. My vegan version is made from rice paper (a blend of tapioca starch and rice flour). While this may seem odd, the rice paper offers the translucency and sheen of thinly sliced pork-based prosciutto. For this recipe, use square rice paper sheets if you can find them. Round sheets will work too but the square sheets will yield more uniform slices. My original recipe yields three 3"x9" strips of mock prosciutto crudo.

Ingredients

- 3 sheets rice paper (preferably square sheets)
- ¼ cup white shoyu (Japanese white soy sauce)
- ¼ cup water
- 2 tsp Worcestershire Sauce (page 27) or commercial vegan equivalent
- ¼ tsp beet powder
- olive oil

Preparation

Combine the white shoyu, water, Worcestershire sauce and beet powder in a cup and then pour into a large, shallow baking dish.

Stack the three sheets of rice paper together and then immerse in the marinade. Allow to soak until most of the marinade has been absorbed and the rice paper is moist and supple and nicely colored, about 10 minutes. The sheets will stick together – this is desirable. The three sheets of rice paper will yield one sheet of prosciutto.

Carefully transfer the mock prosciutto to a baker's cooling rack to drain briefly. Transfer again to a work surface and slice into 3 strips. Rub the strips generously with olive oil to keep them moist and supple. The oil is essential and is not optional; without it the texture will be quite rubbery.

For the best texture experience, use the mock prosciutto immediately if possible. The strips can be stored in a food storage bag in the refrigerator but will acquire a chewier texture during storage. Use in your favorite recipe as desired. Mock prosciutto works well for baked appetizers too.

Lemon Tempeh

This dish is a vegan variation of Chinese lemon chicken. The tempeh can also be subbed with pressed extra-firm tofu or vegan chikun. The sauce is lemony, sweet, savory and has just a hint of heat.

Ingredients for the Tempeh

- 1 package (8 oz) tempeh
- 2 T tamari, soy sauce or Bragg Liquid Aminos™
- 2 T Shaoxing wine, dry sherry, sweet mirin, or water
- 2 T cornstarch or unmodified potato starch
- 2 T all-purpose flour or rice flour
- toasted sesame seeds for garnish (optional)

For the Sauce

- 1 T peanut oil or other cooking oil, plus more for frying
- 2 cloves garlic, minced
- 2 tsp grated ginger
- 1 cup chikun simmering broth (page 41) or commercial vegan equivalent
- ¼ cup fresh lemon juice
- 2 T organic sugar, or to taste
- 1 tsp fresh lemon zest
- 1 tsp sambal oelek, Sriracha™ or other hot red pepper sauce
- 4 tsp cornstarch or unmodified potato starch, dissolved in just enough water to create a slurry
- sea salt or kosher salt, to taste

Preparation

Slice the tempeh in half crosswise and simmer in enough water to cover for 10 minutes. This will help soften the tempeh and remove bitterness. Drain on paper towels until cooled. Slice the tempeh into bite-size cubes. Place the cubes into a food storage bag and add the tamari and wine/mirin. Seal and marinate in the refrigerator for a minimum of 1 hour.

Drain the excess marinade from the bag and add 2 tablespoons starch and the flour. Seal and gently toss to coat evenly. Place on a plate to dry while the sauce is prepared.

Add the 1 tablespoon oil to a medium saucepan and place over medium-low heat. Add the garlic and ginger and sauté for 30 seconds. Add the remaining sauce ingredients except for the starch slurry. Bring to a boil, whisk in the starch slurry and stir until thickened. Taste the sauce and add additional sugar or salt as desired. Reduce the heat to low to keep warm while frying the tempeh.

In a wok or deep skillet, heat 1-inch of oil over medium-high heat. When the oil begins to shimmer, carefully add the cubed tempeh and fry until golden brown. Transfer to a plate lined with paper towels to drain. Add the fried tempeh to the lemon sauce and toss gently to coat. Serve immediately and sprinkle with the toasted sesame seeds.

What are Soy Curls?

Butler Soy Curls™ are a commercial meat analogue. They have a texture similar to textured soy/vegetable protein chunks, but are fundamentally different because they are made with non-GMO whole soybeans, as opposed to textured soy/vegetable protein (which is the extruded by-product of soybean oil production). As such, they are processed differently according to their own proprietary method.

When seasoned and prepared properly, Butler Soy Curls™ produce an amazing meat analogue (left unseasoned, the strips have an inherent mild sweetness; proper seasoning helps mask this sweetness). If you cannot obtain the soy curls, textured vegetable/soy protein nuggets can be substituted but the finished appearance and texture will be different.

Soy Steak Strips
featuring Butler Soy Curls™

Soy steak strips are made with Butler Soy Curls™. This product and recipe offer an amazing grilled steak-like texture and flavor. For gluten-free diets, use wheat-free tamari in the seasoning broth. Omit the vegan Worcestershire if commercial varieties are not gluten-free; or prepare the Worcestershire sauce found in this cookbook using wheat-free tamari.

Primary Ingredient

- 1 pkg (8 oz) Butler Soy Curls™

Seasoning Broth

- 3 cups water
- 3 T tamari, soy sauce or Bragg Liquid Aminos™*
- 4 tsp onion powder
- 2 tsp garlic powder
- 2 tsp nutritional yeast flakes
- 2 tsp mushroom powder (porcini or portabella)
- 2 tsp Browning Liquid (page 28) or commercial equivalent
- 1 tsp Worcestershire Sauce (page 27) or commercial vegan equivalent
- ½ tsp paprika
- a few grinds of fresh ground black pepper

*Reduce the tamari to 2 tablespoons if you intend to serve the strips in a sauce, such as BBQ or teriyaki; or use reduced-sodium tamari or soy sauce.

Tex-Mex Variation

Omit the paprika and add the following ingredients to the seasoning broth:

- 2 tsp ancho chili powder (mild chili powder)
- 1 tsp ground cumin

- optional for spicy: chipotle chili powder to taste

Additional Ingredients for Sautéing

- 2 T cooking oil
- sea salt or kosher salt as desired
- additional coarse ground pepper as desired
- additional herbs and spices of your choice

Preparation

In a large saucepan, whisk together the seasoning broth ingredients and bring to a boil. Remove the saucepan from the heat and add the dry soy curls. Fold well in the broth and cover the saucepan. Allow to cool for 30 minutes to allow proper absorption of the seasoning and the color. Fold occasionally to ensure that all pieces are rehydrated and seasoned.

Drain the excess liquid (about ½ cup) and reserve if desired for enhancing vegetable broths or for seasoning other foods.

Add the cooking oil to a large skillet and place over medium heat. Add the seasoned steak strips and any additional herbs and spices as desired (a splash of red wine is always a nice touch too). Sauté, turning frequently until most of the liquid has evaporated and the strips are nicely browned (the steak strips hold a great deal of flavored broth even after draining the excess, so browning may take a bit longer than other meat analogues). Taste and add salt and pepper as desired.

If you wish to toss the strips with sautéed onions or other vegetables, prepare them in a separate skillet and combine with the steak strips before serving.

Note: To shred the steak strips, pulse a few times in a food processor fitted with a standard chopping blade. Process in two batches so as not to overcrowd the processor bowl.

Mongolian No-Beef

Tender vegan "beef" is stir-fried with a savory and sweet, tamari and ginger-based sauce and garnished with chopped scallions.

Ingredients

- 1 recipe Soy Steak Strips* (page 100), drain and reserve any remaining seasoning liquid
- 1 T peanut oil or neutral vegetable oil
- 2 tsp fresh grated ginger root
- 1 T minced garlic (3 cloves)
- ¾ cup water
- 3 T tamari, soy sauce or Bragg Liquid Aminos™
- 2 tsp cornstarch or unmodified potato starch dissolved in 1 T water to create a slurry
- ¼ cup light brown sugar
- ¼ cup high-temp cooking oil for frying
- whole scallions, sliced lengthwise

*12 oz of sliced Steak Bites (page 53) can be substituted for the soy steak strips.

Preparation

Prepare the sauce by heating 1 tablespoon oil in a medium saucepan over medium-low heat. Don't get the oil too hot.

Add the ginger and garlic to the pan and sauté for 30 seconds. Quickly add the water, reserved seasoning liquid, tamari and the starch slurry before the garlic scorches. Whisk well to combine.

Dissolve the brown sugar in the sauce. Raise the heat to medium and simmer the sauce for 2-3 minutes or until the sauce thickens. Remove from the heat and set aside.

In a skillet or wok, heat the high-temp oil over medium heat until hot but not smoking. Add the steak strips to the oil and fry for a few minutes until nicely browned. Be careful turning, as to not break the slices too much.

Use a large slotted spoon to transfer the beaf onto paper towels to drain any excess oil. Discard the oil out of the wok or skillet into the trash (not the drain).

Place the pan back over the heat, add the steaks strips back to the pan with the sauce and cook for one minute while stirring. Add the scallions and cook for a few more minutes until wilted, then remove the beaf and scallions with tongs or a slotted spoon to a serving plate. Leave the excess sauce behind in the pan. Serve over steamed jasmine rice.

Soy "Pulled" Porq Strips
featuring Butler Soy Curls™

"Pulled" porq strips are made with Butler Soy Curls™. This product and recipe offer an amazing pulled pork-like texture and roasted pork flavor. For gluten-free diets, replace the white shoyu with 2 tablespoons wheat-free tamari in the seasoning broth and add salt to taste. This recipe yields about 1 and ½ lbs.

Primary Ingredient

- 1 pkg (8 oz) Butler Soy Curls™

Seasoning Broth

- 3 cups water
- ¼ cup white shoyu (white soy sauce)*
- 4 tsp onion powder
- 2 tsp garlic powder
- 2 tsp nutritional yeast flakes
- 2 tsp mushroom powder (porcini or portabella)
- a few grinds of fresh ground black pepper
- 1 bay leaf

If you cannot obtain white shoyu, substitute with 2 tablespoons tamari, soy sauce or Bragg Liquid Aminos™ and add salt to taste.

Additional Ingredients for Sautéing

- 2 T cooking oil
- sea salt or kosher salt as desired
- additional coarse ground pepper as desired
- additional herbs and spices of your choice

Preparation

In a large saucepan, whisk together the seasoning broth ingredients, add the bay leaf and bring to a boil. Cover the saucepan, reduce the heat to a simmer and cook 10 minutes. Remove the saucepan from the heat and add the dry soy curls. Fold well in the broth and cover the saucepan. Allow to cool for 30 minutes to allow proper absorption of the seasoning and the color. Fold occasionally to ensure that all pieces are rehydrated and seasoned.

Drain the excess liquid (about ½ cup) and reserve if desired for enhancing vegetable broths or for seasoning other foods.

Add the olive oil to a large skillet and place over medium heat. Add the seasoned porq strips and any additional herbs and spices as desired (a splash of white wine is always a nice touch too). Sauté, turning frequently until most of the liquid has evaporated and the strips are nicely browned (the strips hold a great deal of flavored broth even after draining the excess, so browning may take a bit longer than other meat analogues). Taste and add salt and pepper as desired.

If you wish to toss the strips with sautéed onions or other vegetables, prepare them in a separate skillet and combine with the strips before serving.

Note: To shred the porq strips, tear the larger individual strips in half lengthwise with your fingers. While this takes a few extra minutes, it yields a better shredded texture than pulsing them in a food processor (which chops rather than shreds).

Cuban Porq Variation

Ingredients

- ¼ cup fresh orange juice
- 2 T fresh lime juice
- 2 T cooking oil
- 1 large onion, halved and thinly sliced
- 9 cloves garlic, minced (3 T)
- 1 T fresh minced oregano or 1 tsp dried oregano
- 1 tsp fresh orange zest, loosely packed
- 1 tsp fresh lime zest loosely packed
- sea salt or kosher salt and coarse ground black pepper to taste

Cuban Porq Preparation

Combine the citrus juices in a small bowl; set aside.

Add the oil to a large non-stick skillet or wok and place over medium heat; sauté the onion until tender and translucent. Add the garlic, oregano, orange zest and lime zest and sauté 30 seconds.

Add the porq strips and sauté, tossing frequently, until lightly browned. Drizzle in the citrus juices and toss well to distribute. Continue to sauté until almost all the liquid has evaporated and the strips are beginning to brown in spots (this will take several minutes); season with salt and pepper to taste. Transfer to a serving platter. Garnish with lime wedges.

Levantine Soy Shawarma with Tahini Sauce
featuring Butler's Soy Curls™

Shawarma is a Levantine meat preparation cooked on a rotisserie. Shavings of the meat are served in a sandwich, or on a plate with accompaniments such as tabbouleh or fattoush. Shawarma is often eaten as a fast food, made up into a sandwich wrap with flatbread together with vegetables and dressing. A variety of vegetables accompany the shawarma, and can include any combination of cucumber, onion, tomato, lettuce, parsley, pickled turnips, pickles, shredded cabbage or French fries. Please note that while shawarma shares similarities to Greek gyros and Turkish döner kebab, it is seasoned differently and is therefore not the same dish.

Vegan Levantine Shawarma is prepared using Butler Soy Curls™. For gluten-free diets, use wheat-free tamari in the seasoning broth. This recipe yields about 1 and ½ lbs.

Primary Ingredient

- 1 pkg (8 oz) Butler Soy Curls™

Seasoning Broth

- 3 cups water
- 3 T tamari, soy sauce or Bragg Liquid Aminos™*
- 2 T fresh lemon juice
- 1 T raw apple cider vinegar
- 4 tsp onion powder
- 2 tsp garlic powder
- 2 tsp mushroom powder
- 2 tsp Browning Liquid (page 28) or commercial equivalent
- 1 tsp ground cumin
- ½ tsp dried thyme leaves
- ¼ tsp ground cardamom
- ¼ tsp ground nutmeg
- ¼ tsp ground black pepper
- pinch ground cloves
- pinch ground cinnamon
- pinch cayenne or ground red pepper

Additional Ingredients for Pan-Browning

- 2 T olive oil
- sea salt or kosher salt as desired
- additional coarse ground pepper as desired

Preparation

In a large saucepan, whisk together the seasoning broth ingredients and bring to a boil. Remove the saucepan from the heat and add the dry soy curls. Fold well in the broth and cover the saucepan. Allow to cool for 30 minutes to allow proper absorption of the seasoning and the color. Fold occasionally to ensure that all pieces are rehydrated and seasoned. The strips can be refrigerated in the broth for up to 5 days before finishing.

Browning the Strips

Drain the excess liquid and discard. Add the olive oil to a large skillet and place over medium heat. Add the seasoned shawarma strips and sauté, turning frequently until most of the liquid has evaporated and the strips are nicely browned (the strips hold a great deal of flavored broth even after draining the excess, so browning may take a bit longer than other meat analogues). Taste and add salt and additional ground black pepper as desired.

Wrap the shawarma strips in flatbread with additional ingredients of your choice, as mentioned in the recipe description (for the photo, I used a skillet cooked mixture of potatoes, onions and halved grape tomatoes), and top with a generous drizzle of tahini sauce and a garnish of chopped parsley.

Drizzle tahini sauce over the shawarma and vegetable toppings and garnish with the chopped parsley.

Tahini Sauce

Tahini is a condiment made from toasted ground hulled sesame. Tahini is used in the cuisines of the Mediterranean, Middle East and parts of North Africa.

Ingredients

- ½ cup sesame tahini
- 6 T water, or more as needed to thin consistency
- 2 T fresh lemon juice
- 1 clove raw garlic
- ¼ tsp fine sea salt or kosher salt, or more to taste
- chopped fresh parsley for garnish

Preparation

For the tahini sauce, process the ingredients, except for the parsley, in a blender until smooth. Chill until ready to use. After chilling, thin with a little water if needed to achieve a saucy consistency.

Corned Soy Brisket Strips
featuring Butler's Soy Curls™

Corned brisket strips are made with Butler Soy Curls™. This unique product and recipe offer a texture and flavor that is reminiscent of seasoned corned beef brisket. For gluten-free diets, replace the white shoyu with wheat-free tamari in the seasoning brine. This recipe yields about 1 and ½ lbs.

Primary Ingredient

- 1 pkg (8 oz) Butler Soy Curls™

Additional Ingredients for Sautéing

- 2 T cooking oil
- sea salt or kosher salt as desired
- coarse ground pepper as desired

Seasoning Brine

- 3 cups water
- ¼ cup white shoyu (white soy sauce)*
- 4 tsp onion powder
- 2 tsp garlic powder
- 2 tsp nutritional yeast flakes
- 1 tsp coriander seeds
- ½ tsp ground ginger
- ½ tsp dry ground mustard
- 1 bay leaf
- 10 whole cloves
- 10 whole black peppercorns
- 5 whole allspice berries
- 5 juniper berries, lightly crushed
- 1 T beet powder

*If you cannot obtain white shoyu, substitute with tamari, soy sauce or Bragg Liquid Aminos™, however the finished product will be darker.

Preparation

In a large saucepan, whisk together the seasoning brine ingredients (except for the beet powder), add the bay leaf and bring to a boil.

Cover the saucepan, reduce the heat to a simmer and cook 20 minutes. Remove the saucepan from the heat, add the beet powder and stir until dissolved.

Strain the mixture through a fine mesh sieve into a large bowl; discard the spices.

Add the dry soy curls. Fold well in the brine and cover the bowl. Allow to cool for 30 minutes to allow proper absorption of the seasoning and the color. Fold occasionally to ensure that all pieces are rehydrated and seasoned.

Drain and discard the excess seasoning brine. Add the cooking oil to a large skillet and place over medium-low heat. Add the seasoned strips and sauté, turning frequently until most of the liquid has evaporated. Browning the strips is not necessary. Taste and add salt and pepper as desired.

Italian Soy Sausage Bits
featuring Butler's Soy Curls™

Soy sausage bits are made with Butler Soy Curls™. This unique product and recipe offer a texture and flavor that is reminiscent of Italian sausage. For gluten-free diets, use wheat-free tamari in the seasoning broth. This recipe yields about 1 and ½ lbs.

Primary Ingredient

- 1 pkg (8 oz) Butler Soy Curls™

Seasoning Broth

- 3 cups water
- 3 T tamari, soy sauce or Bragg Liquid Aminos™
- 4 tsp onion powder
- 2 tsp garlic powder
- 2 tsp nutritional yeast flakes
- 2 tsp dried basil leaves
- 1 tsp dried oregano leaves
- 1 tsp ground fennel seed
- ½ tsp whole fennel seed
- ½ tsp crushed red pepper flakes (or more for spicy sausage)
- a few grinds of fresh ground black pepper

Additional Ingredients for Pan-Browning

- 2 T olive oil
- sea salt or kosher salt as desired
- coarse ground pepper as desired

Preparation

In a large saucepan, whisk together the seasoning broth ingredients and bring to a boil. Remove the saucepan from the heat and add the dry soy curls. Fold well in the broth and cover the saucepan. Allow to cool for 30 minutes to allow proper absorption of the seasoning and the color. Fold occasionally to ensure that all pieces are rehydrated and seasoned.

Drain the excess liquid (about ½ cup) and reserve if desired for enhancing vegetable broths or for seasoning other foods. Add the seasoned curls to a food processor and pulse a few times until reduced into bits (avoid over-processing to retain texture). Alternately, chop the curls with a knife.

Add the cooking oil to a large skillet and place over medium heat. Add the sausage bits and sauté, turning frequently until most of the liquid has evaporated and the bits are lightly browned (the bits hold a great deal of flavored broth even after draining the excess, so browning may take a bit longer than other meat analogues). Taste and add salt and pepper to taste. Use in your favorite recipes as desired.

Seasoned Textured Soy Crumbles

Seasoned textured soy crumbles are an excellent soy-based meat alternative for any recipe calling for cooked and crumbled ground beef, such as pasta with "meat" sauce, chili, casseroles, Mexican cuisine, etc. Additional seasonings can be added while cooking the crumbles to accommodate different regional cuisines.

This recipe yields about 3 cups. Refrigerate any unused portion and consume within 1 week.

Seasoning Ingredients

- 1 and ½ cup water
- 1 T dried minced onion
- 2 T tamari, soy sauce or Bragg Liquid Aminos™
- 1 T olive oil
- 2 tsp onion powder
- 2 tsp mushroom powder
- 1 tsp garlic powder
- 2 tsp Worcestershire Sauce (page 27) or commercial vegan equivalent
- 1 cup dry TVP/TSP granules (textured vegetable/soy protein)
- optional fresh or dried herbs and spices as desired
- sea salt or kosher salt and coarse ground black pepper, to taste

Preparation

In a medium saucepan, whisk together the first 8 ingredients and place over medium-high heat to come to a brief boil. The dry powders may tend to clump; don't worry about it as this will resolve once the TVP/TSP granules have been added.

Add the dry TVP/TSP granules and mix well. Add any optional herbs and spices you desire and stir well. Reduce the heat to low and cover the saucepan for 10-15 minutes; stir occasionally. Season the crumbles with salt and pepper to taste. Use in your favorite recipe as desired.

Greek Moussaka

A hearty casserole, vegan Greek moussaka features layers of potato, eggplant, savory beaf crumbles cooked with onion, crushed tomatoes, parsley and red wine, and an enriched and creamy cashew-based Béchamel that's baked until golden brown. My plant-based variation is an adaptation of a generational family recipe from the Greek village of Ardactos on the island of Crete. I tried to stay as true to the flavors of the dish as possible. This recipe requires several components, which can be prepare separately and then assembled prior to baking the dish; however, I've written the recipe so the dish can be prepared seamlessly from start to finish.

Ingredients for the Eggplant Layer

- 2 medium eggplants (aubergine), about 3 lbs, peeled or unpeeled as desired
- olive oil as needed
- coarse sea salt or kosher salt
- coarse ground black pepper

Ingredients for the Potato Layer

- 3 medium russet potatoes
- sea salt or kosher salt

Ingredients for the Meatless Meat Layer

- 2 T olive oil
- 1 large onion, peeled and diced
- ¾ cup water
- ½ cup dry red wine (such as Cabernet Sauvignon, Merlot, etc.)
- 2 T tamari, soy sauce or Bragg Liquid Aminos™
- 1 T mushroom powder
- 1 T Worcestershire Sauce (page 27) or commercial vegan equivalent
- 1 cup dry TVP/TSP granules (textured vegetable protein/textured soy protein)
- 1 cup crushed tomatoes (fresh peeled or canned)
- 1 T tomato paste
- ¼ cup finely chopped parsley
- sea salt or kosher salt and coarse ground black pepper, to taste

Ingredients for the Enriched Béchamel

- 2 and ⅔ cup plain unsweetened non-dairy milk
- ⅓ cup olive oil
- ½ cup (2.5 oz/71 grams) raw cashews (pre-soaking unnecessary)
- 4 tsp nutritional yeast flakes
- 1 T mellow white miso paste
- 1 T fresh lemon juice
- 1 tsp sea salt or kosher salt
- 1 tsp onion powder
- 1 tsp garlic powder
- ¼ tsp ground nutmeg

Preparation

Slice the eggplant crosswise about ¼-inch thick. Place a colander into the sink and add layer of eggplant slices. Sprinkle generously with the coarse salt and repeat with layers of eggplant and salt (don't worry about using too much salt as it will be rinsed away later). Let the eggplant drain about 30 minutes and up to 1 hour to remove bitterness. Rinse well and pat dry on several layers of paper towels.

Position an oven rack in the center of the oven and preheat to 350°F/175°C. Line a baking sheet with parchment paper and place layer of eggplant on the parchment. Brush with olive oil and season with a bit of salt and pepper. Repeat the layers as needed. Bake uncovered in the oven for 40 minutes. Remove to cool.

While the eggplant is baking, peel and slice the potatoes about ¼-inch thick. Immediately place into a large cooking pot with plenty of cold water to cover. Add 2 teaspoons salt and bring to a full boil. Drain in the colander and set aside to cool.

Next, add 2 tablespoons olive oil to a large skillet and place over medium heat. Sauté the onions until tender and lightly golden. Add the water, red wine, tamari, mushroom powder and Worcestershire. Bring to a boil and add the TVP/TSP granules, crushed tomatoes and tomato paste. Stir well, reduce the heat to medium low, cover the skillet and cook about 20 minutes. Stir occasionally.

To prepare the Béchamel, add all ingredients to a blender and process on high speed for 2 full minutes. Transfer to a medium saucepan and cook over medium-low heat until the mixture comes to a simmer. Do not boil. Reduce the heat to low to keep warm.

Assembling the Moussaka

Preheat the oven to 350°F/175°C (if not already heated).

Lightly oil a 9"x13" shallow baking dish. Arrange the potatoes in an even layer on the bottom of the baking dish, overlapping as you layer. Spread about ⅔ cup Béchamel sauce over the potatoes.

Next, layer the eggplant slices as you did the potatoes and spread about ⅔ cup Béchamel sauce over the eggplant.

Spread the meatless meat mixture over the eggplant and top with the remaining Béchamel sauce. Season with a little coarse ground black pepper and bake for 50 to 60 minutes or until golden brown on top.

Let rest at room temperature for at least 30 minutes before slicing and serving.

Sloppy Gentle Joes

A compassionate twist on the classic American hot sandwich filling consisting of seasoned meatless crumbles combined with onions, bell pepper and seasonings in a tangy tomato sauce.

Seasoning Mixture Ingredients

- 1 cup water
- 1 T packed dark brown sugar
- 2 T tamari, soy sauce or Bragg Liquid Aminos™
- 1 T Worcestershire Sauce (page 27) or commercial vegan equivalent
- 1 T prepared yellow mustard
- 2 tsp mushroom powder
- 1 tsp onion powder
- 1 tsp dried oregano leaves
- 1 tsp dried basil leaves

Basic Ingredients

- 2 T olive oil
- 1 medium onion, finely diced
- ½ green bell pepper, finely diced
- 3 cloves garlic, minced
- 1 cup dry TVP/TSP granules (textured vegetable/soy protein)
- 1 can (15 oz) tomato sauce
- sea salt or kosher salt and coarse ground black pepper, to taste
- 4 white or whole grain Kaiser rolls or burger buns, split and lightly toasted

Preparation

In a bowl, whisk together the seasoning mixture ingredients; set aside.

Add the oil to a skillet and place over medium heat. Sauté the onion and bell pepper until tender, about 5 to 7 minutes. Add the minced garlic and sauté an additional minute.

Add the seasoning mixture to the skillet. Stir thoroughly to combine and bring the mixture to a boil. Add the TVP/TSP and mix well. Reduce the heat to low and cover the skillet for 10 minutes.

Stir the tomato sauce into the skillet mixture. The mixture will be very saucy. Bring to a simmer and cook, stirring frequently (to prevent scorching) until nicely thickened, about 10 minutes. Season the mixture with salt and pepper to taste. Spoon onto the toasted buns, and serve immediately.

Introduction to Individual Hand-Rolled Sausages

To create individual hand-rolled sausages, seasoned gluten dough is divided into individual portions, rolled and sealed in aluminum foil and then steamed in a conventional steamer or pressure cooker. After steaming, the sausages are chilled to firm and enhance their texture before browning in a skillet or on the grill.

Pop-up aluminum foil (9"x 10¾") is recommended for wrapping the sausages prior to steaming. Pop-up foil is commonly used in the restaurant industry for wrapping baked potatoes. It's very convenient because cutting foil to create wrappers is not required. While pop-up foil is not available in all supermarkets, it is commonly used in hair salons for hair coloring and can be found in beauty supply stores. It can also be purchased online. Pop-up foil is very thin and flimsy, so double or triple wrapping the sausages is required so they do not burst open while steaming.

If you don't have pop-up foil, standard and heavy-duty aluminum foil can be used; however, the foil will need to be cut with scissors to create eight 8"x10" wrappers. The sausages only need to be wrapped once when using standard or heavy-duty foil (unless the foil tears when twisting the ends).

If you don't want the dough coming into contact with aluminum foil, the dough can first be wrapped in parchment paper to create a barrier, and then in the aluminum foil. The aluminum foil is required.

For steaming, you will need a large cooking pot with a lid and a steamer insert, or an electric pressure cooker with a trivet stand (e.g., Instant Pot™). Add enough water to the cooking pot to just reach the bottom of the steamer insert. Do not overfill or the foil packages will be sitting in water. For the pressure cooker, add 2 to 3 cups of water and insert the trivet stand.

The sausage recipes are formulated with as much liquid as possible, beyond the point of saturation. This saturation is necessary for creating a juicy and meaty sausage. It's not uncommon to have a small amount of excess liquid remaining in the bottom of the mixing bowl after mixing the dough. Resist the urge to add more gluten to absorb the extra liquid as this will make the finished sausages dry and bread-like. However, handling and rolling the soft, wet dough in foil can be a little tricky, at least initially. So be patient when learning to wrap the sausages. Like any skill, it takes a little practice.

Meat-based sausages use a casing to contain the meat and give the sausage its shape. Plant-based sausages on the other hand, have no casing and since they are hand-rolled in aluminum foil, imperfections in their appearance are to be expected. However, these surface imperfections will not detract from their excellent taste and texture. Browning the sausages before serving actually creates a light "casing", so to speak, that significantly improves their appearance and minimizes these imperfections.

Steamed sausages require cooling to room temperature and then refrigeration for a minimum of 8 hours before browning and serving, so plan accordingly. Chilling reinforces the gluten structure thus firming and enhancing the sausage texture. The sausages will be soft and fragile after steaming, so refrigerate them in their foil wrappers until they have firmed up.

The prepared sausages are at their best when browned in the skillet with cooking oil before serving, but they are ideal for grilling too. Just be sure to brush them with cooking oil to keep them moist while grilling. Do not grill the sausages over open flames - hot embers are best; and avoid over-cooking as this can cause excessive dryness.

For even more vegan sausages, please refer to my Seitan and Beyond Cookbook.

Louisiana Hot Link Sausages

Louisiana Hot Link Sausages were inspired by the spicy sausages of Louisiana Cajun cuisine, and are heavily seasoned with garlic, black pepper and cayenne pepper. The sausages can be cooked in a conventional steamer or an electric pressure cooker. This recipe yields 8 plump sausages.

Dry Ingredients

- 1 and ½ cup (225 grams) vital wheat gluten
- 2 T cornstarch or unmodified potato starch
- 2 T dried minced onion
- 2 T nutritional yeast flakes
- 1 T onion powder
- 2 tsp garlic powder

Wet Ingredients

- 2 cups (480 ml) water
- 3 T tamari, soy sauce or Bragg Liquid Aminos™
- 2 T neutral vegetable oil
- 1 T minced fresh garlic (about 3 large cloves)
- 2 tsp liquid smoke
- 1 tsp Aromatica (page 40) or commercial poultry seasoning
- 1 tsp coarse ground black pepper
- 1 tsp ground cayenne or red pepper
- ¾ tsp fine sea salt or kosher salt

Additional Items Needed

- cooking pot with steamer basket insert; or electric pressure cooker with trivet stand
- foil wrappers (see page 113)

Preparing the Dough

Please be sure to review the *Introduction to Individual Hand-Rolled Sausages* on page 113 before proceeding.

Thoroughly combine the dry ingredients in a large mixing bowl. Combine the wet ingredients in a separate bowl or measuring cup.

Pour the wet mixture into the dry ingredients and combine thoroughly with a silicone spatula to develop the gluten. The dough will be soft and very wet. Let the dough rest for 10 minutes to allow the dry ingredients to absorb as much liquid as possible. There may be liquid in the bottom of the mixing bowl; this is normal.

Flatten the dough evenly in the mixing bowl and divide with the edge of the spatula into 8 roughly equal portions.

Foil Wrapping the Dough

Place a portion of dough onto a foil square and with your fingers shape the dough into a rough sausage shape. The dough will be very wet, so keep a moist paper towel on hand to wipe your

fingers as you work. Don't worry too much about shaping perfection, as the dough will expand to conform to the cylindrical shape of the foil package when steamed.

Roll the dough inside the foil to create a cylinder while simultaneously pinching the ends closed. Twist the ends tightly to seal. When using pop-up foil, roll again in a second, and if needed, a third foil wrapper. If the foil should tear while twisting the ends, roll again in additional foil. The dough needs to be securely sealed in the foil to prevent moisture from leaking out but also to prevent steam moisture from entering the packages. Repeat with the remaining pieces of dough.

Conventional Steamer

Add enough water to the cooking pot to almost reach the bottom of the steamer basket. Bring the water to a rolling boil. Place the foil packages in the steamer basket, place over the boiling water and cover. The water must be boiling to generate the proper amount of steam heat to cook the sausages thoroughly and evenly. Set a timer for 50 minutes. Check the water level in the cooking pot at the 25-minute mark and replace if needed with very hot water. Do not the let the pot boil dry!

Remove the packages to cool for about 1 hour and then chill for a minimum of 8 hours before browning and serving.

Pressure Cooker

Place the trivet stand inside your pressure cooker and add a few cups of water. The water level should not exceed the height of the trivet.

Add the foil packages and pressure cook on high for 30 minutes. Turn the unit off but do not release the steam valve or open the unit. Set a timer for 20 minutes and let the steam pressure subside naturally. Remove the packages to cool for about 1 hour and then chill for a minimum of 8 hours before browning and serving.

Browning the Sausages

Bring the foil packages to room temperature, about 30 minutes. The sausages can be browned whole, but also try slicing them on the bias (diagonal) before browning. Sliced and browned hot links are superb for adding to vegan Cajun-style stews.

Remove the foil and recycle. In a non-stick skillet or well-seasoned cast iron skillet, brown the sausages in two tablespoons of cooking oil over medium heat. A teaspoon of tamari, soy sauce or Bragg Liquid Aminos™ will encourage browning, but this is optional. Transfer to a plate lined with paper towels to blot any excess oil. The sausages are ready to eat or use in your favorite recipe.

For grilling, brush the whole sausages with cooking oil and grill over hot embers until lightly browned, or until grill marks appear. Avoid direct flames and do not overcook.

Polska Kielbasa

This sausage recipe is a personal favorite from my Seitan and Beyond Cookbook but I have made some revisions for larger, plumper kielbasa. They're made with my special blend of Polish sausage seasonings, with an abundance of black pepper and garlic, and the recipe yields 8 plump kielbasa. The sausages can be cooked in a conventional steamer or an electric pressure cooker.

Dry Ingredients

- 1 and ½ cup (225 grams) vital wheat gluten
- 2 T cornstarch or unmodified potato starch
- 2 T dried minced onion
- 1 T onion powder
- 2 tsp garlic powder
- 1 and ½ tsp coarse ground black pepper

Wet Ingredients

- 2 cups (480 ml) water
- 3 T tamari, soy sauce or Bragg Liquid Aminos™
- 2 T neutral vegetable oil
- 1 T minced fresh garlic (about 3 large cloves)
- 2 tsp liquid smoke
- 2 tsp dried summer savory or marjoram (or 1 tsp each)
- ¾ tsp fine sea salt or kosher salt
- ½ tsp ground allspice
- ¼ tsp ground nutmeg

Additional Items Needed

- cooking pot with steamer basket insert; or electric pressure cooker with trivet stand
- foil wrappers (see page 113)

Preparing the Dough

Please be sure to review the *Introduction to Individual Hand-Rolled Sausages* on page 113 before proceeding.

Thoroughly combine the dry ingredients in a large mixing bowl. Combine the wet ingredients in a separate bowl or measuring cup.

Pour the wet mixture into the dry ingredients and combine thoroughly with a silicone spatula to develop the gluten. The dough will be soft and very wet. Let the dough rest for 10 minutes to allow the dry ingredients to absorb as much liquid as possible. There may be liquid in the bottom of the mixing bowl; this is normal.

Flatten the dough evenly in the mixing bowl and divide with the edge of the spatula into 8 roughly equal portions.

Foil Wrapping the Dough

Place a portion of dough onto a foil square and with your fingers shape the dough into a rough sausage shape. The dough will be very wet, so keep a moist paper towel on hand to wipe your fingers as you work. Don't worry too much about shaping perfection, as the dough will expand to conform to the cylindrical shape of the foil package when steamed.

Roll the dough inside the foil to create a cylinder while simultaneously pinching the ends closed. Twist the ends tightly to seal. When using pop-up foil, roll again in a second, and if needed, a third foil wrapper. If the foil should tear while twisting the ends, roll again in additional foil. The dough needs to be securely sealed in the foil to prevent moisture from leaking out but also to prevent steam moisture from entering the packages. Repeat with the remaining pieces of dough.

Conventional Steamer

Add enough water to the cooking pot to almost reach the bottom of the steamer basket. Bring the water to a rolling boil. Place the foil packages in the steamer basket, place over the boiling water and cover. The water must be boiling to generate the proper amount of steam heat to cook the sausages thoroughly and evenly. Set a timer for 50 minutes. Check the water level in the cooking pot at the 25-minute mark and replace if needed with very hot water. Do not the let the pot boil dry! Remove the packages to cool for about 1 hour and then chill for a minimum of 8 hours before browning and serving.

Pressure Cooker

Place the trivet stand inside your pressure cooker and add a few cups of water. The water level should not exceed the height of the trivet.

Add the foil packages and pressure cook on high for 30 minutes. Turn the unit off but do not release the steam valve or open the unit. Set a timer for 20 minutes and let the steam pressure subside naturally. Remove the packages to cool for about 1 hour and then chill for a minimum of 8 hours before browning and serving.

Browning the Sausages

Bring the foil packages to room temperature, about 30 minutes. The sausages can be browned whole, but also try slicing them on the bias (diagonal) before browning. Sliced kielbasa are excellent when browned in an oiled skillet with chopped onion and green bell peppers.

Remove the foil and recycle. In a non-stick skillet or well-seasoned cast iron skillet, brown the sausages in two tablespoons of cooking oil over medium heat. A teaspoon of tamari, soy sauce or Bragg Liquid Aminos™ will encourage browning, but this is optional. Transfer to a plate lined with paper towels to blot any excess oil. The sausages are ready to eat or use in your favorite recipe.

For grilling, brush the whole sausages with cooking oil and grill over hot embers until lightly browned, or until grill marks appear. Avoid direct flames and do not overcook.

Deutschewurst

Deutschewurst (which literally means 'German sausage") are tasty meatless sausages made with my special blend of German-inspired seasonings and are reminiscent of knackwurst. They're perfect for celebrating Oktoberfest, but are delicious any time of the year. The sausages can be cooked in a conventional steamer or an electric pressure cooker. This recipe yields 8 plump sausages.

Dry Ingredients

- 1 and ½ cup (225 grams) vital wheat gluten
- 2 T cornstarch or unmodified potato starch
- 2 T onion powder
- 2 tsp garlic powder

Wet Ingredients

- 2 cups (480 ml) water
- 3 T tamari, soy sauce or Bragg Liquid Aminos™
- 2 T neutral vegetable oil
- 1 and ½ tsp smoked paprika
- 1 tsp Aromatica (page 40) or commercial poultry seasoning
- 1 tsp liquid smoke
- ¾ tsp fine sea salt or kosher salt
- ½ tsp ground allspice
- ½ tsp ground mace or nutmeg
- ½ tsp ground white pepper

Additional Items Needed

- cooking pot with steamer basket insert; or electric pressure cooker with trivet stand
- foil wrappers (see page 113)

Preparing the Dough

Please be sure to review the *Introduction to Individual Hand-Rolled Sausages* on page 113 before proceeding.

Thoroughly combine the dry ingredients in a large mixing bowl. Combine the wet ingredients in a separate bowl or measuring cup.

Pour the wet mixture into the dry ingredients and combine thoroughly with a silicone spatula to develop the gluten. The dough will be soft and very wet. Let the dough rest for 10 minutes to allow the dry ingredients to absorb as much liquid as possible. There may be liquid in the bottom of the mixing bowl; this is normal.

Flatten the dough evenly in the mixing bowl and divide with the edge of the spatula into 8 roughly equal portions.

Foil Wrapping the Dough

Place a portion of dough onto a foil square and with your fingers shape the dough into a rough sausage shape. The dough will be very wet, so keep a moist paper towel on hand to wipe your

fingers as you work. Don't worry too much about shaping perfection, as the dough will expand to conform to the cylindrical shape of the foil package when steamed.

Roll the dough inside the foil to create a cylinder while simultaneously pinching the ends closed. Twist the ends tightly to seal. When using pop-up foil, roll again in a second, and if needed, a third foil wrapper. If the foil should tear while twisting the ends, roll again in additional foil. The dough needs to be securely sealed in the foil to prevent moisture from leaking out but also to prevent steam moisture from entering the packages. Repeat with the remaining pieces of dough.

Conventional Steamer

Add enough water to the cooking pot to almost reach the bottom of the steamer basket. Bring the water to a rolling boil. Place the foil packages in the steamer basket, place over the boiling water and cover. The water must be boiling to generate the proper amount of steam heat to cook the sausages thoroughly and evenly. Set a timer for 50 minutes. Check the water level in the cooking pot at the 25-minute mark and replace if needed with very hot water. Do not the let the pot boil dry!

Remove the packages to cool for about 1 hour and then chill for a minimum of 8 hours before browning and serving.

Pressure Cooker

Place the trivet stand inside your pressure cooker and add a few cups of water. The water level should not exceed the height of the trivet.

Add the foil packages and pressure cook on high for 30 minutes. Turn the unit off but do not release the steam valve or open the unit. Set a timer for 20 minutes and let the steam pressure subside naturally. Remove the packages to cool for about 1 hour and then chill for a minimum of 8 hours before browning and serving.

Browning the Sausages

Bring the foil packages to room temperature, about 30 minutes. The sausages can be browned whole, but also try slicing them on the bias (diagonal) before browning. Sliced Deutschewurst are excellent when browned in an oiled skillet with chopped onion and sauerkraut.

Remove the foil and recycle. In a non-stick skillet or well-seasoned cast iron skillet, brown the sausages in two tablespoons of cooking oil over medium heat. A teaspoon of tamari, soy sauce or Bragg Liquid Aminos™ will encourage browning, but this is optional. Transfer to a plate lined with paper towels to blot any excess oil. The sausages are ready to eat or use in your favorite recipe.

For grilling, brush the whole sausages with cooking oil and grill over hot embers until lightly browned, or until grill marks appear. Avoid direct flames and do not overcook.

Portuguese Sausages

These sausages are reminiscent of Linguiça, a sausage which originated in Portugal. My vegan Portuguese sausages are flavored with smoked paprika and heavily seasoned with garlic. The sausages are mild in spiciness; to add spicy heat incorporate some cayenne pepper into the wet ingredients before mixing the dough. The sausages can be cooked in a conventional steamer or an electric pressure cooker. This recipe yields 8 plump sausages.

Dry Ingredients

- 1 and ½ cup (225 grams) vital wheat gluten
- 2 T cornstarch or unmodified potato starch
- 2 T dried minced onion
- 1 T onion powder
- 2 tsp garlic powder

Wet Ingredients

- 2 cups (480 ml) water
- 3 T tamari, soy sauce or Bragg Liquid Aminos™
- 1 T minced fresh garlic (about 3 large cloves)
- 2 T olive oil
- 2 tsp dried oregano leaves
- 1 tsp smoked paprika
- 2 tsp liquid smoke
- ¾ tsp sea salt or kosher salt
- ½ tsp fresh ground black pepper

Additional Items Needed

- cooking pot with steamer basket insert; or electric pressure cooker with trivet stand
- foil wrappers (see page 113)

Preparing the Dough

Please be sure to review the *Introduction to Individual Hand-Rolled Sausages* on page 113 before proceeding.

Thoroughly combine the dry ingredients in a large mixing bowl. Combine the wet ingredients in a separate bowl or measuring cup.

Pour the wet mixture into the dry ingredients and combine thoroughly with a silicone spatula to develop the gluten. The dough will be soft and very wet. Let the dough rest for 10 minutes to allow the dry ingredients to absorb as much liquid as possible. There may be liquid in the bottom of the mixing bowl; this is normal.

Flatten the dough evenly in the mixing bowl and divide with the edge of the spatula into 8 roughly equal portions.

Foil Wrapping the Dough

Place a portion of dough onto a foil square and with your fingers shape the dough into a rough sausage shape. The dough will be very wet, so keep a moist paper towel on hand to wipe your

fingers as you work. Don't worry too much about shaping perfection, as the dough will expand to conform to the cylindrical shape of the foil package when steamed.

Roll the dough inside the foil to create a cylinder while simultaneously pinching the ends closed. Twist the ends tightly to seal. When using pop-up foil, roll again in a second, and if needed, a third foil wrapper. If the foil should tear while twisting the ends, roll again in additional foil. The dough needs to be securely sealed in the foil to prevent moisture from leaking out but also to prevent steam moisture from entering the packages. Repeat with the remaining pieces of dough.

Conventional Steamer

Add enough water to the cooking pot to almost reach the bottom of the steamer basket. Bring the water to a rolling boil. Place the foil packages in the steamer basket, place over the boiling water and cover. The water must be boiling to generate the proper amount of steam heat to cook the sausages thoroughly and evenly. Set a timer for 50 minutes. Check the water level in the cooking pot at the 25-minute mark and replace if needed with very hot water. Do not the let the pot boil dry!

Remove the packages to cool for about 1 hour and then chill for a minimum of 8 hours before browning and serving.

Pressure Cooker

Place the trivet stand inside your pressure cooker and add a few cups of water. The water level should not exceed the height of the trivet.

Add the foil packages and pressure cook on high for 30 minutes. Turn the unit off but do not release the steam valve or open the unit. Set a timer for 20 minutes and let the steam pressure subside naturally. Remove the packages to cool for about 1 hour and then chill for a minimum of 8 hours before browning and serving.

Browning the Sausages

Bring the foil packages to room temperature, about 30 minutes. The sausages can be browned whole, but also try slicing them on the bias (diagonal) before browning. Sliced Portuguese sausages are excellent when browned in an oiled skillet and served with vegan eggz for breakfast.

Remove the foil and recycle. In a non-stick skillet or well-seasoned cast iron skillet, brown the sausages in two tablespoons of cooking oil over medium heat. A teaspoon of tamari, soy sauce or Bragg Liquid Aminos™ will encourage browning, but this is optional. Transfer to a plate lined with paper towels to blot any excess oil. The sausages are ready to eat or use in your favorite recipe.

For grilling, brush the whole sausages with cooking oil and grill over hot embers until lightly browned, or until grill marks appear. Avoid direct flames and do not overcook.

Big Bangers

Bangers are a type of sausage common to the United Kingdom. Bangers are often an essential part of pub food, as they are quick to prepare and Bangers and Mash is the traditional British Isles favorite (sausages with mashed potatoes and onion gravy). The term "bangers" is attributed to the fact that sausages, particularly the kind made during World War II under rationing, were made with water so they were more likely to explode under high heat if not cooked carefully. Fortunately, this isn't an issue with their plant-based counterparts. This recipe yields 8 plump sausages. The recipe for Savory Onion Gravy can be found on page 140.

Dry Ingredients

- 1 and ½ cup (225 grams) vital wheat gluten
- 2 T cornstarch or unmodified potato starch
- 2 T dried minced onion
- 1 T onion powder
- 1 tsp garlic powder
- 1 tsp coarse ground black pepper

Wet Ingredients

- 2 cups (480 ml) water
- 3 T tamari, soy sauce or Bragg Liquid Aminos™
- 2 T neutral vegetable oil
- 1 T minced fresh garlic (about 3 large cloves)
- 1 tsp liquid smoke
- 1 and ½ tsp fresh grated lemon zest (loosely packed)
- 1 tsp Aromatica (page 40) or commercial poultry seasoning
- ¾ tsp fine sea salt or kosher salt
- ¾ tsp ground ginger
- ½ tsp ground nutmeg

Additional Items Needed

- cooking pot with steamer basket insert; or electric pressure cooker with trivet stand
- foil wrappers (see page 113)

Preparing the Dough

Please be sure to review the *Introduction to Individual Hand-Rolled Sausages* on page 113 before proceeding.

Thoroughly combine the dry ingredients in a large mixing bowl. Whisk together the wet ingredients in a separate bowl or measuring cup.

Pour the wet mixture into the dry ingredients and combine thoroughly with a silicone spatula to develop the gluten. The dough will be soft and very wet. Let the dough rest for 10 minutes to allow the dry ingredients to absorb as much liquid as possible. There may be liquid in the bottom of the mixing bowl; this is normal.

Flatten the dough evenly in the mixing bowl and divide with the edge of the spatula into 8 roughly equal portions.

Foil Wrapping the Dough

Place a portion of dough onto a foil square and with your fingers shape the dough into a rough sausage shape. The dough will be very wet, so keep a moist paper towel on hand to wipe your fingers as you work. Don't worry too much about shaping perfection, as the dough will expand to conform to the cylindrical shape of the foil package when steamed.

Roll the dough inside the foil to create a cylinder while simultaneously pinching the ends closed. Twist the ends tightly to seal. When using pop-up foil, roll again in a second, and if needed, a third foil wrapper. If the foil should tear while twisting the ends, roll again in additional foil. The dough needs to be securely sealed in the foil to prevent moisture from leaking out but also to prevent steam moisture from entering the packages. Repeat with the remaining pieces of dough.

Conventional Steamer

Add enough water to the cooking pot to almost reach the bottom of the steamer basket. Bring the water to a rolling boil. Place the foil packages in the steamer basket, place over the boiling water and cover. The water must be boiling to generate the proper amount of steam heat to cook the sausages thoroughly and evenly. Set a timer for 50 minutes. Check the water level in the cooking pot at the 25-minute mark and replace if needed with very hot water. Do not the let the pot boil dry! Remove the packages to cool for about 1 hour and then chill for a minimum of 8 hours before browning and serving.

Pressure Cooker

Place the trivet stand inside your pressure cooker and add a few cups of water. The water level should not exceed the height of the trivet.

Add the foil packages and pressure cook on high for 30 minutes. Turn the unit off but do not release the steam valve or open the unit. Set a timer for 20 minutes and let the steam pressure subside naturally. Remove the packages to cool for about 1 hour and then chill for a minimum of 8 hours before browning and serving.

Browning the Sausages

Bring the foil packages to room temperature, about 30 minutes. The sausages can be browned whole, but also try slicing them on the bias (diagonal) before browning.

Remove the foil and recycle. In a non-stick skillet or well-seasoned cast iron skillet, brown the sausages in two tablespoons of cooking oil over medium heat. A teaspoon of tamari, soy sauce or Bragg Liquid Aminos™ will encourage browning, but this is optional. Transfer to a plate lined with paper towels to blot any excess oil. The sausages are ready to eat or use in your favorite recipe.

For grilling, brush the whole sausages with cooking oil and grill over hot embers until lightly browned, or until grill marks appear. Avoid direct flames and do not overcook.

Italiano Sausages
"Sweet" or "Hot"

Classic Italian seasonings give these sausages their characteristic flavor. The seasoning blend offers options for "sweet" (mild) sausages or "hot" and spicy sausages. The sausages can be cooked in a conventional steamer or an electric pressure cooker. This recipe yields 8 plump sausages.

Dry Ingredients

- 1 and ½ cup (225 grams) vital wheat gluten
- 2 T cornstarch or unmodified potato starch
- 2 T dried minced onion
- 1 T onion powder
- 1 and ½ tsp whole fennel seeds*

Blender Ingredients

- 2 cups (480 ml) water
- 3 T tamari, soy sauce or Bragg Liquid Aminos™
- 2 T olive oil
- 2 tsp dried oregano leaves
- 1 and ½ tsp whole fennel seeds*
- 1 tsp dried basil leaves
- 1 tsp liquid smoke
- ¾ tsp sea salt or kosher salt
- ½ tsp ground white pepper for "sweet" (mild) sausages
  or 1 T crushed red pepper flakes for "hot" (spicy) sausages

Additional Ingredient

- 1 T minced fresh garlic (about 3 large cloves)

*Some of the fennel seeds are left whole, while some are finely ground with the blender ingredients. This is not a misprint.

Additional Items Needed

- cooking pot with steamer basket insert; or electric pressure cooker with trivet stand
- foil wrappers (see page 113)

Preparing the Dough

Please be sure to review the *Introduction to Individual Hand-Rolled Sausages* on page 113 before proceeding.

Thoroughly combine the dry ingredients in a large mixing bowl.

Process the blender ingredients to pulverize the fennel seeds, about 30 seconds. It's not essential that they be ground completely. Stir in the minced garlic but do not continue to process.

Pour the blender mixture into the dry ingredients and combine thoroughly with a silicone spatula to develop the gluten. The dough will be soft and very wet. Let the dough rest for 10 minutes to allow the dry ingredients to absorb as much liquid as possible. There may be liquid in the bottom of the mixing bowl; this is normal. Flatten the dough evenly in the mixing bowl and divide with the edge of the spatula into 8 roughly equal portions.

Foil Wrapping the Dough

Place a portion of dough onto a foil square and with your fingers shape the dough into a rough sausage shape. The dough will be very wet, so keep a moist paper towel on hand to wipe your fingers as you work. Don't worry too much about shaping perfection, as the dough will expand to conform to the cylindrical shape of the foil package when steamed.

Roll the dough inside the foil to create a cylinder while simultaneously pinching the ends closed. Twist the ends tightly to seal. When using pop-up foil, roll again in a second, and if needed, a third foil wrapper. If the foil should tear while twisting the ends, roll again in additional foil. The dough needs to be securely sealed in the foil to prevent moisture from leaking out but also to prevent steam moisture from entering the packages. Repeat with the remaining pieces of dough.

Conventional Steamer

Add enough water to the cooking pot to almost reach the bottom of the steamer basket. Bring the water to a rolling boil. Place the foil packages in the steamer basket, place over the boiling water and cover. The water must be boiling to generate the proper amount of steam heat to cook the sausages thoroughly and evenly. Set a timer for 50 minutes. Check the water level in the cooking pot at the 25-minute mark and replace if needed with very hot water. Do not the let the pot boil dry!

Remove the packages to cool for about 1 hour and then chill for a minimum of 8 hours before browning and serving.

Pressure Cooker

Place the trivet stand inside your pressure cooker and add a few cups of water. The water level should not exceed the height of the trivet.

Add the foil packages and pressure cook on high for 30 minutes. Turn the unit off but do not release the steam valve or open the unit. Set a timer for 20 minutes and let the steam pressure subside naturally. Remove the packages to cool for about 1 hour and then chill for a minimum of 8 hours before browning and serving.

Browning the Sausages

Bring the foil packages to room temperature, about 30 minutes. The sausages can be browned whole, but also try slicing them on the bias (diagonal) before browning. Sliced Italiano sausages are excellent when browned in an oiled skillet, added to your favorite pasta sauce and served over cooked pasta.

Remove the foil and recycle. In a non-stick skillet or well-seasoned cast iron skillet, brown the sausages in two tablespoons of cooking oil over medium heat. A teaspoon of tamari, soy sauce or Bragg Liquid Aminos™ will encourage browning, but this is optional. Transfer to a plate lined with paper towels to blot any excess oil. The sausages are ready to eat or use in your favorite recipe.

For grilling, brush the whole sausages with cooking oil and grill over hot embers until lightly browned, or until grill marks appear. Avoid direct flames and do not overcook.

Pressure-Cooker Pepperoni

Pepperoni is a hard sausage. I feel that the flavor of my plant-based pepperoni rivals the best of its meat-based counterpart. This recipe also appears in my Seitan and Beyond Cookbook but I've included it here because the cooking method is different and, in my opinion, improved. With this method there is no risk of the foil rupturing, which can occur with oven-baking. The dough is divided into two portions and wrapped individually so the packages will fit inside the pressure cooker. Buon Appetito!

Dry Ingredients

- 1 cup (150 grams) vital wheat gluten
- 1 T onion powder

Blender Ingredients

- ½ cup (120 ml) water
- 3 T olive oil
- 3 T tamari, soy sauce or Bragg Liquid Aminos™
- 2 T tomato paste
- 2 tsp red wine vinegar or raw apple cider vinegar
- 2 tsp smoked paprika
- 2 tsp organic sugar
- 2 tsp whole fennel seeds
- 1 tsp crushed red pepper flakes (or more or less to taste)
- 1 tsp dry ground mustard

Additional Wet Ingredient

- 1 T minced fresh garlic (about 3 large cloves)

Additional Items Needed

- electric pressure cooker (e.g., Instant Pot™) with trivet stand
- 18-inch wide heavy-duty aluminum foil

Preparation

Place the trivet inside your pressure cooker and add a few cups of water. The water level should not exceed the height of the trivet.

Combine the dry ingredients in a large mixing bowl.

Process the blender ingredients until the fennel is coarsely ground. Stir the minced garlic into the blender mixture. Do not process once the garlic has been added.

Pour the blender mixture into the dry ingredients and combine thoroughly with a silicone spatula. Knead the dough in the bowl until it exhibits some elasticity, about 1 minute. Divide the dough in half.

Tear off 2 sheets of foil (about 12-inches each) and place a sheet on your work surface. Shape one portion of the dough into a slender log about 6-inches long and place it near the edge of the foil.

Lift the edge of the foil over the dough and begin rolling into a tight cylinder, pinching the ends closed simultaneously while rolling. The goal is to create a slender cylindrical package. Twist the ends tightly to seal, being careful not to tear the foil. Bend the twisted ends in half to lock them tight.

Wrap the additional portion of dough with the second sheet of foil. There is no need to rewrap with additional foil.

Place the packages into the pressure cooker and cook on high for 1 hour. Turn the cooker off but **do not** release the steam. Set a timer for 30 minutes and let the steam pressure release naturally.

Remove the packages from the cooker and let cool about 1 hour. Never attempt to open the packages while they are hot or steam burns can result. Refrigerate the pepperoni in its foil wrappers for a minimum of 8 hours before using. This will firm and enhance the texture and make thin slicing easier.

After chilling, remove the foil and recycle. The pepperoni is ready to eat or use in recipes; it does not require any additional finishing. Simply slice thick or thin and use as needed. Store the pepperoni sealed tightly in plastic wrap in the refrigerator and consume within 10 days or freeze for up to 3 months.

Italian Cauliflower "Sausage Bits"

A unique and simple crumbled "sausage" for your favorite Italian dishes. Superb on pizza!

Ingredients

- 1 large head cauliflower
- 2 T mild olive oil or cooking oil
- 2 T tamari, soy sauce
  or Bragg's Liquid Aminos™
- 1 and ½ tsp ground fennel
- 1 tsp onion powder
- 1 tsp garlic powder
- 1 tsp dried basil leaves
- 1 tsp dried oregano leaves
- 1 tsp Worcestershire Sauce (page 27)
  or commercial vegan equivalent
- 1 tsp Browning Liquid (page 28)
  or commercial equivalent (optional)
- ¾ tsp sea salt or kosher salt
- ½ tsp liquid smoke
- ¼ tsp ground red pepper for spicy or
  ¼ tsp ground white pepper for mild

Preparation

Preheat the oven to 375°F/190°C.

Cut away the rough florets from the stems and core and coarsely crumble the florets into a mixing bowl. Don't crumble too small. Discard or compost the stems and core.

Combine the remaining ingredients in a small dish. Add the mixture to the crumbles and toss well so that the crumbles are evenly and lightly coated. Transfer the crumbles to a baking sheet and spread evenly.

Bake for 20 minutes and stir the mixture Continue to bake another 15 minutes or until the crumbles are browned and tender but still retain a slight chewiness. Use as desired.

Foil-Wrap Technique for Deli-Style Luncheon Slices

Deli-style luncheon slices are a plant-based alternative to deli-style luncheon meat. The bologna, smoky turky and roast beaf luncheon slices are made from a blend of wheat protein from gluten and select seasonings. An electric deli-slicer is recommended for creating uniformly thin slices. The slices can be served hot or cold, as desired.

To prepare, seasoned gluten dough is rolled and sealed in aluminum foil before being cooked in an Instant Pot™ or other electric pressure cooker. The foil-wrapped dough can also be oven-baked if preferred. Parchment paper can be used as a barrier between the dough and the foil if desired.

It is very important to use heavy-duty aluminum foil when cooking gluten, especially when oven-baking. Regular foil can easily rupture from expansion of the gluten as it cooks, and from steam pressure which builds up inside the foil. Always err on using too much foil rather than not enough. When in doubt, rewrap with an additional one or two sheet(s) of foil.

Foil Wrap Technique

On a work surface, lay out a large sheet of heavy-duty aluminum foil (18-inch wide). Place the dough directly on top.

With your hands, form the dough into a round mass. The dough will be very soft and wet and will tend to spread out but try as best as you can to keep it as a round mass. Now, before the dough begins to spread out, lift the edge of the foil over the dough and begin to roll the dough inside the foil, pinching the ends closed simultaneously while rolling. The goal is to create a thick, compact package, not a thin sausage shape. This may take a little bit of practice, so be patient.

Now twist the ends tightly to seal, being careful not to tear the foil. Bend the ends inward to lock them tight. This will also help the package fit inside the pressure cooker chamber, if using this cooking method. For baking, rewrap with 1 or 2 additional large sheet(s) of foil and twist the ends very tight to completely seal the dough, and once again, bend the ends inward to lock them tight.

When using an electric pressure cooker, place the foil package on the trivet in the pressure cooker. Make sure the unit contains 2 to 3 cups of water before closing and cooking. Also, be sure the steam release valve is in the closed position.

When oven-baking, place the package directly onto the middle rack of the preheated oven.

Deli-Style Bologna

While my plant-based bologna lacks the nitrate pink color of its meat-based counterpart, it has a comparable texture and flavor and makes a tasty and natural vegan alternative to meat bologna. Keep in mind that it has been decades since I've consumed meat-based bologna, so my seasonings are based upon what I know to be traditional as well as what I can remember. Feel free to adjust or modify the seasonings as desired. Prepared mustard is a classic condiment with sliced bologna and fried bologna is always a treat.

For this recipe, an Instant Pot™ or other electric pressure cooker is recommended for cooking the bologna. The bologna can also be oven-baked, but consider triple-wrapping with foil to reduce the risk of the package bursting open while baking. This recipe yields about 1 and ½ lbs.

Dry Ingredients

- 1 and ½ cups (225 grams) vital wheat gluten

Blender Ingredients

- 2 cups (480 ml) water
- ½ cup tapioca starch/flour
- 1 T onion powder
- 1 T garlic powder
- 2 T mellow white miso paste
- 3 T neutral vegetable oil
- 2 tsp sea salt or kosher salt
- 1 tsp smoked paprika
- 1 tsp Aromatica (page 40) or commercial poultry seasoning
- ¾ tsp ground nutmeg
- 1 tsp liquid smoke
- ½ tsp ground coriander

Preparation

Please be sure to review the *Foil-Wrap Technique for Deli-Style Luncheon Slices* on page 129 before proceeding.

For pressure-cooking, add 2 to 3 cups water to the cooker and place the trivet inside. Be sure the water level is lower than the height of the trivet. For baking, preheat the oven to 350°F/175°C.

Add the gluten to a large mixing bowl.

Process the blender ingredients until completely smooth.

Add the blender ingredients to the gluten and mix well to form the dough. Let the dough rest for 10 minutes to allow the gluten to absorb as much liquid as possible.

Knead the dough in the bowl with a sturdy spatula or spoon to develop the gluten, about 2 minutes, or until some resistance can be felt in the dough. The dough will be very soft and wet.

Roll the dough in a large sheet of heavy-duty aluminum foil to create a cylinder and twist the ends tightly to seal. The goal is to keep the cylinder package as thick and compact as possible. Rewrap in a second layer of foil and again twist the ends tightly to seal. You will need to bend the twisted ends inward so that the package fits into the pressure cooker chamber. If baking the roast, rewrap in an additional large sheet(s) of foil, twist the ends tightly to seal and bend the ends inward to lock them tight.

Pressure-cooking

Pressure cook on high 1 hour and 45 minutes. Turn the unit off but do not release the steam valve or open the unit. Set a timer for 30 minutes and let the steam pressure subside naturally. Remove the package to cool for about 1 hour and then chill for a minimum of 8 hours before slicing and serving.

An electric deli-slicer is recommended for creating uniformly thin slices. Please note that the bologna roll will have a rustic, rough surface; that's normal and will be fine once sliced. Use within 10 days or freeze for up to 3 months.

Oven-Baking

Bake directly on the middle rack of the oven at 350°F/175°C for 1 hour and 45 minutes. Remove the package to cool for about 1 hour and then chill for a minimum of 8 hours before slicing and serving.

An electric deli-slicer is recommended for creating uniform slices. Please note that the bologna roll will have a rustic, rough surface; that's normal and will be fine once sliced. Use within 10 days or freeze for up to 3 months.

Deli-Style Smoky Turky

Deli-Style Smoky Turky has a mellow smoked flavor and can be served hot or cold. For peppered smoky turky, add 2 teaspoons coarse ground black pepper to the dry ingredients before mixing the dough.

For this recipe, an Instant Pot™ or other electric pressure cooker is recommended for cooking the roast. The roast can also be oven-baked, but consider triple-wrapping with foil to reduce the risk of the package bursting open while baking. This recipe yields about 2 lbs.

Dry Ingredients

- 2 cups (300 grams) vital wheat gluten
- ¼ cup all-purpose flour
- 2 T onion powder
- 2 tsp garlic powder
- 1 tsp Aromatica (page 40) or commercial poultry seasoning

Wet Ingredients

- 2 and ⅔ cups (640 ml) water
- 1 T nutritional yeast flakes
- 1 T liquid smoke
- 2 T neutral vegetable oil
- 2 tsp fine sea salt or kosher salt

Preparation

Please be sure to review the *Foil-Wrap Technique for Deli-Style Luncheon Slices* on page 129 before proceeding.

For pressure-cooking, add 2 to 3 cups water to the cooker and place the trivet inside. Be sure the water level is lower than the height of the trivet. For baking, preheat the oven to 350°F/175°C.

Combine the dry ingredients in a large mixing bowl.

Mix the liquid ingredients in a separate bowl or measuring cup.

Add the liquid ingredients to the dry ingredients and mix well. Knead the dough in the bowl with a sturdy spatula or spoon to develop the gluten, about 2 minutes, or until resistance can be felt in the dough.

Roll the dough in a large sheet of heavy-duty aluminum foil to create a cylinder and twist the ends tightly to seal. The goal is to keep the cylinder package as thick and compact as possible. Rewrap in a second layer of foil and again twist the ends tightly to seal. You will need to bend the twisted ends inward so that the package fits into the pressure cooker chamber. If baking the roast, rewrap in an additional large sheet(s) of foil, twist the ends tightly to seal and bend the ends inward to lock them tight.

Pressure-Cooking

Pressure cook on high for 2 hours. Turn the unit off but do not release the steam valve or open the unit. Set a timer for 30 minutes and let the steam pressure subside naturally. Remove the package to cool for about 1 hour and then chill for a minimum of 8 hours before slicing and serving.

An electric deli-slicer is recommended for uniformly thin slices. The smoky turky is at its best when the slices are shaved as thin as possible. Use within 10 days or freeze for up to 3 months.

Oven-Baking

Bake directly on the middle rack of the oven at 350°F/175°C for 2 hours. Remove the package to cool for about 1 hour and then chill for a minimum of 8 hours before slicing and serving.

An electric deli-slicer is recommended for creating uniform slices. The smoky turky is at its best when the slices are shaved as thin as possible. Use within 10 days or freeze for up to 3 months.

Deli-Style Roast Beaf

Tender, flavorful slices of roast beaf can be served hot or cold. For peppered beaf, add 2 teaspoons coarse ground black pepper to the dry ingredients before mixing the dough.

For this recipe, an Instant Pot™ or other electric pressure cooker is recommended for cooking the roast. The roast can also be oven-baked, but consider triple-wrapping with foil to reduce the risk of the package bursting open while baking. This recipe yields about 2 lbs.

Dry Ingredients

- 2 cups (300 grams) vital wheat gluten
- ¼ cup all-purpose flour
- 2 T mushroom powder
- 2 T nutritional yeast flakes
- 2 T onion powder
- 1 T garlic powder

Liquid Ingredients

- 2 and ⅓ cups (560 ml) water
- 3 T tamari, soy sauce or Bragg Liquid Aminos™
- 2 T neutral vegetable oil
- 1 T Worcestershire Sauce (page 27) or commercial vegan equivalent
- ¾ tsp sea salt or kosher salt

Preparation

Please be sure to review the *Foil-Wrap Technique for Deli-Style Luncheon Slices* on page 129 before proceeding.

For pressure-cooking, add 2 to 3 cups water to the cooker and place the trivet inside. Be sure the water level is lower than the height of the trivet. For baking, preheat the oven to 350°F/175°C.

Combine the dry ingredients in a large mixing bowl. Mix the liquid ingredients in a separate bowl or measuring cup.

Add the liquid ingredients to the dry ingredients and mix well. Knead the dough in the bowl with a sturdy spatula or spoon to develop the gluten, about 2 minutes, or until resistance can be felt in the dough.

Roll the dough in a large sheet of heavy-duty aluminum foil to create a cylinder and twist the ends tightly to seal. The goal is to keep the cylinder package as thick and compact as possible. Rewrap in a second layer of foil and again twist the ends tightly to seal. You will need to bend the twisted ends inward so that the package fits into the pressure cooker chamber. If baking the roast, rewrap in an additional large sheet(s) of foil, twist the ends tightly to seal and bend the ends inward to lock them tight.

Pressure-Cooking

Pressure cook on high for 2 hours. Turn the unit off but do not release the steam valve or open the unit. Set a timer for 30 minutes and let the steam pressure subside naturally. Remove the package to cool for about 1 hour and then chill for a minimum of 8 hours before slicing and serving.

An electric deli-slicer is recommended for uniformly thin slices. The beaf is at its best when the slices are shaved as thin as possible. Try serving hot on toasted roll with Horsey Sauce or 'Jus' (recipes follow). Use within 10 days or freeze for up to 3 months.

Oven-Baking

Bake directly on the middle rack of the oven at 350°F/175°C for 2 hours. Remove the package to cool for about 1 hour and then chill for a minimum of 8 hours before slicing and serving.

An electric deli-slicer is recommended for creating uniform slices. The beaf is at its best when the slices are shaved as thin as possible. Try serving hot on toasted roll with Horsey Sauce or 'Jus' (recipes follow). Use within 10 days or freeze for up to 3 months.

More Sauces and Gravies

Horsey Sauce

A classic sauce for hot or cold deli-style beaf sandwiches. This recipe yields 1 cup.

Ingredients

- ¾ cup No-Eggy Mayo (page 263) or commercial vegan mayonnaise
- ¼ cup Instant Sour Cream (page 176), Cultured Sour Cream (page 177) or commercial non-dairy equivalent
- 2 T prepared horseradish (not creamed), or more to taste
- 2 T fresh lemon juice (about 1 small lemon)
- sea salt or kosher salt, to taste

Preparation

Whisk together the ingredients in a small bowl until smooth and creamy. Transfer to a sealable container and refrigerate to blend the flavors and use within 1 week.

Chef's tip: To optimize the juice you get from a lemon or lime, roll it hard under your palm for a minute before juicing.

'Jus'

Jus (pronounced "zhoo") is French for juice and "au jus" literally means "with (its own) juice". In American cuisine, the term generally refers to the broth itself, which may be served with the food or placed on the side for dipping.

Ingredients

- 1 T olive oil
- 1 shallot, minced or 2 T minced red onion
- 1 T all-purpose flour or rice flour
- 2 T dry sherry, optional
- 3 cups beaf simmering broth (page 56)

Preparation

Add the olive oil to a medium saucepan and place over medium heat. Add the shallot or red onion and sauté until tender. Reduce the heat to low and whisk in the flour until a smooth paste forms (roux). Cook until the flour emits a nutty aroma, about 1 minute. Incorporate the broth in increments while vigorously whisking the mixture until smooth. Add the optional sherry and bring the sauce to a brief boil, stirring frequently. Reduce the heat to low until ready to serve.

Classic Golden Cheese Sauce

This velvety cheese sauce has a mild cheddar-like flavor that will please the entire family. It's ideal for topping hot meatless meat sandwiches or for preparing macaroni and cheese and cheesy rice. Try pouring over freshly steamed vegetables or baked potatoes too. This recipe yields about 2 cups of sauce.

Ingredients

- 1 and ¾ cup plain unsweetened soymilk or almond milk
- 5 T tapioca starch
- ¼ cup neutral vegetable oil
- ¼ cup nutritional yeast flakes
- 2 T mellow white miso paste
- 12 drops natural orange food color (e.g., India Tree™) or 1 T tomato paste or 2 tsp tomato powder
- 2 tsp raw apple cider vinegar
- ¾ tsp fine sea salt or kosher salt, or more to taste
- ½ tsp dry ground mustard
- ½ tsp onion powder

Tip: For a tangier sauce, add ½ tsp lactic acid powder or 2 teaspoons fresh lemon juice.

Preparation

Whisk the ingredients together in a small saucepan until smooth. Place over medium-low heat and stir slowly and continually with a flexible spatula until the mixture becomes bubbly, thickened, smooth and glossy.

Please note that the golden color will develop as the cheese sauce cooks. Taste the sauce and season with additional salt as desired.

Reduce the heat to low to keep warm until ready to serve, stirring occasionally.

Queso Blanco Sauce
(Mexican White Cheese Sauce)

This Mexican-style white cheese sauce is flavored with mild green chilies and is wonderful for dipping warm tortillas or tortilla chips, or for pouring over your favorite Mexican or Tex-Mex foods. This recipe yields about 2 cups of sauce.

Ingredients

- 1 and ¾ cup plain unsweetened soymilk or almond milk
- ¼ cup neutral vegetable oil
- 3 T tapioca starch
- 1 T nutritional yeast flakes
- 1 tsp ground cumin
- 1 tsp fine sea salt or kosher salt
- 2 tsp raw apple cider vinegar
- 1 can (4 oz) diced mild green chilies
- 2 T finely minced onion
- 1 to 2 T chopped fresh cilantro (optional)

Preparation

Add all ingredients except for the chilies, minced onion and cilantro to a small saucepan and whisk until smooth. Stir in the chilies and minced onion and place over medium-low heat. Stir slowly and continually with a flexible spatula until the mixture becomes bubbly, thickened and glossy.

Taste and add salt as desired and/or additional soymilk to lighten the consistency to your preference. Reduce the heat to low to keep warm until ready to serve, stirring occasionally. Stir in the optional cilantro just before serving.

Queso Nacho Sauce

As the name implies, this Mexican-style cheese sauce is perfect for topping nachos. This recipe yields about 2 cups of sauce.

Ingredients

- 1 and ¾ cup plain unsweetened soymilk or almond milk
- ¼ cup nutritional yeast flakes
- ¼ cup tapioca starch
- ¼ cup neutral vegetable oil
- 1 T mellow white miso paste
- 1 tsp fine sea salt or kosher salt
- 1 tsp ancho chili powder
- 2 tsp raw apple cider vinegar
- ½ tsp onion powder
- ¼ tsp ground red pepper or cayenne pepper

Preparation

Whisk the ingredients together in a small saucepan until smooth. Place over medium-low heat and stir slowly and continually with a flexible spatula until the mixture becomes bubbly, thickened, smooth and glossy.

Please note that the golden color will develop as the cheese sauce cooks. Taste and add salt as desired and/or additional soymilk to lighten the consistency to your preference. Reduce the heat to low to keep warm until ready to serve, stirring occasionally.

Classic Hollandaise Sauce

Hollandaise sauce is one of the classic French "mother" sauces. This buttery, lemony sauce is remarkably similar in texture and flavor to its egg-based counterpart; but unlike its counterpart, the emulsion will not curdle or break. Hollandaise is excellent served over pan-grilled meatless meats and cooked vegetables. This recipe yields about 1 cup.

Ingredients

- 1 T nutritional yeast flakes
- 1 and ½ tsp cornstarch or unmodified potato starch
- ¼ tsp sodium alginate, guar gum or xanthan gum
- ½ tsp sea salt or kosher salt
- ⅛ tsp cayenne pepper
- ⅛ tsp ground turmeric
- ¼ cup (2 oz) non-dairy butter or margarine
- ¾ cup plain unsweetened soymilk or almond milk
- 4 tsp fresh lemon juice

Preparation

Combine the nutritional yeast, starch, alginate or gum, salt, cayenne pepper and turmeric in a small dish.

In a small saucepan, melt the butter or margarine over low heat. Whisk in the seasoning blend and stir until smooth.

Whisk in the milk. Increase the heat to medium-low and cook, stirring frequently until the sauce comes to a low simmer. Do not boil! Whisk in the lemon juice and reduce the heat to low to keep warm until ready to serve, stirring occasionally.

Savory Onion Gravy

Ingredients

- 2 T mild olive oil
- 2 medium onions, peeled, halved and then thinly sliced
- 1 tsp organic sugar
- 2 T non-dairy butter or margarine
- ¼ cup all-purpose flour or rice flour
- 2 cups porq simmering broth (page 77) or any well-seasoned vegetable broth
- 1 tsp dark balsamic vinegar
- sea salt or kosher salt and
- coarse ground black pepper, to taste

Preparation

Add the olive oil to a saucepan and place over medium heat. Add the onions, sugar and a pinch of salt; sauté until very tender and golden brown in color.

Add the butter or margarine and stir until melted.

Sprinkle in the flour and stir until a thick paste forms (roux). Cook the mixture until the flour is golden and emits a nutty aroma, about 2 minutes. The flour will stick to the bottom of the saucepan, but don't worry, as it will release when the broth is incorporated.

Incorporate the broth in increments, stirring well after each addition. Add the balsamic vinegar and bring the mixture to a boil, stirring frequently. Reduce the heat and simmer, about 5 minutes.

Ladle half of the mixture into a blender and put the lid in place. For safety, cover the lid with a dish towel, hold down firmly and start the blender on low-speed, gradually increasing speed.

Return the blended gravy to the saucepan and season with salt and pepper to taste. Keep warm over low heat until ready to serve.

Hearty Brown Gravy

Ingredients

- 2 cups beaf simmering broth (page 56) or any well-seasoned vegetable broth
- 2 T olive oil
- 2 T non-dairy butter or margarine
- ¼ cup all-purpose flour or rice flour
- Browning Liquid (page 28), or commercial equivalent as needed for color
- sea salt or kosher salt and coarse ground black pepper, to taste

Preparation

Add the olive oil to a small saucepan and place over medium heat. Add the butter or margarine and stir until melted.

Whisk in the flour to create a thick paste (roux) and cook until the flour is golden and emits a nutty aroma, about 2 minutes. The flour will stick to the bottom of the saucepan, but don't worry, as it will release when the broth is incorporated.

Incorporate the broth in increments while vigorously stirring. Add small amounts of browning liquid as needed for depth of color. Bring to a simmer and continue to stir until the mixture thickens. Add salt and pepper to taste. Reduce heat to low until ready to serve; stir occasionally.

Chef's note: This cooking method should discourage lumps from forming in the gravy. However, should this occur, simply process the gravy on low speed in a blender until smooth and return to saucepan to heat through.

Golden Gravy

Ingredients

- 2 cups chikun simmering broth (page 41) or commercial vegan equivalent
- 2 T neutral vegetable oil
- 2 T non-dairy butter or margarine
- ¼ cup all-purpose flour or rice flour
- sea salt or kosher salt and coarse ground black pepper, to taste

Preparation

Add the olive oil to a small saucepan and place over medium heat. Add the butter or margarine and stir until melted. Whisk in the flour to create a thick paste (roux) and cook until the flour is golden and emits a nutty aroma, about 2 minutes. The flour will stick to the bottom of the saucepan, but don't worry, as it will release when the broth is incorporated.

Incorporate the broth in increments while vigorously stirring. Bring to a simmer and continue to stir until the mixture thickens. Add salt and pepper to taste. Reduce heat to low until ready to serve; stir occasionally.

Chef's note: This cooking method should discourage lumps from forming in the gravy. However, should this occur, simply process the gravy on low speed in a blender until smooth and return to saucepan to heat through.

Country Mushroom Gravy

Country mushroom gravy is a classic for preparing holiday Green Bean Casserole.

Ingredients

- 2 T olive oil
- 8 oz mushrooms of your choice, sliced or chopped
- 2 T non-dairy butter or margarine
- ¼ cup all-purpose flour or rice flour
- 1 and ½ cup chikun simmering broth (page 41) or vegetable broth
- ½ tsp dried thyme leaves
- ½ cup plain unsweetened soymilk or almond milk
- sea salt or kosher salt and coarse ground black pepper, to taste

Preparation

Add the olive oil to a large saucepan and place over medium heat. Add the mushrooms and sauté until the liquid has evaporated and the mushrooms begin to brown. Stir in the butter until melted.

Sprinkle in the flour and stir until a thick paste forms (roux). Cook the mixture until the flour is golden and emits a nutty aroma, about 2 minutes. The flour will stick to the bottom of the saucepan, but don't worry, as it will release when the broth is incorporated.

Incorporate the broth in increments, stirring well after each addition. Add the thyme and bring the mixture to a boil, stirring frequently. Reduce the heat and simmer, about 5 minutes.

Add the milk and return to a gentle simmer. Season the gravy with salt and pepper to taste. Keep warm over low heat until ready to serve.

Chef's Best BBQ Sauce

A thick tangy tomato-based sauce with just the right balance of savory and sweet, superb for basting your favorite grilled and broiled meat analogues.

Ingredients

- ¼ cup non-dairy butter or margarine
- 6 cloves garlic, minced (2 T)
- 1 can (6 oz) tomato paste
- ½ cup dark brown sugar
- ½ cup water
- ¼ cup raw apple cider vinegar
- 1 T dried minced onion
- 1 T Worcestershire Sauce (page 27) or commercial vegan equivalent
- 1 T hickory liquid smoke
- 1 tsp fine sea salt or kosher salt
- 1 tsp prepared Dijon or spicy mustard
- ½ tsp hot red pepper sauce, or more to taste

Preparation

Melt the butter or margarine in a small saucepan over medium-low heat and sauté the garlic for 1 minute.

Whisk in the remaining ingredients and bring the mixture to a simmer. Reduce heat to low and cook uncovered, stirring occasionally, for about 1 hour until the sauce is thickened. Let cool and refrigerate to further thicken before using.

Jack D's BBQ Sauce Variation

Follow the recipe for the sauce but replace the water with a good quality whiskey or bourbon.

Vodka Blush Sauce

Vodka blush sauce is a creamy tomato-based pasta sauce flavored with vodka. This is my own variation which can be prepared with either cashew cream or soy cream. Sweet red pepper was included for flavor. Serve over penne, rigatoni or spiral pasta.

Ingredients

- ¼ cup raw cashews*
- ½ cup water*
- 2 T olive oil
- 1 medium onion, peeled and chopped
- 1 large sweet red pepper, seeded and chopped
- 3 cloves garlic, chopped
- 1 can (28 oz) diced tomatoes with liquid
- ¼ cup premium vodka
- 2 T tomato paste
- 1 tsp dried basil leaves
- 1 tsp fine sea salt or kosher salt, or more to taste
- ½ tsp dried oregano leaves
- ½ tsp crushed red pepper flakes
- grated Hard Parmesano (page 208), or Grated Sunflower Parmesan (page 212) or commercial vegan equivalent for garnish
- julienned fresh sweet basil for garnish (optional)
- fresh ground black pepper, to taste
- cooked pasta of your choice (penne is commonly used)

The cashews and water can be substituted with ½ cup Soy Cream (page 171).

Preparation

In a blender, process the cashews and water on high speed for 2 full minutes. Transfer to a cup and chill until ready to use. Alternately, the cashew cream mixture can be replaced with ½ cup soy cream.

Add the olive oil to a skillet and place over medium heat. Add the onions and sweet red pepper and sauté until the onions are translucent. Add the garlic and sauté an additional minute or two.

Stir in the diced tomatoes with liquid, vodka, tomato paste, dried basil, salt, dried oregano and the red pepper flakes. Bring to a gentle simmer and cover the skillet. Reduce the heat to low and cook for 45 minutes, stirring occasionally.

Transfer the skillet mixture to the blender. Begin processing on low speed, gradually increasing to high. Process the contents until smooth and then transfer back to the skillet, placing over medium heat.

Stir in the cashew or soy cream and cook until heated through. Season the sauce with additional salt as needed to taste. Ladle the sauce over cooked pasta, sprinkle with parmesan and fresh ground black pepper and garnish with the optional fresh basil.

Chef's Best Alfredo Sauce

Alfredo sauce is a creamy and rich white sauce traditionally served over fettuccini. It's a classic complementary sauce for tossing with slices of pan-grilled Chikun cutlets and serving over hot cooked pasta.

Dairy parmesan cheese is a primary ingredient in traditional Alfredo sauce; however, non-dairy parmesan won't provide the same texture and richness; therefore, non-dairy parmesan is reserved for garnishing the final dish.

Chef's Best Alfredo Sauce is very easy to prepare and achieves the ideal nappe consistency for serving over pasta with pan-grilled or sautéed vegan seafoods and/or cooked vegetables. This recipe yields about 2 and ¼ cups.

Ingredients

- 2 cups plain unsweetened soymilk
- 1.5 oz/43 grams (about ⅓ cup) raw cashews (pre-soaking unnecessary)
- ¼ cup mild olive oil
- 1 T nutritional yeast flakes
- 1 T mellow white miso paste
- 1 and ½ tsp onion powder
- 1 tsp garlic powder
- ¾ tsp fine sea salt or kosher salt, or more to taste
- ¼ tsp ground white pepper
- 2 T chopped fresh parsley
- grated Hard Parmesano (page 208), or Grated Sunflower Parmesan (page 212) or commercial vegan equivalent for garnish

Preparation

Process all ingredients except for the parsley and parmesan in a blender on high speed for 2 full minutes. Strain through a fine mesh sieve into a saucepan and cook over medium-low heat, stirring slowly and continually, until the mixture just comes to a simmer.

Reduce the heat to low to keep warm until ready to serve; stir occasionally.

Garnish with the parmesan and fresh parsley when serving.

Chef's Best Marinara Sauce

A classic tomato-based sauce for dressing fresh cooked pasta; as an ingredient in a wide variety of Italian cuisine; or as a condiment for dipping.

Ingredients

- 2 T olive oil
- 1 medium onion, diced
- 3 cloves minced garlic
- 1 can (28 oz) crushed tomatoes
- or 2 lbs vine-ripened tomatoes, peeled* and crushed
- ½ cup dry white wine (e.g., Chardonnay, Sauvignon Blanc)
- 2 T tomato paste
- 1 T organic sugar
- 1 tsp sea salt or kosher salt
- 1 tsp dried basil or 1 T fresh basil, finely minced
- 1 tsp dried oregano or 1 T fresh oregano, finely minced
- ¼ tsp coarse ground black pepper, or more to taste

To peel fresh tomatoes, blanch them by immersing them in boiling water for 1 minute. Immediately immerse them in an ice-water bath. The skins should slip off easily. Pulse the tomatoes a few times in a food processor to crush.

Preparation

In a large saucepan, sauté the onions in olive oil over medium heat until translucent. Add the garlic and sauté an additional 2 minutes.

Add the crushed tomatoes, tomato paste, white wine, sugar, salt, herbs and pepper. The sugar is important, as it tempers the acidity of the tomatoes, so do not omit unless you are diabetic. Bring to a simmer, cover and reduce the heat to just above low. Cook for about 45 minutes and season with additional salt and pepper as desired. The marinara sauce is now ready to use.

Bolognese Sauce

Bolognese is a meat-based sauce originating from Bologna, Italy, hence the name. In Italian cuisine, it is customarily used to dress broad, flat pasta shapes, such as tagliatelle, pappardelle or fettuccine.

For Bolognese sauce, prepare the marinara sauce in the preceding recipe but add 1 diced carrot and one diced rib of celery to the onion sauté. Add ½ cup dry TVP/TSP granules, ½ cup water and 2 tablespoons tamari or soy sauce when adding the crushed tomatoes and other ingredients. Simmer as directed. Ten minutes before serving, stir in ½ cup Soy Cream (page 171) or Raw Cashew Milk (page 168). Season with additional salt and pepper as desired. Serve over the hot cooked pasta.

Chimichurri Sauce

Chimichurri sauce is one of my personal favorites. It is an aromatic herb sauce that originated in Argentina and is traditionally used for grilled meat. In vegan gastronomy, it can be used as a sauce for dressing a wide variety of meat alternatives such as shredded beaf; grilled seitan, tofu, tempeh, portabella mushrooms or cauliflower "steak". It's also wonderful as a dip for crusty bread or for marinating cooked beans.

Ingredients

- ¼ cup water
- ¼ cup white wine vinegar or champagne vinegar
- 2 T red wine vinegar
- 2 cups chopped flat leaf parsley, loosely packed
- ½ cup roasted red pepper, skin removed plus additional for garnish if desired
- ¼ cup fresh chopped oregano, loosely packed or 4 tsp dried oregano
- 1 shallot, chopped
- 2 cloves garlic, chopped
- 1 tsp minced habanero or jalapeno pepper
- 1 tsp sea salt or kosher salt
- 1 tsp sweet paprika
- ¼ tsp ground cumin
- ½ cup extra-virgin olive oil

Preparation

Prepare and then chill the stewing beaf according to the cookbook directions.

Remove the foil and recycle. Using your hands, bend the roast in half to split it lengthwise; this will reveal the "grain". Tear the roast in half following where it has been split. Bend and tear those pieces in half lengthwise.

Now, with your fingers, pull the beaf into long strings or shreds, following the grain as much as possible. Tear those pieces into smaller bite-size shreds.

Process all sauce ingredients in a food processor but leave little bit of texture. Add salt as needed to taste.

Store the sauce in an airtight container in the refrigerator until ready to use; shake well to re-emulsify before using.

Gentle Seafoods

Scallopz

Scallopz are a soy protein (from tofu) and konjac-based seafood alternative and can be used in any recipe just as you would real sea or bay scallops. They're very easy to make and are a good starting point when first learning to prepare the seafood analogues. Basic instructions for marinating and pan-searing the scallopz are included (any marinade of your choice can also be used). This recipe yields about 10 ounces.

Blender Ingredients

- 1 T glucomannan (konjac) powder
- 3 oz/85 grams **pressed** extra-firm tofu (not silken tofu)
- 1 and ¾ cup wakame infusion or water
  (see preparation instructions for the optional wakame infusion)
- 1 and ½ tsp organic sugar
- 1 and ¼ tsp sea salt or kosher salt
- ½ tsp agar powder
- ¼ tsp onion powder
- ¼ tsp pickling lime powder (calcium hydroxide)

Optional Wakame Infusion Ingredients

- 2 cups (480 ml) water
- 2 T (6 grams) dried wakame flakes

Additional Items Needed

- assorted round cutters: 2-inch for jumbo scallopz,
- 1 and ½-inch for standard scallopz, and 1-inch for bay scallopz
- blender
- standard loaf pan
- flexible silicone spatula

Preparation

The wakame infusion is optional but will enhance seafood flavor. To prepare the infusion, bring the water and wakame to a brief boil in a small saucepan. Remove from the heat, cover and let cool completely. Strain into a measuring cup and measure 1 and ¾ cup (420 ml) liquid. Press the wakame with the back of a spoon to extract the liquid. Compost or discard the wakame as it will have lost most of its flavor.

Measure the glucomannan powder and set aside near your blender.

Add the wakame infusion or water and the remaining blender ingredients to the blender (except for the glucomannan powder) and process until completely liquefied. Reduce the blender speed, add the glucomannan powder and process to the count of 5. Pour the mixture into the medium saucepan and place over medium heat.

Slowly stir the mixture with the spatula. As the mixture begins to thicken, begin slowly folding and stirring the mixture with the spatula. As the mixture begins to stiffen, fold and knead the mixture with the spatula. A thin "skin" of protein will begin to adhere to the bottom and sides of the saucepan and may dislodge while stirring; simply work it into the mixture as it cooks.

The mixture needs to be cooked past the creamy stage and when sufficiently cooked, should have a very stiff but moist consistency. It is important to cook the mixture to this stage or it will set not set properly. However, avoid cooking to the point where the cohesive mass begins to break apart into clumps.

Transfer the mixture to the loaf pan and use the spatula to press the mixture evenly into the pan. Let the mixture cool about 10 minutes and turn the gel onto a work surface.

Forming the Scallopz

Using a desired size round cutter, cut discs from the gel while it is still warm (this will create softer edges than cold gel). Any ragged edges can be trimmed away with kitchen shears. Create one or two shallow snips along the edges of each scallop with kitchen shears for a more natural appearance. Any remnants can be chopped, lightly sautéed and added to recipes, if desired. Unlike most of the other konjac-based analogues in this cookbook, scallopz do not require simmering in water to complete their preparation process (as this would overcook them and make them tough).

Refrigerate the scallopz and any chopped remnants, with or without a marinade, in a sealed container or food storage bag until ready to use in recipes. Use within 5 days or freeze up to 3 months. When including sautéed scallopz in soups or stews, add them just before serving so they don't become overcooked and tough.

Marinating and Pan-Searing the Scallopz

Marinade Ingredients

- ½ cup semi-sweet or semi-dry white wine such as Moscato or Riesling or ⅓ cup water plus the juice of 1 large lemon (about 2 T)
- 1 T tamari, soy sauce or Bragg Liquid Aminos™
- 1 tsp Gentle Bay Seasoning (page 150) or commercial Old Bay™ seasoning, plus additional for seasoning the scallopz after pan-searing if desired
- 2 garlic cloves, minced

Pan-Searing Ingredients

- 1 T olive oil
- 1 T non-dairy butter or margarine

Place the scallopz in a food storage bag and add the marinade. Press out the excess air, seal the bag and chill for a minimum of 1 hour (longer marinating will increase the flavor).

Remove the scallopz from the marinade and gently pat them dry.

Add the butter and oil to a skillet and place over medium heat. When the butter has melted, place the scallopz in the skillet and cook until they are lightly browned on each side. Sprinkle with additional seasoning if desired. Transfer the scallopz to serving plates and serve immediately.

Gentle Bay Seasoning

A homemade variation of the commercial Old Bay™ seasoning, which is popularly used for seasoning seafood dishes.

Ingredients

- 2 T celery salt (or 4 tsp coarse sea salt or kosher salt and 2 tsp celery seed)
- 1 T paprika
- 1 tsp coarse ground black pepper
- 2 dried bay leaves (also known as laurel leaves), crumbled
- ¼ tsp ground red pepper

Preparation

Process the ingredients in a dry blender or spice grinder until finely powdered. Store in a small airtight container. This recipe yields about 3 tablespoons.

Classic Cocktail Sauce

A classic condiment dipping sauce for your favorite vegan seafoods.

Ingredients

- 1 cup tomato ketchup
- 1 to 2 T prepared horseradish (to taste)
- 1 T fresh lemon juice
- 1 tsp Worcestershire Sauce (page 27), or commercial vegan equivalent
- dash ground white pepper
- sea salt or kosher salt to taste

Preparation

Whisk the ingredients together and season with salt to taste. Chill to blend the flavors before serving.

Shrymp

Shrymp are a soy protein (from tofu) and konjac-based seafood alternative and can be used in any recipe just as you would real shrimp.

Blender Ingredients

- 1 T glucomannan (konjac) powder
- 3 oz/85 grams **pressed** extra-firm tofu (not silken tofu)
- 1 and ¾ cup (420 ml) wakame infusion or water
  (see preparation instructions for the optional wakame infusion)
- 1 and ¼ tsp sea salt or kosher salt
- 1 tsp agar powder
- ¼ tsp onion powder
- ¼ tsp pickling lime powder (calcium hydroxide)

Optional Wakame Infusion Ingredients

- 2 cups (480 ml) water
- 2 T (6 grams) dried wakame flakes

Additional Items Needed

- 8" square baking dish
- paprika for dusting the bottom of the baking dish
- blender
- sturdy silicone spatula
- 2-inch round cutter for standard shrymp; 1-inch round cutter for bay shrymp
- common teaspoon, kitchen shears and a sharp paring knife for detailing standard shrymp; miniature cocktail spoon for detailing bay shrymp

Preparation

The wakame infusion is optional but will enhance seafood flavor. To prepare the infusion, bring the water and wakame to a brief boil in a small saucepan. Remove from the heat, cover and let cool completely. Strain into a measuring cup and measure 1 and ¾ cup (420 ml) liquid. Press the wakame with the back of a spoon to extract the liquid. Compost or discard the wakame as it will have lost most of its flavor.

Dust the bottom of the baking dish with a thin layer of paprika. Using your fingertips, dab the paprika to create a stippling effect. Set aside. Measure the glucomannan powder and set aside near your blender.

Add the wakame infusion or water and the remaining blender ingredients to the blender (except for the glucomannan powder) and process until completely liquefied. Reduce the blender speed, add the glucomannan powder and process to the count of 5. Pour the mixture into the medium saucepan and place over medium heat.

Slowly stir the mixture with the spatula. As the mixture begins to thicken, begin slowly folding and stirring the mixture with the spatula. As the mixture begins to stiffen, fold and knead the mixture with the spatula. A thin "skin" of protein will begin to adhere to the bottom and sides of the saucepan and may dislodge while stirring; simply work it into the mixture as it cooks. The mixture needs to be cooked past the creamy stage and when sufficiently cooked, should have a very stiff but moist consistency. It is important to cook the mixture to this stage or it will set not set properly. However, avoid cooking to the point where the cohesive mass begins to break apart into clumps.

Transfer the mixture to the baking dish and use the spatula to press the mixture evenly into the pan. Do not use a spreading motion. Do not worry about completely smoothing the surface of the gel as some bumpy irregularity will enhance the finished appearance of the shrymp.

Let the mixture cool about 10 minutes and turn the gel onto a work surface.

Cutting and Detailing the Shrymp

Using a round cutter, cut discs from the gel while it is still slightly warm (any remnants of the gel can be simmered with the shrymp and chopped later for use in any recipe calling for chopped shrimp). If desired, the sharp edges of the cut disc can be lightly beveled using kitchen shears to create a softer, rounded edge, but this is purely optional.

To begin detailing, use the tip of a common teaspoon to cut a small loop from each disc (the curvature of the spoon will help create the rounded loop). For smaller bay shrimp, use a miniature cocktail spoon to cut the loop. It's okay if the edges of the loop are a little ragged, as this adds to the natural appearance of the shrymp.

Fine Detailing the Shrymp

With a sharp paring knife, make a shallow cut down the back of each shrymp from "head to tail". Don't cut too deep. With kitchen shears, create shallow snips crosswise and ¼-inch apart along the back of the shrymp from "head to tail". Don't snip too deep. Please note that fine detailing is not necessary for small bay shrymp due to their size.

Final Preparation Step

Bring 6 cups water to a boil in a large saucepan and add the shrymp. Reduce to a simmer and cook uncovered for 5 minutes. Remove with a slotted spoon and drain on paper towels until cool. Chill in a sealed food storage container or bag until ready to use. Use within 5 days or freeze up to 3 months.

Golden Fried Shrymp

Deliciously vegan. Serve with Classic Cocktail Sauce (page 150) for dipping.

Ingredients

- 1 recipe Shrymp (page 151)
- cooking oil for frying

Dipping Ingredients

- 1 cup plain unsweetened soymilk or almond milk
- 1 and ½ tsp Gentle Chef Vegan Eggz Essentials A
- ½ tsp Gentle Chef Vegan Eggz Essentials B

If you don't have the Gentle Chef Vegan Eggz Essentials on hand, whisk together these alternate dipping ingredients: ½ cup plain unsweetened soymilk or almond milk and ½ cup No-Eggy Mayo (pg. 263) or commercial vegan equivalent.

Dredging Ingredients

- ¾ cup panko-style bread crumbs
- ¾ cup all-purpose flour
- 1 T nutritional yeast
- 1 T Gentle Bay Seasoning (page 150) or commercial Old Bay™ seasoning

Preparation

Place the shrymp into a sealable food storage bag.

Process the dipping ingredients in a mini-blender for 20 seconds. If using the alternate ingredients, whisk them in a bowl until smooth. Pour the mixture into the bag, seal and turn the bag to coat the shrymp thoroughly.

Combine the dredging ingredients in a roomy food storage container. Add the shrymp, seal the container and shake until well coated. Open the container to allow the breading to dry while the cooking oil is heating.

In a deep skillet or wok, add about 2-inches of oil and place over medium-high heat. To test the oil for the proper frying temperature, drop a few breadcrumbs into the hot oil. If they begin to sizzle and brown, the oil is ready. Carefully place the breaded shrymp into the hot oil; avoid over-crowding. Fry until golden brown, turning occasionally with a wire spider or slotted spoon and place on a plate lined with paper towels to drain. Repeat with any remaining shrymp. If the oil gets too hot, simply reduce the heat a bit. Serve with cocktail sauce for dipping.

Ceviche

Ceviche (pronounced "seh-VEE-chay") is a Latin American dish which traditionally consists of raw fish or shellfish marinated in citrus juice (usually lime and/or lemon juice). The acid in the citrus juice coagulates (denatures) the proteins in the seafood, effectively cooking it.

My plant-based version does not rely upon acid to cook the "seafood", since it is already cooked, but is rather intended to capture the flavor, texture and appearance of the traditional finished dish. It is served cold as a refreshing appetizer with crispy corn tortilla chips. This recipe yields enough ceviche for 2 to 3 guests; for more simply multiply the recipe.

Ingredients

- 1 and ½ cup chopped Shrymp (page 151)
- 2 tsp (2 grams) dried wakame flakes
- ½ cup peeled and small diced tomato
- ½ cup peeled, seeded and small diced cucumber
- ¼ cup small diced onion
- ¼ cup chopped cilantro
- 1 clove garlic, minced
- 1 small Jalapeno or Serrano chili, seeded and finely minced
- juice of 1 lime (2 T)
- 1 T mild olive oil
- ½ tsp sea salt or kosher salt, or more to taste
- ¼ tsp fresh ground black pepper
- ¼ tsp ground cumin
- ½ ripe but firm avocado, diced

Preparation

Place the chopped seafood into a mixing bowl.

In a separate small bowl, soak the wakame flakes in warm water until rehydrated. Squeeze dry in your hand, finely chop and add to the mixing bowl.

Add the remaining ingredients except for the avocado and toss well to combine. Refrigerate for several hours to marinate the ingredients and blend the flavors.

Add the diced avocado just before serving and toss well.

Season the ceviche with additional salt as desired. Serve with crunchy tortilla chips.

Shrymp Scampi

This is my vegan variation of the simple, classic dish. Homemade vegan shrymp are sautéed in a delectable garlicky, buttery sauce and garnished with parsley. Serve with plenty of crusty bread for soaking up the fragrant sauce.

Ingredients

- 1 recipe Shrymp (page 151)
- 2 T non-dairy butter or margarine
- 2 T olive oil
- 4 garlic cloves, minced
- 1 cup dry white wine or vegetable broth
- pinch crushed red pepper flakes, or to taste
- fresh ground black pepper
- 2 T chopped parsley
- 1 T fresh lemon juice
- sea salt or kosher salt, to taste
- crusty bread for soaking up the sauce

Preparation

In a large skillet, melt the butter with olive oil. Add the garlic and sauté until fragrant, about 1 minute.

Add the wine or broth, red pepper flakes and plenty of black pepper and bring to a simmer. Let the liquid reduce by half, about 2 minutes.

Add the shrymp and sauté until heated through, about 2 minutes. Stir in the parsley and lemon juice and season with salt to taste. Serve with crusty bread.

Shrymp Bisque

Shrymp Bisque is a creamy mock seafood and tomato-based soup flavored with dry sherry or white wine. This recipe yields 4 to 6 servings.

Ingredients

- 1 and ½ cup coarsely chopped Shrymp
- ¼ cup olive oil
- 1 medium-sized sweet yellow onion, chopped
- 2 ribs celery, chopped
- ½ cup dry sherry or dry white wine
- ¼ cup all-purpose flour or rice flour
- 4 cups Fumet (page 163)
- 1 can (15 oz) diced tomatoes with liquid
  or 2 cups blanched, peeled and diced fresh tomatoes
- 2 T tomato paste
- 1 tsp Gentle Bay Seasoning (page 150) or commercial Old Bay™ seasoning
- 2 sprigs fresh thyme leaves or ½ tsp dried thyme
- pinch ground white pepper
- 1 cup Raw Cashew Milk (page 168) or Soy Cream (page 171)
- sea salt or kosher salt to taste
- fresh snipped chives for garnish

Preparation

Add the olive oil to a large cooking pot and place over medium heat. Add the onions and celery and sauté until the onions are translucent. Add the sherry or wine and bring to a simmer. Cook until the liquid is reduced by about half.

Sprinkle in the flour. Stir until blended and cook until the flour emits a nutty aroma, about 1 minute.

Incorporate the fumet in small increments while vigorously stirring. Transfer the mixture to a blender and add the tomatoes and tomato paste. Blend until smooth and then transfer back to the cooking pot.

Add the bay seasoning, thyme and white pepper and bring the mixture to a gentle simmer. Cover the pot and cook about 20 minutes, stirring occasionally.

Stir in the chopped shrymp. Add the cashew milk or soy cream and stir until heated through. Season the bisque with salt to taste.

Ladle into individual serving bowls and garnish with the snipped chives.

Shrymp Étouffée

Étouffée is a spicy seafood stew found in both Cajun and Creole cuisine typically served over white long grain rice. Étouffée is most popular in Louisiana and in the coastal counties of Mississippi, Alabama, and eastern Texas.

Ingredients

- 1 recipe Shrymp (page 151)
- 2 T neutral vegetable oil
- 1 large onion, diced
- 1 green bell pepper, diced
- 1 red bell pepper, diced
- 2 ribs celery, diced
- 5 garlic cloves, minced
- 2 tsp (2 grams) dried wakame flakes
  rehydrated in warm water, squeezed dry and finely chopped
- 2 T non-dairy butter or margarine
- ¼ cup all-purpose flour or rice flour
- 1 and ¾ cup Fumet (page 163) or vegetable broth
- 1 tsp Browning Liquid (page 28) or commercial equivalent, or more to enrich color
- ½ tsp cayenne pepper, or more or less to taste
- sea salt or kosher salt to taste
- 4 scallions, chopped
- cooked long grain rice

Preparation

Add the olive oil to a large deep skillet and place over medium heat. Add the onion, bell peppers and celery and sauté until the vegetables have softened and the onions are translucent. Add the garlic and wakame and sauté an additional minute.

Add the butter and stir until melted. Sprinkle in the flour, mix well and cook until the flour is golden and emits a nutty aroma.

Incorporate the broth in increments while stirring vigorously. Add the browning liquid, white pepper and cayenne. Simmer the mixture uncovered for 20 minutes.

Add the bay shrymp and continue to cook for 10 minutes; season with salt to taste.

Ladle into individual serving bowls, add a scoop of rice and garnish with the chopped scallions.

Sweet Clamz

Sweet Clamz are a soy protein (from tofu) and konjac-based seafood alternative and can be used in any recipe just as you would real clams.

Blender Ingredients
- 1 T glucomannan (konjac) powder
- 5 oz/142 grams **pressed** extra-firm tofu (not silken tofu)
- 1 and ¾ cup (420 ml) nori infusion
- 1 T nutritional yeast flakes
- 2 tsp organic sugar
- 1 and ½ tsp sea salt or kosher salt
- 1 tsp agar powder
- ¼ tsp onion powder
- ¼ tsp pickling lime powder (calcium hydroxide)

Nori Infusion Ingredients
- 2 and ½ cups (600 ml) water
- 4 sheets sushi nori seaweed

Additional Items Needed
- blender
- standard loaf pan
- flexible silicone spatula

Preparation

To prepare the nori infusion, tear the nori into pieces and add to a medium saucepan with the water. Bring to brief boil, cover and remove from the heat to cool completely. Strain the amber colored liquid through a fine mesh sieve into a measuring cup. Press the nori with the back of a spoon to extract the liquid and measure 1 and ¾ cup (420 ml). Add water if necessary. Compost or discard the nori.

Measure the glucomannan powder and set aside near your blender.

Add the nori infusion and the remaining blender ingredients to the blender (except for the glucomannan powder) and process until completely liquefied. Reduce the blender speed, add the glucomannan powder and process to the count of 5. Pour the mixture into the medium saucepan and place over medium heat.

Slowly stir the mixture with the spatula. As the mixture begins to thicken, begin slowly folding and stirring the mixture with the spatula. As the mixture begins to stiffen, fold and knead the mixture with the spatula. A thin "skin" of protein will begin to adhere to the bottom and sides of the saucepan and may dislodge while stirring; simply work it into the mixture as it cooks.

The mixture needs to be cooked past the creamy stage and when sufficiently cooked, should have a very stiff but moist consistency. It is important to cook the mixture to this stage or it will set not set properly.

Transfer the mixture to the loaf pan and use the spatula to press the mixture evenly into the pan.

Let the mixture cool about 10 minutes and turn the gel onto a work surface. Using a scraping motion with a dull table knife, cut thin fragments from the gel.

Bring 6 cups water to a boil in a large saucepan. Add the fragments, reduce the heat to a simmer and cook uncovered for 5 minutes. Remove the clamz with a spider or slotted spoon and transfer to a plate lined with paper towels to drain. Let drain and cool completely and then transfer to a storage container to chill before using in recipes. Use the clamz within 5 days or freeze up to 3 months.

New England Clamz Chowdah

Tender diced potatoes, celery, onions and diced clamz are combined in this creamy and satisfying chowder. The special broth needs to be prepared ahead of time, so plan accordingly. This recipe yields 4 to 6 servings.

Ingredients

- ¼ cup neutral vegetable oil
- 1 large onion, diced
- 2 ribs celery, diced
- 2 russet potatoes, peeled and diced into ½-inch cubes
- 2 garlic cloves, minced
- 10 oz diced Sweet Clamz (page 158)
- ¼ cup all-purpose flour or rice flour
- 4 cups Fumet (page 163)
- 1 bay leaf
- ¼ tsp fresh ground black pepper, or more to taste
- 2 cups homemade raw cashew milk*
- sea salt or kosher salt, to taste

*Homemade raw cashew milk is used because of its richness and ability to naturally thicken soups. To prepare the cashew milk, process ½ cup raw cashews (no pre-soaking necessary) with 2 and ¼ cups water in a blender on high speed for 2 full minutes. Strain through a fine-mesh nut milk bag. Substitute with plain unsweetened soymilk if preferred. Other commercial non-dairy milks are not recommended as they are too watery for this purpose.

Preparation

Add the olive oil to a large cooking pot and place over medium heat. Add the onions, celery, potatoes and garlic and toss well. Cover the pot and sweat the vegetables for 20 minutes, stirring occasionally.

Raise the heat to medium and sprinkle in the flour. Stir until blended and cook until the flour emits a nutty aroma, about 1 minute.

Incorporate the fumet in small increments while vigorously stirring.

Add the diced clamz, bay leaf and black pepper. Bring the chowder to a gentle simmer. Cover the pot and cook about 30 minutes, stirring occasionally, or until the potatoes are very tender.

Add the cashew milk (or soymilk) and stir until heated through. Season the chowder with salt and pepper to taste.

Fried Sweet Clamz

Tender sweet clamz are battered and fried and served with your choice of Tartar Sauce or Cocktail Sauce.

Ingredients

- 1 recipe Sweet Clamz (page 158)
- ¼ cup plain non-dairy milk
- ½ cup fine dry breadcrumbs
- ½ cup all-purpose flour, divided in half
- 1 tsp sea salt or kosher salt
- ½ tsp sweet paprika
- ½ tsp ground white pepper
- high-heat cooking oil for frying

Preparation

Prepare your choice of dipping sauce and keep refrigerated until ready to use.

Combine ¼ cup all-purpose flour with the breadcrumbs in a bowl. Mix in the salt, paprika and white pepper; set aside.

Place the clamz into a food storage bag and add the remaining ¼ cup flour. Seal and shake well to coat.

Add the milk to the food storage bag, seal and shake until the clamz are coated.

Dredge the clamz in the breadcrumb mixture until well-coated. Set aside to dry on a plate for about 15 minutes; this will help the breading adhere better when frying.

In a deep wok or skillet, heat about ½-inch of oil over medium-high heat until the oil begins to shimmer. Fry the clams until golden. Remove with a spider or slotted spoon and drain on a plate lined with paper towels. Serve hot with lemon wedges and the sauce of your choice for dipping.

Battered Flaky Tofysh Filets
(Gluten-Free)

Tender and flaky tofysh filets are battered and fried and served with the condiments of your choice. This recipe yields 6 filets.

Filet Ingredients

- 10 oz/284 grams **pressed** extra-firm tofu (not silken tofu)
- 6 oz/170 grams extra-firm **silke**n tofu
- 2 T cornstarch or unmodified potato starch
- 1 T neutral vegetable oil
- 1 and ½ tsp fine sea salt or kosher salt
- ½ tsp onion powder
- ¼ tsp garlic powder
- ¼ tsp ground white pepper
- 1 tsp (1 gram) dried wakame flakes, rehydrated in warm water, squeezed dry and very finely minced (optional)*

*Please note that flecks of wakame will be visible in the finished filets. The wakame is necessary for adding a seafood flavor to the filets. The wakame can be omitted if a seafood flavor is undesirable.

Dredging Ingredient

- ⅓ cup cornstarch or unmodified potato starch

Batter Ingredients

- ½ cup rice flour
- ¾ cup club soda or beer
- 2 tsp Old Bay™ or Chesapeake Bay™ seasoning
- 1 tsp baking powder (preferably aluminum-free)
- 1 tsp dried kelp powder

Additional Items Needed

- baking sheet
- standard cheese/vegetable grater
- parchment paper or silicone baking mat

Preparation

Drain the silken tofu on a plate lined with several paper towels for 30 minutes. Firmly blot the silken tofu with additional towels to remove as much moisture as possible; set aside.

Using the largest holes on a standard cheese/vegetable grater, shred the pressed extra-firm block tofu (not the silken tofu) into a large mixing bowl; set aside.

Preheat the oven to 375°F/190°C. Line a baking sheet with parchment paper or a silicone baking mat.

In a small bowl, mash the silken tofu (not the shredded tofu) with a fork into a smooth paste. Add the starch, oil, salt, onion and garlic powder, white pepper and minced wakame. Mix well.

Add the seasoned tofu paste to the shredded tofu in the mixing bowl and fold to combine the ingredients with a sturdy silicone spatula until the mixture begins to hold together. If the mixture is extremely dry, add water a tablespoon at a time until the mixture holds together. Press the mixture evenly into the bottom of the bowl and divide into 6 roughly equal portions using the edge of the spatula.

Scatter the dredging starch on a plate. With your hands, compress a portion of the tofu mixture into a ball. Flatten and shape the ball into a narrow patty about ½-inch thick. Carefully dredge the filet in the starch on the plate, gently pressing the starch into the filet. Place the filet on the parchment paper or baking mat. Repeat with the remaining portions.

Bake uncovered on the middle rack of the oven for 30 minutes or until lightly golden and firm to the touch. Remove from the oven to cool for a minimum of 20 minutes to allow the filets to "set" before proceeding. Don't handle them until they have cooled a bit or they can break.

Battering and Frying the Filets

Whisk together the batter ingredients in a large bowl until smooth.

Dip the filets in the batter and fry in hot cooking oil until golden brown and crispy. They will brown quickly. Drain on paper towels. Serve while still hot with a wedge of lemon and cocktail sauce, Tartar sauce (page 162), or malt vinegar for dipping. The fried filets are also ideal for soft tacos.

Tartar Sauce

A classic condiment sauce for fried Clamz and breaded and battered Tofysh filets.

Ingredients

- ½ cup No-Eggy Mayo (page 263) or commercial vegan mayonnaise
- 2 T finely diced cucumber dill pickle or prepared relish
- 1 T fresh lemon juice
- 1 T finely minced sweet onion
- ½ tsp Dijon mustard or coarse-grain mustard
- coarse sea salt or kosher salt, to taste
- coarse ground black pepper, to taste

Preparation

Whisk all ingredients together and chill to blend flavors for a minimum of 1 hour before using.

Fumet

Fumet (pronounced "foo-may", a French culinary term which refers to a flavorful and aromatic condensed stock) is a concentrated vegetable and sea vegetable-based stock used for preparing vegan seafood soups and stews. Fumet contains no added salt (other than the salt which is inherent in the miso), so be sure to season with salt to taste when preparing soups or stews. This recipe yields about 4 cups of stock.

Ingredients

- 6 cups water
- ¼ cup dry white wine (optional)
- 3 T mellow white miso paste
- ¼ cup (12 grams) dried wakame flakes rehydrated in ½ cup warm water
- 2 extra large onions, outer paper removed and then quartered
- 2 leafy ribs celery, chopped
- 1 small carrot, unpeeled and chopped
- 1 four to six-inch piece dried kombu*
- small handful parsley stems
- 4 garlic cloves, crushed
- 2 sprigs fresh thyme or ½ tsp dried thyme leaves
- 1 bay leaf
- 1 tsp whole black peppercorns

*Kombu is a sea vegetable, or edible variety of kelp. It has a mild ocean aroma and flavor and leathery texture.

Preparation

Bring the ingredients to a boil in large cooking pot. Reduce the heat to a simmer and cook partially covered for 40 minutes. If using immediately, strain the stock through a fine mesh sieve into another cooking pot and season with sea salt or kosher salt to taste. Discard the solids.

To clarify the stock, let the mixture cool and then strain though a fine mesh sieve into a large sealable container. Chill overnight to let any sediment settle. Decant the clear portion and use in recipes as desired, seasoning with sea salt or kosher salt to taste. The stock can be refrigerated for 1 week or frozen for up to 3 months.

Linguini with Clamz Sauce

An Italian-American classic reinvented with plant-based diced clamz and non-dairy butter. This recipe yields 4 servings.

Ingredients

- 1 pound dry linguini
- 2 T olive oil
- 1 shallot, minced (or 2 T minced red onion)
- 4 garlic cloves, finely chopped
- ½ cup dry white wine (e.g., Chardonnay; Sauvignon Blanc)
- ½ tsp dried basil
- ½ tsp dried oregano
- 6 T non-dairy butter or margarine
- 8 oz diced Sweet Clamz (page 158)
- sea vegetable broth (see preparation instructions included)
- sea salt or kosher salt and fresh ground black pepper, to taste
- 3 T chopped parsley
- grated Hard Parmesano (page 208), or Grated Sunflower Parmesan (page 212) or commercial vegan equivalent for garnish

Sea Vegetable Broth Ingredients

- ¾ cup vegetable broth
- 1 T (3 grams) dried wakame flakes

Preparation

For the sea vegetable broth, bring the vegetable broth and wakame to a simmer in a small saucepan. Remove from the heat to cool. Strain the broth into a bowl and set aside. Finely chop the wakame and set aside in a small dish.

Bring a large pot of salted water to a boil and cook the pasta, using the package instructions as a guideline, until desired tenderness (be sure to test the pasta yourself).

While the water is coming to a boil to cook the pasta, add the olive oil to a skillet and place over medium heat. Add the diced clamz and the shallot and sauté until the shallot is softened, about 2 to 3 minutes. Add the garlic, basil, oregano and chopped wakame and sauté an additional 2 minutes. Add the wine, bring to a simmer and allow it to cook about 2 minutes to eliminate some of the alcohol.

Add the butter or margarine and stir until melted. Add the reserved sea vegetable broth and bring back to a simmer. Cook until the sauce reduces a bit, about 10 minutes; season with salt and pepper to taste. Keep warm over low heat until the pasta is cooked.

Drain the pasta, place back in the cooking pot. Add 2 tablespoons parsley and half of the sauce. Distribute the pasta on serving plates and top with the remaining sauce. Top with the parmesan and garnish with the remaining parsley; serve immediately.

Watuna Sashimi

Seedless watermelon is remarkably transformed to create this amazing "tuna" sashimi. Typically, modern gastronomists use a vacuum chamber called a Cryovac™ to produce this effect, but the equipment is very expensive and not practical for most household budgets. With some experimentation, I discovered a simple and inexpensive way to create this same effect at home.

Watermelon that is not quite in season works best, since it has a lower sugar content than ripe summer watermelon. Also, the flesh needs to be firm and crisp. Watuna sashimi is wonderful when used for sushi too.

Ingredients

- 1 seedless watermelon
- 4 tsp sea salt or kosher salt

Marinade Ingredients

- 6 T tamari, soy sauce or Bragg Liquid Aminos™
- 6 T water
- 2 T mirin (Japanese sweet rice wine)
- 1 T (3 grams) dried wakame flakes
- 1 tsp sesame oil

Preparation

Cut 2 or 3 rectangular blocks from the center of the watermelon.

Each block should be about 4-inches long and no more than 1 and ½-inch thick.

Keep in mind that even seedless watermelon contains some pale, soft seeds and there's simply no way to remove them completely.

Bring 2 quarts of water to a rapid boil in a large cooking pot. Add 4 teaspoons of salt. Add the blocks of watermelon, reduce the heat to a soft boil and cook for 15 minutes. Gently turn the blocks occasionally as they cook.

While the watermelon cooks, add the marinade ingredients to a small saucepan and bring to a simmer. Remove from the heat to cool.

Transfer the blocks of watermelon to a plate lined with several layers of paper towels or a lint-free kitchen towel to drain. As the watermelon cools and drains, the texture will change and become remarkably like the texture of raw tuna (boiling ruptures the cells of the watermelon and draining on the towel(s) pulls water from the ruptured cells by absorption). Change the towel(s) occasionally as a substantial amount of water will be absorbed.

When the watermelon has drained sufficiently and the marinade has cooled, place the watermelon in a food storage bag or sealable container, add the marinade, seal and refrigerate for several hours.

When ready to use, drain the sashimi on a few paper towels to absorb the excess marinade (and excess saltiness). If using the Watuna for Hawaiian Poke, reserve the marinade. Gently press the "filets" in lightly toasted sesame seeds if desired. Slice and serve with your favorite Asian condiments, such as pickled ginger and wasabi; or use for making sushi.

Non-Dairy Delights

Soymilk

Soymilk is a beverage made from soybeans. It is produced by soaking dry soybeans, cooking them in water, processing them in a blender with fresh water and then straining out the solid pulp which is called okara. For drinking purposes, a natural sweetener can be added to suit your taste. "Laura" soybeans are a specific variety of soybeans that are said to produce a mild soymilk.

This recipe will yield as many quarts of soymilk as you desire. The soybeans can also be cooked ahead of time in bulk, frozen and then conveniently used as needed for making fresh soymilk. Soymilk has a refrigerator shelf life of up to 10 days.

Ingredients

- ½ cup dry organic non-GMO soybeans for each quart of soymilk, or 1 and ¼ cup cooked soybeans for each quart of soymilk
- 3 and ½ cup (840 ml) water for each quart of soymilk
- ¼ tsp fine sea salt or kosher salt for each quart of soymilk

You will also need a blender for processing and a nylon nut milk bag to strain the okara (pulp) from the milk. A strainer lined with 4-layers of cheesecloth and a large spoon can be used in place of the nut milk bag.

Preparation

Rinse the beans to make sure they are clean and then place them into a mason jar (home canning jar) or other sealable container and fill the container with plenty of cold water to cover. Refrigerate for a minimum of 6 hours, with 12 hours being ideal. After soaking, drain the water from the beans and pour them into a large cooking pot. Add plenty of fresh water to cover the soybeans.

Bring the pot of soybeans and water to a rapid boil. Reduce the heat to a soft boil and set a timer for 30 minutes.

After cooking, drain the soybeans in a strainer or colander. Place the cooking pot into the sink, add the soybeans and fill the pot with cold water. Vigorously stir the soybeans in the water. This will help loosen some of the soybean skins. Removing the skins will reduce the amount of oligosaccharides in the finished soymilk. Oligosaccharides are starch compounds responsible for causing excessive intestinal gas whenever beans are consumed, since the human GI tract cannot break down the compounds completely.

After stirring, the soybeans will sink to the bottom of the pot while the loosened skins will float towards the top. Alternately, the soybeans can be rubbed between the palms of your hands to loosen the skins while submerged in the water.

Pour off the water into the sink, which in turn will carry most of the loosened skins with it. It's not essential to remove all the skins, just the excess. Now transfer the soybeans back to the strainer or colander to drain completely.

Next, the beans will need to be processed in a blender with fresh water. It is recommended to process and strain each quart individually. Place 1 and ¼ cup (7.5 oz by weight) cooked soybeans into a blender (if using pre-cooked frozen soybeans, be sure to thaw them first). Add 3 and ½ cup of fresh water and the salt and process the contents on high speed for 2 full minutes.

The soymilk will now need to be strained to remove the okara. To do this, pour the soymilk into the nut milk bag over a large container.

While holding the top of the bag with one hand, firmly knead and squeeze the bag with your other hand to help the milk pass through the fine mesh and to extract as much of the milk as you can from the okara. This may take a few minutes, so be patient.

Optionally, place a strainer lined with 4-layers of cheesecloth over a large container and pour the milk (in increments) into the strainer. Stir the milk with a large spoon to help it pass through the cheesecloth.

Discard or compost the okara in the bag or cheesecloth or save for other uses as desired.

Transfer the milk to a sealable container and refrigerate until chilled. Initially, the bean aroma of the milk may be distinct but will diminish after chilling.

Raw Cashew Milk

Many varieties of nuts and seeds can be used to make milk, but in my humble opinion, raw cashews produce the mildest, creamiest milk with just the right amount of natural sweetness that additional sweeteners are generally unnecessary. However, if you've adapted to commercial nut milks with sweeteners for drinking purposes, this milk may taste a bit bland and a natural sweetener can always be added to suit your taste.

Cashew milk thickens naturally when heated and aside from drinking purposes, works well as a dairy cream substitute when preparing delicate cooked sauces. This recipe yields about 1 quart of cashew milk. Cashew milk has a refrigerator shelf life of up to 5 days.

Ingredients

- 1 cup (5 oz/142 grams) raw cashews
- 3 and ½ cups (840 ml) water
- ¼ tsp fine sea salt or kosher salt (optional)

You will also need a blender and a nylon nut milk bag to strain the fine solids from the milk. A strainer lined with 4-layers of cheesecloth and a large spoon can be used in place of the nut milk bag.

Preparation

Rinse the cashews to remove any dust or debris, drain thoroughly and place them in a high-powered blender. Pre-soaking of the cashews is not required. Add the salt and process the contents on high speed for 2 full minutes.

The milk will now need to be strained to remove the solids. To do this, pour the milk into the nut milk bag over a large container.

While holding the top of the bag with one hand, gently knead the bag to help the milk pass through the ultra-fine mesh - but don't force the milk through.

Optionally, the milk can be poured (in increments) into a strainer lined with 4-layers of cheesecloth placed over a large container. Stir the milk gently with a spoon to help it pass through the layers of cheesecloth.

Cashews break down significantly when processed into milk, so there won't be much solid residue remaining in the nut milk bag or strainer (compared to soymilk or almond milk, which leaves a great deal of solid residue). Discard or compost the cashew solids.

For drinking purposes, sweeten the milk to taste if desired. Transfer to a sealable container and refrigerate. Shake well before using.

Almond Milk

Commercial almond milk can be purchased easily enough, but commercial versions contain very little almond and usually include a significant amount of sweeteners, emulsifiers and stabilizers to keep them homogenized, and thickeners to compensate for their watery consistency.

Almond meal/flour, blanched almonds or whole raw almonds can be used to prepare almond milk at home. Homemade almond milk has a mild, nutty flavor and slightly astringent aroma. It has a rich consistency that is very different from its commercial counterpart and is the only recommended alternative to soymilk for preparing the non-dairy recipes in this cookbook.

Un-blanched whole raw almonds can be used if preferred, but be aware that the almond skins can impart a bitter undertaste. Almond milk lacks the natural sweetness of raw cashew milk; therefore, for drinking purposes a natural sweetener can be added to suit your taste.

Almond meal/flour requires no presoaking prior to preparation; however blanched almonds or whole raw almonds require presoaking in water for a minimum of 8 hours to soften them before processing. This recipe yields 1 quart of fresh almond milk. Almond milk has a refrigerator shelf life of up to 5 days.

Ingredients

- 1 cup (5 oz/142 grams) almond meal/flour or 5 oz/142 grams blanched almonds
- 3 and ¾ cup (900 ml) water
- ¼ tsp fine sea salt or kosher salt (optional)

You will also need a blender and a nylon or cotton muslin nut milk bag to strain the fine solids from the milk. A strainer lined with 4-layers of cheesecloth and a large spoon can be used in place of the nut milk bag.

Preparation

If using blanched almonds, or whole raw almonds, place them into a container with a lid and add plenty of water to cover. Refrigerate for a minimum of 8 hours to soften. Drain and discard the soaking water and add the almonds to a blender with 3 and ¾ cup fresh water and the salt. If using almond meal/flour, presoaking is unnecessary. Add the almond meal/flour directly to the blender with the water and the salt. Process the contents on high speed for 2 full minutes.

The milk will now need to be strained to remove the solids. To do this, pour the milk into the nut milk bag over a large container.

While holding the top of the bag with one hand, vigorously knead the bag to help the milk pass through the ultra-fine mesh, squeezing as much of the milk as possible from the ground almonds.

Optionally, the milk can be poured (in increments) into a strainer lined with 4-layers of cheesecloth placed over a large container. Stir and press with a spoon to help the milk pass through the layers of cheesecloth.

Almonds don't break down as easily as cashews when preparing milk, so there will be a significant amount of residue remaining in the nut milk bag or strainer. If you don't have residue, the weave on the nut milk bag is too large. Discard or compost the solids or reserve for other uses.

For drinking purposes, sweeten the milk to taste; it will need it. Transfer the milk to a sealable container and refrigerate. Like other nut milks, almond milk tends to separate upon standing so shake well before using.

Chocolate Almond Milk and Hot Chocolate

Kids will love this recipe and your "inner child" will love it too. Chocolate almond milk is delicious served cold or hot. This recipe yields about 1 quart. Chocolate almond milk has a refrigerator shelf life of about 5 days.

Ingredients

- 1 cup (5 oz/142 grams) almond meal/flour or 5 oz/142 grams blanched almonds
- 3 and ¾ cups (900 ml) filtered/purified water
- ⅔ cup organic sugar, or more to taste
- ⅓ cup unsweetened cocoa powder
- 1 tsp real vanilla extract
- ½ tsp guar gum or xanthan gum (optional; adds body)

You will also need a blender and a nylon or cotton muslin nut milk bag to strain the fine solids from the milk. A strainer lined with 4-layers of cheesecloth and a large spoon can be used in place of the nut milk bag.

Preparation

Place the almond meal or dry almonds into a high-powered blender. Pre-soaking of the almonds is not required. Process the contents on high speed for 2 full minutes.

The milk will now need to be strained to remove the solids. To do this, pour the milk into the nut milk bag over a large container. While holding the top of the bag with one hand, gently knead the bag to help the milk pass through the ultra-fine mesh, but don't force the milk through.

Optionally, the milk can be poured (in increments) into a strainer lined with 4-layers of cheesecloth placed over a large container. Stir the milk gently with a spoon to help it pass through the cheesecloth.

Pour the strained milk back into the blender and discard or compost the solids in the bag or cheesecloth. Add the sugar to taste, cocoa powder, vanilla, optional food gum and salt to the blender and process until smooth. Store the milk in a covered container in the refrigerator. Almond milk tends to separate upon standing so shake well before serving.

For hot chocolate, gently heat the chocolate almond milk in a saucepan while continually stirring. Do not let the milk boil!

Soy Cream

Soy cream is an all-purpose cream for use in any cooking application. It works beautifully when preparing cooked sauces, as it will not cause delicate sauces to over-thicken. It has a silky-smooth texture with no discernible grit and is very quick and easy to prepare. It's also a superb creamer for coffee and tea. Soy cream has a refrigerator shelf life of up to 10 days. Cashew milk can be used as an alternate to soy cream for cooked sauces since it has natural thickening properties when heated. This recipe yields 2 cups of cream.

Ingredients

- 1 and ¾ cups (420 ml) plain unsweetened soymilk, room temperature
- ¼ cup **refined** coconut oil, melted (not virgin coconut oil)

Preparation

The soymilk must be at room temperature to emulsify properly with the coconut oil. If necessary, gently warm the milk in a saucepan over low heat or briefly in the microwave. If cold soymilk is used, the melted coconut oil will congeal when it comes into contact with the cold liquid and disrupt the emulsification process.

Pour the milk into a blender, put the cover in place but remove the center insert. Begin blending on low speed, gradually increasing to high speed (if the milk is splashing too much in the blender jar, reduce the speed slightly). Pour the melted coconut oil slowly into the milk through the opening in the blender jar's lid. Continue to process for 10 seconds after the oil has been incorporated to ensure homogenization.

Transfer the cream to a sealable container and refrigerate until well-chilled. The cream will thicken to the proper texture upon refrigeration. Shake well before using and consume within 10 days.

Whipped Cream

At last, a non-dairy whipping cream that whips just like dairy whipping cream! The whipped cream produced from this recipe has a lighter texture and mouth feel comparable to dairy whipped cream, as opposed to the dense texture of whipped coconut cream. Regardless, consume moderately as this is not a low fat or low-calorie topping! This recipe yields 2 cups of heavy whipping cream which will produce about 3 cups of the finest non-dairy whipped cream. This recipe requires sufficient chilling time for the cream to whip properly, preferably overnight, so please plan accordingly.

Ingredients for Preparing the Heavy Whipping Cream

- 1 cup plain soymilk, **room temperature**
- 1 cup organic refined or virgin coconut oil*, melted
- ½ tsp guar gum or xanthan gum (acts as a stabilizer)

Ingredients for Whipping the Cream

- ⅓ cup Organic Powdered Sugar (recipe follows) or commercial equivalent
- 1 tsp real vanilla extract

Special Equipment Needed

- ceramic or metal mixing bowl
- stand mixer with whip attachment or electric rotary hand mixer

*Please note that virgin coconut oil will impart a subtle coconut undertaste.

Preparing the Whipping Cream

The soymilk must be at room temperature to emulsify properly with the coconut oil. If necessary, gently warm the milk in a saucepan over low heat or briefly in the microwave. If cold soymilk is used, the coconut oil will congeal when it comes into contact with the cold liquid.

Measure the melted coconut oil and set aside.

Pour the milk into a blender, put the cover in place but remove the center insert. Begin blending on low speed, gradually increasing to high speed (if the milk is splashing too much in the blender jar, reduce the speed slightly). Pour the coconut oil slowly into the milk through the opening in the blender jar's lid. Continue to process for 20 seconds after the oil has been incorporated to ensure homogenization.

Pour the cream into a sealable container and refrigerate until very cold before whipping, preferably overnight.

Whipping the Cream

Place a metal or ceramic mixing bowl and 2 beaters from an electric rotary mixer or the metal bowl and wire whip attachment from a stand mixer into the refrigerator. Chill until very cold. Blenders and food processors will not work for this recipe, as they will not whip air into the cream.

Pour or scoop the chilled cream into the chilled bowl and begin whipping with the electric mixer or stand mixer on low speed, gradually increasing to high speed. Whip until soft peaks begin to form. This can take several minutes, so be patient. Begin incorporating the powdered sugar, in increments, and add the vanilla. Continue to whip just until stiff peaks begin to form. Avoid over-processing because the liquid portion will eventually separate and the cream will turn into sweet butter.

Transfer the whipped cream to a covered container and refrigerate until ready to use. Whipped cream will retain its whipped texture as long as it is refrigerated. Consume within 1 week.

Organic Powdered Sugar

Ingredients

- 2 cups organic sugar (evaporated cane juice)
- 1 T cornstarch or unmodified potato starch

Preparation

In a **dry** blender, add the sugar and starch and process at high speed into a very fine powder. Store the sugar in an airtight, dry container until ready to use.

Cultured Buttermilk

I realize I'm in the minority, but buttermilk was one of the things I missed the most when I adopted a strict plant-based diet. If you've ever missed drinking a cold glass of refreshing buttermilk, then this recipe is for you too. Cultured raw buttermilk is rich in probiotics and living enzymes which are beneficial for nurturing digestive health. Cultured raw buttermilk is also excellent for raw cuisine and cold food applications, such as salad dressings or dips. The cashews do not require pre-soaking. This recipe yields about 1 quart of the finest cultured buttermilk.

Ingredients

- 1 cup (5 oz/142 grams) raw cashews (pre-soaking unnecessary)
- 3 and ½ cups (840 ml) filtered/purified water
- contents of 2 vegan probiotic capsules*
- ½ tsp fine sea salt or kosher salt

You will also need a blender and a nylon nut milk bag to strain the fine solids from the buttermilk. A strainer lined with 4-layers of cheesecloth and a large spoon can be used in place of the nut milk bag.

*If possible, choose vegan probiotic capsules that offer several strains of Lactobacillus bacteria, as well as beneficial Streptococcus thermophilus and Bifidobacterium strains. This will create a more complex buttermilk flavor than using Lactobacillus acidophilus alone.

Preparation

Rinse the cashews to remove any dust or debris, drain thoroughly and place them in a high-powered blender. Add the filtered/purified water and the salt and process on high speed for 2 full minutes. Wash your hands thoroughly or wear disposable gloves (so as not to contaminate the mixture when pressing the milk through the nut milk bag). Pour the milk into the nut milk bag over a large container.

While holding the top of the bag with one hand, gently knead the bag to help the milk pass through the ultra-fine mesh. Optionally, the milk can be poured in increments into a strainer lined with 4-layers of cheesecloth placed over a large container. Stir the milk gently with a spoon to help it pass through the cheesecloth. Discard or compost the solids in the bag or cheesecloth.

Now stir in the contents of the probiotic capsules. Pour the milk into a mason jar or other similar container and cover loosely with a lid. Set aside to culture at room temperature for 24 to 36 hours (culturing will take longer at cooler temperatures and more rapidly during the warmer months). The mixture will separate while culturing; this is normal.

Occasionally tighten the lid and give the mixture a good shake. Be sure to loosen the lid slightly after shaking and continue to culture (loosening the lid will allow the escape of carbon dioxide gas produced during fermentation).

Smell the liquid after 24 hours; the scent of sour milk will indicate that the buttermilk is ready to be refrigerated. Use a clean spoon and taste the mixture. If the milk does not smell or taste sour, continue to culture for an additional 12 hours. If the milk is not culturing, the bacterial strains in the probiotic capsules are no longer active; purchase fresh product.

After culturing, tighten the lid and shake thoroughly. Slightly loosen the lid and refrigerate. Chill for 12 hours before using and be sure to re-tighten the lid before shaking.

Quick Buttermilk

This quick and easy-to-make buttermilk has a tangy, refreshing flavor and does not require culturing. Soymilk is essential for this formula since it thickens in the presence of lactic acid, which adds body to the buttermilk. It's excellent for breading and battering chikun for frying, or for any baking purpose. It's superb for salad dressings and dips too. This recipe yields 2 cups of buttermilk.

Ingredients

- 2 cups (480 ml) plain unsweetened soymilk
- 1 tsp lactic acid powder (sorry, no substitutes)
- ¼ tsp fine sea salt or kosher salt

Preparation

Add the ingredients to a sealable container. Shake well and refrigerate until chilled before using. Quick buttermilk has a shelf life of up to 2 weeks.

Buttermilk Ranch Dressing and Dip

This recipe yields about 1 and ½ cup of tangy and creamy dressing or 1 and ⅓ cup dip.

Ingredients

- ½ cup (120 ml) Cultured Buttermilk (page 174) or Quick Buttermilk (page 175) for dressing; or ⅓ cup (80 ml) for dip
- 1 cup No-Eggy Mayo (page 263) or commercial vegan equivalent
- 1 tsp Dijon mustard
- ½ tsp onion powder
- ¼ tsp garlic powder
- ¼ tsp fine sea salt or kosher salt, or more to taste
- ¼ tsp coarse ground black pepper, or more to taste
- ¼ tsp Worcestershire Sauce (page 27) or commercial vegan equivalent
- 1 T finely chopped fresh chives or 1 tsp dried
- 1 T finely chopped fresh parsley or 1 tsp dried
- 1 and ½ tsp finely chopped fresh dill or a ½ tsp dry

Preparation

In a mixing bowl, whisk all the ingredients together except for the herbs until smooth. The ingredients can also be combined in a shaker cup with a tight-fitting lid. Taste and add additional salt or pepper or thin with additional buttermilk to suit your taste. Stir in the herbs and pour into a sealable container (or store in the shaker cup). Refrigerate for a few hours to blend the flavors.

Instant Sour Cream

This easy-to-make, instant, non-dairy sour cream is my smoothest and creamiest uncultured sour cream recipe to date. Please note that there is no alternative to using soymilk or lactic acid in this recipe. Thickening is dependent upon the curdling action of soymilk when lactic acid is introduced. Other plant milks will not react to the acid in the same manner and fruit acids (lemon juice; vinegar) will not yield the same flavor as lactic acid. Lactic acid powder can be purchased online from ModernistPantry.com. This recipe yields 2 cups sour cream.

Ingredients

- ¾ cup **refined** coconut oil, melted (not virgin coconut oil)
- 1 and ¼ cup plain soymilk (sorry, no substitutes), room temperature
- ½ tsp guar gum or xanthan gum
- ¼ tsp fine sea salt or kosher salt
- 2 tsp lactic acid powder (sorry, no substitutions)

Preparation

Measure the melted coconut oil and set aside.

Measure the lactic acid and set aside in a small dish.

Add the soymilk, food gum and salt to a high-powered blender, cover and process on high speed. With the blender running, add the coconut oil through the hole in the lid in a slow but steady stream. Continue to process for 15 seconds. Add the lactic acid powder all at once and process no more than 5 seconds; turn the blender off.

Transfer the sour cream to an airtight container, seal and refrigerate until well-chilled and further thickened. Consume within 10 days of preparation.

Cultured Sour Cream

Rich, tangy and velvety smooth, this recipe yields about 2 cups of the finest cultured sour cream. Although extremely easy to prepare, a high-powered blender is recommended for producing the smoothest texture.

Ingredients

- 1 and ½ cup (7.5 oz/213 grams) raw cashews
- ¾ cup (180 ml) filtered/purified water
- ½ tsp fine sea salt or kosher salt
- contents of 2 vegan probiotic capsules*

*If possible, choose vegan probiotic capsules that offer several strains of Lactobacillus bacteria, as well as beneficial Streptococcus thermophilus and Bifidobacterium strains. This will create a more complex sour cream flavor than using Lactobacillus acidophilus alone.

Preparation

Soak the cashews for a minimum of 8 hours with enough filtered/purified water to cover (refrigeration is not needed unless soaking time exceeds 8 hours). Drain the cashews, discarding the soaking water, and add them to the blender. Add the fresh filtered/purified water and the salt.

Process the contents until completely smooth, stopping to stir or scrape down the sides of blender as necessary. Add the contents of the probiotic capsules and process briefly to blend.

Transfer the mixture to a roomy container with a lid and cover. The cream may develop an "airy" texture and expand during culturing. This is caused by the release of carbon dioxide gas during fermentation and is perfectly normal. Every 12 hours or so, burp the lid of the container to release carbon dioxide.

Let the cream culture at room temperature for 24 to 48 hours or until the desired level of tanginess is achieved. Do not heat the mixture in a yogurt maker or similar device in an attempt to accelerate the process. This will alter the starch in the cashews and adversely affect the texture. Warm room temperatures will accelerate the culturing process, and cooler room temperatures will slow the process, so taste test after 24 hours and then every 12 hours after that. Viability of the probiotic culture can also affect culturing time, so be sure to use a fresh product that has been stored in the refrigerator.

After culturing, stir the sour cream thoroughly. Seal the container and place in the refrigerator to chill for 8 hours to thicken properly before using.

Cultured Cajou Cheese

Cajou is a semi-soft, cultured cashew cheese with a tangy, refreshing flavor. While delicious on its own, Cajou also serves as a wonderful cheese base for rolling in various dried or fresh herbs, spices, and crushed raw or toasted nuts and seeds to create unique variations of flavor. A high-powered blender is essential for the smoothest finished texture. This recipe yields two 6-ounce portions (each portion can be flavored differently if desired).

Ingredients

- 1 and ½ cup (7.5 oz/213 grams) raw cashews
- ¼ cup **refined** coconut oil, melted (not virgin coconut oil)
- ¼ cup filtered/purified water
- 1 T mellow white miso paste
- 1 T nutritional yeast flakes
- 1 tsp fine sea salt or kosher salt
- contents of 2 vegan probiotic capsules*

*If possible, choose vegan probiotic capsules that offer several strains of Lactobacillus bacteria, as well as beneficial Streptococcus thermophilus and Bifidobacterium strains. This will create a more complex cultured cheese flavor than using Lactobacillus acidophilus alone.

Preparation

Soak the cashews for a minimum of 8 hours with enough filtered/purified water to cover (refrigeration is not needed unless soaking time exceeds 8 hours). Drain the cashews, discarding the water, and add them to the blender with the melted coconut oil, fresh filtered/purified water, miso, nutritional yeast and salt.

Process the contents beginning on low-speed to break down the cashews. Gradually increase to high-speed and process until completely smooth. The mixture will be very thick, so stop to scrape down the sides of the blender and push the mixture down into the blades as necessary. Use a tamper tool if provided with your blender to keep the mixture turning in the blades.

Add the contents of the probiotic capsules and process briefly until blended.

Transfer the cheese mixture to a clean container with a lid (be sure to use a container with extra room, as the mixture will expand when culturing due to the release of carbon dioxide gas). Cover and let the cheese culture at room temperature for 48 hours (warmer weather will accelerate the culturing process, so taste-test after 36 hours). For a tangier cajou, let the cheese culture for up to 72 hours.

After culturing, stir the cheese mixture until creamy, cover and place the container in the refrigerator to chill for 24 hours until the cheese is very firm.

After firming the cheese, lay out a sheet of plastic wrap. Scoop up half of the cheese mixture from the container and place on the wrap. With your fingers, form the mixture into a small log shape (keep a moist towel nearby to wipe your hands). Don't worry about shaping perfection, as the wrap will shape the log for you when rolled.

Roll the cheese log in the wrap, twist the ends tightly and place the cheese in the refrigerator for a minimum of 48 hours to fully ripen. Repeat the procedure with the remaining portion of cheese. To serve, simply remove the wrap and place on a serving plate.

Cajou Variations

Peppercorn Cajou

First, prepare the cajou; culture and refrigerate until firm as instructed on page 178.

After firming the cheese, lay out a sheet of plastic wrap. Sprinkle the wrap with 1 teaspoon of cracked pepper. Scoop up half of the cheese mixture from the container and place on the pepper. With your fingers, form the mixture into a small log shape (keep a moist towel nearby to wipe your hands). Don't worry about shaping perfection, as the wrap will shape the log for you when rolled. Sprinkle with an additional teaspoon of cracked pepper and press the pepper into the cheese with your fingers.

Roll the cheese log in the wrap, twist the ends tightly and place the cheese in the refrigerator for a minimum of 48 hours to fully ripen. Repeat the procedure with the remaining portion of cheese or reserve for flavoring with different seasonings. To serve, simply remove the wrap and place on a serving plate.

Cajou with Fines Herbes

First, prepare the cajou; culture and refrigerate until firm as instructed on page 178.

After firming the cheese, lay out a sheet of plastic wrap. Sprinkle the wrap with 1 teaspoon of dried fine herbes. Scoop up half of the cheese mixture from the container and place on the herbs. With your fingers, form the mixture into a small log shape (keep a moist towel nearby to wipe your hands). Don't worry about shaping perfection as the wrap will shape the log for you when rolled. Sprinkle with an additional teaspoon of herbs and press the herbs into the cheese with your fingers.

Roll the cheese log in the wrap, twist the ends tightly and place the cheese in the refrigerator for a minimum of 48 hours to fully ripen. Repeat the procedure with the remaining portion of cheese or reserve for flavoring with different seasonings. To serve, simply remove the wrap and place on a serving plate.

Fresh Almond Milk Ricotta

Fresh Almond Milk Ricotta is a basic, soft curd, Italian-style cheese. While dairy ricotta is made from the whey left over from cheese production and is very low yield, almond milk ricotta is made by acidifying the milk itself and then draining the whey from the curds. This makes it a high yield cheese.

Typically, almond milk does not curdle by simply introducing acid; but, when sea salt or kosher salt is added to the milk in the proper ratio, it acts as a catalyst for the acid to induce curdling. This would seemingly create a salty finished cheese; however most of the salt is carried away with the whey when the curds are drained. This recipe yields about 10 ounces.

Please note: Commercial almond milk will not work for this recipe.

Ingredients

- 1 and ½ packed cup almond meal/flour
  or 7.5 oz/213 grams blanched almonds (pre-soaking unnecessary)
- 1 qt (4 cups) water
- 2 tsp fine sea salt or kosher salt (do not omit!)
- 2 T fresh lemon juice (fresh only; do not use reconstituted)

Special Supplies Needed

- a standard or high-powered blender
- an ultra-fine mesh nut milk bag for straining the almond milk
- a commercial Greek yogurt strainer or a large sieve lined with fine muslin
  or high-quality double-layered cheesecloth for draining the curds

Preparation

Add the almond meal or blanched almonds, water and salt to a blender and process on high speed for 2 full minutes.

Pour the almond milk into a nut milk bag over a large saucepan. While holding the top of the bag with one hand, vigorously knead the bag to help the milk pass through the ultra-fine mesh, squeezing as much of the milk as possible from the ground almonds.

Optionally, the milk can be poured (in increments) into a sieve lined with fine muslin or 4-layers of cheesecloth placed over the saucepan. Stir and press with a large spoon to help the milk pass through the cloth.

Almonds don't break down as easily as cashews when preparing milk, so there will be a significant amount of solids remaining in the nut milk bag or sieve. Discard, compost or save the solids for other uses as desired.

Place the saucepan over medium heat and bring the milk to a brief boil while stirring frequently. Do not walk away from the heating milk as it can boil over easily when the boiling temperature is reached. Remove the saucepan from the heat and stir in the lemon juice. Gently stir a few more times to ensure that the lemon juice is evenly dispersed. Let the saucepan cool uncovered for 30 minutes to allow curdling. Please note that the curds will be quite fine and may not be apparent to the eye.

While the milk is curdling, set aside a commercial Greek yogurt strainer or line a large sieve with the muslin or double-layered cheesecloth and place over a large, deep bowl.

Pour the curdled almond milk into the sieve and allow draining for 2 hours at room temperature, or until the desired texture is achieved. Discard the whey as it will be very salty.

The acidity of the finished ricotta can be enhanced by stirring in small amounts of lactic acid powder or fresh lemon juice.

Chill in a sealed container until ready to use. Prepared almond ricotta has a refrigerator shelf life of about 1 week.

Enriched Ricotta Variation

If you prefer to enrich the flavor of the ricotta, stir the following ingredients into the prepared ricotta before using in recipes:

- 1 T extra-virgin olive oil
- 2 tsp nutritional yeast flakes
- ¼ tsp ground white pepper
- 1 tsp each of dried basil, parsley, and oregano (optional)
- fine sea salt or kosher salt to taste

Amande Cheese

Amande is my almond milk-based version of fresh chèvre (goat's milk cheese). It has a creamy mouthfeel and a mild lactic acidity and is delightfully fresh and tangy. Dried herbs, spices or other dry seasonings can be blended, if desired, into the cheese before shaping into a log. Small amounts of wine, vinegar or fruit syrup reductions can be swirled into the cheese; or the finished cheese can be rolled in fresh or dried herbs and/or spices before serving. Lactic acid powder can be purchased from ModernistPantry.com and other online retailers such as Amazon.com.

Please note: Commercial almond milk will not work for this recipe.

Ingredients

- 1 and ½ packed cup almond meal/flour
  or 7.5 oz/213 grams blanched almonds (pre-soaking unnecessary)
- 1 qt (4 cups) water
- 2 tsp fine sea salt or kosher salt (do not omit!)
- 1 T lactic acid powder or ¼ cup fresh lemon juice (fresh only; do not use reconstituted)

Special Supplies Needed

- a standard or high-powered blender
- an ultra-fine mesh nut milk bag for straining the almond milk
- a large sieve lined with fine muslin or high-quality double-layered cheesecloth for draining the curds
- a tofu press or a tofu box with a heavy weight for pressing

Preparation

Add the almond meal or blanched almonds, water and salt to a blender and process on high speed for 2 full minutes.

Pour the almond milk into a nut milk bag over a large saucepan. While holding the top of the bag with one hand, vigorously knead the bag to help the milk pass through the ultra-fine mesh, squeezing as much of the milk as possible from the ground almonds.

Optionally, the milk can be poured (in increments) into a large sieve lined with fine muslin or 4-layers of cheesecloth placed over the saucepan. Stir and press with a large spoon to help the milk pass through the cloth.

Almonds don't break down as easily as cashews when preparing milk, so there will be a significant amount of solids remaining in the nut milk bag or sieve. Discard, compost or save the solids for other uses as desired.

Place the saucepan over medium heat and bring the milk to a brief boil while stirring frequently. Do not walk away from the heating milk as it can boil over easily when the boiling temperature is reached. Remove the saucepan from the heat and stir in the lactic acid powder or fresh lemon juice. Gently stir a few more times to ensure that the acid is evenly dispersed. Let the saucepan cool uncovered for 30 minutes to allow curdling. Please note that the curds will be quite fine and may not be apparent to the eye.

While the milk is curdling, line a large sieve with the muslin or double-layered cheesecloth and place over a large, deep bowl.

Pour the curdled almond milk into the sieve and allow draining for 2 hours at room temperature. When draining is complete, lift the cloth from each corner and transfer to the tofu press.

Fold the cloth over the curds and put the spring plate or heavy weight in place. Place the press into the refrigerator and allow pressing for a minimum of 8 hours to sufficiently remove most of the whey. Pour off and discard the whey occasionally while pressing if you have the opportunity.

Remove the cheese from the press and unwrap. At this point, dried herbs, spices or other dry seasonings can be stirred directly into the cheese if desired. Small amounts of wine, vinegar or fruit syrup reductions can also be swirled into the cheese.

The cheese can then be transferred to a serving container and served in that manner; or the cheese can be formed into a log.

To shape the cheese into a log, place the mixture onto a sheet of plastic wrap. Fold the wrap over the cheese and using your fingers, shape the cheese into a log using the wrap as a barrier. Don't worry about shaping perfection, as the wrap will shape the log when rolled and the ends twisted tight.

Continue to roll the cheese in the wrap, twist the ends tightly and place the cheese in the refrigerator for several hours to re-firm. To serve, simply remove the wrap, roll the cheese in fresh or dried herbs and/or spices if desired, and place on a serving plate.

Fresh Paneer
(Basic Almond Curd Cheese)

Paneer is a fresh, uncultured, un-aged, acid-set, non-melting curd cheese popular in Indian, Pakistani and Bangladeshi cuisines. It is made by curdling heated milk with food acid and then draining and pressing the resulting curds into a block of cheese.

My non-dairy paneer is produced in a similar manner by curdling fresh almond milk with lemon juice and then pressing the resulting the curds into a solid block. Typically, almond milk does not curdle by simply introducing acid; but, when sea salt or kosher salt is added to the milk in the proper ratio, it acts as a catalyst for the acid to induce curdling. This would seemingly create a salty finished cheese, however most of the salt is carried away with the whey when the curds are drained and pressed.

In order to create a solid and well-formed block of paneer cheese, a box-shaped tofu press is required to maintain the block shape of the cheese while pressing. The TofuXpress® works exceptionally well for this purpose because of its compact design which can be placed into the refrigerator while pressing. A tofu box, used for preparing tofu at home, can also be used but will require a heavy weight to be placed on top of the box for pressing. This can be bulky and will require additional room in your refrigerator.

The cheese is very simple to prepare but it does require 2 to 3 days of pressing and drying before it is ready to use, so plan ahead. This is a high-yield cheese; in other words, 7.5 ounces of almonds yields about 8 ounces of fresh paneer. Fresh paneer also serves as the foundation for several other cheeses in this cookbook.

Please note: Commercial almond milk will not work for this recipe.

Ingredients

- 1 and ½ packed cup almond meal/flour
  or 7.5 oz/213 grams blanched almonds (pre-soaking unnecessary)
- 1 qt (4 cups) water
- 2 tsp fine sea salt or kosher salt (do not omit!)
- 2 T fresh lemon juice (fresh only; do not use reconstituted)

Special Supplies Needed

- a standard or high-powered blender
- an ultra-fine mesh nut milk bag for straining the almond milk
- a large sieve lined with fine muslin or high-quality double-layered cheesecloth for draining and pressing the curds
- a box-shaped tofu press, such as a TofuXpress®
  or a tofu box with a heavy weight for pressing
- paper towels

Preparation

Add the almond meal or blanched almonds, water and salt to a blender and process on high speed for 2 full minutes. Pour the almond milk into a nut milk bag over a large saucepan. While holding the top of the bag with one hand, vigorously knead the bag to help the milk pass through the ultra-fine mesh, squeezing as much of the milk as possible from the ground almonds.

Optionally, the milk can be poured (in increments) into a large sieve lined with fine muslin or 4-layers of cheesecloth placed over the saucepan. Stir and press with a large spoon to help the milk pass through the cloth. Almonds don't break down as easily as cashews when preparing milk, so there will be a significant amount of solids remaining in the nut milk bag or sieve. Discard, compost or save the solids for other uses as desired.

Place the saucepan over medium heat and bring the milk to a brief boil while stirring frequently. Do not walk away from the heating milk as it can boil over easily when the boiling temperature is reached. Remove the saucepan from the heat and stir in the lemon juice. Gently stir a few more times to ensure that the lemon juice is evenly dispersed. Let the saucepan cool uncovered for 30 minutes to allow curdling. Please note that the curds will be quite fine and may not be apparent to the eye.

While the milk is curdling, line a large sieve with the muslin or double-layered cheesecloth and place over a large, deep bowl. Pour the curdled almond milk into the sieve and allow draining for 2 hours at room temperature. When draining is complete, lift the cloth from each corner and transfer to the tofu press. Use a spoon or spatula to push the corners of the cloth into the corners of the box. This will ensure an evenly shaped block of cheese.

Fold the cloth over the curds and put the spring plate in place. Place the box into the refrigerator and allow pressing for about 8 hours to sufficiently remove most of the whey. Pour off and discard the liquid occasionally while pressing if you have the opportunity.

Remove the cheese from the box and unwrap. The paneer will still be quite moist at this point. Transfer the cheese to several layers of paper towels and fold securely in the towels. Place into a food storage bag and refrigerate a minimum of 8 hours. Repeat the process again until the cheese is quite firm and semi-dry. Slice the cheese into cubes and use in your favorite recipes as desired.

Saag Paneer
(Indian Creamed Spinach and Mustard Greens with Fresh Paneer Cheese)

Every Indian chef and home cook, or lover of Indian cuisine, has their own recipe and technique for preparing saag. Over the years I have studied different ways to prepare this dish and then developed my own recipe and technique. The recipe calls for garam masala, which is an Indian spice blend. It can be found in specialty food stores or in the ethnic section of some supermarkets. You really have to try this dish; the flavors are amazing!

Dry Spice Mix

- 1 tsp garam masala
- 2 tsp whole cumin seeds or 1 tsp ground cumin
- ½ tsp ground coriander
- ½ tsp ground fenugreek
- ¼ tsp cayenne pepper, or more to taste

Basic Ingredients

- 1 block fresh Paneer (page 184), cut into bite-size cubes
- 10 oz fresh spinach (or one 10 oz package frozen spinach, thawed)
- 10 oz fresh mustard greens
- sea salt or kosher salt
- 1 tsp organic sugar
- ¼ cup (60 ml) olive oil
- 1 large onion, diced
- 1 small jalapeno or serrano pepper, seeds removed and chopped (if you like it hot, leave some of the seeds!)
- 3 cloves garlic, chopped
- 2 T tomato paste
- 1 T fresh grated ginger root
- 1 T fresh lemon juice
- optional: ½ cup Raw Cashew Milk (page 168) or Soy Cream (page 171)

Note: For Palak Paneer, omit the mustard greens and use 20 ounces fresh spinach or two 10-ounce packages frozen spinach, thawed.

Preparation

In a small dish, combine the dry spices and set aside.

Place a large stockpot with about 1 gallon of water over high heat. Add 1 teaspoon salt and 1 teaspoon organic sugar (the salt and sugar will help maintain the bright green color of the greens). When the water comes to a boil, add the greens. As they begin to wilt, submerge them in the water completely with a large spoon. Bring back to a boil and cook for 4 minutes. Drain the greens thoroughly in a colander but do not press. Set aside.

While the cooked greens are draining, add the olive oil to a large skillet and place over medium heat. Add the onions and green chili pepper to the skillet with 1 teaspoon salt and sauté until the onions are soft and beginning to take on a golden color, about 5 to 7 minutes. Add the garlic and dry spice mixture and continue to sauté one minute. The mixture will be very fragrant. Stir in the tomato paste and lemon juice and mix well. Cook an additional minute or two.

Place the cooked and drained greens into a blender. Add the skillet mixture and process the contents until almost smooth. Transfer the mixture back to the skillet and place over medium-low heat. Cook uncovered for 10 minutes to blend the flavors, stirring occasionally.

Meanwhile, spray a non-stick skillet with cooking oil and place over medium heat. Add the cubed paneer in a single layer and cook until golden brown on one side only. Carefully remove the paneer to a plate. Be careful not to dislodge the browned crust from the cubes.

Stir the optional cashew milk or soy cream into the saag for a creamier dish. Season with salt to taste and add a bit more cayenne pepper to intensify the heat if desired. Cook an additional 5 minutes. Gently fold in the paneer, reserving several cubes for garnishing the dish. Serve immediately.

Fresh Almond Curd Cottage Cheese

A delightfully fresh and creamy cottage-style cheese produced from fresh pressed almond curd and fresh raw cashew milk. Cashew milk is used in this cheese because of its richness and natural sweetness. Lactic acid powder can be purchased from ModernistPantry.com and other online retailers such as Amazon.com. Fresh cottage cheese has a refrigerator shelf-life of about 1 week.

Ingredients

- 1 block fresh Paneer (page 184)
- ½ cup Raw Cashew Milk (page 168), or more as needed for creaminess
- ½ tsp lactic acid powder or 2 tsp fresh lemon juice
- a pinch or two of fine sea salt or kosher salt, or more to taste

Preparation

Crumble the paneer into a bowl and fold in the remaining ingredients until blended. Fold in additional cashew milk as needed for creaminess; season with salt to taste. Try stirring in fresh snipped chives before serving or serve with chunks of fresh pineapple for a naturally sweet treat.

Easy Cream Cheese
(Tofu and Cashew Base)

This recipe produces a velvety smooth cream cheese that rivals its commercial non-dairy counterparts; and since no culturing is involved, it's much quicker to make than cultured non-dairy cream cheese. The cheese mixture will be very thick and therefore a high-powered blender is recommended for efficient processing.

Lactic acid powder can be purchased from ModernistPantry.com and other online retailers such as Amazon.com. Please do not replace the soymilk with other non-dairy milks since the curdling reaction of the lactic acid with the soymilk is essential to the final texture. This recipe yields about 2 cups.

Ingredients

- ¾ cup (3.75 oz/160 grams) raw cashews
- ½ cup plain unsweetened soymilk
- 5 oz/142 grams **pressed** extra-firm tofu (not silken tofu)
- ¼ cup **refined** coconut oil, melted (not virgin coconut oil)
- 2 tsp lactic acid powder
- ½ tsp raw apple cider vinegar
- ½ tsp fine sea salt or kosher salt

Preparation

Rinse the cashews to remove any dust or debris and drain thoroughly. In a covered container, soak the cashews in the soymilk for a minimum of 8 hours in the refrigerator.

Tip: Let the cashews, soymilk and tofu come to room temperature before blending as this will make processing easier.

Add the cashews, soymilk and melted coconut oil to a high-powered blender and process the contents on high speed until completely smooth and creamy, stopping to scrape down the sides of the blender jar and push the mixture down into the blades as necessary (the mixture will be very thick, so use a tamper tool if you have one).

Crumble the tofu into the blender and add the lactic acid, vinegar and salt. Continue to process on high speed until completely smooth and creamy, stopping to scrape down the sides of the blender jar and push the mixture down into the blades as necessary (the mixture will be extremely thick at this point, so use a tamper tool if you have one). Transfer the cheese mixture to a container with a lid and refrigerate until chilled.

Variations: For cream cheese with onion and chives, stir in 1 tablespoon dried minced onion and 1 tablespoon freeze-dried minced chives before chilling. For fruit flavored cream cheese, mix ¼ cup all-fruit jam into the cream cheese after it has chilled and firmed.

Neufchâtel Cream Cheese
(cultured cashew base)

This recipe produces the finest, cultured non-dairy cream cheese. Neufchâtel is actually a French cream cheese with flavor nuances of mushroom (replicated with truffle oil in this recipe), while the American version lacks the mushroom nuance. A high-powered blender is required for the smoothest finished texture. This recipe yields about 12 ounces.

Ingredients

- 1 and ½ cups (7.5 oz/213 grams) raw cashews
- ¼ cup **refined** coconut oil, melted (not virgin coconut oil)
- ⅓ cup filtered/purified water
- ½ tsp fine sea salt or kosher salt
- contents of 2 vegan probiotic capsules*
- ⅛ tsp truffle oil (optional)

*If possible, choose vegan probiotic capsules that offer several strains of Lactobacillus bacteria, as well as beneficial Streptococcus thermophilus and Bifidobacterium strains. This will create a more complex cultured cream cheese flavor than using Lactobacillus acidophilus alone.

Preparation

Soak the cashews for a minimum of 8 hours with enough filtered/purified water to cover (refrigeration is not needed unless soaking time exceeds 8 hours). Drain the cashews, discarding the water, and add them to the blender with the melted coconut oil, fresh filtered/purified water and salt.

Process the contents beginning on low-speed to break down the cashews. Gradually increase to high-speed and process until completely smooth. The mixture will be very thick, so stop to scrape down the sides of the blender and push the mixture down into the blades as necessary. Use a tamper tool if provided with your blender to keep the mixture turning in the blades.

Add the contents of the probiotic capsules and process briefly until blended.

Transfer the mixture to a clean, roomy container with a lid. Cover and let the cheese culture at room temperature for 24 hours. The cream cheese mixture will expand and develop an "airy" texture during culturing. This is caused by the release of carbon dioxide gas during fermentation and is perfectly normal.

After culturing, stir the cream cheese thoroughly. Smooth the surface with the back of a spoon and place a layer of plastic wrap directly in contact with the cheese. This will discourage the harmless surface discoloration that may occur during extended storage. Now seal the container and place in the refrigerator to chill for 12 hours before using. The cream cheese will continue to develop flavor as it chills.

Almond Cream Cheese

Almond Cream Cheese is a soft and spreadable, mild-tasting, rich and creamy, fresh cheese. A food processor is recommended for efficient processing. This recipe yields about 10 ounces.

Ingredients

- 1 block fresh Paneer (page 184)
- 3 T **refined** coconut oil, melted (not virgin coconut oil)
- ½ tsp lactic acid powder, or more to taste
- ¼ tsp fine sea salt or kosher salt, or more to taste

Preparation

Crumble the paneer into a food processor and set aside.

Add the melted coconut oil to the food processor with the remaining ingredients and process the contents until very smooth. Taste the cheese and add more lactic acid and/or salt as desired.

Transfer the cheese mixture to a sealable container and refrigerate for several hours to chill and firm. Prepared almond cream cheese has a refrigerator shelf life of about 10 days.

Variations: For cream cheese with onion and chives, stir in 1 tablespoon dried minced onion and 1 tablespoon freeze-dried minced chives before chilling. For fruit flavored cream cheese, mix ¼ cup all-fruit jam into the cream cheese after it has chilled and firmed.

Greek Feta
(Almond Curd and Tofu Variations)

Greek Feta can be made with either homemade pressed fresh paneer (almond curd) or pressed extra-firm tofu. It has a very tangy, salty flavor and is wonderful for topping Mediterranean salads, pizza or for using in recipes such as Greek Spanakopita. A food processor is recommended for efficient processing.

You will also need a silicone, glass, ceramic, metal or BPA-free plastic container that will hold a minimum of 2 cups liquid to act as a form to shape the cheese. Line the form with plastic wrap or a double layer of cheesecloth, leaving plenty of excess hanging over the sides. This will help lift the cheese from the form after firming. This recipe yields about 10 ounces.

Ingredients

- 1 block fresh Paneer (page 184) or 8 oz **pressed** extra-firm tofu (not silken tofu)
- ¼ cup **refined** coconut oil, melted (not virgin coconut oil)
- 1 T white wine vinegar or raw apple cider vinegar
- ¾ tsp lactic acid powder or 1 T fresh lemon juice
- 1 and ¼ tsp fine sea salt or kosher salt
- ¼ tsp onion powder

Mediterranean Herbed Feta Variation

Process the cheese mixture as directed below and then add the following ingredients and pulse a few times to blend:

- 1 tsp dried basil
- 1 tsp dried marjoram
- 1 tsp dried oregano

Preparation

Crumble the paneer or tofu into a food processor.

Add the melted coconut oil with the remaining ingredients and process the contents until very smooth.

Transfer the cheese mixture to the lined form. Pack the mixture with the back of a spoon and smooth the surface as best you can. Cover with plastic wrap and refrigerate for a minimum of 8 hours. This will ensure that the coconut oil has completely solidified. Once firmed, lift the cheese from the container and crumble as needed.

When using as a topping for salads, toss the salad first with the dressing and then add the crumbles. Cubed feta is wonderful drizzled with olive oil and served with falafel and other Mediterranean favorites. Store in a food storage bag or wrapped tightly in plastic wrap in the refrigerator.

Creamy Feta Salad Dressing

This creamy and tangy dressing is also excellent when served as a dip for crudités (assorted sliced raw vegetables).

Ingredients

- 4 oz Greek Feta (page 191)
- 1 cup No-Eggy Mayo (page 263) or commercial vegan mayonnaise
- 3 T Instant Sour Cream (page 176) or Cultured Sour Cream (page 177)
- 1 T red wine vinegar
- 1 T plain unsweetened soymilk or almond milk, or more to adjust consistency
- ¼ tsp coarse ground black pepper, or more to taste
- ¼ tsp fine sea salt or kosher salt, or more to taste
- 2 T minced red onion

Preparation

Add half of the crumbled feta cheese (2 ounces) and the remaining ingredients to a food processor or blender, except for the red onion, and process the contents until smooth. Transfer to a sealable container.

Stir in the minced red onion and the remaining crumbled feta cheese and season with additional salt and pepper to taste.

If you wish to thin the consistency, stir in small amounts of plain unsweetened non-dairy milk until the desired consistency is achieved. Cover and refrigerate for several hours to blend the flavors and chill the dressing before using.

Garlic Herb Gournay

This garlicky, semi-soft cheese can be made with either fresh almond curd or pressed extra-firm tofu. It makes a flavorful spread for crackers or crusty bread. The texture is similar to Boursin™, a trademarked brand of Gournay cheese. A food processor is recommended for efficient processing. This recipe yields about 8 ounces.

Ingredients

- 1 block fresh Paneer (page 184) or 8 oz **pressed** extra-firm tofu (not silken)
- 3 T **refined** coconut oil, melted (not virgin coconut oil)
- ¾ tsp lactic acid powder or 1 T fresh lemon juice
- 1 tsp white wine vinegar or raw apple cider vinegar
- 1 clove garlic, chopped
- 2 tsp dried parsley
- 2 tsp dried minced chives
- 1 tsp dried basil
- 1 tsp fine sea salt or kosher salt
- ½ tsp onion powder
- ½ tsp coarse ground black pepper
- ¼ tsp dried thyme leaves

Preparation

Crumble the paneer into a food processor or mixing bowl.

Add the melted coconut oil with the remaining ingredients. Process the contents until very smooth or mash thoroughly in the bowl until blended.

Transfer the mixture to a container with a lid. Cover and refrigerate for a minimum of 6 hours to allow the flavors to blend and the cheese to firm. If desired, transfer the cheese to a decorative container and allow the cheese to soften for about 15 minutes at room temperature before serving.

Gournay should be thick, yet spreadable. If the cheese is dry and crumbly, stir in small amounts of non-dairy milk until the desired consistency is achieved.

Cultured Yogurt
(Soymilk or Almond Milk)

This recipe yields a creamy, tangy, plain yogurt from soymilk or almond milk and requires no additional thickening agents such as food starches, gums or gels. So why make your own yogurt? Because most commercial non-dairy yogurts have sugar and/or fruit added, which makes them unsuitable for preparing yogurt-based cheeses or savory condiments. Of course, when not being used to make cheese or savory condiments, this yogurt can also be sweetened to your liking with organic sugar, natural syrups, fresh fruit or fruit preserves.

The yogurt can also be strained to remove the liquid whey, which results in a thick Greek-style yogurt consistency.

This yogurt is made with plain, pure homemade or commercial soymilk - or pure homemade almond milk (do not use commercial almond milk; it's too watery and too low in protein for coagulation).

It may seem odd for plain, unsweetened yogurt to include brown rice syrup in its preparation but there is a sound reason for this: Brown rice syrup is rich in dextrose, a natural sugar similar to glucose. It's not used to sweeten the yogurt but rather to provide a food source for the yogurt culture (beneficial lacto-bacteria). Pure soymilk and almond milk are too low in natural sugar to provide this food source. As the soy or almond milk cultures, the lacto-bacteria consume the dextrose in the brown rice syrup and convert it to lactic acid. This gives the yogurt its familiar tanginess. If cultured for the recommended period of time, you should not detect any sweetness in the finished yogurt.

Brown rice syrup can be found in natural and health food stores and sometimes in the natural foods section of major supermarkets. If you cannot source it locally, it can be purchased through the internet. Agave syrup will also work but may leave a slight agave undertaste.

You will need a commercial vegan yogurt starter to prepare your first batch. Despite what the package directions may state, you will not need a new sachet of starter to culture another batch of yogurt. As long as ¼ cup of yogurt is reserved from a previous batch, a new batch can be made once or twice successfully. For subsequent batches, it's a good idea to begin with a new sachet to renew the bacterial strain.

Vegan yogurt starter can be purchased from CulturesforHealth.com. It is very affordable and they ship quickly. You may also be able to locate vegan yogurt starter elsewhere by doing a little internet searching. Commercial non-dairy yogurt can be used as a starter, as long as the culture is viable and the yogurt is plain and not sweetened excessively.

For consistent results, I recommend using a commercial yogurt maker. Yogurt makers maintain the yogurt at a specific temperature for an extended period of time and are convenient and reasonably affordable. If your yogurt maker uses individual glass jars, set them aside. In this case, the yogurt needs to be cultured in a glass bowl that will fit inside the yogurt maker with the unit lid in place.

A commercial Greek-style yogurt strainer is a handy tool should you desire to thicken the yogurt. The yogurt can also be strained in a large sieve lined with fine muslin or a double layer of high-quality cheesecloth which has been placed over a large, deep bowl.

It is important to make sure all your containers and working tools are very clean before you begin so as not to contaminate the yogurt with undesirable bacteria or molds. This recipe yields about 3 cups or six ½-cup servings of plain Greek-style yogurt (be sure to reserve ¼ cup for starting your next batch!)

Ingredients for Soymilk Yogurt

- 4 cups plain, pure homemade or commercial soymilk
- ½ tsp sea salt or kosher salt
- 2 T brown rice syrup
- 1 sachet vegan yogurt culture or ¼ cup almond milk yogurt (from a previous batch)

Ingredients for Almond Milk Yogurt*

- 4 cups filtered/purified water
- 1 and ½ packed cup almond meal
  or 7.5 oz/213 grams blanched almonds (pre-soaking not necessary)
- ½ tsp sea salt or kosher salt
- 2 T brown rice syrup
- 1 sachet vegan yogurt culture or ¼ cup almond milk yogurt (from a previous batch)

*Do not use commercial almond milk; it's too watery and too low in protein for coagulation.

Preparing the Milk

When you are ready to begin, switch on the power to warm the yogurt maker. For preparing soymilk yogurt, pour the soymilk into a large saucepan and then skip to the section titled "Heating the Milk".)

For almond milk, add the almond meal or blanched almonds, water and salt to a blender and process on high speed for 2 full minutes. Pour the almond milk into a nut milk bag over a large saucepan. While holding the top of the bag with one hand, vigorously knead the bag to help the milk pass through the ultra-fine mesh, squeezing as much of the milk as possible from the ground almonds.

Optionally, the milk can be poured (in increments) into a large sieve lined with fine muslin or 4-layers of cheesecloth placed over the saucepan. Stir and press with a large spoon to help the milk pass through the cloth.

Almonds don't break down as easily as cashews when preparing milk, so there will be a significant amount of solids remaining in the nut milk bag or sieve. Discard, compost or save the solids for other uses as desired.

Heating the Soymilk or Almond Milk

Stir the brown rice syrup into the milk in the saucepan and place over medium heat. Bring the milk to a brief simmer while stirring frequently. Do not walk away from the heating milk as it can boil over easily if left unattended. Remove the saucepan from the heat to cool for 30 minutes. Stir occasionally while cooling to help the milk cool evenly.

After 30 minutes of cooling, feel the bottom of the saucepan. If it is comfortably warm to the touch proceed to the next step; otherwise, let cool an additional 5 to 10 minutes and then test again. If desired, test the temperature of the mixture with an instant-read thermometer. It should not exceed 110°F/43°C (if the mixture is too hot, it will destroy the culture).

Culturing the Soymilk or Almond Milk

Whisk in the yogurt starter or reserved yogurt until thoroughly blended. Pour the mixture into the yogurt maker. Put the unit lid in place and culture for 12 hours. No more; no less.

After culturing, refrigerate the yogurt in a covered container for a minimum of 8 hours or overnight. This will further develop the flavor and assist thickening. Stir the yogurt vigorously until smooth before serving.

Consume or use the yogurt within 3 weeks (because yogurt is a cultured food, it may stay fresh longer, but 3 weeks is a rough guideline). Be sure to reserve ¼ cup for starting your next batch.

Straining the Yogurt (Optional)

Have a commercial Greek yogurt strainer ready or line a large sieve with the muslin or double-layered cheesecloth and place over a large, deep bowl.

Pour the chilled yogurt into the strainer or sieve and allow draining for 2 hours at room temperature. Transfer it back to its storage container and refrigerate.

Consume or use the yogurt within 3 weeks (because yogurt is a cultured food, it may stay fresh longer, but 3 weeks is a rough guideline). Be sure to reserve ¼ cup for starting your next batch.

Chef's note: Reserve the whey and chill in a sealed container if desired. I have discovered that the whey is a superb gluten-free alternative to rejuvelac for preparing cultured cashew-based cheeses. Recipes for rejuvelac-cultured cheeses can be found in my Non-Dairy Evolution Cookbook. It's also good as a probiotic drink for maintaining intestinal health. The whey will stay fresh and active for about 5 days. Over time it will turn to vinegar and is no longer useable.

Yogurt Ranch Dressing

Non-dairy yogurt offers a tangy base for this refreshing homemade ranch dressing.

Ingredients

- 1 cup unstrained Cultured Yogurt (page 194)
- 1 T fresh lemon juice
- 1 tsp onion powder
- 1 tsp garlic powder
- 1 and ½ tsp minced fresh parsley or ½ tsp dried
- 1 and ½ tsp minced fresh chives or ½ tsp dried
- ¾ tsp minced fresh dill or ¼ tsp dried
- ½ tsp sea salt or kosher salt or more to taste
- a few grinds of coarse ground black pepper

Preparation

Whisk together all ingredients until blended. Refrigerate for several hours to blend the flavors before using.

Greek Tzatziki

Greek Tzatziki is a cucumber sauce used as a condiment for Greek and other Mediterranean cuisine. This recipe is my own variation and yields about 2 and ½ cups.

Ingredients

- 1 English cucumber, peeled, split lengthwise and seeds removed
- 2 cups Cultured Yogurt (page 194)
- 2 T extra-virgin olive oil
- 2 T minced sweet yellow onion
- 2 cloves minced garlic (2 tsp)
- 1 T red wine vinegar or raw apple cider vinegar
- 1 tsp fine sea salt or kosher salt, or more to taste
- ½ tsp coarse ground black pepper, or more to taste
- 2 tsp minced fresh dill

Preparation

Grate the cucumber on the largest holes of a box grater. Place the grated cucumber into a fine sieve and gently press with the back of a spoon to remove the excess juice. The cucumber water can also be removed using a tofu press.

In a bowl, whisk the olive oil into the yogurt until emulsified. Stir in the cucumber and remaining ingredients and season with additional salt and pepper to taste. Chill for a minimum of two hours to blend the flavors before serving.

Indian Raita

Raita is an Indian, Pakistani and Bangladeshi condiment used to temper the heat of Indian spices. I also enjoy eating it on its own as a refreshing non-dairy treat. This recipe is my own variation and yields about 2 and ½ cups.

Ingredients

- 1 English cucumber, peeled, split lengthwise and seeds removed
- 2 cups Cultured Yogurt (page 194)
- 2 T minced green onion, including the green top
- 1 T fresh lemon juice
- 1 tsp fine sea salt or kosher salt, or more to taste
- ¾ tsp ground cumin
- ¼ tsp ground coriander
- 2 T chopped fresh mint

Preparation

Grate the cucumber on the largest holes of a box grater. Place the grated cucumber into a fine sieve, gently press with the back of a spoon to remove the excess water and then transfer to a bowl. The cucumber water can also be removed using a tofu press.

Add the remaining ingredients and stir until blended; season with additional salt as desired. Chill for a minimum of two hours to blend the flavors before serving.

Yogurt Butter

Yogurt Butter is a cultured, non-dairy yogurt-based, palm oil-free butter with a flavor that is remarkably similar to artisan-crafted European dairy butter.

The lactic acid in this butter is naturally produced during the culturing process of the yogurt. This natural lactic acid eliminates the need for commercially produced lactic acid (or fruit acids) to add flavor to the butter. My signature recipe produces a butter that looks, tastes and melts like dairy butter and can be used in any recipe, including baked goods, as you would dairy butter.

Since Yogurt Butter contains live bacterial cultures and enzymes, it is a "living food" and will continue to develop flavor as it chills in the refrigerator.

Just like its dairy counterpart, Yogurt Butter browns and burns when exposed to high heat and therefore should not be used for high-heat sautéing; it works best with low to medium heat.

The best kitchen appliance for emulsifying the butter ingredients is an immersion blender. A food processor will also work. The ingredients can also be emulsified using a standard or high-speed blender; however, retrieving the thick butter from around the blades can be difficult.

This recipe yields about 2 cups of butter.

Ingredients

- 1 cup **refined** coconut oil, melted (not virgin coconut oil)
- ⅔ cup unstrained Cultured Yogurt (page 194), room temperature
- ⅓ cup neutral vegetable oil
- 4 tsp/20 ml liquid soy lecithin or liquid sunflower lecithin*;
  or 24 grams soy or sunflower lecithin powder (about 2 T plus 2 tsp);
  or 24 grams soy or sunflower lecithin granules ground into a fine powder
- ¼ tsp to 1 tsp fine sea salt or kosher salt, to taste
- ¼ tsp guar gum, sodium alginate or xanthan gum

Preparation

You will need a 2-cup minimum food storage container with a lid to store the butter. If you prefer, the butter can be shaped in a flexible silicone form, or divided into several forms, and released after hardening.

Immersion Blender Method

Measure 1 cup of the melted coconut oil into a 2-cup measuring cup or other suitable container with a pouring "lip". Add ⅓ cup neutral vegetable oil to the coconut oil and set aside.

Add the remaining ingredients to a 4-cup glass measuring cup or heavy glass/ceramic bowl. Insert the immersion blender and process the mixture for about 15 seconds.

With the immersion blender running on high speed, begin slowly pouring the mixed oils into the blending cup or bowl. Move the blender gently up and down and side to side as you add the oils. Continue blending until the mixture is emulsified and thick. Transfer to a sealable container, cover and refrigerate until solid (if using one or several silicone molds, cover with plastic wrap).

For individual forms: Once solid, release the butter from the forms by wiggling the sides a bit to loosen and then press out onto a plate. Keep refrigerated until ready to use.

Food Processor Method

Measure 1 cup of the melted coconut oil into a 2-cup measuring cup or other suitable container with a pouring "lip". Add ⅓ cup neutral vegetable oil to the coconut oil and set aside.

Add the remaining ingredients to the processor and turn on the processor. Now, slowly pour the mixed oils into the mixture through the food chute. Continue to process until the mixture is emulsified and thick.

Transfer to a sealable container, cover and refrigerate until solid (if using one or several silicone molds, cover with plastic wrap).

For individual forms: Once solid, release the butter from the forms by wiggling the sides a bit to loosen and then press out onto a plate. Keep refrigerated until ready to use.

Fresh Churned Butter

Dairy butter is an emulsion that consists of butterfat, milk protein and water. It is made by churning fresh or lightly fermented cream. Lightly fermented cream, along with salt, adds flavor to the butter.

Non-dairy fresh churned butter is an emulsion consisting of plant fat, soymilk protein and water. Lactic acid is added to produce the lightly fermented quality and add flavor, along with salt. No additional emulsifiers (such as lecithin) or stabilizers (such as guar gum) are required. It looks like dairy butter; it tastes like dairy butter; it behaves in cooking just like dairy butter; and it can be used in any recipe just as you would use dairy butter.

Fresh churned butter is prepared with soy-based extra-heavy whipping cream. The composition of this cream is remarkably similar to heavy dairy cream, which makes it ideal for home-churning butter. Do not use any other form of non-dairy cream; it will not produce the same results and most likely will not work at all.

You will also need a stand mixer with a wire whisk attachment or an electric handheld rotary mixer (the rotary mixer is not as efficient as a stand mixer and will take longer to produce butter). Do not attempt with a food processor or blender; they won't work. Please read through the instructions completely at least once before beginning. Lactic acid powder can be purchased from ModernistPantry.com or other online sources such as Amazon.com.

Ingredients

- 1 cup plain soymilk, room temperature (sorry, no substitutions)
- 1 tsp fine salt or kosher salt (reduce or omit as desired)
- 1 cup **refined** coconut oil, melted (not virgin coconut oil)
- ½ tsp lactic acid powder

Preparation

The soymilk must be at room temperature to emulsify properly with the coconut oil. If necessary, gently warm the milk in a saucepan over low heat or briefly in the microwave. If cold soymilk is used, the coconut oil will congeal when it comes into contact with the cold liquid

Measure the coconut oil and set aside.

Pour the soymilk into a blender and add the salt. Put the cover in place but remove the center insert. Begin blending on low speed, gradually increasing to high speed (if the milk is splashing too much in the blender jar, reduce the speed slightly). Pour the coconut oil in a slow but steady stream into the milk through the opening in the blender jar's lid. After the oil has been incorporated, add the lactic acid.

Continue to process for a few seconds until the mixture thickens (this should occur instantaneously). The mixture will resemble crème fraîche. Transfer the thickened cream to a sealable container and refrigerate until very cold (a minimum of 6 hours). Cold cream is essential to the success of churning butter. Also place the metal bowl and balloon whip attachment from a stand mixer or a metal or ceramic mixing bowl and 2 beaters from an electric rotary mixer into the refrigerator. Chill until very cold.

Please note that the thickened cream may taste somewhat salty; don't worry, as a substantial portion of the salt is carried away with the buttermilk when the liquid separates from the butter. The finished butter should have a well-balanced flavor; however, the salt can always be adjusted to taste. For baking purposes, reducing or omitting the salt is recommended.

Scoop the cold thickened cream into the chilled bowl and begin whipping with the electric mixer or stand mixer on high speed. Using a stand mixer, it will take about 7 minutes for a stiff, grainy-appearing texture to form. From there it will begin to clump as the buttermilk separates from the butter. Total churning time is about 9 to 10 minutes. Using an electric rotary mixer, it will take about 12 to 14 minutes for a stiff, grainy-appearing texture to form. From there it will begin to clump as the buttermilk separates from the butter. Total churning time is about 15 to 17 minutes. This requires patience - but it will turn into butter.

Tips: When using a stand mixer, drape a kitchen towel over the mixing bowl while processing to protect from excessive splashing when the buttermilk begins to separate from the butter solids. When using a handheld rotary mixer, occasionally scrape the sides towards the bottom of the bowl with a flexible spatula as the mixture is whipped.

Press the butter to one side of the bowl with a spatula or the back of a spoon and then pour off the buttermilk (about ½ cup). The buttermilk can be discarded if you wish, but I enjoy drinking it - it's rich, tangy, salty and delicious.

Transfer and pack the solid butter into a container. As the butter is packed down, a small amount of residual buttermilk will rise to the top of the container; simply pour this off. Store the butter in the refrigerator until ready to use. The butter will stay fresh for several weeks. It can also be stored in the freezer for up to 3 months.

Tip: The butter will be quite solid and hard after refrigeration; simply let it sit out at room temperature to soften before using.

Better Butter

Better Butter is a superior tasting, palm oil-free alternative to dairy butter and commercial dairy and non-dairy margarine. This recipe produces a buttery spread that looks like, tastes like and melts like dairy butter or margarine and can be used in any recipe, including baking, as you would dairy butter or margarine. Better Butter will brown and burn when exposed to high heat and therefore should not be used for high-heat sautéing; it works best with low to medium heat.

The best kitchen appliance for emulsifying the ingredients is an immersion blender. A food processor will also work. The ingredients can also be emulsified using a standard or high-speed blender; however, retrieving the thick spread from around the blades can be difficult. This recipe yields about 2 cups.

Ingredients

- 1 cup **refined** coconut oil, melted (not virgin coconut oil)
- ⅓ cup neutral vegetable oil
- ⅔ cup plain unsweetened soymilk or almond milk
- 4 tsp/20 ml liquid soy lecithin or liquid sunflower lecithin;
  or 24 grams soy or sunflower lecithin powder (about 2 T plus 2 tsp);
  or 24 grams soy or sunflower lecithin granules ground into a fine powder
- 1 tsp organic sugar
- ½ tsp lactic acid powder (or 1 tsp raw apple cider vinegar and 1 tsp fresh lemon juice)
- ¼ tsp to 1 tsp fine sea salt or kosher salt, according to taste
- 1 tsp nutritional yeast flakes
- ½ tsp guar gum, sodium alginate or xanthan gum

Sunflower lecithin can be substituted for the soy lecithin for those who prefer a soy-free butter. However, sunflower lecithin lacks the rich golden hue of soy lecithin, so expect a color variation.

Soy lecithin powder, lactic acid powder, and guar gum, sodium alginate and xanthan gum are all available from ModernistPantry.com and other online retailers such as Amazon.com.

Preparation

You will need a 2-cup minimum food storage container with a lid to store the butter. If you prefer, the butter can be shaped in a flexible silicone form, or divided into several forms, and released after hardening.

Pour 1 cup of the melted coconut oil into a 2-cup measuring cup or other suitable container with a pouring "lip". Add the neutral vegetable oil to the coconut oil and set aside.

Immersion Blender Method

Add the remaining ingredients to a 4-cup glass measuring cup or heavy glass/ceramic bowl. Insert the immersion blender and process the mixture for about 15 seconds. With the immersion blender running on high speed, begin slowly pouring the mixed oils into the blending cup or bowl. Move the blender up and down and side to side as you add the oils. Continue blending until the mixture is emulsified and thick. Transfer to a sealable container.

If soymilk was used as a base, cover the container and refrigerate until solid (if using one or several silicone molds, cover with plastic wrap). The butter can also be stored in the freezer for to 3 months. To release the butter from a form, simply wiggle the sides a bit to loosen and then press out onto a plate.

If almond milk was used as a base, cover and freeze until solid (if using one or several silicone molds, cover with plastic wrap). Once frozen, place the butter in the refrigerator until thawed before using; or it can be stored in the freezer for up to 3 months. To release the butter from a form, simply wiggle the sides a bit to loosen and then press out onto a plate.

Food Processor Method

Add the remaining ingredients to the processor and turn on the processor. Now begin to slowly pour the mixed oils into the mixture through the food chute. Continue to process until the mixture is emulsified and thick. Transfer to a sealable container.

If soymilk was used as a base, cover the container and refrigerate until solid (if using one or several silicone molds, cover with plastic wrap). The butter can also be stored in the freezer for to 3 months. To release the butter from a form, simply wiggle the sides a bit to loosen and then press out onto a plate.

If almond milk was used as a base, cover and freeze until solid (if using one or several silicone molds, cover with plastic wrap). Once frozen, place the butter in the refrigerator until thawed before using; or it can be stored in the freezer for up to 3 months. To release the butter from a form, simply wiggle the sides a bit to loosen and then press out onto a plate.

Seasoned Butter

Seasoned Butter is a blend of non-dairy butter or margarine and specially selected herbs and spices. It's wonderful for sautéing and adding a flavorful crust to pan-seared meat analogues. It's also excellent for topping potatoes, corn on the cob, cooked grains and cooked vegetables.

Ingredients

- ½ cup non-dairy butter or margarine, softened to room temperature
- 1 T fresh lemon juice
- 1 tsp Worcestershire Sauce (page 27) or commercial vegan equivalent
- ½ tsp onion powder
- ½ tsp garlic powder
- ¼ tsp coarse ground black pepper
- ¼ tsp sweet paprika
- ¼ tsp fine sea salt or kosher salt
- 2 tsp minced fresh herbs of your choice (optional)

Preparation

Mash all ingredients together in a bowl. Refrigerate in a covered container until ready to use.

Black Garlic Truffle Butter

Black garlic is a slow-roasted and fermented form of garlic. It possesses a unique combination of molasses-like sweetness and tangy garlic undertones with a tender, creamy texture similar to soft dried fruit. Truffle oil has deep, earthy, mushroom undertones. This rich butter is superb for pan-browning beaf. It's also superb as a spread for crackers or toasted bread. Try topping with non-dairy parmesan for a uniquely different garlic bread; or drizzle the melted butter over freshly popped popcorn, sprinkle with sea salt and toss well. Black garlic and truffle oil can be found in gourmet and specialty food markets or purchased online.

Ingredients

- ½ cup non-dairy butter or margarine, softened to room temperature
- 1 head black garlic, peeled and mashed
- 1 tsp black or white truffle oil (optional)
- sea salt or kosher salt, to taste (optional)

Preparation

With a fork, mash the ingredients together in a small bowl. Cover and refrigerate until ready to use.

Honee Butter

Melted honee butter is superb for basting meat analogues when grilling to keep them moist and tender; or try brushing a little melted honee butter over fried chikun. Also serve on toast, warm rolls, scones, corn bread, waffles, pancakes, etc.

Ingredients

- ½ cup non-dairy butter or margarine, chilled
- 3 T organic raw agave syrup
- 1 T real maple syrup

Preparation

Whip the ingredients with an electric beater until fluffy. Transfer to a sealable container and chill to re-firm until ready to use.

Yomage
(Cultured Yogurt Cheese)

"Yomage" is a hybrid of the word "yogurt" and "fromage", the French word for "cheese". While straining yogurt to create a simple soft cheese is not new, pressing the strained yogurt to condense it and firm it takes this simple concept to a new level. Yomage has a rich, dense cream cheese texture and a tangy, cultured yogurt flavor. In its simplest form, it makes a wonderful alternative to dairy cream cheese. It's also rich in probiotics which helps maintain optimum digestive health.

The basic pressed cheese can also be used as a base for blending with any variety of low-moisture seasonings to create different flavors. Blending with refined coconut oil will create a firmer texture. The cheese can also be rolled into balls with herbs to create Labneh, a Middle Eastern treat (recipe follows).

A box-shaped tofu press is required for pressing the whey from the yogurt. The TofuXpress® works exceptionally well for this purpose because of its compact design which can be placed into the refrigerator while pressing. A tofu box, used for preparing tofu at home, can also be used but will require a heavy weight to be placed on top of the box for pressing. This can be bulky and will require additional room in your refrigerator.

The cheese is very simple to prepare but it does require 2 to 3 days of pressing and drying before it is ready to use, so plan ahead. This is a fairly high-yield cheese; in other words, 2 cups of yogurt will yield about 8 ounces of cheese.

Ingredients

- 2 cups prepared Greek-style (strained) Cultured Yogurt (page 194)
- fine sea salt or kosher salt to taste

Special Supplies Needed

- fine muslin or high-quality double-layered cheesecloth
- a tofu press, such as a TofuXpress®, or a tofu box with a heavy weight for pressing
- paper towels

Preparation

Line the tofu press or tofu box with the muslin or cheesecloth, leaving plenty of excess hanging over the sides.

Add the yogurt and spread evenly with a spoon. Fold the cloth over the yogurt and put the spring plate in place. Place the box into the refrigerator and allow pressing for about 8 hours to sufficiently remove most of the whey. Pour off the whey occasionally while pressing if you have the opportunity.

Chef's note: Reserve the whey and chill in a sealed container if desired. I have discovered that the whey is a superb gluten-free alternative to rejuvelac for preparing the cultured cashew-based cheeses in my Non-Dairy Evolution Cookbook. It's also good as a probiotic drink for maintaining intestinal health. The whey will stay fresh and active for about 5 days. Over time it will turn to vinegar and is no longer useable.

Remove the cheese from the box and unwrap. The pressed yogurt will still be quite moist at this point. Transfer the cheese to several layers of paper towels and fold securely in the towels. Place into a food storage bag and refrigerate a minimum of 8 hours. Repeat the process again until the cheese is quite firm and semi-dry.

When sufficiently firm and semi-dry, transfer the cheese to a mixing bowl and mash with a fork; season with salt to taste and mix well. At this point, dried herbs, spices or other dry seasonings can be stirred directly into the cheese if desired. Small amounts of wine or vinegar reductions, or fruit syrup reductions, can also be swirled into the cheese.

The cheese can then be transferred to a serving container and served in that manner; or the cheese can be formed into a log.

To shape the cheese into a log, place the mixture onto a sheet of plastic wrap. Fold the wrap over the cheese and using your fingers, shape the cheese into a log using the wrap as a barrier. Don't worry about shaping perfection, as the wrap will shape the log when rolled and the ends twisted tight.

Continue to roll the cheese in the wrap, twist the ends tightly and place the cheese in the refrigerator for several hours to re-firm. To serve, simply remove the wrap, roll the cheese in fresh or dried herbs and/or spices if desired, and place on a serving plate.

Labneh

Labneh is a popular Middle Eastern dish, often served for breakfast. It consists of straining yogurt to create a thick cheese which is then formed into balls, and sometimes covered with herbs or spices and stored in olive oil. A popular sandwich in the Middle East consists of labneh, mint, thyme, and olive on pita bread.

Ingredients

- Yomage cheese (see preceding recipe)
- za'atar (a Middle Eastern spice blend)
- sprig or two fresh thyme
- a strip or two of fresh lemon peel
- 1 clove garlic, lightly crushed
- good quality extra-virgin olive oil

Preparation

Roll the Yomage into walnut-sized balls and then dust with the za'atar spice blend. Place into a storage container, add the garlic clove, rosemary sprig and lemon peel. Add enough olive oil to cover completely. Seal and chill to blend flavors.

Hard Parmesano

Hard Parmesano is a hard block cheese with a Parmesan cheese-like flavor. Hard Parmesano can be finely shredded or grated and is ideal for topping or garnishing your favorite Italian foods. Homemade cultured yogurt is used as a base for this cheese. The yogurt imparts a natural lactic aroma and flavor that cannot be achieved using commercial lactic acid powder alone. However, for the sake of convenience, you can replace the yogurt with 1 cup plain unsweetened soymilk or almond milk and ¾ tsp lactic acid powder.

The cheese is very easy to prepare since it does not rely upon stirring or emulsification during cooking. It also does not rely upon gels for firming and is therefore free of carrageenan or agar.

For this recipe you will need a flexible silicone form/cheese mold that will hold a minimum of 2 cups liquid. Avoid using a metal or Pyrex™ container because the cheese will be very hard after chilling and difficult to remove. Do not use a plastic form as it will not be able to withstand the cooking temperature. You will also need a cooking pot with a lid and an open steamer basket for steaming the cheese in the mold.

Ingredients

- 1 cup unstrained Cultured Yogurt (page 194), room temperature
- 1 cup unmodified potato starch or corn starch
- ½ cup **refined** coconut oil, melted (not virgin coconut oil)
- 2 T nutritional yeast flakes
- 2 T mellow white miso paste
- 1 and ½ tsp sea salt or kosher salt
- 1 tsp onion powder
- 2 tsp white wine vinegar or raw apple cider vinegar
- ½ tsp garlic powder

Preparation

Add water to the pot, but just below the bottom of the steamer basket, and place over high heat to bring the water to a boil.

Process all ingredients in a blender until very smooth. Transfer to the cheese mold and rap the mold gently on a firm surface to settle the mixture and remove any air bubbles.

Place the uncovered mold into the steamer basket. Place the basket into the pot over the boiling water and cover with the lid. Set a timer for 30 minutes.

Remove the mold from the steamer and allow to cool about 1 hour. The cheese mixture will have a puffy appearance but will settle upon cooling. If steam condensation has settled on the surface of the cheese, very gently blot with a paper towel to remove it. The cheese will be very sticky until fully chilled and hardened. It will also have a translucent appearance but will become opaque upon cooling. Cover the mold with plastic wrap and refrigerate until hardened. This will take upwards of 12 hours with 24 hours being ideal.

Remove the cheese from the flexible silicone form and shred or grate as desired. Wrap in a dry paper towel and store airtight in the refrigerator. Change the towel every few days. Stored properly, the cheese will last for weeks.

Halloumi

Halloumi is an unripened cheese which originated in Cyprus and is eaten throughout the Middle East. It has a tangy, salty flavor which can be likened to feta cheese. Halloumi is often used in cooking and can be fried until brown without melting, owing to its higher-than-normal melting point. This makes it an excellent cheese for frying or grilling (like Greek Saganaki). It can be served on its own as an appetizer; served with vegetables; or used as an ingredient in salads. Cypriots like eating halloumi with watermelon in the warm months.

Homemade cultured yogurt is used as a base for this cheese. The yogurt imparts a natural lactic aroma and flavor that cannot be achieved using commercial lactic acid powder alone. However, for the sake of convenience, you can replace the yogurt with 1 cup plain unsweetened soymilk or almond milk and ¾ tsp lactic acid powder.

The cheese is very easy to prepare since it does not rely upon stirring or emulsification during cooking. It also does not rely upon gels for firming and is therefore free of carrageenan or agar. Please note that while this cheese will soften when heated, it will not melt completely, which makes it particularly well suited for this application.

For this recipe you will need a flexible silicone form/cheese mold that will hold a minimum of 2 cups liquid. Avoid using a metal or Pyrex™ container because the cheese will be very hard after chilling and difficult to remove. Do not use a plastic form as it will not be able to withstand the cooking temperature. You will also need a cooking pot with a lid and an open steamer basket for steaming the cheese in the mold.

Ingredients

- 1 cup unstrained Cultured Yogurt (page 194), room temperature
- 1 cup unmodified potato starch or corn starch
- ¼ cup **refined** coconut oil, melted (not virgin coconut oil)
- ¼ cup neutral vegetable oil
- 2 and ½ tsp sea salt or kosher salt
- 2 tsp white wine vinegar or raw apple cider vinegar

Preparation

Add water to the pot, but just below the bottom of the steamer basket, and place over high heat to bring the water to a boil.

Process all ingredients in a blender until very smooth.

Transfer to the silicone cheese mold and rap the mold gently on a firm surface to settle the mixture and remove any air bubbles.

Place the uncovered mold into the steamer basket. Place the basket into the pot over the boiling water and cover with the lid. Set a timer for 30 minutes.

Remove the mold from the steamer and allow to cool about 1 hour. The cheese mixture will have a puffy appearance but will settle upon cooling. If steam condensation has settled on the surface of the cheese, very gently blot with a paper towel to remove it. The cheese will be very sticky until fully chilled and hardened. It will also have a translucent appearance but will become opaque upon cooling. Cover the mold with plastic wrap and refrigerate until hardened. This will take upwards of 12 hours with 24 hours being ideal.

Remove the cheese from the flexible silicone form and slice and use as desired. Wrap in a dry paper towel and store airtight in the refrigerator. Change the towel every few days. Stored properly, the cheese will last for weeks.

To grill, lightly oil a non-stick grill pan or skillet and grill over medium-high heat until golden brown. Store airtight in the refrigerator.

Shreddin' Chedda'

Shreddin' Chedda' is a hard block cheese with a golden hue and a mild cheddar cheese-like flavor. It is a cold-snacking cheese, which means that although it will soften when heated, it will not melt completely. Shreddin' Chedda' can be finely shredded and is ideal for topping foods where complete melting is not necessary or desirable, such as for topping tacos, taco salads or tostadas. Slices are wonderful for serving on crackers or cold sandwiches.

Homemade cultured yogurt is used as a base for this cheese. The yogurt imparts a natural lactic aroma and flavor that cannot be achieved using commercial lactic acid powder alone. However, for the sake of convenience, you can replace the yogurt with 1 cup plain unsweetened soymilk or almond milk and ¾ tsp lactic acid powder.

The cheese is very easy to prepare since it does not rely upon stirring or emulsification during cooking. It also does not rely upon gels for firming and is therefore free of carrageenan or agar.

The cheese can also be seasoned with additional ingredients to create interesting flavor combinations. Ingredients might include a tablespoon or two of wine, prepared horseradish or hot pepper sauce blended into the liquid mixture before cooking. Dried herbs, spices and low moisture ingredients such as crushed peppercorns, chopped sun-dried tomato, dehydrated garlic, dried minced onion, red pepper flakes, etc., can be stirred into the mixture just before cooking.

For this recipe you will need a flexible silicone form/cheese mold that will hold a minimum of 2 cups liquid. Avoid using a metal or Pyrex™ container because the cheese will be very hard after chilling and difficult to remove. Do not use a plastic form as it will not be able to withstand the cooking temperature. You will also need a cooking pot with a lid and an open steamer basket for steaming the cheese in the mold.

Ingredients

- 1 cup unstrained Cultured Yogurt (page 194), room temperature
- 1 cup unmodified potato starch or corn starch
- ¼ cup **refined** coconut oil, melted (not virgin coconut oil)
- ¼ cup neutral vegetable oil
- ¼ cup nutritional yeast flakes
- 2 T mellow white miso paste

- 12 drops natural orange food color (e.g., India Tree™) or 1 T tomato paste or 2 tsp tomato powder
- 2 tsp raw apple cider vinegar
- 1 and ½ tsp sea salt or kosher salt
- 1 tsp onion powder
- ½ tsp dry ground mustard
- optional additional low-moisture ingredients (2 T maximum)

Preparation

Add water to the pot, but just below the bottom of the steamer basket, and place over high heat to bring the water to a boil.

Process all ingredients, including any optional wet flavor ingredients such as prepared horseradish or red pepper sauce, in a blender until very smooth. If adding herbs and spices, stir them in after blending.

Transfer to the cheese mold and rap the mold gently on a firm surface to settle the mixture and remove any air bubbles.

Place the uncovered mold into the steamer basket. Place the basket into the pot over the boiling water and cover with the lid. Set a timer for 30 minutes.

Remove the mold from the steamer and allow to cool about 1 hour. The cheese mixture will have a puffy appearance but will settle upon cooling. If steam condensation has settled on the surface of the cheese, very gently blot with a paper towel to remove it. The cheese will be very sticky until fully chilled and hardened. It will also have a translucent appearance but will become opaque upon cooling. Cover the mold with plastic wrap and refrigerate until hardened. This will take upwards of 12 hours with 24 hours being ideal.

Remove the cheese from the flexible silicone form and slice or shred as desired. Wrap in a dry paper towel and store airtight in the refrigerator. Change the towel every few days. Stored properly, the cheese will last for weeks.

Grated Sunflower Parmesan
Soy and Nut-Free

Sunflower Parmesan is prepared from sunflower seeds and is a tasty alternative to grated dairy Parmesan for those abstaining from dairy products and for those who cannot consume tree nuts due to allergies. It has a granular texture reminiscent of a grated dairy Parmesan cheese. While it lacks the pungent aroma of its dairy counterparts, it has its own unique identity and savory flavor.

Since Sunflower Parmesan is made with miso, a fermented product or "living" food, the flavor will continue to develop during refrigeration. It will also stay fresh in the refrigerator for several weeks or more if stored in an airtight container. Lactic acid powder can be purchased from ModernistPantry.com and other online retailers such as Amazon.com.

Ingredients

- 3 oz natural raw sunflower seeds
- ¼ cup white rice flour
- 1 T nutritional yeast flakes
- 1 T chickpea miso paste
- ¾ tsp lactic acid powder
- ½ tsp fine sea salt or kosher salt
- ½ tsp onion powder
- ¼ tsp garlic powder

Preparation

Place the sunflower seeds and the white rice flour into a food processor and process until finely ground, about 1 minute. Add the remaining ingredients and continue to process until well-blended. Refrigerate in a covered container until ready to use.

Roquefort Cheese

Dairy Roquefort is a type of bleu cheese. It has a tangy, salty flavor and a distinct, pungent aroma created by the mold Penicillium roqueforti, as well as by specially cultivated bacteria. This mold is also responsible for the blue-green "veins" within the cheese.

Although it lacks some of the pungency of dairy Roquefort normally created by the Penicillium mold, non-dairy Roquefort has a sharp, tangy flavor, a semi-firm crumbly texture and the characteristic blue-green "veins".

A high-powered blender is required for efficient processing. This recipe yields about 12 ounces.

Chef's Note: If you have access to a non-dairy source of Penicillium roqueforti culture, you can experiment with creating the blue-green veining yourself. To do this, culture the cheese as directed. Before chilling the cheese, sprinkle the surface with a small amount of the live mold culture. Place the cheese in roomy storage container, seal and refrigerate. In about a week, the surface of the cheese should be coated with the blue-green mold. Simply fold that into the cheese to create the "veins". Repack into another container lined with plastic wrap to shape the cheese and chill until firm.

Ingredients

- 1 and ½ cup (7.5 oz/213 grams) raw cashews
- ½ cup **refined** coconut oil, melted but not hot (not virgin coconut oil)
- ¼ cup sauerkraut juice (preferably live)
- 1 T mellow white miso paste
- 1 tsp fine sea salt or kosher salt
- ½ tsp onion powder
- ¼ tsp garlic powder
- contents of 2 vegan probiotic capsules*
- ¼ tsp blue-green algae powder (optional for the veining)
- ¼ tsp kelp powder (optional for the veining)

*If possible, choose vegan probiotic capsules that offer several strains of Lactobacillus bacteria, as well as beneficial Streptococcus thermophilus and Bifidobacterium strains. This will create a more complex cultured cheese flavor than using Lactobacillus acidophilus alone.

Preparation

Soak the cashews for a minimum of 8 hours with enough filtered/purified water to cover (refrigeration is not needed unless soaking time exceeds 8 hours). Drain the cashews, discarding the soaking water, and add them to the blender with the coconut oil, sauerkraut juice, miso, salt, onion powder and garlic powder.

Process the contents beginning on low-speed to break down the cashews. Gradually increase to high-speed and process until completely smooth. The mixture will be very thick, so stop to scrape down the sides of the blender and push the mixture down into the blades as necessary. Use a tamper tool if provided with your blender to keep the mixture turning in the blades.

Add the contents of the probiotic capsules and process briefly until blended.

Transfer the mixture to a clean container with a lid, cover and let the cheese culture at room temperature for 48 to 72 hours (warmer weather will accelerate the culturing process, so taste-test after 48 hours for the proper sharpness). The cheese will develop an "airy" texture during culturing. This is caused by the release of carbon dioxide gas during fermentation and is perfectly normal.

After culturing, remove the lid and stir the cheese until creamy. Mix the algae and kelp powder together and then dot the surface of the cheese in several places with the powder. Now fold (rather than stir) the cheese over a few times to create swirls of blue-green color. Scoop the cheese into another clean container lined with plastic wrap. The plastic wrap will help lift the cheese from the form after chilling and ripening. Pack the cheese into the container and smooth the surface with the back of a spoon. Cover with a lid or plastic wrap and refrigerate for 72 hours.

After 72 hours, lift the cheese from the form and remove the plastic wrap. The cheese is now ready to slice or crumble as needed. Store tightly wrapped in plastic wrap or a food storage bag. The cheese will become firmer, crumblier and the flavor will continue to develop as the cheese ages. Do not freeze.

Chunky Roquefort Dressing

This tangy non-dairy bleu cheese dressing tastes remarkably like commercial dairy Roquefort dressing. This dressing is also excellent when served as a dip for crudités (assorted sliced raw vegetables).

Ingredients

- 4 oz Roquefort Cheese (see preceding recipe)
- 1 cup No-Eggy Mayo (page 263)
- 3 T Instant Sour Cream (page 176) or Cultured Sour Cream (page 177)
- 2 T plain unsweetened non-dairy milk, or more to adjust consistency
- ¼ tsp coarse ground black pepper, or more to taste
- ¼ tsp fine sea salt or kosher salt, or more to taste
- ¼ tsp Worcestershire Sauce (page 27) or commercial vegan equivalent

Preparation

Add ½ of the crumbled Roquefort and the remaining ingredients to a food processor or blender and process the contents until smooth. If you wish to thin the consistency, add small amounts of non-dairy milk until the desired consistency is achieved; season with additional salt and pepper to taste. Transfer to a covered container and stir in the remaining crumbled Roquefort. Seal the container and refrigerate until chilled before using.

Camembrie

Camembrie is inspired by the French dairy cheeses Camembert and Brie. It is a soft, spreadable table cheese with a rich, creamy and buttery flavor. This cheese obtains its rich, cultured flavor from the homemade cultured soy or almond milk yogurt used as one of its base ingredients.

Tapioca flour is used to mimic the exterior white mold bloom; however, if you can obtain a dairy-free version of the mold culture Penicillium candidum, an actual mold rind can be produced on this cheese as it ages. This mold culture provides an authentic Brie/Camembert flavor and aroma. At the time of this writing, I have only found one vegan source for this mold culture in Europe, at www.cashewbert.com, but not in the U.S.

Camembrie is excellent when served at room temperature with fresh fruit and crackers or it can be baked "en croûte" (wrapped in flaky puff pastry with optional toppings and baked until melted).

For this recipe you will need a round, flexible silicone cheese mold to shape the wheel of cheese. Alternately, a round glass, ceramic, metal or BPA-free plastic container which will hold a minimum of 2 cups liquid will also work. If using a rigid form such as glass, ceramic or metal, line the form with plastic wrap with excess hanging over the edge. This will help lift the cheese from the form after firming.

Ingredients

- 1 cup plain unsweetened soymilk or almond milk
- ½ cup unstrained Cultured Yogurt (page 194)
- ¼ cup tapioca flour
- 1 T nutritional yeast flakes
- 1 T mellow white miso paste
- 1 and ¼ tsp kappa carrageenan
- 1 tsp fine sea salt or kosher salt
- ¼ tsp truffle oil (optional)
- ½ cup **refined** coconut oil, melted (not virgin coconut oil)

Set aside an additional 2 T tapioca flour for the mold bloom unless you will be using the *Penicillium candidum* mold culture for a true mold rind.

Preparation

Process all ingredients except for the melted coconut oil in a blender until smooth. Add the coconut oil and pulse once or twice only to blend in the oil.

Transfer to a medium stainless-steel saucepan (avoid non-stick pans). Place over medium-low heat. Stir continuously with a flexible spatula until the mixture is steaming hot, thickened and just beginning to bubble in spots. This may take several minutes, so be patient. Do not increase the heat to speed up the process as this can cause the emulsion to break.

Transfer immediately to the cheese form lined with plastic wrap.

Note: This cheese is dependent upon complete emulsification of the refined coconut oil with the milk mixture during cooking. Should the oil begin to separate from the milk once it has already emulsified (blended together), remove the saucepan from the heat immediately and beat vigorously with the spatula until emulsified, then pour the mixture into the form. If that doesn't work, blitz the mixture with an immersion blender until emulsified and then transfer to the form.

Let the cheese cool about 20 minutes and then refrigerate uncovered for a minimum of 8 hours. This will allow the surface of the cheese to dry slightly while firming in the refrigerator.

To remove the cheese from the container after firming, place a plate over the top of the form and invert, shaking gently. Peel away the plastic wrap and discard. Handle the cheese carefully as it will be soft and rather sticky.

For Imitation Mold Rind

Generously dust the cheese on all sides with tapioca flour. This will help dry the exterior, reduce stickiness and imitate the "mold bloom". Set the cheese on a parchment-lined plate or baker's cooling rack with the driest side on the bottom (the side that was exposed to air while refrigerating). Place the cheese in the refrigerator to air-dry for an additional 8 hours. This will help create a soft "rind".

Let the cheese come to room temperature before serving. Store the cheese in the refrigerator in a food storage bag or securely wrapped in plastic. Consume within 2 weeks.

For Authentic Mold Rind

Gently rub about ¼ tsp of the *Penicillium candidum* mold culture over the cheese. Place the cheese into a cheese culturing box, or a roomy storage container lined with a piece of parchment paper. Seal the container and refrigerate until a thin layer of mold completely covers the exposed surface of the cheese, about 1 week. Don't over-culture; if the mold rind gets too thick it will develop an unappealing gray color and peel away from the cheese.

Let the cheese come to room temperature before serving. Store the cheese in the refrigerator in a food storage bag or securely wrapped in plastic. Consume within 1 week after producing the mold rind.

Melty Mozzarella

Melty Mozzarella is a firm block cheese with a mild lactic acidity and neutral flavor. Its texture is remarkably similar to low-moisture dairy mozzarella, which makes it excellent for fine shredding and melting in many recipes. Kappa carrageenan and lactic acid powder can be purchased from ModernistPantry.com and other online retailers such as Amazon.com.

For this recipe you will need a glass, ceramic, metal or BPA-free plastic container which will hold a minimum of 2 cups liquid; this will act as the form to shape the cheese.

Ingredients

- ¾ tsp lactic acid powder or 1 T fresh lemon juice
- 1 and ½ cup (360 ml) plain unsweetened soymilk or almond milk, room temperature
- ¼ cup tapioca flour/starch
- 1 T kappa carrageenan (sorry, no substitutes)
- 1 and ½ tsp fine sea salt or kosher salt
- ½ cup **refined** coconut oil, melted (not virgin coconut oil)

Preparation

Measure the lactic acid or lemon juice into a small dish and set aside.

Process the remaining ingredients except for the coconut oil in a blender until smooth. Add the melted coconut oil and pulse once or twice only to blend in the oil.

Transfer the mixture to a medium stainless-steel saucepan (avoid non-stick pans). Place over medium-low heat. Stir slowly and continuously with a sturdy but flexible silicone spatula until the mixture heats and lumps begin to appear. This may take several minutes, so be patient. Do not increase the heat to speed up the process as this can cause the emulsion to break.

Once the lumps begin to appear, increase stirring speed incrementally until the mixture is steaming hot and all lumps have disappeared. Cooking is complete when the cheese is thick, stretchy and glossy, like melted cheese. Remove from the heat.

Fold in the lactic acid powder or lemon juice and then whip with the spatula to blend completely. Transfer immediately to the cheese form. Rap the form sharply on the work surface to settle the cheese. It's not necessary to smooth the surface perfectly.

Note: This cheese is dependent upon complete emulsification of the refined coconut oil with the milk mixture during cooking. Should the oil begin to separate from the milk once it has already emulsified (blended together), remove the saucepan from the heat immediately and beat vigorously with the spatula until emulsified, then fold in the lactic acid or lemon juice and pour the mixture into the form. If that doesn't work, blitz the mixture with an immersion blender until emulsified and then transfer to the form.

Let the cheese cool about 30 minutes and then cover with plastic wrap and refrigerate until completely form and set, about 8 hours. Remove from the form, wrap the cheese in several layers of paper towels to absorb moisture and place in a sealable food storage bag. Chill for 24 hours before shredding and using in your favorite recipes. Store the cheese wrapped in a dry paper towel in the food storage bag in the refrigerator. Change the paper towel every couple of days. Shelf life is 10 days to 2 weeks when stored properly.

Crock Beer Cheese

Crock Beer Cheese is a spreadable sharp non-dairy cheddar enhanced with the flavor of beer. The beer is first reduced to eliminate the alcohol and a good portion of the water thus concentrating its flavor (the beer flavor is not a primary note in the cheese but rather contributes to the overall flavor profile). To spice things up, ground cayenne pepper can be added before cooking the cheese. For a robust cheese, prepared horseradish can be mixed into the cheese after it has set.

Crock Beer Cheese is superb for spreading on crackers, hard or soft pretzels or chunks of crusty bread. It can be melted on sandwiches or used in any application where spreadable sharp cheddar might be used.

Any heat-proof container that will hold a minimum of 2 cups liquid will suffice for chilling and setting the cheese. Kappa carrageenan and lactic acid powder can be purchased from ModernistPantry.com and other online retailers such as Amazon.com.

Ingredients

- 1 bottle (12 oz) beer of your choice, alcoholic or non-alcoholic (please note that dark beers will darken the cheese)
- 1 T raw apple cider vinegar
- ½ tsp lactic acid powder or 2 tsp fresh lemon juice
- ½ cup **refined** coconut oil, melted (not virgin coconut oil)
- 1 cup plain unsweetened soymilk or almond milk
- ¼ cup tapioca flour
- ¼ cup nutritional yeast flakes
- 2 T mellow white miso paste
- 12 drops natural orange food color (e.g., India Tree™) or 1 T tomato paste or 2 tsp tomato powder
- 2 tsp kappa carrageenan
- 1 tsp fine sea salt or kosher salt
- 1 tsp dry ground mustard
- ½ tsp onion powder
- ½ tsp garlic powder
- optional: ¼ tsp ground cayenne pepper, or more to taste
- optional: 1 T prepared horseradish (not creamed) for stirring into the cheese after cooking and chilling

Preparation

First, gather all ingredients. Combine the vinegar with the lactic acid powder or lemon juice in a small dish and set aside near your cooking area. The acid mixture will be added to the cheese mixture after cooking.

In a medium stainless-steel saucepan (avoid non-stick for this recipe), bring the beer to a simmer. Watch carefully while heating, as the beer will foam excessively and possibly boil over if brought to a vigorous boil. Skim and discard any excess foam. Simmer until reduced, about 15 minutes. Let the mixture cool until warm. Measure ⅓ cup and discard any remainder.

Transfer the beer reduction to a blender. Add the soymilk or almond milk with the remaining ingredients (except for the optional horseradish). Do not add the coconut oil or acid to the blender. Process the contents until smooth, stopping as necessary to dislodge any dry powder from the sides of the blender with a flexible spatula.

Now add the coconut oil (but not the acid) to the blender and pulse the mixture once or twice only to disperse the oil but not completely blend. This is important. After pulsing, pour the mixture into the saucepan and place over medium-low heat.

Cook, stirring almost constantly. As the mixture heats, it will begin to form lumps. Continue cooking and stirring until the mixture is hot and smooth and beginning to bubble.

Add the acid mixture to the cooked cheese and stir vigorously until blended. Transfer the cheese mixture to a minimum 2-cup container to set.

Cover with plastic wrap and chill for a minimum of 6 hours. After chilling, transfer the set cheese to a mixing bowl and mash and stir thoroughly with a fork until smooth. Stir in the optional prepared horseradish. Transfer to a crock or other suitable container and chill until ready to serve.

Jarlsberg Cheese Melt

Jarlsberg shares flavor similarities with Swiss cheese and can best be described as mild, buttery and nutty with a hint of sweetness. Do not omit the ground coriander, even though only a small amount is needed, as it is essential to the flavor of this melt. This recipe yields about 1 cup of melted cheese.

Ingredients

- ¾ cup plain unsweetened soymilk or almond milk
- ¼ cup neutral vegetable oil
- 3 T tapioca flour
- 1 T nutritional yeast flakes
- 1 T dry sherry or dry white wine*
- 1 T mellow white miso paste
- ½ T (1 and ½ tsp) sesame tahini
- ¼ tsp fine sea salt or kosher salt
- ¼ tsp guar gum, sodium alginate or xanthan gum
- ¼ tsp ground coriander

The sherry or wine can be omitted for health or ethical reasons, but this will alter the flavor profile.

Preparation

In a small saucepan, vigorously whisk together the ingredients until smooth. Cook the mixture over medium-low heat, stirring slowly and continually with a flexible spatula. As the mixture thickens and curdles (forms lumps), begin stirring vigorously until the curds disappear and the cheese becomes very thick, smooth and glossy. Set aside until ready to use in the recipe.

Golden Cheese Melt

The golden cheese melt can best be described as having a very mild cheddar-like flavor, similar to Colby cheese. It is also excellent as a spread for grilled cheese sandwiches. This recipe yields about 1 cup of melted cheese.

Ingredients

- ¾ cup plain unsweetened soymilk or almond milk
- ¼ cup neutral vegetable oil
- 3 T tapioca starch
- 2 T nutritional yeast flakes
- 1 T mellow white miso paste
- 12 drops natural orange food color (e.g., India Tree™) or 1 T tomato paste or 2 tsp tomato powder
- ½ tsp fine sea salt or kosher salt
- ¼ tsp dry ground mustard
- ¼ tsp onion powder
- ¼ tsp guar gum or xanthan gum

Preparation

In a small saucepan, vigorously whisk together the ingredients until smooth (a blender can also be used to efficiently combine the ingredients). Cook the mixture over medium-low heat, stirring slowly and continually with a flexible spatula. The golden color will develop as the mixture cooks.

As the mixture thickens and curdles (forms lumps), begin stirring vigorously until the curds disappear and the cheese becomes very thick, smooth and glossy. Keep warm over low heat, stirring occasionally, until ready to use. For a spreadable consistency, remove from the heat and allow the melt to thicken.

Monterey Jack Cheese Melt

This popular mild white cheese can be used for a variety of Spanish and Mexican inspired dishes and is excellent as a spread for grilled cheese sandwiches. This recipe yields about 1 cup of melted cheese.

Ingredients

- ¾ cup plain unsweetened soymilk or almond milk
- ¼ cup neutral vegetable oil
- 3 T tapioca flour
- 1 T nutritional yeast flakes
- ½ tsp plus a pinch of fine sea salt or kosher salt
- ½ tsp raw apple cider vinegar
- ¼ tsp lactic acid powder or 1 tsp fresh lemon juice
- ¼ tsp guar gum, sodium alginate or xanthan gum

Preparation

In a small saucepan, vigorously whisk together the ingredients until smooth. Cook the mixture over medium-low heat, stirring slowly and continually with a flexible spatula.

As the mixture thickens and curdles (forms lumps), begin stirring vigorously until the curds disappear and the cheese becomes very thick, smooth and glossy. Keep warm over low heat, stirring occasionally, until ready to use. For a spreadable consistency, remove from the heat and allow the melt to thicken.

Beer Cheese Sauce

Beer cheese sauce is a sharp, non-dairy cheddar sauce enhanced with the flavor of beer. The beer is first reduced to eliminate the alcohol and a good portion of the water thus concentrating its flavor (the beer flavor is not a primary note in the sauce but rather contributes to the overall flavor profile). For a zesty sauce, prepared horseradish can be added when blending the sauce before cooking. To spice things up, ground cayenne pepper can be added too.

Beer cheese sauce is superb for dipping hard or soft pretzels or chunks of crusty bread. It can be used as a topping for hot sandwiches or pasta, or for any application where a tangy cheddar sauce might be used.

Ingredients

- 1 bottle (12 oz) beer of your choice, alcoholic or non-alcoholic (please note that dark beers will darken the sauce)
- 1 and ¼ cup plain unsweetened soymilk or almond milk
- 5 T tapioca flour
- ¼ cup nutritional yeast flakes
- ¼ cup neutral vegetable oil
- 2 T mellow white miso paste
- 12 drops natural orange food color (e.g., India Tree™) or 1 T tomato paste or 2 tsp tomato powder
- 1 T raw apple cider vinegar
- 1 tsp dry ground mustard
- 1 tsp fine sea salt or kosher salt
- ½ tsp lactic acid powder (available from ModernistPantry.com and other online sources) or 2 tsp fresh lemon juice
- ½ tsp onion powder
- ½ tsp garlic powder
- optional: 1 T prepared horseradish (not creamed)
- optional: ¼ tsp ground cayenne pepper, or more to taste

Preparation

In a medium saucepan, bring the beer to a simmer. Watch carefully while heating, as the beer will foam excessively and possibly boil over if brought to a vigorous boil. Skim and discard any excess foam. Simmer until reduced, about 15 minutes. Let the mixture cool until warm. Measure ½ cup and discard any remainder (if any).

Transfer the beer reduction to a blender. Add the remaining ingredients and process until smooth and then transfer the blended mixture back to the saucepan.

Place the saucepan over medium-low heat. Stir slowly and continually with a flexible spatula until the mixture becomes bubbly, thickened and glossy. Reduce the heat to low to keep warm until ready to serve or keep warm in a mini crock pot or heated chafing dish, stirring occasionally.

Cheddar and Sour Cream Seasoning Powder

This cheesy, creamy and mildly tangy seasoning powder was created specifically for dusting pre-salted potato chips and popcorn. For unsalted chips and popcorn, consider increasing and even doubling the amount of salt in the recipe. Freeze-dried minced chives can be added for a "loaded baked potato" flavor. This recipe yields about 1 cup of seasoning.

Ingredients

- ¾ cup nutritional yeast flakes
- ¼ cup soymilk powder (do not use soy protein powder or soy flour)
- 3 T tomato powder
- 2 T onion powder
- 4 tsp fine sea salt or kosher salt, or more to taste
- 1 and ½ tsp lactic acid powder (available from ModernistPantry.com)
- ½ tsp dry ground mustard
- ⅛ tsp garlic powder

Preparation

Process the ingredients in a dry blender until finely powdered. Store the seasoning blend in an airtight container at room temperature in a cool, dry place for up to 6 months (but you'll never keep it around that long!)

To season a large bag of commercial potato chips, open the bag and add about 3 tablespoons of seasoning. Close the bag tightly and gently shake and turn to distribute the seasoning. Open the bag and enjoy.

Alternately, add the seasoning powder to a shaker dispenser and season your favorite foods and snacks according to taste.

Loaded Baked Potato Variation

Process the ingredients in a dry blender until finely powdered. Add 1 tablespoon freeze-dried minced chives and process again until the chives are reduced to small particles but not completely powdered. Season the chips as directed above.

Breakfast and Brunch

Introduction to Gentle Chef Vegan Eggz Essentials

Gentle Chef Vegan Eggz Essentials is used in this chapter to create remarkably realistic simulations of cooked eggs. It's also used in several recipes in this cookbook to function in a similar manner as eggs. Vegan Eggz Essentials is 100% plant-based, egg-free, dairy-free, nut-free and gluten-free and contains no nutritional value of its own other than dietary fiber.

Vegan Eggz Essentials is not an egg replacer or complete mix like other commercial egg replacer products on the market. The product consists of 2 special ingredients portioned and sealed in their own individual pouches (labeled "Essentials A" and "Essentials B") and sold in one convenient package.

These two ingredients are then used in recipes with other ingredients to simulate eggs or function like eggs in cooking (a good analogy would be lactic acid and kappa carrageenan used in non-dairy cheesemaking; they're not a complete mix, but rather two ingredients which make the cheese recipe work).

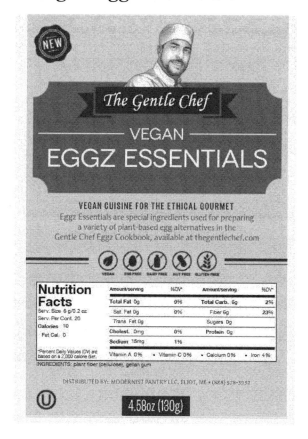

The recipes in this chapter using Vegan Eggz Essentials are the result of my quest to create home-prepared egg alternatives that have the appearance, flavor and texture of real eggs but which can also be cooked like real eggs. The exciting thing about these alternatives is that they are easily prepared using soymilk or almond milk and can be customized for different culinary purposes.

Eggz mixtures prepared with Vegan Eggz Essentials can be blended in advance (up to 1 week) and cooked at your convenience. The eggz mixtures can also be used to replace the functionality of real eggs as a binder in some cooking applications. However, the eggz mixtures are not formulated to act as an egg replacer in baked goods (breads, cakes, muffins, etc.), or in other recipes that rely on the protein structure of eggs to create lift (such as soufflés), since their chemical and structural composition is not the same as real eggs. For baked goods you may want to experiment with aquafaba, commercial egg replacers or other ingredients such as flaxseed emulsion, applesauce and bananas.

Tofu-based egg alternative recipes are also included in this cookbook for variety. Tofu is a good source of concentrated and complete plant protein, so it is always a good option. In some cases, tofu is required for functionality of the recipes. Please be aware that if you have an allergy to soy, you will only be able to prepare the recipes which use almond milk as an option.

Ingredients in the eggz recipes such as Vegan Eggz Essentials, soymilk or almond milk, tofu, water, starch and food gums are functional ingredients, so for the best results do not modify the amounts suggested or substitute with other ingredients; and always use accurate level measurements. Other ingredients such as nutritional yeast, kala namak, paprika and turmeric are flavoring and coloring ingredients and they can be adjusted to suit your taste - but please try the recommended measurements first.

Regarding nutrition: The new egg alternatives offered in this cookbook are not nutritionally equivalent to real eggs. They were created for those who miss the appearance, flavor and texture of real eggs and not as a primary protein source in the plant-based diet. The protein and other nutritional values of these alternatives are equivalent to the nutritional value of the primary ingredients being used, whether soymilk, almond milk or tofu. Be sure to consume a wholesome, varied and balanced plant-based diet in order to satisfy your nutritional requirements.

To prepare the eggz mixtures, Eggz Essentials A and B are blended with soymilk or almond milk and other ingredients as specified in the recipes for flavor and/or color. A mini blender or immersion blender is required for blending the eggz mixtures, since the Essentials do not mix readily in cool liquids simply by stirring. For dishes such as quiches and frittatas, starch is added to assist setting of the eggz mixtures when cooked. This is necessary when non-dairy cheeses, cooked vegetables and/or meat analogues are combined with the eggz mixtures before cooking.

As a general rule for simulating cooked eggs, the blended eggz mixtures need to chill and thicken before cooking. This allows the ingredients in the Essentials to absorb the water in the soymilk or almond milk, which in turn ensures proper setting of the eggz mixtures when cooked. However, the eggz mixtures do not require chilling when used for some cooking applications, such as eggz-dipping and breading. Please follow the recommendations in the individual recipes.

Will other non-dairy milks work in the recipes? Possibly, but experiment at your own risk. Plain unsweetened soymilk and almond milk, either homemade or commercial, are recommended because of their higher protein content and lower starch content than other plant milks. Other commercial plant milks are almost always sweetened and are usually loaded with additives for homogenization and mouthfeel. Cashew milk thickens significantly when heated and this may cause an adverse effect in the eggz texture.

Remember to keep your expectations realistic because these recipes can only mimic eggs to a certain degree. If you expect exact replicas, you are setting yourself up for disappointment. Creating high quality plant-based egg alternatives is a complex art and there is no doubt that I have many discoveries to make in the future. I've just begun exploring the potential of the Vegan Eggz Essentials. The recipes will continue to evolve as I continue to learn, so expect revisions in future cookbooks.

Vegan Eggz Essentials is my first product sold under The Gentle Chef label and is solely available by mail order through ModernistPantry.com. The product can be shipped worldwide.

Scrambled Eggz

Cooked scrambled eggz bear a remarkable resemblance to real cook scrambled eggs - with no tofu required. The eggz mixture consists of Gentle Chef Vegan Eggz Essentials blended with soymilk or almond milk and other ingredients for flavor and color and the mixture is cooked just as you would real beaten eggs.

The scrambled eggz mixture needs to be blended and refrigerated for a minimum of 2 hours for proper setting when cooked, so plan accordingly. For breakfast preparation convenience, blend and chill the eggz mixture the night before.

Please note that the scrambled eggz mixture is only intended for preparing scrambled eggz and omelets and as a binder in some cooked foods. The formula needs to be customized for eggz quiches and frittatas (page 249).

The scramble mixture will not work as an egg replacer in baked goods (breads, cakes, muffins, etc.), or in other recipes that rely on the protein structure of eggs to create lift (such as soufflés). For baked goods you may want to experiment with aquafaba, commercial egg replacers, flaxseed emulsion, bananas or applesauce.

After the eggz have set, try folding in some shredded non-dairy cheese that melts before serving; or blend in one of the cheese melts featured in this cookbook. If desired, top with sautéed vegetables; chopped herbs; or slices of fresh avocado and salsa. For a classic American breakfast, serve with hash browns, vegan bacon or sausages and whole grain toast with non-dairy butter. This recipe yields about 4 servings.

Ingredients

- 2 cups (480 ml) plain unsweetened soymilk or almond milk
- 2 T nutritional yeast flakes
- 2 T (8 grams) Eggz Essentials A
- 2 tsp (5 grams) Eggz Essentials B
- ¾ tsp kala namak (Himalayan black salt)
- scant ¼ tsp paprika
- scant ¼ tsp ground turmeric

Preparation

Add the eggz ingredients to a blender and process for 20 seconds (a mini-blender is ideal for this purpose). An immersion blender can also be used. The mixture will be pale in color (the "egg" color will develop when the mixture is cooked). Resist adding more turmeric or paprika as this will create a very unnatural finished color appearance. Please note that the raw mixture will be thicker than real beaten eggs.

Transfer the mixture to a sealable container and chill for a minimum of 2 hours. This is essential in order for the mixture to set properly when cooked. The blended mixture can be stored in the refrigerator for up to 1 week and then used to prepare scrambles at your convenience. After chilling, the mixture will be quite thick and somewhat gelatinous. It will also separate after extended chilling. So, before using stir vigorously to loosen and/or recombine the mixture and also break up any air bubbles that formed during blending. If the mixture has been chilled for extended periods, let it warm up to room temperature a bit. This will also help loosen the mixture and improve flow.

Mist a non-stick skillet with cooking oil or melt a tablespoon or two of non-dairy butter or margarine over medium-low gas flame (electric stoves may require a higher setting to heat the skillet sufficiently). Spread the desired amount of the eggz mixture in the skillet (½ cup for each serving). Increase the heat to medium.

After thirty seconds, push against the edge of the mixture with a flexible spatula to test for setting. If still liquid check again in thirty seconds. Once the mixture begins to set, push and fold the edges in towards the center with a flexible spatula. Break up the mixture with the edge of the spatula and continue to fold and cook until the eggz are set.

Plate, season and garnish as desired; serve immediately.

Classic Tofu Scramble

I'm always looking for ways to improve the texture of certain plant-based foods and the classic tofu scramble has been one of them. When scrambled eggs are made with real eggs (or my new vegan scrambled eggz in the preceding recipe), the spatula scrapes the beaten egg mixture into curds as the eggs cook and begin to set, thus creating the scrambled texture.

So rather than crumbling the tofu (which always resembles crumbled tofu rather than scrambled eggs), the tofu is sliced into very thin fragments before cooking. This takes a couple more minutes than crumbling, but the finished texture is remarkable.

The other secret to a velvety scramble is to avoid pressing all the water out of the tofu. You'll want to press the excess water, but some water is essential for a velvety texture. After cooking, try folding in some shredded non-dairy cheese that melts before serving; or blend in one of the cheese melts featured in this cookbook.

If desired, top with sautéed vegetables; chopped herbs; or slices of fresh avocado and salsa. For a classic American breakfast, serve with skillet potatoes, vegan bacon or sausages and whole grain toast with non-dairy butter. This recipe yields 2 to 4 servings.

Ingredients

- 1 block (about 14 oz before pressing) medium to firm tofu (not silken tofu)
- ¼ cup plain unsweetened soymilk or almond milk
- non-dairy butter or margarine for cooking

Scramble Seasonings

- 2 T nutritional yeast flakes
- 1 tsp kala namak (Himalayan black salt)
- ½ tsp ground turmeric
- ½ tsp paprika
- ¼ tsp onion powder (optional)

Preparation

Drain and press the tofu on paper towels or in a tofu press to remove excess water, about 20 minutes (the goal is to retain some of the moisture in the tofu which is beneficial to the scramble texture, so avoid pressing completely). Stand the block of tofu upright on a work surface and with a knife, slice or scrape thin sheets from the block. Use a light touch and glide the knife through the surface of the tofu. Uniform sheets are unnecessary and imperfection will look more natural.

Whisk together the scramble seasonings with the non-dairy milk in a small dish and set aside.

Melt 2 tablespoons non-dairy butter or margarine in a non-stick skillet over low heat. Add the seasoned milk mixture and whisk until smooth.

Add the thinly sliced sheets of tofu and "scramble" (push, lift and fold the contents of the skillet with a spatula; don't mash) until the tofu is evenly coated with the seasoning mixture.

Increase the heat to medium and continue to gently push and fold the mixture. It will take a minute or two for the tofu to begin absorbing the color from the seasoning mixture. Pushing and folding will usually break up solid sheets into natural looking "curds" but use the edge of the spatula if necessary. Cook until the mixture is heated through, the color is evenly dispersed and the tofu resembles scrambled eggs. Plate, season and garnish as desired. Serve immediately.

Broken Yolx

Broken Yolx is a rich, liquid egg yolk alternative that remarkably resembles lightly-cooked egg yolk. It's superb for drizzling over cooked eggz whites or silken tofu to create a "broken yolk" effect; or used to create a liquid "egg yolk" center in oven-cooked eggz, poached eggz and shirred eggz. It's also wonderful for dipping toast, vegan bacun or sausage.

This recipe yields about 1 cup. The recipe can be doubled if desired and stored in the refrigerator for up to 7 days and then reheated at your convenience. For whole yolx, please refer to the following recipe on page 230.

Ingredients

- 2 T nutritional yeast flakes
- ¾ tsp sodium alginate, guar gum or xanthan gum
- ½ tsp ground turmeric
- ¼ tsp kala namak (Himalayan black salt)
- 4 drops natural orange food color (e.g., India Tree™) or ½ tsp paprika
- 2 T vegan butter or margarine
- ½ cup water
- ½ cup plain unsweetened soymilk or almond milk

Preparation

In a small dish, combine the nutritional yeast, alginate or gum, turmeric, kala namak and optional paprika.

In a small saucepan, melt the butter or margarine over low heat. Whisk in the mixed dry ingredients to create a paste. If using natural food color instead of paprika, add the drops at this time.

In small increments, whisk in the water and milk until smooth. Increase the heat to medium-low and stir occasionally until the mixture is heated through. Reduce the heat to low to keep warm until ready to serve, stirring occasionally.

Whole Yolx

This recipe produces delicate spheres filled with a golden liquid egg yolk alternative which remarkably resembles whole egg yolks. While the ingredients for the whole yolx mixture appear identical to the Broken Yolx sauce, sodium alginate is required for this technique to work successfully and cannot be replaced with other food gums such as guar gum or xanthan gum.

The relatively simple process for creating the spheres is known as "spherification", a popular technique in modern gastronomy. The sodium alginate in the yolx mixture reacts with the calcium chloride in the water bath to create the delicate edible membrane which contains the liquid yolx. Whole yolx are intended to remain in a liquid state and will not cook firm like real egg yolks.

Whole yolx are ideal for creating an authentic egg appearance, texture and flavor in skillet-cooked, oven-cooked and poached eggz. Although simple and straightforward, the technique requires a little practice and patience for mastery. Any remaining whole yolx liquid not used for creating the spheres can be gently heated in a small saucepan and used as an extra dipping sauce; or the remaining liquid can be refrigerated for up to 1 week in a sealable container and used to create additional whole yolx at your convenience. Simply stir the thickened mixture thoroughly before using.

The spheres require a minimum of 5 minutes firming time in the activation bath before using, so plan cooking the eggz accordingly. For convenience, the spheres can be prepared a maximum of 1 hour in advance and left in the rinsing bath until ready to use. While this recipe and technique may seem daunting at first, it's actually very easy and will become second nature with practice. Once mastered, the yolx can be made quickly.

Ingredients for the Yolx Mixture

- 2 T nutritional yeast flakes
- ¾ tsp sodium alginate
  (specific for spherification; no substitutions)
- ½ tsp ground turmeric
- ½ tsp kala namak (Himalayan black salt)
- 4 drops natural orange food color (e.g., India Tree™)
  or ½ tsp paprika
- 2 T non-dairy butter or margarine
- ½ cup water
- ½ cup plain unsweetened soymilk or almond milk

Ingredients for the Activation Bath

- 2 cups water
- 1 tsp calcium chloride granules

Special Supplies Needed

- whisk
- 2 shallow bowls that hold 2 cups water each
- a rounded tablespoon
- a small slotted spoon; or a spherification spoon

Spherification Spoon

Preparation

In a small dish, combine the nutritional yeast, alginate, turmeric, kala namak and paprika (if using food color wait until the next step).

In a small saucepan, melt the butter or margarine over low heat. Immediately remove the saucepan from the heat once the butter or margarine is melted. Do not overheat.

Whisk in the mixed dry yolx ingredients to create a paste. If using natural food color instead of paprika, add the drops at this time.

In small increments, whisk in the water and milk until completely smooth. Transfer the mixture to a small measuring cup or other suitable container with a pouring "lip". The mixture will thicken upon standing.

For the activating bath, add 2 cups cool water and 1 teaspoon calcium chloride granules to one bowl and stir until dissolved. For the rinsing bath, add 2 cups cool water to a second bowl.

Hold a round tablespoon over the activation bath and pour in just enough of the yolx mixture to fill the tablespoon. Lower the tablespoon just below the surface of the activation bath. Slowly turn the tablespoon over and lift slowly from the bath to release the mixture into the solution, thus creating the sphere. Repeat to create as many spheres as desired. It's always a good idea to create extra in case a sphere breaks when handling. Allow to set for 5 minutes (10 minutes is recommended until the technique is mastered). This will create a membrane that is sturdy enough for cooking using the various eggz techniques.

Chef's Tip: If perfectly shaped spheres are a priority, any tendrils of the yolx mixture attached to the spheres can be snipped off using kitchen shears while submerged in the activation bath; the "wounds" will self-seal.

Using a spherification spoon (available from ModernistPantry.com) or slotted spoon, gently lift the spheres one at a time from the activation bath and lower into the rinsing bath. Leave in the rinsing bath until ready to use (up to 1 hour).

When ready to use in the various eggz recipes, fold a paper towel and hold in one hand. With the other hand, lift a sphere from the rinsing bath with the spherification spoon or slotted spoon and set the spoon (not the sphere) on the paper towel. This will wick away any excess water which would cause the eggz white mixture to seep liquid when cooking. Use the whole yolx in the recipes as instructed.

Chef's Tip: If the yolx membranes break too easily when handling or cooking, try increasing the activation bath time to 10 minutes. Mastery of the technique requires practice.

Firm-Set Yolx

The firm set yolx mixture is formulated to set when cooked, similar to a real egg yolk (unlike whole yolx which retain their liquid center when heated). Firm-set yolx can be used for both oven-cooked and skillet-cooked eggz.

Ingredients

- ½ cup plain unsweetened soymilk or almond milk, chilled
- 1 T non-dairy butter or margarine, melted
- 1 T nutritional yeast flakes
- 1 and ½ tsp (2 grams) Eggz Essentials A
- ½ tsp (1.25 grams) Eggz Essentials B
- ¼ tsp ground turmeric
- 2 drops natural orange food color (e.g., India Tree™) or ¼ tsp paprika
- ⅛ tsp kala namak (Himalayan black salt)

Preparation

With an immersion blender, process the yolx ingredients in a measuring cup or other suitable container until completely smooth. A mini-blender can also be used. Refrigerate the mixture for a minimum of 2 hours. Stir the mixture vigorously before using.

Bacun Grease

Bacun grease is essentially a "bacon" flavored, non-hydrogenated vegetable shortening. Use for any cooking purpose just as you would real bacon grease; store in an airtight container in the refrigerator and use within 1 year. This recipe yields 1 cup.

Ingredients

- ⅔ cup **refined** coconut oil (not virgin coconut oil), melted
- ⅓ cup neutral vegetable oil
- 2 tsp tamari, soy sauce or Bragg Liquid Aminos™
- 1 tsp dark brown sugar or real maple syrup
- ½ tsp liquid smoke
- ¼ tsp coarse ground black pepper
- ¼ tsp guar gum or xanthan gum (acts as an emulsifier and stabilizer - do not omit!)

Preparation

If using brown sugar, dissolve the brown sugar with the tamari and liquid smoke in a small dish.

Process all ingredients in a mini-blender or in a heavy measuring cup using an immersion blender until emulsified. Transfer to a sealable container and freeze until hardened and then transfer to the refrigerator for storage until ready to use.

Eggz Whites

Cooked eggz whites bear a remarkable resemblance in appearance, flavor and texture to real cooked egg whites. Eggz whites can be used for preparing skillet-cooked eggz, oven-cooked eggz, poached eggz, shirred eggz and eggz white omelets. Cold-served eggz are prepared differently using agar as a setting agent; please see appropriate recipes. Eggz whites consist of Vegan Eggz Essentials blended with soymilk or almond milk, and kala namak to impart the characteristic egg-like flavor and aroma. No tofu is required.

The eggz white mixture needs to be blended and refrigerated for a minimum of 2 hours before cooking, so plan accordingly. For breakfast preparation convenience, blend and chill the eggz mixture the night before. This recipe yields 5 to 6 eggz whites (the recipe can be doubled or tripled if desired).

Please note that the eggz white mixture is only intended for preparing skillet-cooked eggz, oven-cooked eggz, poached eggz, shirred eggz and eggz white scrambles and omelets. While it will work as a binder in some cooked foods, it doesn't have the structure for creating fluffy meringues (aquafaba is recommended for meringues). It also will not work as an egg white replacer in baked goods (breads, cakes, muffins, etc.) or in other recipes that rely on the protein structure of eggs to create lift (such as soufflés). For baked goods you may want to experiment with aquafaba, commercial egg replacers or flaxseed emulsion.

Ingredients

- 1 cup plain unsweetened soymilk or almond milk
- 1 T (4 grams) Eggz Essentials A
- 1 tsp (2.5 grams) Eggz Essentials B
- ½ tsp kala namak (Himalayan black salt)

Preparation

Add the ingredients to a blender and process for 20 seconds (a mini-blender is ideal for this purpose). An immersion blender can also be used. Please note that the raw eggz white mixture will be opaque and much creamier, thicker and less slimy than real egg whites.

Transfer the mixture to a sealable container and chill for a minimum of 2 hours. This is essential in order for the mixture to set properly when cooked. The blended mixture can be stored in the refrigerator for up to 1 week and then used at your convenience. After chilling, the mixture will be quite thick and somewhat gelatinous. Before using, stir vigorously to loosen the mixture and break up any air bubbles that formed during blending. If the mixture has been chilled for extended periods, let it warm up to room temperature a bit. This will also help loosen the mixture and improve flow.

Basic Skillet-Cooked Eggz Whites

Mist a non-stick or cast-iron skillet with cooking oil or melt 1 to 2 tablespoons bacun grease over a medium-low gas flame. If using an electric stove, a higher setting may be needed to preheat the skillet sufficiently.

Vigorously stir the chilled eggz whites to loosen the mixture and remove any air bubbles. For each eggz white, spoon 2 generous tablespoons of the mixture into the skillet. If necessary, use the back of a spoon to spread the mixture into a circular or oval shape. Increase the heat to medium and cook until the whites are firm to the touch. Flip the eggz with a flexible spatula and cook for another 10 to 15 seconds. Transfer to a serving plate and season and garnish as desired. Serve immediately.

Skillet-Cooked Eggz

Skillet-cooking is a classic method for preparing individual eggz. The eggz whites can be prepared with a whole yolx center for eggz sunnyside-up and "over-easy"; a firm-set yolx center for eggz over-hard, or simply cooked and served with a broken yolx topping. The eggz can also be cooked and basted in oil or vegan bacun grease for an authentic fried egg experience.

Ingredients

- Eggz White mixture (page 233), chilled for a minimum of 2 hours
- Broken Yolx (page 229); Whole Yolx (page 230) or Firm-Set Yolx (page 232)
- cooking oil or Bacun Grease (page 232)
- sea salt or kosher salt and coarse ground black pepper, to taste

Note: The eggz already contain salt, so season with additional salt sparingly.

Skillet-Cooked Eggz with Broken Yolx (easiest option)

Prepare the eggz white mixture and chill for a minimum of 2 hours. Prepare the broken yolx and keep warm over low heat until ready to serve.

Mist a non-stick or well-seasoned cast-iron skillet with cooking oil or melt 1 to 2 tablespoons bacun grease over a medium-low gas flame. If using an electric stove, a higher setting may be needed to preheat the skillet sufficiently.

Vigorously stir the chilled eggz whites to loosen the mixture and remove any air bubbles. For each eggz white, spoon 2 generous tablespoons of the mixture into the skillet. If necessary, use the back of a spoon to spread the mixture into a circular or oval shape. Increase the heat to medium and cook until the whites are firm to the touch.

Flip the eggz with a flexible spatula and cook for another 10 to 15 seconds. Transfer to a serving plate and top with the broken yolx mixture; season and garnish as desired. Serve immediately.

Skillet-Cooked Eggz Sunnyside-Up

Prepare the eggz white mixture and chill for a minimum of 2 hours. Prepare the whole yolx and leave in the rinsing bath until ready to use (up to 1 hour before cooking the eggz).

Mist a non-stick or well-seasoned cast-iron skillet with cooking oil or melt 1 to 2 tablespoons bacun grease over a medium-low gas flame. If using an electric stove, a higher setting may be needed to preheat the skillet sufficiently. If you wish to baste the eggz for a more authentic "fried egg" experience, use enough oil or bacun grease to create a 1/8-inch layer on the bottom of the skillet (about 1/4 cup or more depending on the size of the skillet). This will allow a sufficient amount of oil or grease for spooning over the eggz as they cook.

Vigorously stir the chilled eggz whites to loosen the mixture and remove any air bubbles. For each eggz white, spoon 2 generous tablespoons of the mixture into the skillet. If necessary, use the back of a spoon to spread the mixture into a circular or oval shape.

Working quickly, use the spherification spoon or slotted spoon to gently place one yolx in the center of each eggz white (be sure to blot the bottom of the spoon against a paper towel to wick away any excess water from the rinsing bath before adding to the eggz whites). Quickly spoon an additional teaspoon of the eggz white mixture around the perimeter base of each yolx sphere. As the whites set, this will help hold the yolx in place (but it's not a guarantee).

Increase the heat to medium and cook until the whites are firm to the touch. For fried eggz, baste with the hot oil or grease while cooking until the whites are set. Keeping a spatula level, lift the eggz from the skillet and transfer to a serving plate. This will help keep the yolx from sliding off (but it's not a guarantee). Season and garnish as desired and serve immediately.

Skillet-Cooked Eggz "Over-Easy" (no flipping required)

Prepare the eggz white mixture and chill for a minimum of 2 hours. Prepare the whole yolx and leave in the rinsing bath until ready to use (up to 1 hour before cooking the eggz).

Mist a non-stick or cast-iron skillet with cooking oil or melt 1 to 2 tablespoons bacun grease over a medium-low gas flame. If you wish to baste the eggz for a more authentic "fried egg" experience, use enough oil or bacun grease to create a ⅛-inch layer on the bottom of the skillet (about ¼ cup or more depending on the size of the skillet). This will allow a sufficient amount of oil or grease for spooning over the eggz as they cook. If using an electric stove, a higher setting may be needed to preheat the skillet sufficiently.

Vigorously stir the chilled eggz whites to loosen the mixture and remove any air bubbles. For each eggz white, spoon 2 tablespoons of the mixture into the skillet. If necessary, use the back of a spoon to spread the mixture into a circular or oval shape.

Working quickly, use the spherification spoon or slotted spoon to gently place one yolx in the center of each eggz white (be sure to blot the bottom of the spoon against a paper towel to wick away any excess water from the rinsing bath before adding to the eggz whites). Quickly spoon 2 teaspoons of the eggz white mixture over each yolx sphere.

Increase the heat to medium and cook until the whites are firm to the touch. For fried eggz, baste with the hot oil or grease while cooking until the whites are set. Keeping a spatula level, lift the eggz from the skillet and transfer to a serving plate. This will help keep the yolx from sliding off (but it's not a guarantee). Season and garnish as desired and serve immediately.

Skillet-Cooked Eggz Over-Hard

Prepare the eggz white mixture and chill for a minimum of 2 hours. Prepare the firm-set yolx mixture and chill for a minimum of 2 hours.

Mist a non-stick or well-seasoned cast-iron skillet with cooking oil or melt 1 to 2 tablespoons bacun grease over a medium-low gas flame. If using an electric stove, a higher setting may be needed to preheat the skillet sufficiently. If you wish to baste the eggz for a more authentic "fried egg" experience, use enough oil or bacun grease to create a ⅛-inch layer on the bottom of the skillet (about ¼ cup or more depending on the size of the skillet). This will allow a sufficient amount of oil or grease for spooning over the eggz as they cook.

Vigorously stir the chilled eggz whites to loosen the mixture and remove any air bubbles. For each eggz white, spoon 2 generous tablespoons of the mixture into the skillet. If necessary, use the back of a spoon to spread the mixture into a circular or oval shape.

Stir the firm-set yolx mixture vigorously. Add 1 tablespoon of the yolx mixture to the center of each white. Increase the heat to medium and cook until the whites feel firm to the touch. Flip the eggz with a flexible spatula and cook for another 10 to 15 seconds. Transfer to a serving plate; season and garnish as desired. Serve immediately.

Oven-Cooked Eggz

Oven-cooking is an easy method for preparing individual eggz. The eggz are baked in a greased muffin tin which creates their perfectly formed shape. Oven-cooked eggz make a lovely presentation when served over toast or English muffins. This cooking method is ideal for serving more than two guests, since any number of eggz can be cooked simultaneously and presented at the same time.

The eggz can be prepared with a broken yolx liquid center (simplest technique); with a whole yolx liquid center (for a more authentic, structured appearance); or with a firm-set yolx center.

Ingredients

- Eggz White mixture (page 233), chilled for a minimum of 2 hours
- Broken Yolx (page 229); Whole Yolx (page 230); or Firm-Set Yolx (page 232)
- cooking oil spray, non-dairy butter, margarine, or Bacun Grease (page 232)
- sea salt or kosher salt and coarse ground black pepper, to taste

Note: The eggz already contain salt, so season with additional salt sparingly.

Special Supplies Needed

- standard muffin tin

Preparation

Oven-Cooked Eggz with Broken Yolx

Preheat the oven to 375°F/190°C. Grease the muffin tin with non-dairy butter, margarine, cooking oil or bacun grease.

Prepare the broken yolx mixture and set aside until ready to use. Heating the mixture is not necessary. Vigorously stir the chilled eggz whites to loosen the mixture and remove any air bubbles.

For each eggz serving, spoon 2 generous tablespoons of the eggz white mixture into the tin. Place in the oven and bake for exactly 3 minutes.

Remove from the oven (caution: the muffin tin will be hot!) and spoon 1 tablespoon of the broken yolx mixture into the center of each eggz white. The yolx mixture should sink almost completely.

Spoon a small amount of the eggz white mixture (about 1 teaspoon) over any of the exposed yolx to completely cover.

Lightly mist with cooking oil; or if desired, top with ½ teaspoon butter, margarine or bacun grease. Return to the oven and bake for 10 minutes. Remove from the oven and let cool for 1 to 2 minutes. Use a spoon to gently loosen the eggz around the edges and lift from the muffin tin. Transfer to a serving plate and season and garnish as desired. Serve immediately.

Oven-Cooked Eggz with Whole Yolx

Preheat the oven to 375°F/190°C. Grease the muffin tin with non-dairy butter, margarine, cooking oil or bacun grease.

Prepare the whole yolx spheres and leave in the rinsing bath until ready to use. Vigorously stir the chilled eggz whites to loosen the mixture and remove any air bubbles.

For each eggz serving, spoon 2 generous tablespoons of the eggz white mixture into the tin. Place in the oven and bake for exactly 3 minutes and then remove from the oven (caution: the muffin tin will be hot!)

Using the spherification spoon or slotted spoon, gently place one yolx in the center of each eggz white (be sure to blot the bottom of the spoon against a paper towel to wick away any excess water from the rinsing bath before adding to the eggz whites).

Top the yolx with an additional teaspoon of the eggz white mixture. This will create a film over the yolx and prevent the membrane from drying out when exposed to the dry heat of the oven.

Lightly mist with cooking oil; or if desired, top with ½ teaspoon butter, margarine or bacun grease. Return to the oven and bake for 10 minutes. Remove from the oven and let cool for 1 to 2 minutes. Use a spoon to gently loosen the eggz around the edges and lift from the muffin tin. Plate, season and garnish as desired. Serve immediately.

Oven-Cooked Eggz with Firm-Set Yolx

Preheat the oven to 375°F/190°C. Grease the muffin tin with non-dairy butter, margarine, cooking oil or bacun grease.

Prepare the Firm-Set Yolx mixture and chill for a minimum of 2 hours before using. Vigorously stir the chilled eggz whites to loosen the mixture and remove any air bubbles.

For each eggz serving, spoon 2 generous tablespoons of the eggz white mixture into the tin. Place in the oven and bake for exactly 3 minutes. Remove from the oven (caution: the muffin tin will be hot!) and spoon 1 tablespoon of the firm-set yolx mixture into the center of each eggz white. Spoon a small amount of the eggz white mixture (1 to 2 teaspoons) over the exposed yolx to completely cover.

Lightly mist with cooking oil; or if desired, top with ½ teaspoon butter, margarine or bacun grease. Return to the oven and bake for 10 minutes.

Remove from the oven and let cool for 1 to 2 minutes. Use a spoon to gently loosen the eggz around the edges and lift from the muffin tin. Transfer to a serving plate and season and garnish as desired. Serve immediately.

Silken Tofu Eggz

Delicate slices of silken tofu are lightly seasoned with kala namak (Himalayan black salt), gently pan-seared and then topped with either broken yolx (easiest option), or whole yolx for sunnyside-up.

Ingredients

- 12 oz extra-firm **silken** tofu
- kala namak (Himalayan black salt)
- cooking oil spray
- Whole Yolx (page 230) or Broken Yolx (page 229)

Preparation

If using whole yolx, prepare the spheres and leave in the rinsing bath until ready to use (up to 1 hour before cooking the tofu eggz).

Drain any water from the silken tofu. Handle it carefully as it is very delicate and will break easily. Transfer the tofu to a work surface, turn the block on its side and slice lengthwise to create 4 even slabs. Place the slabs on a plate lined with several layers of paper towels or a lint-free kitchen towel to drain for a minimum of 20 minutes. If desired, cut each slab into a round using a 3-inch ring mold or biscuit cutter. Discard the tofu remnants or save for another recipe.

If using broken yolx, prepare the mixture while the tofu is draining and keep warm over low heat, stirring occasionally. Place a small amount of kala namak into a small dish and with a water-moistened fingertip carefully rub some of the salt over the tofu slices. If using whole yolx, scoop a shallow indentation with a spoon on one side of the tofu slice. This will help hold the yolx in place (but it's not a guarantee). Set aside.

Silken Tofu Eggz Sunnyside-Up

Mist a non-stick skillet with cooking oil spray and place over medium heat. When the skillet is hot, add the tofu slices with the indentation side down. Pan-sear until lightly golden and then flip over. Reduce the heat to medium-low.

Working quickly, use the spherification spoon or slotted spoon to gently place one yolx in the indentation of each tofu slice (be sure to blot the bottom of the spoon against a paper towel to wick away any excess water from the rinsing bath before adding to the eggz whites). Cook a few more minutes. This will allow time for the whole yolx to sufficiently heat through from contact with the tofu. Keeping a spatula level, lift the tofu eggz from the skillet and transfer to a serving plate. This will help keep the yolx from sliding off (but it's not a guarantee). Season and garnish as desired and serve immediately.

Silken Tofu Eggz with Broken Yolx (easiest option)

Mist a non-stick skillet with cooking oil spray and place over medium heat. When the skillet is hot, add the tofu slices and pan-sear until lightly golden on both sides. Transfer the slices to a serving plate and spoon a generous tablespoon of the yolx onto the center of each slice; season and garnish as desired. Pour additional sauce into individual serving cups on each plate for dipping if desired.

Huevoz Rancheroz

Huevoz Rancheroz is my vegan variation of Huevos Rancheros (Spanish for "rancher's eggs"). The basic dish consists of layers of refried beans, pinto beans or black beans, homemade chunky salsa and lightly fried corn tortillas. The layers are topped with skillet-cooked or oven-cooked eggz of your choice and garnished with sliced avocado and cilantro. Mexican rice (page 240) is a suggested accompaniment. This recipe yields 2 to 4 servings.

Ingredients

- Skillet-Cooked Eggz (page 234), Oven-Cooked Eggz (page 236) or Silken Tofu Eggz (page 238) - 1 or 2 eggz per serving
- 1 can (16 oz) pinto beans, black beans or vegetarian or fat-free refried beans
- cooking oil
- 2 corn tortillas per serving
- sliced avocado (optional)
- chopped cilantro for garnish, optional

Salsa Ingredients

- olive oil
- ½ medium onion, chopped (about ½ cup)
- 3 cloves garlic, minced
- ½ tsp sea salt or kosher salt, or more to taste
- 1 can (15 oz) diced tomatoes, preferably fire-roasted, with juice or 2 large vine-ripened tomatoes, when in season*
- 1 can (4 oz) diced mild green chilies
- 1 tsp ancho chili powder (or ½ tsp ancho and ½ tsp chipotle for a spicier sauce)
- ½ tsp ground cumin

Blanch fresh tomatoes in boiling water for 1 minute and then plunge in an ice water bath to ease removal of the skins before dicing.

Preparation

If using skillet or oven-cooked eggz, prepare the eggz white mixture and chill for a minimum of 2 hours. If using silken tofu, slice as directed and let drain for a minimum of 20 minutes prior to cooking. Season the tofu slices with kala namak.

If using broken yolx to top the eggz (easiest option), prepare as directed and set aside until ready to use. If using whole yolx, prepare them and leave in the rinsing bath until ready to use (up to 1 hour before cooking the eggz).

Next, prepare the salsa (for convenience, this can be done ahead of time, refrigerated and re-warmed prior to serving). Commercial chunky salsa can be substituted, if desired, and warmed gently in a small saucepan.

To prepare the salsa, add 2 tablespoons of cooking oil to a skillet and place over medium heat. Add the onions and ½ teaspoon salt and sauté until translucent. Add the garlic and sauté an additional minute. Add the tomatoes and any juice from the tomatoes. If you are using fresh tomatoes, chop them first and then add. Stir in the chopped green chilies and the spices. Bring to a simmer and cook for 15 to 20 minutes. Reduce heat to low to keep warm until ready to serve. Stir occasionally and season with salt to taste.

Next, warm the beans in a covered saucepan over low heat. Add a little water if necessary to loosen the refried beans.

Now prepare the tortillas. Heat the oven to its lowest setting and place serving plates in the oven to keep warm. Heat 2 tablespoons of cooking oil in a large non-stick or well-seasoned cast-iron skillet on medium high, tip and rotate the skillet to coat evenly with the oil. One by one, heat the tortillas in the skillet for a minute or two on each side until they are heated through and softened (add additional oil as necessary). Stack them on one of the warming plates in the oven to keep warm.

Cook the eggz as directed in the appropriate recipe.

To serve, spoon some of the salsa onto a warmed plate. Top with a tortilla, some beans and another tortilla. Place the eggz on top of the tortilla and spoon additional salsa around the eggz. Garnish with optional avocado slices and optional cilantro.

Mexican Rice

This recipe yields 4 to 6 servings.

Ingredients

- 2 T olive oil
- ½ medium onion, diced
- ½ red bell or sweet red pepper, diced
- ½ green bell pepper, diced
- 1 jalapeno or serrano chili, seeded and diced
- 1 (15 oz) can diced tomatoes with liquid
- 1 and ½ cup chikun simmering broth (page 41) or vegetable broth
- 1 cup jasmine rice
- 2 tsp mild chili powder
- 1 tsp dried oregano leaves
- 1 tsp onion powder
- 1 tsp ground cumin
- ½ tsp garlic powder
- ½ tsp sea salt or kosher salt

Preparation

Add the oil to a skillet with a lid and place over medium-high heat. Add the diced onion, peppers and chili pepper and sauté until softened. Add the remaining ingredients and stir well. Bring to boil and then reduce to a lazy simmer (just above low). Cover and cook 20 minutes. Uncover and continue to cook until any excess moisture is reduced. Fluff with a fork and serve.

Eggz Omelet

Fluffy and delicate eggz omelets can be filled with your choice of ingredients. For omelets, the eggz mixture needs to be blended and refrigerated for a minimum of 2 hours before cooking, so plan accordingly. For breakfast preparation convenience, blend and chill the eggz mixture the night before. This recipe yields 4 omelets.

Note: If you prefer an eggz white omelet, prepare the Eggz White mixture as directed on page 233 and use ½ cup mixture for each omelet.

Eggz Ingredients

- 2 cups (480 ml) plain unsweetened soymilk or almond milk
- 2 T (8 grams) Eggz Essentials A
- 1 T nutritional yeast flakes
- 2 tsp (5 grams) Eggz Essentials B
- ¾ tsp kala namak (Himalayan black salt)
- scant ¼ tsp paprika
- scant ¼ tsp ground turmeric
- optional: 1 tsp dried parsley, chives or other aromatic herbs of your choice

Filling Ingredients

- sautéed vegetables and/or diced vegan meats; non-dairy cheese shreds or melts

Preparation

Add the eggz ingredients to a blender and process for 20 seconds (a mini-blender is ideal for this purpose). An immersion blender can also be used. The mixture will be pale in color (the "egg" color will develop when the mixture is cooked). Resist adding more turmeric or paprika as this will create a very unnatural finished color appearance. Please note that the raw mixture will be thicker than real beaten eggs.

Transfer the mixture to a sealable container and chill for a minimum of 2 hours. This is essential in order for the mixture to set properly when cooked. The blended mixture can be stored in the refrigerator for up to 1 week and then used to prepare omelets at your convenience.

After chilling, the mixture will be quite thick and somewhat gelatinous. Before using, stir vigorously to loosen the mixture and break up any air bubbles that formed during blending. If the mixture has been chilled for extended periods, let it warm up to room temperature a bit. This will also help loosen the mixture and improve flow.

Prepare the omelet fillings and set aside. Vegetables that have high moisture content, such as mushrooms, spinach and other greens, zucchini, diced tomatoes, etc., should be sautéed until they have released most of their liquid. Transfer the vegetables and other fillings to a separate bowl and set aside. If using shredded cheese, mix the shreds with the warm filling to assist melting before filling the omelet. Prepare any garnishes and set aside.

Mist a non-stick omelet pan with cooking oil or melt a tablespoon of non-dairy butter or margarine over medium-low gas flame (electric stoves may require a higher heat setting to heat the pan sufficiently). Spread about ½ cup of the eggz mixture evenly in the pan. Let the mixture cook until the surface is just dry to the touch. With a wide flexible spatula, carefully flip the omelet over.

Top with fillings on one side of the omelet and fold the other side of the omelet over the fillings. Cover the pan with a lid and continue to cook an additional minute or two to allow any shredded cheese to melt or fillings to reheat.

Transfer to a plate and keep warm in a low oven while preparing additional omelets. Season and garnish as desired; serve immediately.

Silken Tofu Omelet

Fluffy and delicate silken tofu omelets can be filled with your choice of ingredients. The omelets are oven-baked for ease and efficiency, rather than the traditional omelet pan preparation. This also allows all omelets to be prepared at the same time.

This recipe yields two fluffy omelets, so two standard pie plates will be needed to prepare two omelets at the same time. For additional omelets, simply double or triple the recipe and use additional pie plates for each omelet (most large ovens can accommodate six pie plates with three on each rack). Alternately, a large baking sheet can be used to prepare one or two omelets or two baking sheets to prepare up to four omelets.

Eggz Ingredients

- 12 oz extra-firm silken tofu
- 3 T cornstarch or unmodified potato starch
- 1 T melted non-dairy butter or margarine
- 1 T nutritional yeast flakes
- ¾ tsp kala namak (Himalayan black salt)
- scant ¼ tsp paprika
- scant ¼ tsp ground turmeric
- optional: 1 tsp dried parsley, chives or other aromatic herbs of your choice

Filling Ingredients

- sautéed vegetables and/or diced meatless meats; non-dairy cheese shreds or melts

Preparation

Drain any water from the tofu. Slice the tofu into 4 slabs and place the slabs on a plate lined with several layers of paper towels or a lint-free kitchen towel to drain for a minimum of 20 minutes. Firmly blot the tofu with additional towels to remove as much moisture as possible. This step is very important or the omelets will not set properly.

Crumble the tofu into a food processor* and add the starch, nutritional yeast, butter or margarine, kala namak and onion powder. Process the contents until smooth and fluffy, with a texture similar to mayonnaise. Stop to scrape down the sides of the processor bowl as necessary. The ingredients will form a thick, pale cream (the egg color will develop when the mixture is cooked). Transfer the mixture to a bowl and set aside; if desired, stir in any optional dried herbs.

Preheat the oven to 375°F/190°C.

Prepare the omelet fillings and set aside. Vegetables that have a high moisture content, such as mushrooms, spinach, zucchini, diced tomatoes, etc., should be sautéed until they have released most of their liquid. Transfer the vegetables and other fillings to a separate bowl and set aside. If using shredded cheese, mix the shreds with the warm filling to assist melting before filling the omelet. Prepare any garnishes and set aside.

Pie Plate Technique

Grease each pie plate with 1 teaspoon non-dairy butter or margarine or lightly mist with cooking oil spray. Add half of the mixture (about ¾ cup) to each plate. With the back of large spoon or flexible spatula, pat and spread the mixture evenly to the interior edges of the plate. Place the pie plate(s) into the oven and bake uncovered for 10 minutes.

Test the omelets by touching the center; the center should feel dry to the touch. If it feels moist, bake an additional minute or two until just dry to the touch. Remove from the oven and spoon the filling onto one side of the omelet.

With a flexible spatula, carefully lift the opposite side of the omelet over the filling. Return the omelet(s) to the oven for 3 to 5 minutes. Slide the omelet(s) onto a serving plate and top and/or garnish as desired. Serve immediately.

Baking Sheet Technique

Grease a non-stick baking sheet with non-dairy butter or margarine or lightly mist with cooking oil spray. Spoon half of the tofu mixture onto one side of the baking sheet and spread to create a smooth, round "disc" about 8-inches in diameter. Repeat with the remaining mixture on the other side of the sheet. Place the baking sheet into the oven and bake uncovered for 10 minutes.

Test the omelets by touching the center; the center should feel dry to the touch. If it feels moist, bake an additional minute or two until just dry to the touch.

Remove from the oven and spoon the filling onto one side of the omelet. With a flexible spatula, carefully lift the opposite side of the omelet over the filling. Return the omelet(s) to the oven for 3 to 5 minutes. Slide the omelet(s) onto a serving plate and top and/or garnish as desired. Serve immediately.

Spanish Omelet

Spanish omelet is the English name for a popular Spanish dish called "Tortilla Española" or "Tortilla de Patatas", which in this case consists of an open-faced omelet made with the eggz scramble mixture, and the traditional toppings of potato, onion and parsley.

This dish is very easy to prepare since it is cooked in a 9-inch cake pan or pie plate and baked in the oven. This omelet yields 3 to 4 servings.

Eggz Ingredients

- 1 and ½ cup (360 ml) plain unsweetened soymilk or almond milk
- 4 and ½ tsp (6 grams) Eggz Essentials A
- 2 tsp nutritional yeast flakes
- 1 and ½ tsp (3.75 grams) Eggz Essentials B
- ½ tsp kala namak (Himalayan black salt)
- ⅛ tsp paprika
- ⅛ tsp ground turmeric

Skillet Ingredients

- 2 T cooking oil
- 3 average-size waxy potatoes (new, gold or red potatoes; about 1 lb), peeled and thinly sliced
- 1 medium onion, peeled and thinly sliced
- sea salt or kosher salt and coarse ground black pepper to taste
- ¼ cup fresh chopped flat leaf parsley
- cooking oil spray, for misting the omelet surface

Preparation

Add the eggz ingredients to a blender and process for 20 seconds (a mini-blender is ideal for this purpose). An immersion blender can also be used. The mixture will be pale in color (the "egg" color will develop when the mixture is cooked). Resist adding more turmeric or paprika as this will create a very unnatural finished color appearance. Please note that the raw mixture will be thicker than real beaten eggs.

Transfer the mixture to a sealable container and chill for a minimum of 2 hours. This is essential in order for the mixture to set properly when cooked. Before using, stir vigorously to loosen the mixture and break up any air bubbles that formed during blending.

To prepare the omelet, add the cooking oil to a skillet and place over medium-low heat. Add the potatoes and onions and toss to coat with the oil. Cover with a lid and cook for 20 minutes, stirring occasionally. Remove the lid, increase the heat to medium and cook until the potatoes and onions are lightly golden, tender and have released most of their moisture; season with salt and coarse ground black pepper to taste and set aside to cool.

Meanwhile, heat the oven to 375°F/190°C. Grease a 9-inch cake pan or pie plate with cooking oil.

Spread the skillet contents in the pan or plate, top with the parsley and then add the eggz mixture in an even layer. Mist with cooking oil spray to prevent the omelet surface from drying out during baking. Bake on a middle oven rack for 35 minutes or until the surface of the omelet is puffed and golden. Remove from the oven and let rest for 10 minutes. Run a table knife or narrow flexible spatula around the edges of the omelet to loosen. Invert a serving plate over the top of the pan and flip to remove the omelet. Serve immediately.

Poached Eggz

Poached eggz require an egg poacher since the eggz white mixture containing the yolx cannot be cooked directly in water. An egg poacher consists of a pan fitted with a tray insert that holds individual egg cups. Other similar methods you may be familiar with will also work (such as setting individual silicone egg cups directly into shallow boiling water).

The eggz mixture is added to the individual cups and the cups are placed into the tray insert. Water is added to the pan, and the pan is heated on the stove. When the water comes to a boil, the tray insert is placed over the water in the pan to cook the eggz. Whole yolx will provide a more structured appearance with the top of the yolx sphere peeking through the top of the poached eggz. Broken yolx will provide a less structured appearance with the broken yolx liquid center hidden within the poached eggz whites.

The results are similar to the baking technique using the muffin tin, but this method avoids heating the oven (which is ideal in the summer months).

Ingredients

- Eggz White mixture (page 233), chilled for a minimum of 2 hours
- Whole Yolx (page 230) or Broken Yolx (page 229)
- non-dairy butter, margarine or cooking oil
- sea salt or kosher salt and coarse ground black pepper, to taste

> *Note: The eggz already contain salt, so season with additional salt sparingly.*

Preparation

Prepare the eggz white mixture and chill for a minimum of 2 hours. Prepare the whole yolx and leave in the rinsing bath until ready to use (up to 1 hour before poaching the eggz).

If using broken yolx, prepare as directed and set aside until ready to use.

Whole Yolx Technique

Whole yolx will provide a more structured appearance with the top of the yolx sphere peeking through the top of the poached eggz. To prepare, set the insert tray and the eggz cups aside. Grease the eggz cups with butter, margarine or cooking oil. Fill the poaching pan half full with water and place over high heat.

Vigorously stir the chilled eggz whites to loosen the mixture and remove any air bubbles. For each poached eggz serving, spoon 2 generous tablespoons of the mixture into each eggz cup. Place the cups into the insert tray and set the tray into the pan over the boiling water. Do not cover! Cook for exactly 2 minutes.

Working quickly, use the spherification spoon or slotted spoon to gently place one yolx in the center of each eggz white (be sure to blot the bottom of the spoon against a paper towel to wick away any excess water from the rinsing bath before adding to the eggz whites).

Season the eggz with salt and pepper to taste and continue cooking uncovered for 10 minutes. After 10 minutes, cover the pan with a lid and cook for 1 minute only.

With a heatproof glove, remove the lid and the tray insert holding the eggz cups. Let the cups cool about 2 minutes. Carefully remove the poached eggz using a spoon. Plate and garnish as desired.

Broken Yolx Technique

Broken yolx will provide a less structured appearance with the broken yolx liquid center hidden within the poached eggz whites. To prepare, set the insert tray and the eggz cups aside. Grease the eggz cups with butter, margarine or cooking oil. Fill the poaching pan half full with water and place over high heat.

Vigorously stir the chilled eggz whites to loosen the mixture and remove any air bubbles. For each poached eggz serving, spoon 2 generous tablespoons of the mixture into each eggz cup. Place the cups into the insert tray and set the tray into the pan over the boiling water. Do not cover! Cook for 2 minutes.

Working quickly, spoon one tablespoon of the broken yolx mixture into the center of the eggz white mixture. Spoon a small amount (about 1 teaspoon) of additional eggz white mixture over the yolx mixture. This will help seal in the yolx mixture.

Season the eggz with salt and pepper to taste and continue cooking uncovered for 10 minutes. After 10 minutes, cover the pan with a lid and cook for 1 minute only.

With a heatproof glove, remove the lid and the tray insert holding the eggz cups. Let the cups cool about 2 minutes. Carefully remove the poached eggz using a spoon. Plate and garnish as desired.

Eggz Florentine with Mushrooms

This is my own variation of a classic brunch favorite. Toasted artisan bread or English muffins are layered with sautéed mushrooms, sliced tomato, sautéed spinach or greens and topped with poached eggz or oven-cooked eggz. The finished dish is crowned with Hollandaise sauce and garnished as desired; serves 2 to 4.

Ingredients

- 4 Poached Eggz (page 245) or Oven-Cooked Eggz (page 236)
- Classic Hollandaise Sauce (page 139)
- 2 T cooking oil
- 8 oz sliced white or cremini mushrooms
- 4 slices fresh tomato
- 8 oz fresh spinach (or try arugula, baby mustard greens or baby kale)
- 2 large slices artisan bread, cut in half or 2 English muffins, split
- coarse ground black pepper to taste
- optional garnishes: paprika, snipped chives, chopped parsley

Preparation

Prepare the eggz white mixture and chill for a minimum of 2 hours. Prepare the whole yolx and leave in the rinsing bath until ready to use (up to 1 hour before poaching the eggz). If using broken yolx, prepare as directed and set aside until ready to use.

Next, prepare the Hollandaise sauce. Reduce the heat to low to keep warm until ready to serve. Stir occasionally.

Fill the eggz cups as directed in the recipe with the eggz white mixture. Set aside in the insert tray.

Add the cooking oil to a skillet and place over medium heat. Add the mushrooms and a pinch of salt and sauté until golden. Remove to a bowl, cover to keep warm and set aside.

Next, set the poaching pan over high heat to bring the water to a boil. Do not place the eggz cups over the water yet.

Add the spinach or other greens to the same skillet used for the mushrooms and sauté over medium heat until the moisture has been removed and the spinach/greens are cooked through. Remove from the heat and set aside to keep warm in the skillet.

Place the insert tray with the eggz cups over the boiling water. Add the whole yolx or broken yolx as directed in the recipe. Cook as directed. While the eggz are poaching, toast the bread or English muffins.

To assemble: Divide the sautéed mushrooms between the toasted bread or muffin slices. Add a tomato slice on top of the mushrooms and top the tomato slice with the sautéed greens. Top the greens with the poached eggz. Spoon the Hollandaise sauce over the eggz and garnish with a dusting of paprika and ground black pepper. Serve immediately.

Shirred Eggz

Shirred Eggz refers to baked eggz with liquid yolx centers served in individual ramekins (the portion equivalent of 2 eggs per serving). The finished dish is reminiscent of soft-boiled eggs. One cup eggz white mixture will be more than enough to yield 2 servings (2 ramekins). For additional servings, simply double or triple the eggz whites recipe. This recipe is so easy to prepare and so delicious; you really must try it.

Ingredients

- Eggz White mixture (page 233), prepared and chilled for a minimum of 2 hours
- Broken Yolx (page 229)
- cooking oil spray, non-dairy butter or margarine
- sea salt or kosher salt and coarse ground black pepper, to taste
- optional garnishes, such as paprika, minced chives and chopped parsley

Note: The eggz already contain salt, so season with additional salt sparingly.

Special Supplies Needed

- 2 individual ½-cup ceramic ramekins
- baking sheet

Preparation

Preheat the oven to 375°F/190°C. Grease the ramekins with cooking oil, non-dairy butter or margarine and place on a baking sheet.

Vigorously stir the chilled eggz whites to loosen the mixture and remove any air bubbles. Spoon four generous tablespoons of the eggz white mixture into each greased ramekin. Place in the oven for exactly 3 minutes. Remove from the oven but leave the oven on.

For each ramekin, spoon 2 tablespoons of the broken yolx liquid into the center of the eggz white mixture. Spoon a small amount (about 2 teaspoons) of additional eggz white mixture over any exposed yolx mixture to completely cover. This will seal in the yolx mixture when b

Lightly mist with cooking oil; or if desired, top with ½ teaspoon butter or margarine; or try topping with a tablespoon or two of shredded non-dairy cheese that melts. Season with salt, coarse ground black pepper and a dash of paprika, if desired.

Return to the oven and bake for 15 minutes. Remove from the oven and transfer the ramekins to a serving plate. Garnish as desired and serve immediately. Non-dairy buttered toast is recommended for dipping.

Eggz Frittata and Eggz Quiche

Quiche is French in origin. Here it consists of an open-faced pastry crust filled with a savory mixture of velvety eggz custard combined with non-dairy cheese, cooked vegetables and/or meatless meats. Frittata, which is Italian in origin, is essentially a quiche without the crust.

The basic difference between the two, other than the presence or lack of crust, is that frittatas are traditionally cooked in a skillet on the stove and then finished in the oven, while a quiche is entirely oven-baked. However, in this case the frittata is also oven-baked for ease and proper setting of the eggz mixture. The eggz mixture for frittatas and quiches is customized for these applications.

For the quiche you will need a 9-inch vegan pastry/pie crust. For the frittata you will need a greased 9-inch pie plate or cake pan.

Customized Eggz Ingredients for Frittatas and Quiches

- 2 cups (480 ml) plain unsweetened soymilk or almond milk
- 2 T (8 grams) Eggz Essentials A
- 2 T cornstarch or unmodified potato starch
- 1 T nutritional yeast flakes
- 2 tsp (5 grams) Eggz Essentials B
- 1 tsp kala namak (Himalayan black salt)
- ⅛ tsp paprika
- ⅛ tsp ground turmeric

Filling Ingredients

- 1 to 1 and ½ cup cooked diced or chopped vegetables, greens and/or meatless meats of your choice (see preparation instructions)
- ½ tsp dried thyme leaves
- ¼ tsp coarse ground black pepper
- 4 oz shredded Melty Mozzarella, about 1 cup (page 217)*
- non-dairy butter, margarine or cooking oil for greasing the pan
- cooking oil spray for oiling the surface of the frittata or quiche prior to baking

*Chef's note: I recommend Melty Mozzarella for the quiche and frittata because it functions like dairy cheese, yielding a light and fluffy finished texture. Commercial non-dairy cheeses are made differently and may yield unfavorable results. Proceed at your own risk when using commercial products.

Preparation

Add the customized eggz ingredients to a blender and process for 20 seconds (a mini-blender is ideal for this purpose). An immersion blender can also be used. The mixture will be pale in color (the "egg" color will develop when the mixture is cooked). Resist adding more turmeric or paprika as this will create a very unnatural finished color appearance.

Transfer the mixture to a sealable container and chill for a minimum of 2 hours. This is essential in order for the mixture to set properly when cooked. After chilling, the mixture will be quite thick and somewhat gelatinous.

In a skillet over medium heat, sauté diced or chopped vegetables and/or greens of your choice in 2 tablespoons cooking oil until most of their moisture has been released. For meatless meats, lightly brown in the oil. It is essential that vegetables be cooked thoroughly and their excess moisture evaporated or the eggz will fail to set properly. Use no more than 1 and ½ cup cooked vegetables and/or meatless meats for the frittata filling (or the eggz may not hold the frittata together) and no more than 1 cup for the quiche filling (otherwise there may be too much combined filling for the pastry/pie crust).

Stir in the thyme and black pepper and set aside to cool.

While the skillet mixture is cooling, preheat the oven 375°F/190°C. If preparing a quiche, prebake the pastry crust for 15 minutes. For a frittata, grease the baking pan with non-dairy butter, margarine or cooking oil.

Stir the eggz mixture vigorously and add to the cooled skillet mixture. Add the shredded cheese and mix thoroughly.

For the Frittata

Transfer the combined mixture to the greased pan, smooth the surface, season with a little ground black pepper if desired and then lightly mist the surface of the frittata with cooking oil to encourage browning.

Bake uncovered on the middle rack of the oven for 45 to 50 minutes or until the surface is golden and slightly puffed. Let the frittata cool for 10 minutes before transferring to a serving plate for slicing and serving. To remove, run a table knife around the edges of the frittata to loosen from the pan. Invert a plate over the pan and flip. Place a serving plate over the frittata and flip again. Serve immediately.

If the frittata needs to be reheated, cover securely with foil and heat in the oven at 350°F/175°C for 15 to 20 minutes. Slices can also be reheated in the microwave.

For the Quiche

Spoon the combined mixture into the pre-baked pastry crust, smooth the surface, season with a little ground black pepper if desired and then lightly mist the surface of the quiche with cooking oil to encourage browning.

Bake uncovered on the middle rack of the oven for 50 to 55 minutes or until the surface is golden and slightly puffed. Let the quiche cool for 10 minutes before slicing and serving. If the quiche needs to be reheated, cover securely with foil and heat in the oven at 350°F/175°C for 15 to 20 minutes. Slices can also be reheated in the microwave.

Pancakes

Light, fluffy, eggless and dairy free. Blueberries can also be added if desired.

Ingredients

- 1 and ¼ cups all-purpose flour
- 2 tsp baking powder
- ½ tsp salt
- 1 and ½ cups soymilk or almond milk
- 2 T real maple syrup, agave syrup, brown rice syrup or organic sugar
- 2 T neutral vegetable oil
- 1 tsp real vanilla extract
- optional: 1 cup fresh blueberries (or thawed from frozen)

Preparation

If using frozen blueberries, thaw them and place on a paper towel to drain any excess liquid. Set aside.

Sift the flour, baking powder and salt into a large bowl. Mix the liquid ingredients together in a separate bowl.

Make a well in the center of the dry ingredients, and pour in the liquid ingredients. Stir thoroughly until no large lumps of flour remain (very small lumps are okay). The batter may seem a little thin - this is how it should be. If using blueberries, fold them in now.

Heat a lightly oiled griddle over medium-high heat until very hot. Drop batter by the large spoonful onto the griddle, and cook until bubbles form and the edges are dry. Flip, and cook until browned on the other side. Repeat with remaining batter. Serve with non-dairy butter or margarine and warm syrup.

French Crêpes

Crêpes are delicate, thin French pancakes which can be dressed up with sweet or savory toppings and any number of flavorful fillings. Gentle Chef Vegan Eggz Essentials are required for this recipe.

Dry Ingredients

- 1 cup all-purpose flour
- 1 T organic sugar (for dessert crêpes)
- ¼ tsp salt

Wet Ingredients

- 1 cup plain soymilk or almond milk
- ½ cup water
- 2 T non-dairy butter or margarine, melted
- 1 and ½ tsp (2 grams) Gentle Chef Vegan Eggz Essentials A
- ½ tsp (1.25 grams) Gentle Chef Vegan Eggz Essentials B

Preparation

Combine the dry ingredients in a mixing bowl.

Process the wet ingredients in a blender for 30 seconds. A mini-blender is ideal for this purpose.

Fold the wet ingredients into the dry ingredients and stir until smooth. Chill the batter for 30 minutes before proceeding.

Lightly grease a crêpe pan, griddle or frying pan with cooking oil and place over medium-high heat.

Pour or ladle about ¼ cup for a small pan or ½ cup for a large pan of the chilled batter onto the pan. Tilt the pan with a circular motion so that the batter coats the surface evenly.

Cook the crepe for about 2 minutes, until the bottom is lightly browned. Loosen with a spatula, turn and cook the other side about 1 minute. Slide onto a serving plate, cover with a paper towel to keep warm while cooking the remaining crêpes. If desired, keep warm in a low oven until ready to serve.

Eggz-Dipped Pain Perdu

Pain Perdu (literally meaning "lost bread" in French) is a plant-based reincarnation of a breakfast and brunch classic. It consists of sliced bread dipped in my special eggz batter, pan-fried until golden brown and garnished with toppings of your choice. If you don't have access to my Gentle Chef Vegan Eggz Essentials, try the following recipe for Classic Silken French Toast.

Primary Ingredients

- 6 slices of bread*
- cooking oil
- toppings of your choice, such as non-dairy butter or margarine, real maple syrup, coconut syrup, fruit syrup, jam or marmalade; or top with fruit compote and dust with organic powdered sugar

Eggz Dip Ingredients

- 1 and ½ cup plain or vanilla soymilk or almond milk
- 1 T (4 grams) Eggz Essentials A
- 1 T organic sugar, maple syrup or brown rice syrup
- 2 tsp nutritional yeast flakes
- 1 tsp (2.5 grams) Eggz Essentials B
- 1 tsp real vanilla extract
- pinch of fine sea salt or kosher salt
- optional: ½ tsp cinnamon (or try pumpkin pie spice)

Preparation

In a blender, process the eggz mixture ingredients for 20 seconds and then pour into a pie plate or wide, shallow bowl. Chilling the eggz mixture is not necessary for this technique.

Add 2 tablespoons cooking oil to a large non-stick skillet. Crumple a paper towel and wipe the oil around the skillet (reserve the oily paper towel to re-wipe the skillet in between batches of toast). Place the skillet over medium-low heat. The key is to cook the toast slowly so the eggz batter browns nicely without scorching. If the oil begins to smoke, reduce the heat.

Dip a bread slice briefly into the batter. Coat both sides but do not soak. Gently shake the slice of bread to remove excess batter. Add the bread slice to the skillet and repeat with another slice. Fry until golden brown on each side, turning with a spatula.

Tip: Mist the spatula with cooking oil so that it doesn't dislodge the eggz batter crust.

Transfer to a plate and place in a low oven while repeating the process with additional slices. Re-wipe the skillet with the oily paper towel before adding more battered bread (add a little more oil if needed).

Serve hot with a dab of non-dairy butter or margarine and the toppings of your choice.

Classic Silken French Toast

French toast is a classic breakfast and brunch favorite. My egg and dairy-free version consists of sliced bread dipped in a special silken tofu-based batter, pan-fried until golden brown and garnished with toppings of your choice.

Primary Ingredients

- 6 slices of bread*
- cooking oil
- toppings of your choice, such as non-dairy butter or margarine, real maple syrup, coconut syrup, fruit syrup, jam or marmalade; or top with fruit compote and dust with organic powdered sugar

*Bread that is a day or two old is best (but not stale). Whole grain bread has a heartier texture but I'm a traditionalist and prefer thick slices of homemade white bread.

Batter Ingredients

- 6 oz extra-firm silken tofu, drained
- ¾ cup plain or vanilla non-dairy milk
- 3 T cornstarch or unmodified potato starch
- 1 T nutritional yeast flakes
- 1 T neutral vegetable oil
- 1 T organic sugar, maple syrup or brown rice syrup
- 1 tsp real vanilla extract
- pinch of fine sea salt or kosher salt
- optional: ½ tsp cinnamon (or try pumpkin pie spice)

Preparation

Place the tofu into a blender, add the remaining batter ingredients and process until completely smooth. Pour the blender mixture into a pie plate or wide, shallow dish.

Add 2 tablespoons cooking oil to a non-stick skillet. Crumple a paper towel and wipe the oil around the skillet (reserve the oily paper towel to re-wipe the skillet in between batches of French toast). Place the skillet over medium-low heat. The key to this recipe is to cook the toast low and slow so the batter cooks through without scorching. In other words, don't use high heat.

Dip a bread slice briefly into the batter. Coat both sides but do not soak. Gently shake the slice of bread to remove excess batter. Add the bread slice to the skillet and repeat with another slice. Fry until golden brown on each side (if the toast is taking an excessively long time to brown, the heat may be too low; increase the heat slightly).

Test each piece in the center with your finger to make sure the batter is cooked through and toast has firmed up. Transfer to a plate and place in a low oven while repeating the process with additional slices. Re-wipe the skillet with the oily paper towel before adding more battered bread (add a little more oil if needed).

Serve hot with a dab of non-dairy butter or margarine and the toppings of your choice.

Belgian Waffles

Egg-free and dairy-free waffles with a crispy exterior and fluffy, tender interior. This recipe yields 4 large Belgian-style waffles.

Ingredients

- 2 cups all-purpose flour
- 2 T organic sugar
- 4 tsp baking powder
- ½ tsp sea salt or kosher salt
- 1 and ¾ cups soymilk or almond milk
- ¼ cup water
- ¼ cup non-dairy butter or margarine, melted
- 2 T neutral vegetable oil
- 2 tsp vanilla extract

Tip: For a heartier texture, use 1 and ½ cup all-purpose flour and ½ cup whole wheat flour.

Preparation

Preheat the Belgian waffle iron.

In a large mixing bowl, combine the flour, sugar, baking powder and salt.

In a bowl, whisk together the milk and water with the melted butter, oil and vanilla.

Add the wet mixture to the dry mixture and whisk just until blended (small lumps are normal and fine). Avoid overmixing or the waffles will be tough.

Spray the waffle iron with non-stick cooking spray. Ladle the mixture onto the hot waffle iron. Cook until golden brown. If necessary keep warm or reheat in a 200°F/100°C oven. Serve hot with warm syrup, or sliced strawberries and non-dairy whipped cream.

Italian Farinata/French Socca

Farinata, or socca, is a type of thin, savory, unleavened and gluten-free crêpe or flat bread made from garbanzo bean (chickpea) flour, which is also known as gram or besan flour. It originated in Genoa, Italy and later became a typical street food of the sea coast region, stretching from Nice, France to Pisa, Italy.

Farinata, or socca, is made by stirring water into a mixture of chickpea flour, seasonings and olive oil to form a loose batter. Traditionally it is cooked in an open oven; however, for this version it is cooked on the stove. It is then cut into triangle-shaped wedges and eaten. With the inclusion of the rosemary, the crêpes have a flavor reminiscent of Middle Eastern falafel and are wonderful served with hummus or baba ghannouj.

The crêpes can also be topped with cooked vegetables and/or non-dairy cheese and folded over like an omelet, and as such are ideal for those who cannot consume tofu-based omelets. It is essential to cook the vegetables so that all of their excess moisture is removed, otherwise the moisture will make the crêpes soggy. Please note that if you have issues with texture, chickpea flour is not as smooth as other flours and a slight grittiness can be detected on the tongue. This recipe yields four crêpes.

Ingredients

- 1 cup garbanzo bean (chickpea) flour
- ¾ tsp sea salt
- ½ tsp onion powder
- ½ tsp coarse ground black pepper
- ¼ tsp garlic powder
- ¼ tsp smoked paprika
- 1 and ¼ cup warm water
- 2 T olive oil
- 1 tsp fresh minced rosemary (optional)
- vegan butter or margarine for the skillet (cooking oil can be substituted but the crêpes will not brown as nicely)

Preparation

In a large bowl, whisk together the garbanzo bean (chickpea) flour, salt, onion powder, black pepper, garlic powder and paprika. Whisk in the warm water and olive oil (and optional rosemary, if desired). Cover and place in the refrigerator for a minimum of 30 minutes and up to 12 hours (the longer, the better).

In a 10-inch non-stick or well-seasoned cast-iron skillet, add 2 teaspoons butter or margarine and melt over medium heat. Use the tip of a flexible pancake spatula to spread the butter around the pan.

Pour a fourth of the batter (½ cup) into the center of the skillet. Tilt and rotate the skillet slightly to spread the batter evenly into a circular shape. Avoid spreading the batter all the way to the curve of the skillet, if possible, as this will make it easier to loosen the edges of the crêpe with the spatula and flip it over. Reduce the heat to medium-low and cook until the surface appears dry. This will take a few minutes.

Using the flexible spatula, gently loosen under the edges of the crêpe. Slide the spatula under the crêpe and quickly but carefully flip it over. Continue to cook another 30 seconds to 1 minute. Slip the spatula under the crêpe and carefully slide it onto a serving plate. Place the plate in a lightly warmed oven to keep the crêpe warm while preparing the additional crêpes.

Repeat the procedure for the additional crêpes but reduce the butter or margarine to 1 teaspoon.

Cut the crêpes into wedges and serve warm.

To serve as an "omelet"

After flipping the crêpe, top with shredded cheese or cooked vegetables and fold the crêpe in half over the toppings. If using cheese, cover with a lid, and continue to warm for a minute or two to allow the cheese to melt. Serve immediately.

Potato and Onion Latkes
(Gluten-Free)

Latkes, or potato pancakes, are commonly associated with traditional cuisines of Germany, Austria and Eastern Europe. The term "latkes" is Yiddish in origin. Most traditional recipes call for freshly grated potatoes and are mixed with egg and flour to bind them. I experimented with the freshly grated potatoes and found the pancakes to be very gummy, even after rinsing away and squeezing out the excess starch. So, I opted for canned whole new potatoes, which are already cooked until tender. They seem to work amazingly well for creating a light and crispy pancake. Of course, you can always peel and boil a pound of fresh new potatoes just until tender if you prefer. This recipe is gluten-free and yields about 8 to 10 latkes.

Ingredients

- 1 can (about 15 oz) whole new potatoes
- ½ medium onion, thinly sliced and then finely chopped (about ⅔ cup)
- 1/3 cup garbanzo bean (chickpea) flour
- 2 T plain unsweetened soymilk or almond milk
- ¾ tsp fine sea salt or kosher salt
- ½ tsp coarse ground black pepper
- cooking oil to cover the bottom of a large skillet
- garnish of your choice, such as applesauce, sour cream, chopped scallions, etc.

Preparation

Preheat oven to 250°F/120°C.

Drain the water from the potatoes. Blot them on a paper towel and then coarsely grate them on a standard cheese/vegetable grater. Place the shreds in a large bowl.

Add the remaining ingredients, mix thoroughly and let the mixture sit for 15 minutes. Form the potato mixture into golf size balls and set on a work surface.

Heat the oil in the skillet over medium-high heat until the oil begins to shimmer.

In the palm of your hand, flatten a potato ball with your other hand and shape into a patty. Gently place the patty in the hot oil and repeat with the other potato balls. Don't crowd the skillet; fry them in 2 batches of 4 at a time until golden brown and crispy, about 3 to 5 minutes per side. Handle them carefully; remember, there is no egg to bind them, so they're more delicate.

Remove them with a slotted spoon and transfer to a plate lined with paper towels to drain. Lightly salt the patties. Place in the oven to keep warm while you finish frying the remaining patties. Serve with your favorite condiment.

Corned Beaf Hash

Top the Corned Beaf Hash with Sunny-Side Ups, Eggz Over-Easy or Eggz/Tofu Scramble.

Ingredients

- 3 T non-dairy butter or margarine
- 1 small onion, finely diced (about ⅔ cup)
- 2 cloves garlic, minced (2 tsp)
- 8 oz Corned Soy Brisket Strips (page 107), drained well
- 1 can (14.5 oz) whole new potatoes or
  1 lb potatoes of choice, peeled, cut into large chunks and boiled just until tender
- sea salt or kosher salt and coarse ground black pepper to taste
- 2 T finely chopped fresh parsley

Preparation

Finely dice the potatoes and set aside. Dice the corned brisket strips or pulse in a food processor until minced. Set aside.

Melt the butter or margarine in a large non-stick or cast-iron skillet over medium heat. Add the onion and sauté until translucent. Add the garlic and sauté an additional minute.

Mix in the corned beef, potatoes and parsley. Spread out evenly over the pan. Increase the heat to medium-high and press down on the mixture with a spatula.

Do not stir the mixture. The goal is to achieve browning. After a few minutes, use the spatula to flip sections over in the skillet to brown the opposite side. Press down again with the spatula. If the mixture is sticking, add a little more butter or margarine to the pan. Continue to cook in this manner until the potatoes and the corned beef are nicely browned.

Remove from heat and salt and pepper to taste. Garnish with chopped parsley just before serving.

Maple Sage Breakfast Sausage Patties

The wonderful flavors of rubbed sage and maple syrup complement these tasty breakfast sausage patties. They're perfect served alongside scrambles, pancakes, waffles or French toast.

For this recipe, the sausage roll is pre-cooked in a pressure cooker (recommended) or oven-baked, refrigerated for a minimum of 8 hours to firm and enhance texture, and then sliced into patties and browned in a skillet. The sausage roll can also be broken into crumbles or ground in a food processor, browned in a skillet and used in your favorite recipes as desired.

Dry Ingredients

- 1 and ½ cup (225 grams) vital wheat gluten
- 2 T cornstarch or unmodified potato starch
- 2 T dried minced onion
- 1 T onion powder
- 1 tsp coarse ground black pepper

Blender Ingredients

- 1 and ¾ cups (420 ml) water
- ¼ cup tamari, soy sauce or Bragg Liquid Aminos™
- 3 T real maple syrup
- 2 T olive oil
- 1 T dry rubbed sage or 1 tsp ground sage*
- 1 tsp Aromatica (page 40) or commercial poultry seasoning
- ¾ tsp ground nutmeg
- ½ tsp sea salt or kosher salt
- ½ tsp paprika

*If using ground sage, a blender is not needed. Simply whisk together the blender ingredients.

Additional Ingredients

- 1 T minced fresh garlic (3 large cloves)

Additional Items Needed

- heavy-duty aluminum foil

Preparing the Dough

Place the trivet inside your pressure cooker and add a few cups of water. The water level should not exceed the height of the trivet. For oven-baking, preheat the oven to 350°F/175°C.

Combine the dry ingredients in a large mixing bowl.

Process the blender ingredients briefly until the sage is coarsely ground.

Stir the minced garlic into the blender mixture. Do not process once the garlic has been added.

Pour the blender mixture into the dry ingredients and combine thoroughly with a silicone spatula. Knead the dough in the bowl until it exhibits some elasticity, about 1 minute.

Tear off a sheet of foil (about 18-inches) and place it on your work surface. Place the dough directly on top.

Now, lift the edge of the foil over the dough and begin rolling into a cylinder, pinching the ends closed simultaneously while rolling. The goal is to create a cylindrical package about 3-inches in diameter. This may take practice, so be patient. Twist the ends tightly to seal, being careful not to tear the foil. Bend the twisted ends in half to lock them tight.

Wrap with an additional large sheet of foil and twist the ends tightly to completely seal the package. For oven-baking, rewrap in a third sheet of foil.

Pressure Cooking

Place the foil package on the trivet, seal the lid, close the steam valve and set the cooker on high (or the setting for cooking meat) for 1 hour and 45 minutes (with most programmable cookers, you will need to manually override the preset cooking time). After cooking, turn the cooker off and let the steam naturally release for 30 minutes. Do not release the steam valve until the 30 minutes is completed. Remove from the cooker to cool. Refrigerate the sausage roll in the foil wrapper for a minimum of 8 hours before finishing. This will firm and enhance the texture.

Oven Baking

Place the foil package directly on the middle rack of the oven and set a timer for 1 hour and 45 minutes. Remove from the oven to cool. Refrigerate the sausage roll in the foil wrapper for a minimum of 8 hours before finishing. This will firm and enhance the texture.

Slicing and Browning the Sausage

Remove the foil and recycle. Slice the sausage roll into ¼-inch thick patties. In a non-stick skillet or well-seasoned cast iron skillet, brown the patties in two tablespoons of cooking oil over medium heat. Transfer to a plate lined with paper towels to blot any excess oil before serving.

For sausage crumbles, remove the foil and recycle. Slice into 1-inch chunks. Place the chunks into a food processor and pulse to grind to desired texture. For larger crumbles, break the chunks apart with your fingers. In a skillet over medium heat, lightly brown the sausage crumbles in two tablespoons of cooking oil. Use in your favorite recipe as desired.

Chile Relleno Chimichangas

This breakfast/brunch dish is an original creation and is based upon the classic Chile Relleno; but rather than stuff the Poblano or Anaheim peppers with cheese and then batter them, the peppers are roasted and wrapped in soft tortillas with non-dairy Monterey Jack cheese melt and flash-fried in a small amount of cooking oil (rather than deep-frying in a large amount of oil).

The results are delicious and so much less greasy than the traditional dish. I chose the cheese melt over shredded block cheese since the chimichanga is flash-fried very quickly, which wouldn't give the shredded cheese enough time to melt. The cheese melt is quick and easy to make too. Try adding Scrambled Eggz or Classic Tofu Scramble (from this chapter) as a variation.

Ingredients

- 4 large Poblano or Anaheim chilies
- 4 whole wheat or white tortillas (burrito size)
- 1 recipe Monterey Jack Cheese Melt (page 221)
- Chunky Garden Vegetable Salsa (recipe follows) or salsa of your choice
- toppings and garnishing of your choice, such as diced avocado or guacamole, chopped cilantro and/or non-dairy sour cream

Items Needed

- 8 toothpicks for securing
- large skillet with ¼-inch of cooking oil

Preparation

Prepare the salsa first since it requires about 45 minutes of cooking time. If using pre-prepared salsa, skip to the next step.

Roast the chilies on a hot grill or under a broiler. Turn them occasionally until the skins are blackened and charred. When the skins of the chilies have sufficiently charred and blistered, place them on a plate and cover with foil until cool. The residual heat will steam the peppers under the foil and fully cook them through. When cool, peel the skin from the chilies (they will remove easily) and blot them with a paper towel to remove any excess moisture. Cut the peppers into strips (you will need the strips of 1 pepper per tortilla); set aside.

Prepare the cheese melt according to the directions and keep warm over low heat until ready to assemble the dish.

Next, place a tortilla directly on the stove burner set to low heat. Flip after about 15 seconds and repeat as necessary until the tortilla is heated through and is soft and pliable*.

*An alternate method for heating the tortillas is to preheat the oven to 350°F/175°C. Wrap the tortillas in aluminum foil and warm them in the oven for approximately 15 minutes. The tortillas can also be wrapped in a damp towel and warmed in the microwave for about 15 seconds; or they can be misted with a spritz of water and heated briefly in a hot non-stick or cast-iron skillet.

Place a tortilla on a work surface and place the pepper strips on top. Spread ¼ cup of the melted cheese over the peppers. Begin rolling the tortilla over the pepper/cheese mixture and fold in the sides as you roll (like wrapping a burrito or spring roll). Secure the seam of the tortilla with 2 toothpicks and repeat with the remaining tortillas.

Place the skillet with the oil over medium-high heat. When the oil begins to shimmer, fry the chimichangas until golden brown, turning with a pair of kitchen tongs. They will brown quickly, so turn frequently (it is advisable to only cook 1 or 2 at a time since they brown so quickly). Transfer to a plate lined with paper towels to drain. Remove the toothpicks.

To serve, place on a serving plate and garnish as desired. Serve with the salsa.

Chunky Garden Vegetable Salsa

Salsa is the Spanish word for "sauce". This is a cooked salsa which is served hot and is wonderful for topping a variety of Tex-Mex inspired dishes such as chimichangas, burritos and Tex-Mex tofu scrambles. Despite the inclusion of fresh jalapeno pepper, the sauce is relatively mild. To spice it up add a little chipotle chili powder or minced habanero pepper, to taste.

Ingredients

- 1 can (28 oz) whole tomatoes
- 2 T olive oil
- 1 large carrot, peeled and diced
- 1 medium onion, diced
- 2 ribs celery, diced
- 1 large jalapeno pepper, seeded and minced
- 3 cloves garlic, minced
- 2 tsp ancho chili powder or mild chili powder
- 1 tsp dried oregano
- 1 tsp ground cumin
- sea salt or kosher salt and coarse ground black pepper, to taste

Preparation

Drain the excess juice from the tomatoes (reserve for other uses) and pulse the tomatoes in a food processor until puréed but still chunky. Set aside.

Add the oil to a cooking pot and place over medium heat. Add the carrots and sauté for a few minutes. Now add the onions, celery, jalapeno and a couple pinches of salt and sauté until the onions are translucent and the vegetables have softened, about 10 minutes. Add the garlic and continue to sauté an additional minute.

Add the tomatoes and the chili powder, cumin and oregano. Season with black pepper as desired and bring the mixture to a simmer. Cover the pot and reduce the heat to low. Cook for about 45 minutes or until the carrots are very tender, stirring occasionally. Season the salsa with salt as needed and keep warm until ready to serve.

Salads and Dressings
No-Eggy Mayo

This is my signature recipe for producing an egg-free mayonnaise that rivals real egg mayonnaise in both taste and texture. It's also much less expensive than commercial egg-free mayonnaise. The ingredients are readily available in most markets and an immersion blender or food processor makes this a nearly fool-proof method of preparation.

The advantage of using a food processor is that the machine does most of the work for you. The advantage of using an immersion blender is that the mayonnaise will be thicker, yet requires less oil. The disadvantage of the immersion blender is that your hand and arm may become tired from controlling the blender. The immersion blender method also requires a little dexterity to manage blending with one hand and pouring the oil with the other hand.

I have personally used both methods many times and now favor the immersion blender method for producing the best quality mayonnaise. A standard blender is not recommended for preparing mayonnaise because once the mixture thickens, it's nearly impossible to keep it turning in the blades while adding the oil.

Sunflower, safflower, grapeseed, canola and soybean oil are the best oils for preparing this mayonnaise. Extra-virgin or virgin olive oil will add a bitter undertaste to the mayonnaise. If you wish to include olive oil, reduce the carrier oil by ½ cup and mix ½ cup olive oil into the carrier oil.

This recipe yields about 2 cups.

Note: The recipe can be reduced by half for a 1 cup portion, but an immersion blender is required for preparation. The reduced amount of soymilk and oil will not provide sufficient volume for the food processor to blend and emulsify the mixture properly.

Ingredients

- ½ cup plain soymilk, chilled
  (sorry, no substitutions; other plant milks will not emulsify properly)
- 1 T plus 1 tsp fresh lemon juice
- 1 tsp apple cider vinegar
- 2 tsp organic sugar
- 1 tsp dry ground mustard*
- ¾ to 1 tsp fine sea salt or kosher salt
- ¼ ground white pepper
- pinch of sweet paprika or cayenne pepper
- optional: pinch of kala namak (imparts an egg mayonnaise flavor)
- 1 and ½ cup neutral vegetable oil if using an immersion blender;
  or 1 and ¾ cup neutral vegetable oil if using a food processor

*Do not omit this ingredient! Dry ground mustard not only adds flavor but is a natural emulsifier due to its high content of mucilage which coats the droplets of oil, and is therefore essential to the success of this recipe.

Preparation

Measure the oil into a liquid measuring cup (ideally it should have a "lip" for pouring). Set aside.

Immersion Blender Method

Place all of the ingredients except for the oil into a 4-cup glass measuring cup or heavy glass/ceramic bowl. Insert the immersion blender and process the mixture for about 10 seconds.

Now with the immersion blender running on high speed, slowly drizzle the oil into the blending cup or bowl. Move the blender up and down and side to side as you add the oil (you can stop blending to give your arm a rest as long as you stop pouring the oil; then resume when you're ready). Continue blending until all the oil is incorporated and the mixture is emulsified and very thick. Transfer to a glass jar or plastic container and refrigerate.

Note: Because immersion blenders are so efficient at high speed blending, adding the oil all at once may be tempting when using this method and it may produce an acceptable mayonnaise. However, it won't cut down on the blending time and the mayo may not have the same "fluffy" texture or stability as it would when incorporating the oil gradually or in increments. We're not seeking acceptable results here, we're seeking exceptional results. Please note that adding the oil all at once will definitely not work when using the food processor method described below.

Food Processor Method

Place all of the ingredients except for the oil into a food processor and process the mixture for about 10 seconds.

Turn the food processor on continuous run and slowly begin to drizzle the oil into the mixture through the food chute. The addition of the oil will take about 2 minutes, so be patient and don't rush. You should begin to note a change in the consistency of the mixture after about 1 and ¼ cup of oil has been added.

Continue to slowly add the remainder of the oil. As soon as all of the oil has been incorporated, turn the processor off - the mayonnaise is finished. Transfer to a glass jar or plastic container and refrigerate.

Note: I cannot emphasize enough the importance of adding the oil slowly. If you add it too fast, the emulsion may break and revert back to a liquid.

Mediterranean Mixed Green Salad
with Pomegranate Vinaigrette

Ingredients for the Salad

- crumbled Greek Feta (page 191)
- mixed greens of your choice
- pomegranate seeds
- orange segments
- chopped walnuts, raw or lightly toasted
- sea salt or kosher salt and coarse ground black pepper to taste

Ingredients for the Dressing

- 1 and ½ cup pomegranate juice
- 1 cup olive oil
- ¼ cup champagne vinegar, white wine vinegar, rice vinegar or raw apple cider vinegar
- 2 T minced shallot or red onion
- ½ tsp sea salt or kosher salt
- ½ tsp coarse ground black pepper

Preparation

For the dressing, simmer the pomegranate juice in a small saucepan until reduced to approximately ¼ cup. Cool and chill until ready to make the dressing.

Add the pomegranate reduction and the remaining dressing ingredients to a shaker jar and shake until emulsified. Chill thoroughly. Shake the jar thoroughly again before using.

Arrange the salad ingredients on individual plates and drizzle with the dressing; season with salt and pepper to taste.

Greek Potato Salad

Potato salads tossed with red wine vinaigrette are popular in Greece. The potatoes soak up the dressing and the salad is served warm or at room temperature. The addition of capers and lemon zest impart a citrusy, salty flavor.

Ingredients

- 1 and ½ lbs small red potatoes
- sea salt or kosher salt
- 2 T red wine vinegar
- 2 T extra-virgin olive oil
- 1 tsp ground coriander
- 1 tsp fresh lemon zest
- ½ tsp coarse ground black pepper, or more to taste
- ½ cup chopped fresh flat-leaf parsley
- 2 T finely minced shallot or red onion
- 1 T capers, drained and chopped (salt-packed capers should be rinsed and drained)
- 1 T chopped fresh dill
- caperberries for garnish (optional)

Preparation

Cut the smallest red potatoes in half and cut any larger potatoes into 1-inch chunks. Place the cut potatoes into a large cooking pot and add plenty of water to cover. Add 2 teaspoons salt and bring to a boil.

Reduce the heat to a soft boil and cook the potatoes just until fork tender, about 10 to 15 minutes. Avoid overcooking. Drain thoroughly and set aside in a large mixing bowl.

In a non-reactive bowl, whisk together the vinegar, oil, coriander, lemon zest, black pepper and 1 teaspoon salt until emulsified. Pour over the potatoes in the mixing bowl.

Sprinkle in the chopped parsley, shallot or onion, capers and dill. Toss thoroughly and set aside for 20 minutes for the potatoes to absorb the dressing; season with additional salt and pepper to taste.

Serve warm or at room temperature and garnish with caperberries if desired.

Apple, Walnut and Beet Salad
with Citrus Miso Vinaigrette

This salad is a combination of earthy beets, fresh sweet apple, crunchy walnuts and peppery arugula. Mellow white miso adds plenty of umami (the Japanese word used to describe a savory flavor) to the simple citrus vinaigrette.

Dressing Ingredients

- juice of 1 fresh orange
- 2 T mellow white miso paste
- 2 T rice vinegar
- 2 tsp Dijon mustard
- 1 small shallot, minced
- 1 clove garlic, minced
- ½ cup mild salad oil, such as grapeseed, sunflower or safflower
- ½ tsp Asian red pepper sauce (such as Sriracha™)

Salad Ingredients

- 1 lb trimmed medium beets
- coarse sea salt or kosher salt and coarse ground black pepper, to taste
- 8 packed cups arugula (about 8 oz) or mixed baby greens of your choice
- 2 crisp apples, such as Granny Smith, Honeycrisp or Gala
- ½ cup walnuts, toasted and chopped

Preparation

In a shaker bottle or similar sealed container, add all dressing ingredients. Seal and shake vigorously to emulsify the dressing. The dressing will keep for about 1 week, refrigerated. Shake well to re-emulsify before using

In a large cooking pot, place the beets in plenty of water to cover. Bring to a boil, reduce to a vigorous simmer and cook until the beets can be pierced easily with a fork, about 25 minutes. Drain and set aside to cool. Peel the beets, cut them in half and then thinly slice. Arrange them on a platter or on salad plates and season with salt and pepper.

Cut the apples in half and thinly slice. Combine the slices with the arugula (or other greens) in a large mixing bowl; season with salt and pepper and toss with enough vinaigrette to lightly but sufficiently dress the greens and apples. Top the beets with the greens and apple, sprinkle with the walnuts and serve.

Island Shrymp Salad

A refreshing mixed green salad with chilled vegan shrymp, papaya, avocado, cucumber and a zesty Island-inspired dressing.

Ingredients

- 1 recipe Shrymp (page 151)
- 8 cups mixed greens of your choice
- 1 cup cubed papaya
- 1 avocado, cubed
- 1 cucumber, sliced
- ¼ cup thinly sliced scallions
- 2 T toasted pepitas (pumpkin seeds)
- 2 T chopped cilantro (optional)

Marinade and Dressing

- ½ cup neutral vegetable oil
- ¼ cup seasoned rice vinegar
- 2 T Asian chili garlic sauce
- 2 T fresh lime juice
- 2 tsp agave syrup
- 2 tsp grated lime zest
- ½ tsp ground cumin
- ½ tsp sea salt or kosher salt, or to taste

Preparation

Whisk or blend together the marinade/dressing ingredients until emulsified. Marinate the shrymp for several hours to overnight. Drain the marinade but reserve for dressing the salad.

Oil a grill pan or skillet and grill the shrymp over medium-high heat until golden. Set aside to cool.

In a mixing bowl, toss together the greens, papaya, avocado and cucumber with a portion of the dressing. Top with the grilled shrymp and drizzle with additional dressing to taste. Garnish with the scallions, pepitas and cilantro.

Three Bean Salad
with Cumin-Scented Vinaigrette

Fresh cooked green beans, shelled edamame (green soybeans), chickpeas and sliced onion are tossed with a light and refreshing cumin-scented vinaigrette.

Ingredients

- 1 lb. fresh green beans, ends trimmed
- 1 lb. froze shelled edamame (mukimame)
- 1 can (16 oz.) garbanzo beans (chickpeas), rinsed well and drained
- ½ small sweet onion, sliced paper thin
- 1 tsp cumin seeds
- ¼ cup olive oil
- 2 T white wine vinegar
- 2 T fresh lemon juice
- 1 T sesame tahini
- 1 tsp sea salt or kosher salt
- 1 handful fresh parsley
- 1 clove garlic (1 tsp minced)
- ¼ tsp cayenne pepper
- coarse ground black pepper, to taste

Preparation

Steam the green beans until tender crisp. Rinse with cold water to stop the cooking process and drain. Cook the edamame according to the package directions; rinse with cold water and drain.

Add the green beans and the edamame to a large mixing bowl. Add the thoroughly rinsed chickpeas and the sliced onion. Set aside.

In a small skillet, toast the cumin seeds over medium heat until fragrant. Place the cumin seeds in a blender with the remaining ingredients except for the black pepper and process until smooth.

Pour over the beans and gently toss to avoid breaking the green beans. Add the black pepper, to taste, and gently toss again. Chill for a minimum of 30 minutes to blend the flavors before serving.

Singapore Salad

Singapore salad is a refreshing combination of tropical fruits, cherry or grape tomatoes, cucumber and crunchy slivers of jicama with a Malaysian-inspired, oil-free, sweet and spicy chili-lime dressing. The recipe yields ½ cup dressing, which is enough for 2 servings.

Salad Ingredients

- 1 and ½ cup large diced mango
- 1 and ½ cup large diced pineapple
- 1 cup halved cherry or grape tomatoes
- ½ cucumber, peeled, seeds removed and large diced
- ½ cup peeled and julienned jicama
- sesame seeds for garnish (optional: I like to use a combination of white and black)

Dressing Ingredients

- ¼ cup pineapple, mango or orange juice (or a combination)
- ¼ cup fresh lime juice (about 2 large limes)
- 2 T light brown sugar
- 1 T finely minced sweet yellow onion
- 2 tsp tamari, soy sauce or Bragg Liquid Aminos™
- ½ tsp Thai red chili paste or Sriracha™, or more to taste
- ¼ tsp guar gum or xanthan gum

Notes: Fresh pineapple is always preferred but if canned chunk pineapple is used, the juice can be reserved for the dressing. The guar gum or xanthan gum is important to this recipe as it adds viscosity to the dressing which helps it cling to the salad.

Preparation

In a bowl, whisk together the dressing ingredients. The dressing may seem thin at first but will thicken slightly upon standing.

Toss the salad with the dressing and chill for about 15 minutes to let the flavors blend before serving. Garnish with sesame seeds if desired.

Iceberg Wedge Salad
with Chunky Roquefort Dressing

Crisp iceberg lettuce wedges are dressed with a cool and tangy Roquefort dressing and then garnished with diced tomatoes, crispy crumbled vegan bacon and additional Roquefort crumbles. If you prefer, substitute the Roquefort with the Creamy Feta Dressing (page 192) and crumbles of Greek Feta (page 191) and toasted slivered almonds or pistachios.

Ingredients

- 1 head iceberg lettuce
- Chunky Roquefort Dressing (page 214)
- ½ cup crumbled Roquefort Cheese (page 213)
- 1 vine-ripened tomato or several cherry or grape tomatoes, diced
- 1 cup cooked and crumbled vegan bacon or ½ cup slivered smokehouse almonds
- coarse ground black pepper, to taste

Preparation

Remove any loose or torn outer leaves from a head of iceberg lettuce. Cut the head into quarters, cutting from the stem end to the top of the head. Remove the tough core from each quarter but leave enough to hold the wedge together.

On each salad plate, place 1 wedge of lettuce. Drizzle bleu cheese dressing over the wedge and garnish with tomatoes, crumbled Roquefort, crumbled vegan bacon and coarse ground black pepper, to taste.

Cilantro Pepita (Pumpkin Seed) Salad Dressing

A creamy dressing with a South of the Border taste; its beautiful pale green color and fresh herbal flavor will brighten up any green salad. Anaheim green chilies are very mild; if necessary, canned green chilies can be substituted for fresh.

Ingredients

- 2 medium Anaheim chilies, roasted, peeled and seeded
- ¾ cup neutral vegetable
- ¼ cup red wine vinegar
- 5 T roasted pepitas (pumpkin seeds with shells removed), plus additional for garnishing the salad
- ¼ cup water
- 3 cloves fresh garlic (1 T minced)
- ½ tsp coarse ground black pepper, or more to taste
- ½ tsp sea salt or kosher salt, plus additional to taste as desired
- 2 bunches fresh cilantro
- 1 cup No-Eggy Mayo (page 263) or commercial vegan mayonnaise

Preparation

Place all ingredients except for the cilantro and mayonnaise into a blender. Blend approximately 10 seconds. Pack in the cilantro and continue to blend until smooth.

Add the mayo and blend briefly to combine. Season with additional salt and pepper as desired.

Pour into an airtight container and refrigerate until ready to serve. Add small amounts of additional water to thin the dressing to desired consistency, if needed.

Toss with mixed greens and salad veggies of your choice. Use additional whole pepitas to garnish the salad before serving.

Soups and Stews

Chilled Greek Garden Soup

Chilled Greek Garden Soup is a delightfully refreshing spin on the classic Greek salad. This recipe yields about 6 servings.

Soup Ingredients

- 2 cans (28 oz each) whole peeled tomatoes with liquid
- 1 large cucumber
- 1 small red onion
- 1 red bell pepper or large sweet red pepper, chopped
- 6 T extra-virgin olive oil
- 3 T red wine vinegar
- 1 T sherry vinegar or dark balsamic vinegar
- 1 tsp dried basil
- 1 tsp dried oregano
- 1 tsp sea salt or kosher salt, or more to taste
- ½ tsp coarse ground black pepper, or more to taste

Garnishes

- thinly sliced cucumber
- thinly sliced red onion
- pitted Kalamata olives, halved
- micro greens or baby greens of your choice, such as arugula
- crumbled Greek Feta (page 191)
- fresh marjoram leaves (optional)

Preparation

Thinly slice several cucumber rounds with the peel intact. Set aside for the garnish. Peel the remaining cucumber, cut in half and scrape out the seeds with a spoon. Chop the cucumber and add to a blender.

Thinly slice some of the red onion and set aside for the garnish. Chop the remaining onion and add to the blender. Add the chopped red bell pepper.

Add one can of the tomatoes with liquid to the blender. Add the olive oil, vinegars, basil, oregano, salt and pepper.

Process the mixture until smooth and transfer to a large sealable container. Add the remaining tomatoes with liquid to the blender and pulse a few times until puréed but chunky. Stir the chunky tomatoes into the soup mixture in the container; season with additional salt and pepper to taste. Cover and refrigerate until well-chilled to blend the flavors.

To serve, ladle the soup into individual bowls and top with the garnishes. Serve with toasted pita wedges if desired.

Hot and Sour Tofu Vegetable Soup

This is my own adaptation of Chinese hot and sour soup. I've eaten many versions of hot and sour soup throughout my life. Some were very good while others were very gelatinous and/or so acidic that the broth burned the back of my throat. I feel I've struck a nice balance of hot and sour and with just enough starch slurry added to create body without being gelatinous.

I broke tradition and used tender straw mushrooms rather than the tough and chewy Chinese fungus. I also replaced the bamboo shoots with bean sprouts (although you can certainly use bamboo shoots if you prefer). The tofu was shaved into fragments to resemble cooked egg. Julienned bok choy greens were added and the soup garnished with green onions and cilantro. The heat is created with a blend of ground white pepper and sambal oelek (a Southeast Asian red chili pepper sauce).

Ingredients for the Broth

- 8 cups water
- 2 large onions, peeled and quartered
- 3 ribs bok choy (white part only; reserve the greens for the soup)
- 2 large carrots, unpeeled and cut into large pieces
- ½ cup plus 2 T tamari, soy sauce or Bragg Liquid Aminos™
- ¼ cup rice vinegar
- 6 cilantro stems (reserve the leaves for garnish)
- 6 cloves garlic, minced
- 2 T nutritional yeast flakes
- 1 T mushroom powder
- 1 T grated ginger root
- 1 T dark brown sugar
- 2 tsp sambal oelek or Sriracha™
- 1 tsp ground white pepper

Ingredients for the Soup

- ½ block (about 5 oz) **pressed** firm or extra-firm tofu (not silken tofu), shaved with a sharp knife into fragments
- 1 can (15 oz) straw mushrooms, drained and halved lengthwise or 8 oz small button mushrooms, halved
- reserved bok choy greens, julienned into ribbons
- 3 green onions, white and light green parts sliced and set aside in 1 dish and the greens chopped and set aside in another dish for garnishing
- 1 and ½ cup fresh bean sprouts or 1 can (14 oz) bean sprouts, drained well
- 2 T plus 2 tsp cornstarch or unmodified potato starch dissolved in ¼ cup water
- ¼ cup chopped cilantro for garnish

Preparation

Add all broth ingredients to a large soup pot. Cover and bring to a boil. Reduce the heat to a gentle simmer and cook for 1 hour.

With a spider or slotted spoon, remove the large vegetable solids and transfer to a bowl (after the vegetables have cooled a bit, the broth collecting in the bottom of the bowl can be added back to the soup pot). Discard the broth vegetables.

Add the tofu, mushrooms, bok choy greens and green onions (white and light green parts only). Bring the soup back to a simmer, cover and cook for 30 minutes.

10 minutes before the soup is done, add the bean sprouts and stir in the starch slurry to thicken the soup (be sure the broth is simmering). Taste the soup and add salt if needed.

Ladle into individual serving bowls and garnish with the green onions and cilantro.

Cream of Brussels Sprout Soup

Ingredients

- 2 T non-dairy butter or margarine
- 4 cups chikun simmering broth (page 41) or vegetable broth
- ¼ cup dry white wine optional
- 12 oz Brussels sprouts, fresh or thawed and drained from frozen
- 1 medium onion chopped
- 1 pinch nutmeg freshly grated
- ½ tsp ground white pepper
- 1 cup Soy Cream (page 171) or Raw Cashew Milk (page 168)
- sea salt or kosher salt to taste
- chopped chives and coarse ground black pepper for garnish (optional)

Preparation

If using fresh Brussels sprouts, trim the tough stems and outer leaves. Frozen sprouts should be thawed before using.

In a large soup pot, bring the butter, broth, white wine, Brussels sprouts and onions to a rapid simmer. Immediately reduce the heat to a gentle simmer. Partially cover and cook for 30 minutes.

Transfer the mixture to a blender, cover and begin processing on low speed. Hot liquids can expand explosively if the blender is immediately run on high speed, so start on low and hold the lid on the blender with a dish towel for safety). Increase the speed to high and process until smooth.

Return the purée to the soup pot and add the nutmeg and white pepper. Stir in the heavy cashew cream. Add salt to taste. Gently cook on low heat until heated through, stirring frequently. Ladle into soup bowls and garnish with chopped chives if desired.

Thai Yellow Curry

A fragrant Thai chikun (or tofu) and vegetable stew flavored with ginger and yellow curry.

Ingredients

- 4 cups chikun simmering broth (page 41) or commercial vegan equivalent
- 2 medium russet potatoes, peeled and diced
- 1 T grated ginger
- 3 cloves garlic, chopped
- 4 tsp yellow curry powder
- 1 medium onion, peeled and chopped
- 1 large green bell pepper, chopped
- 1 can (14 oz) coconut milk (preferably full fat; not lite)
- ½ cup green peas, fresh or from frozen
- 1 can (15 oz) straw mushrooms, drained; or 6 oz sliced white mushrooms
- 2 tsp sambal oelek (chili paste) or other hot red pepper sauce, or to taste
- a few fresh or dried Thai bird's eye chilies (optional)
- sea salt or kosher salt, to taste
- 1 and ½ cup Shredded Chikun (page 47) torn into bite-size morsels; or bite-size cubes of pressed tofu
- chopped Thai basil or sweet basil for garnish (optional)
- chopped cilantro for garnish (optional)
- cooked jasmine rice for serving

Preparation

In a large soup pot, simmer the potatoes, ginger, garlic and curry powder until the potatoes are tender, about 20 minutes. Transfer to a blender and process until smooth (exercise caution when blending hot liquids; place a kitchen towel over the blender lid and begin on low speed progressing slowly to high speed).

Transfer the purée back to the soup pot. Place over medium-low heat and stir in the coconut milk.

Mist a skillet with cooking oil and sauté the onions and bell pepper over medium heat until softened. Add to the soup pot. Stir in the peas, mushrooms, sambal oelek and optional bird's eye chilies. Cover and simmer about 20 minutes or until the bell pepper is very tender.

Add the optional tofu and simmer an additional 10 minutes; season with salt to taste. If using shredded chikun, stir into the curry just before serving. Garnish with the Thai basil and cilantro.

Warning: Do not eat the bird's eye chilies!

Mushroom Barley Soup

Mushroom barley soup is not only healthy and easy-to-prepare but hearty, comforting and delicious.

Ingredients

- 2 T olive oil
- 1 medium onion, peeled and diced
- 1 large leek, white and light green part, rinsed thoroughly, split lengthwise and sliced into "half-moons"
- 2 medium carrots, peeled and thinly sliced
- 8 oz sliced mushrooms of your choice (about 3 cups)
- 3 cloves garlic, minced
- 2 T all-purpose flour or rice flour
- 2 T dry sherry or dry white wine (optional)
- 6 cups beaf simmering broth (page 56) or vegetable broth
- ½ cup dry pearled barley
- 3 sprigs fresh thyme or ½ tsp dried thyme leaves
- ½ tsp dried marjoram leaves
- sea salt or kosher salt and coarse ground black pepper, to taste
- chopped parsley for garnish (optional)

Preparation

Add the olive oil to large cooking pot and place over medium heat. Sauté the onions, leeks and carrots until the onions are translucent. Add the mushrooms and garlic and sauté until the mushrooms have rendered most of their liquid.

Sprinkle in the flour and mix well. Cook until the flour emits a nutty aroma, about 2 minutes. Add the sherry or wine and cook an additional minute to evaporate the alcohol.

Incorporate the broth in increments while stirring. Add the barley, thyme and marjoram and bring to a boil. Reduce the heat to a low simmer, cover the pot and cook for about 1 hour, or until the barley is tender. Season the soup with salt and pepper to taste. Ladle into individual bowls and garnish with parsley before serving.

Pasta e Fagioli

Pasta e Fagioli (pronounced fa-jo-lee) literally means "pasta and beans" in Italian. My version of this classic soup contains meaty butter beans (large limas) and ditalini pasta in a savory tomato and vegetable-based broth. Garnish with grated non-dairy parmesan and chopped parsley. Fresh oregano leaves or julienned basil leaves are optional garnishes.

Ingredients

- 2 T olive oil
- 1 medium onion, diced
- 2 ribs celery, diced
- sea salt or kosher salt
- 4 large cloves garlic, minced
- 5 cups vegan no-chicken broth or vegetable broth
- 1 can (28 oz) crushed tomatoes with liquid or 3 cups peeled and crushed fresh tomatoes
- 1 tsp dried basil leaves
- 1 bay leaf
- coarse ground black pepper to taste
- 2 cans (15 oz each) butter beans, drained
- 3 oz/⅔ cup dry ditalini pasta
- grated Hard Parmesano (page 208), or Grated Sunflower Parmesan (page 212) or commercial vegan equivalent
- 2 T chopped parsley
- optional garnishes: fresh oregano leaves or julienned basil leaves

Preparation

Add the olive oil to a large soup pot and place over medium heat. Add the onions and celery and a pinch or two of salt. Sauté until the vegetables are softened and the onions are translucent but not browned. Add the garlic and sauté and additional minute.

Add the broth, crushed tomatoes with liquid, dried basil and bay leaf and season with black pepper to taste. Bring to a brief boil and reduce to a simmer. Cover the pot and cook for 20 minutes.

While the soup base is cooking, place the butter beans in large bowl in the sink and fill with cool water. Immerse your hand in the water and swirl the beans to loosen the skins. Work gently so as not to mash or break the beans. Let the beans settle and pour off the water which will carry away any loosened skins. Repeat a few times until most of the skins have been removed. Drain well.

After 20 minutes of cooking, add the beans and the dry pasta. Cover and simmer an additional 20 minutes; season with salt to taste.

Remove and discard the bay leaf and ladle the soup into individual serving bowls. Garnish with the parmesan, parsley and the optional oregano or basil leaves. Serve with crusty Italian bread.

Chickpea Creole Gumbo

Gumbo is a heavily seasoned stew-like dish that originated in southern Louisiana from the Louisiana Creole people during the 18th century. The dish combines ingredients and culinary practices of several cultures, including West African, French, Spanish, German, and Choctaw. Creole Gumbo interacts between all class barriers and ethnicities in the south especially in New Orleans, appearing on the tables of the poor as well as the wealthy. Gumbo traditionally contains spicy meat sausage, chicken and seafood; however, for my plant-based version, all meat proteins were replaced with nutritious and satisfying chickpeas. Kelp powder can be added to impart a subtle seafood taste, if desired. Gumbo is traditionally served with rice.

Note: Gumbo filé, which is dried and ground sassafras leaves, is an ingredient sometimes added to gumbo (but I did not include in this recipe). It imparts an earthy flavor and is also used to thicken the gumbo. After consulting a chef colleague from New Orleans who specializes in Cajun cuisine, she informed me that the filé is purely an optional ingredient. In restaurants it is often contained in a shaker on the table which gives the diner the option to use it as desired. For the home cook, filé can provide thickening when okra is not in season. Feel free to add it to the recipe if you have it on hand.

Ingredients

- ¼ cup cooking oil
- 1 large onion, chopped
- 1 green bell pepper, seeded and chopped
- 3 ribs celery, chopped
- ¼ cup vegan butter or margarine
- ½ cup all-purpose flour (or rice flour for gluten-free)
- 8 cloves garlic, minced
- 4 cups water
- ⅓ cup tamari, soy sauce or Bragg Liquid Aminos
  (use wheat-free tamari or Bragg's for gluten-free)
- ¼ cup Worcestershire Sauce (page 27) or commercial vegan equivalent
- 2 tsp Browning Liquid (page 28) or commercial equivalent
- 1 tsp liquid smoke, or more to taste
- 1 can (15 oz) diced tomatoes with juice or 2 cups peeled and chopped tomatoes
- 3 cups frozen sliced okra
- 2 cans (15 oz each) chickpeas, rinsed and drained
  or about 3 and ½ cups cooked chickpeas
- 3 sprigs fresh thyme leaves or ½ tsp dried thyme
- 1 tsp kelp powder (optional)
- ½ tsp cayenne pepper, or more to taste
- 1 bay leaf
- sea salt or kosher salt and coarse ground black pepper to taste
- 4 green onions, chopped, white and green parts
- ½ cup chopped flat leaf parsley plus chopped leaves for garnish

Preparation

Heat the oil in a large cooking pot over medium heat. Add the onion, bell pepper and celery and sauté until softened, about 10 minutes. Add the garlic and sauté an additional minute. Add the butter or margarine and stir until melted. Sprinkle in the flour, stir to combine and cook until the flour emits a nutty aroma, about 2 minutes.

Incorporate the water in increments while stirring vigorously. Stir in the tamari, Worcestershire, liquid smoke, tomatoes with liquid, okra, chickpeas, thyme, optional kelp powder, cayenne and bay leaf. Bring to a boil then reduce the heat; partially cover and simmer for a minimum of 1 hour. While the gumbo is cooking, prepare white or brown rice, your choice, and keep warm until ready to serve.

Five minutes before serving, stir the green onions and parsley into the gumbo (reserve a little for garnishing). Add salt, black pepper or additional cayenne, kelp powder and/or liquid smoke as desired to taste. To serve, place a scoop of white or brown rice into serving bowls and ladle in the gumbo. Garnish with green onions and parsley.

Spicy Chipotle Pumpkin Soup
with Toasted Pepitas

Chipotle pepper in adobo sauce adds a spicy and smoky kick to this velvety pumpkin soup. For timid palates, the chipotle pepper can be replaced with a mild chili powder.

Ingredients

- 2 T olive oil
- 1 medium onion, chopped
- 2 cloves garlic, chopped
- 1 and ¾ cup roasted and mashed pumpkin* or 1 can (15 oz) pure pumpkin or 1 and ¾ cup roasted and mashed butternut squash
- 4 cups (1 quart) chikun simmering broth (page 41) or vegetable broth
- 1 chipotle pepper in adobo sauce (or 2 if you want to break a sweat; for timid palates omit the chipotle pepper and add 2 tsp mild chili powder)
- 1 tsp ground cumin
- ½ tsp ground coriander
- sea salt or kosher salt to taste
- ¼ cup pepitas (shelled pumpkin seeds)
- cilantro for garnish (optional)

*For fresh roasted pumpkin, cut a sugar pumpkin in half. Scoop out the seeds and strings and place the halves face down on a foil-lined baking sheet. Bake at 350°F until soft, about 45 minutes to 1 hour. Cool and then scoop out the flesh. Freeze any remainder for other recipes. Butternut squash can also be used in this recipe as an alternate to pumpkin. Simply follow the same roasting technique.

Preparation

In a dry skillet, toast the pepitas over medium heat. Stir the seeds frequently to evenly toast and prevent scorching. Set aside.

Add the olive oil to the skillet and place over medium heat. Add the onions and sauté until lightly golden. Add the garlic and sauté an additional minute. Transfer the mixture to a blender.

Add the pumpkin, 2 cups of broth, the chipotle pepper and the cumin and coriander; process until completely smooth. Transfer to a large cooking pot and add the remaining stock/broth. Bring to simmer, partially cover and cook for 30 minutes; season with salt to taste. Ladle into individual bowls and garnish with the toasted pepitas and optional cilantro.

Serve with warm flour tortillas if desired. To warm the tortillas, roll them up securely in foil and place in a 350°F oven for 10 to 15 minutes.

Eggz Flower Soup

Presented here is my compassionate version of the Chinese restaurant classic. Sliced wood ear mushrooms are common in this soup but I opted for more tender straw mushrooms or sliced white mushrooms. If you have the time and inclination, prepare the chikun simmering broth recipe for a delicious homemade flavor, rather than using commercial bouillon paste or cubes for the broth. This recipe yields 4 to 6 servings.

Ingredients for the Eggz White Mixture*

- ½ cup plain unsweetened soymilk or almond milk
- 1 and ½ tsp (2 grams) Gentle Chef Vegan Eggz Essentials A
- ½ tsp (1.25 grams) Gentle Chef Vegan Eggz Essentials B
- ¼ tsp kala namak (Himalayan black salt)

*If you don't have the Vegan Eggz Essentials on hand, the eggz can be replaced with ½ block firm or extra-firm tofu (not silken tofu), shaved paper thin into lacey fragments.

Ingredients for the Soup

- 6 cups chikun simmering broth (page 41) or commercial vegan equivalent
- 1 can (15 oz) straw mushrooms, drained or 6 oz fresh white mushrooms, sliced
- ½ tsp ground ginger
- pinch ground white pepper
- ½ cup fresh peas or frozen peas, thawed
- 3 scallions, chopped
- 2 T cornstarch or unmodified potato starch
- sea salt or kosher salt, to taste

Preparation

Add the broth, mushrooms, ground ginger and white pepper to a large cooking pot and place over medium heat. Bring to a simmer and cook for 10 minutes.

Meanwhile, process the eggz white ingredients in a mini-blender for 20 seconds. Transfer to a small bowl and set aside.

With a large spoon, vigorously stir the eggz mixture to loosen. Lift the spoon from the mixture and allow any excess to drain back into the bowl. Stir the soup with the coated spoon until the white slides off (coating the spatula with a thin layer of the mixture will create the wispy strands of eggz). Repeat this technique until all the eggz mixture has been added. If using tofu, simply stir in the fragments.

In a small dish, dissolve the starch in 3 tablespoons water and then stir into the soup. Stir in the peas and scallions and simmer an additional 3 minutes; season with salt if needed. Ladle the soup into bowls and serve.

Matzo Ball Soup

Matzo is a traditional Jewish unleavened "bread" or cracker. Matzo balls are comprised of matzo meal, which is basically matzo crumbs. The matzo balls are served in a golden broth flavored with thyme, parsley and a mirepoix of carrots, celery and onions; simple and yet delicious. This recipe yields 6 medium-size matzo balls and about 1 quart of soup. Please note that the Gentle Chef Vegan Eggs Essentials is required for creating the matzo balls.

Ingredients for the Matzo Balls

- ½ cup matzo meal
- ½ cup plain unsweetened soymilk or almond milk
- 1 and ½ (2 grams) Eggz Essentials A
- ½ tsp (1.25 grams) Eggz Essentials B
- ½ tsp kosher salt
- 2 T neutral vegetable oil (plus 1 tsp for the mixing bowl)

Ingredients for the Soup

- 6 cups chikun simmering broth (page 41) or commercial vegan equivalent
- 1 large carrot, sliced
- 1 large rib celery, sliced
- 1 small onion, peeled, thinly sliced and then chopped
- ½ tsp dried thyme leaves
- 2 T chopped parsley
- coarse ground black pepper to taste
- kosher salt, to taste as needed

Preparation

Add the matzo meal to a mixing bowl and set aside. Add the remaining matzo ball ingredients (not the soup ingredients) to a blender and process for 20 seconds. Pour the blended eggz mixture into the matzo meal and mix thoroughly. Cover and refrigerate for 10 minutes.

Form the dough into 6 balls. Add 1 teaspoon cooking oil to the mixing bowl and roll the matzo balls in the oil until evenly covered. Cover again and refrigerate for 10 minutes.

Bring 6 cups of salted water to a boil in a cooking pot. Carefully lower the chilled matzo balls into the boiling water. Reduce the heat to a simmer and cook for 15 minutes. When done, remove from the heat and set aside (do not remove from the water).

Bring the broth, carrot, celery and onion to a boil in large cooking pot. Add the thyme, partially cover and reduce the heat to a gentle simmer for 20 minutes. Add the matzo balls to the soup (discard the salted simmering water), partially cover the pot and continue cooking for 20 minutes. Season the soup with pepper and additional salt as needed to taste. Stir in the parsley just before serving.

Appetizers and Small Plates

Bedeviled Eggz

Bedeviled eggz are remarkably similar to deviled eggs in appearance, taste and texture. They make the perfect bite-size finger food for BBQs, picnics and parties. Kala namak, or Himalayan black salt, is essential to impart that familiar egg-like taste.

A blender is required for preparing the "egg whites" and a food processor is recommended for the "yolk filling". You will also need an 8" square baking pan and 1 block (about 14 oz before pressing) extra-firm water-packed tofu (not silken tofu). If you have egg molds, or a heat-proof container that specifically holds deviled eggs, the "egg white" mixture can be poured directly into the molds to create perfect, halved hard-boiled egg shapes. This recipe yields 16 to 24 bedeviled eggz or more depending upon the mold(s) used for the "egg whites".

Ingredients for the "Egg Whites"

- ⅓ block (about 5 oz/142 grams before pressing) extra-firm tofu (not silken tofu)
- ¾ tsp kala namak (Himalayan black salt)
- 2 cups (480 ml) water
- 2 and ¼ tsp agar powder

Ingredients for the "Yolk" Filling

- ⅔ block (about 9 oz/255 grams before pressing) extra-firm tofu (not silken tofu)
- ¼ cup No-Eggy Mayo (page 263) or commercial vegan mayonnaise
- 1 T nutritional yeast flakes
- 1 T dill pickle or sweet pickle relish
- 2 tsp Dijon mustard or spicy golden mustard
- ½ tsp onion powder
- ¼ tsp kala namak* (Himalayan black salt), or more to taste
- ¼ tsp sweet paprika (for extra "bedeviling" add a pinch of cayenne pepper too)
- ¼ tsp ground turmeric

Garnishes

- sweet paprika
- optional: coarse ground black pepper, sliced black olives; fresh snipped chives or "spears"; capers; minced celery; minced onion; chopped cornichons; chopped dill or dill "fronds"

Preparation

Drain and press the tofu until it is not releasing any more liquid. Slice ⅓ of the tofu to use for the "egg whites". The remaining ⅔ will be used for the "yolk" filling.

To prepare the "egg whites", place the "egg white" ingredients into a blender and process until smooth. Pour the mixture into a saucepan and bring to a simmer over medium heat, stirring frequently to avoid scorching the tofu mixture. Avoid boiling as this will cause the soy protein to re-coagulate (a minimal degree of re-coagulation may occur as the mixture is brought to a simmer but will not affect the final appearance or texture). Pour the mixture into the 8" baking pan and set aside to cool. If you have egg molds, or a heat-proof container that specifically holds deviled eggs, pour the tofu mixture directly into the molds and set aside to cool. After cooling a bit, refrigerate until completely set, about 1 hour.

Next, crumble the ⅔ block of pressed tofu into the food processor and add the remaining "yolk" filling ingredients. Process the contents until completely smooth, stopping as necessary to scrape down the sides of the food processor. Alternately, the mixture can be mashed using a fork or a potato masher/ricer, but the mixture will not be as smooth. Taste the mixture and add additional kala namak (or sea salt) as desired.

Transfer the "yolk" mixture to a bowl or food storage container, cover and refrigerate until ready to use.

Now, run a table knife around the perimeter of the baking pan to loosen the "egg white" (or simply pop them out of the egg molds). Invert the baking pan onto a clean work surface. At this point, the "egg white" can be cut into rectangles or cut into rounds or ovals.

For rectangles, cut the "egg whites" into 6 even strips. Turn your cutting surface and make 4 even slices. This will create 24 rectangles. For rounds or ovals, use a 1 and ½-inch to 1 and ¾-inch cookie cutter or ring mold. Any "egg white" remnants can be finely diced and mixed with any of the leftover "yolk" filling for a quick eggless egg salad sandwich.

Spoon a generous teaspoonful of the "yolk" mixture onto the top of each "egg white". Alternately, the mixture can be decoratively piped onto the "egg whites" using a pastry bag. If you don't have a pastry bag, try placing the mixture into a food storage bag, seal and then snip off a tiny piece from the bottom corner of the bag with scissors. Squeeze the bag to pipe the mixture onto the "egg whites".

Sprinkle with paprika and garnish with optional ingredients as desired. Cover gently with plastic wrap and chill thoroughly before serving.

Asian Spring Rolls

Just about any filling can be used for Spring rolls. Raw, steamed or lightly sautéed vegetables should be coarsely chopped or sliced into thin slivers. Fresh herbs are wonderful to use in Spring rolls as well. Try my Soy Ginger Dipping Sauce (recipe follows) for dipping your rolls.

Ingredients

- your choice of slivered tofu, seitan or tempeh, and/or slivered raw or lightly steamed vegetables; sprouts
- Bánh Tráng (rice paper spring roll skins/wrappers)

Preparation

Prepare your fillings and set aside.

Fill a dinner plate with hot water and set next to your work surface.

Submerge a wrapper in the water on the plate. Count to ten and remove the wrapper. It may not feel totally pliable at this point but it will be by the time you wrap your filling. Hold the wrapper by the edge over the plate so the excess water can drain. Gently place the wrapper on your work surface.

Place a few tablespoons of filling in the center of the wrapper, avoiding about 2-inches on each side. Fold the wrapper in half over the filling. With your fingers, press down to compress the filling. Fold the sides in (like a burrito) and then roll up as tightly as you can. This technique takes a little practice so be patient.

Repeat until the filling is used up. If you have a hard time wrapping, try doubling the wrappers. Slice the rolls with a sharp knife on the diagonal. Serve with your favorite dipping sauce.

Soy Ginger Spring Roll Dipping Sauce

Ingredients

- 2 T organic sugar
- ¼ cup soy sauce, tamari or Bragg Liquid Aminos™
- ¾ cup water
- 2 tsp cornstarch mixed with 2 tsp water
- 1 T fresh lime juice
- 2 tsp fresh grated ginger root
- 1 clove garlic, minced (1 tsp)
- 2 T chopped green onions

Preparation

Combine the sugar, soy sauce, and water in a small saucepan. Bring to a boil. Stir in the cornstarch/water paste. Reduce heat to a simmer and add the garlic, ginger, lime juice and green onions. Continue to simmer, stirring frequently, for about 2 minutes to blend the flavors. Chill until ready to serve.

French Onion and Leek Dip

A savory dip made from scratch with caramelized onions and leeks. Serve with crudités, chips or crackers. This recipe yields about 2 and ½ cups.

Ingredients

- 2 T olive oil
- 1 large sweet yellow onion, peeled
- 1 medium leek, white and light green part only
- 2 cloves garlic, minced (2 tsp)
- 1 T tamari, soy sauce, tamari or Bragg Liquid Aminos™
- 1 tsp Worcestershire Sauce (page 27) or commercial vegan equivalent
- ¼ tsp coarse ground black pepper, or more taste
- ¼ tsp dried thyme leaves
- 1 cup Instant Sour Cream (page 176) or Cultured Sour Cream (page 177)
- 1 cup No-Eggy Mayo (page 263) or commercial vegan mayonnaise
- sea salt or kosher salt to taste, if needed
- chopped parsley for garnish (optional)

Preparation

Slice the onions very thin (a mandoline is very helpful) and then chop. Split the leek lengthwise; rinse well to remove any sand and then thinly slice crosswise into "half-moons".

Add the olive oil to a non-stick skillet and place over medium heat. Add the onions and leeks and a pinch of salt and sauté until golden.

Add the garlic, tamari, Worcestershire, black pepper and thyme and continue to sauté until the vegetables are very soft and nicely caramelized. Transfer to a container and refrigerate until chilled.

In a medium mixing bowl, combine the caramelized onion and leek mixture with the sour cream and mayonnaise and mix well. Taste and add salt as needed and additional pepper to taste. Transfer to a serving bowl, cover and chill to blend the flavors. Garnish with chopped parsley before serving if desired.

Mediterranean Lentil Dip

This dip is similar to hummus but is made with cooked red or yellow lentils instead of the traditional chickpeas. It's smooth, creamy and delicious! Sweating the garlic prior to blending mellows the garlic flavor. Serve with warm or toasted pita or other flatbread, and/or crunchy fresh vegetables. This recipe yields about 2 cups.

Ingredients

- 1 cup dried lentils
- 1 T extra-virgin olive oil, plus additional for garnish
- 3 medium cloves garlic, chopped
- ¼ cup sesame tahini
- 1 T fresh lemon juice, or more to taste
- 1 tsp ground cumin
- ½ tsp ground coriander
- ½ tsp fine sea salt or kosher salt, or more to taste
- ¼ tsp ground white pepper
- water sufficient for processing
- 1 T chopped fresh parsley for garnish
- other garnish(es) of your choice*

Other garnishes might include but are not limited to: Greek Feta (page 191); sweet or smoked paprika; powdered sumac; roasted or sautéed minced garlic; chopped roasted red peppers; dairy-free pesto; toasted pine nuts; chopped cilantro or basil.

Preparation

Sort through the dry lentils and remove any foreign matter. Rinse the lentils thoroughly in a sieve, drain and add to a medium cooking pot. Add 4 cups water and 1 teaspoon sea salt or kosher salt and bring to a boil. Stir the lentils, partially cover the pot, reduce the heat to a simmer and cook for 20 minutes or until tender. Drain the cooked lentils thoroughly in the sieve.

While the cooked lentils are draining, add 1 tablespoon olive oil to a small skillet and place over medium-low to low heat. Sweat the garlic about 10 minutes to mellow and sweeten the flavor and remove the raw pungency. If you hear an audible "sizzle" from the oil, the heat is too high; turn it down slightly.

Place the drained lentils into a blender or food processor and add the sautéed garlic and remaining ingredients except for the parsley and other optional garnishes. Process until very smooth. Add water as needed to assist processing. The dip should be creamy and smooth, not thick and pasty.

Taste and add salt or more lemon juice as desired (lemon juice plays a supporting role in flavor development but the dip should not have an obvious lemon flavor). Transfer to a bowl, cover and refrigerate for a minimum of 30 minutes to thicken and blend the flavors before serving, or for up to 1 week. The dip will thicken a little bit upon refrigeration; if it becomes too thick after chilling, simply incorporate a little water.

Drizzle with extra-virgin olive oil and garnish as desired before serving.

Channna Masala Hummus

This unique dip and spread is a flavorful fusion of warm, aromatic Indian spices and creamy Mediterranean hummus. A blender is required for efficient processing.

Ingredients

- ¼ cup olive oil, divided in half
- 1 medium onion, peeled and chopped
- 1 large jalapeno or serrano pepper, seeded and chopped
- 3 cloves garlic, chopped
- 1 T tomato paste
- 2 tsp garam masala
- 1 tsp paprika plus additional for garnish
- 2 tsp fresh grated ginger root
- 1 can (15 oz) garbanzo beans (chickpeas), rinsed well and drained
- ¼ cup cashew butter or sesame tahini
- ¼ cup water
- 2 T fresh lemon juice
- ¾ tsp fine sea salt or kosher salt, or more to taste
- optional garnishes: toasted cumin seeds*; chopped tomato; Hari Chutney (page 326)

*To toast the cumin seeds, place 1 teaspoon whole cumin seeds in a dry skillet and place over medium-low heat. Occasionally shake the skillet back and forth gently until the seeds are very aromatic, about 1 to 2 minutes. Be careful not to burn them. Transfer to a small dish to cool.

Preparation

Add 2 tablespoons olive oil to a skillet and place over medium heat. Add the onions and hot pepper and sauté until the onions are lightly golden, about 4 to 5 minutes. Add the garlic, tomato paste, garam masala, paprika and ginger and stir to combine. Sauté until very fragrant, about 1 minute. Remove from the heat.

Add the garbanzo beans, cashew butter or tahini, water, remaining 2 tablespoons olive oil, lemon juice and salt to a blender. Add the sautéed mixture. Cover and process until very smooth. Add additional water as needed for processing (this shouldn't be necessary).

Taste the mixture and add salt to taste as desired. Transfer to a sealable container and refrigerate until well-chilled. The mixture will thicken upon chilling. To serve, transfer to a serving dish and garnish with toasted cumin seeds. Also garnish with chopped tomato and Hari Chutney, if desired. Serve with wedges of pita or crackers; or use as a dip for fresh vegetables. Channa masala hummus also makes a unique sandwich spread.

Mediterranean Kalamata Olive and Artichoke Hummus

Artichoke hearts and tangy Kalamata olives are blended with chickpeas and Mediterranean herbs to create this savory dip and spread. A food processor is recommended for a textured dip (which is ideal for this recipe) but a high-powered blender can also be used for a smoother texture.

Ingredients

- 1 can (15 oz) garbanzo beans (chickpeas), rinsed thoroughly and drained well
- ¼ cup sesame tahini
- ¼ cup extra-virgin olive oil
- 2 cloves garlic
- juice of 1 lemon
- 1 tsp dried oregano
- 1 tsp dried basil
- ¾ tsp sea salt or kosher salt, or more to taste
- ¼ tsp coarse ground black pepper, or more to taste
- 1 can (about 14 oz) artichoke hearts, rinsed and drained well (about 8 oz after draining)
- ½ cup pitted Kalamata olives, drained well and cut in half to ensure that there are no stray pits
- optional garnish: chopped fresh parsley, chopped Kalamata olives and a drizzle of olive oil

Preparation

Place the chickpeas, tahini, olive oil, garlic, lemon juice, oregano, basil, salt and black pepper into a food processor and process into a coarse paste.

Add the artichoke hearts and olives and process until blended but slightly chunky (or smooth if you prefer); season with additional salt and pepper to taste (keep in mind that the olives are inherently salty). Refrigerate to blend the flavors.

Garnish with chopped fresh parsley, chopped olives and a drizzle of olive oil before serving, if desired. Serve with toasted pita wedges or crackers; or use as a sandwich spread.

Olive Salad Spread

This recipe is my version of the mixed olive tapenade served on the famous New Orleans Muffuletta sandwich. Its bold Mediterranean flavors also pair well with hummus or baba ghannouj on crackers and crusty bread. Or try it on grilled eggplant sandwiches. Ideally it should be made a day in advance to give the flavors time to blend. Stored in an airtight container in the refrigerator, this spread will last for months.

Ingredients

- 1 cup small pimento-stuffed olives, drained
- 1 cup small pitted Kalamata olives, drained
- ½ cup coarsely chopped Giardiniera (page 329), or commercial equivalent
- 2 pepperoncini, stems removed
- 1 T capers, drained
- 2 cloves garlic, chopped
- 3 T olive oil
- 1 T red wine vinegar
- 1 tsp dried oregano
- ½ tsp coarse ground black pepper

Preparation

Place all ingredients in a food processor and pulse until coarsely chopped. Refrigerate to blend flavors before using.

Chef's Favorite Garden Salsa

This fresh chunky garden salsa has a medium heat which can be adjusted to suit your taste. I chose canned whole tomatoes because they are partially stewed during the canning process, thus producing a superb texture for salsa. It's very easy to make and so much better than store-bought. This recipe yields about 4 cups.

Ingredients

- 1 can (28 oz) diced tomatoes, lightly drained
- 3 large scallions or 6 small scallions, white and green parts, chopped
- 1 or 2 cloves garlic
- juice of 1 lime (about 2 T)
- 1 Serrano or jalapeno pepper, coarsely chopped, or more to taste (for a fiery salsa try including the seeds; for a milder salsa reduce or omit altogether)
- ¼ cup chopped cilantro, or more to taste
- 1 tsp fine sea salt or kosher salt, or more to taste
- 1 tsp ground cumin

Preparation

Place all ingredients, except for the tomatoes into a food processor and process until finely minced.

Add the tomatoes and pulse a few times but retain some texture.

Refrigerate for several hours to blend the flavors, ideally overnight.

Taste and add additional salt before serving, as desired. The salsa will keep for about 10 days in the refrigerator. Serve with your favorite tortilla chips; or use as a topping for your favorite Mexican or Tex-Mex recipes.

Fried Mozzarella Sticks

An appetizer favorite, savory breaded and fried mozzarella sticks are served with warm marinara sauce for dipping.

Ingredients

- 1 block Melty Mozzarella (page 217)
- 1 cup plain unsweetened non-dairy milk
- ½ cup all-purpose flour or rice flour
- 1 T nutritional yeast flakes
- 1 cup plain fine dry breadcrumbs
- ½ cup panko-style bread crumbs
- 1 and ½ tsp fine sea salt or kosher salt
- 1 tsp onion powder
- 1 tsp garlic powder
- 1 tsp dried oregano
- 1 tsp dried basil
- ½ tsp coarse ground black pepper
- high-temp cooking oil
- Chef's Best Marinara Sauce (page 146) or commercial favorite, for dipping

Preparation

Cut the mozzarella into sticks and keep chilled until ready to prepare the breading. Prepare the marinara sauce ahead of time so it can be reheated just before serving the fried mozzarella.

In one bowl, whisk the milk, flour and nutritional yeast together until smooth. Set aside.

In another bowl, combine the breadcrumbs and seasonings.

Dip a mozzarella stick into the milk/flour batter, shake off the excess and roll in the breadcrumbs until thoroughly coated. Handle them gently so as to not dislodge the breading. Place the stick on a plate and repeat with the remaining sticks. If the breading is not adhering completely, repeat dipping in the milk/flour mixture and then the breadcrumbs. It's important to achieve complete coverage. Place the plate into the refrigerator uncovered for 30 minutes to allow the breading to dry a bit and thoroughly chill the mozzarella.

Add 1-inch of oil to a deep skillet or wok and place over medium-high heat. Place the marinara sauce over medium heat to warm while frying the mozzarella sticks.

When the oil begins to shimmer, gently lower a few of the sticks into the hot oil and fry until golden brown. Fry the sticks in batches; remove with a slotted spoon and place on a plate lined with paper towels to absorb any excess oil.

Serve immediately with the marinara sauce. If the sticks need to be reheated, place them in a hot oven for about 10 minutes; they also respond well to brief reheating in a microwave (they heat from within, which is very efficient for melting the cheese).

Cheesy Jalapeno Popper Bean Dip

A zesty and cheesy Southwestern bean dip served hot with your favorite chips or bread for dipping.

Ingredients

- 1 can (15 oz) or 2 cups cooked white beans (cannellini, navy or Great Northern)
- cooking oil
- 3 large jalapenos, seeded and diced
- 1 large Anaheim chili, seeded and diced or 1 can (4 oz) diced mild green chilies
- ½ medium onion, diced
- 3 cloves garlic, minced
- 1 and ¾ cup plain unsweetened soymilk or almond milk
- ¼ cup tapioca flour (starch)
- 2 T nutritional yeast flakes
- 1 T mellow white miso paste
- 2 tsp fine sea salt or kosher salt
- 2 tsp lactic acid powder or 2 T fresh lemon juice
- 2 tsp apple cider vinegar
- ½ cup panko bread crumbs or plain, dry breadcrumbs

Note: Use protective gloves when handling jalapeno peppers; or wash your hands thoroughly several times after handling.

Preparation

If using canned beans, rinse thoroughly until all traces of foam disappear. Drain well and set aside.

Preheat the oven to 375°F/190°C. Grease a small, shallow baking dish with cooking oil and set aside.

Add 2 tablespoons of cooking oil to a skillet and place over medium-low heat. Add the jalapeno, fresh Anaheim chili, onion and garlic with a pinch of salt and "sweat" the vegetables until softened (if using canned mild green chilies, set aside for later).

If using canned green chilies, add them at this time. Increase the heat to medium and sauté until any liquid has evaporated and the onions are translucent and lightly golden - do not brown. Transfer to a mixing bowl to cool.

In a small saucepan, whisk together the non-dairy milk, tapioca flour, nutritional yeast, miso, salt and acids. Whisk in 2 tablespoons of cooking oil and place over medium-low heat. Cook, stirring frequently, until the mixture is hot, cheesy, bubbly and smooth (the cheese sauce will be somewhat salty at this stage but will balance out when mixed with the bean purée and vegetables). Keep warm over low heat.

Place the white beans into a food processor and process into a paste. Alternately, mash the beans thoroughly with a potato masher or ricer. Transfer to the mixing bowl.

Add the cheese mixture to the mixing bowl and stir all ingredients thoroughly. Transfer to the greased baking dish, spread evenly and top with the panko crumbs. Season the topping with coarse ground black pepper and mist with cooking oil spray. The oil will help the crumbs brown in the oven.

Place on the middle rack of the oven and bake uncovered for 45 to 50 minutes or until browned and bubbly. To enhance browning if necessary, place under the broiler for about 1 minute.

Serve hot with warm tortilla chips, chunks of crusty bread or crackers. The dip will be saucy when very hot but will thicken substantially as it cools.

Escarfaux
(Mock Escargot)

Oven-roasted mushrooms are bathed in a buttery, garlicky wine sauce and served with crusty bread. Roasting the mushrooms yields a texture similar to escargot.

Ingredients

- ¼ cup olive oil
- ¾ lb small white button or cremini mushrooms
- 2 T non-dairy butter or margarine
- 4 large cloves garlic, minced
- 1 cup dry white wine or red wine, your choice
  (or vegetable broth with 1 T fresh lemon juice)
- ½ tsp coarse ground black pepper
- 2 T chopped fresh parsley
- sea salt or kosher salt, to taste
- crusty bread for soaking up the sauce

Preparation

Preheat the oven to 400°F/200°C. Toss the mushrooms with 2 tablespoons of the olive oil and a pinch or two of salt on a baking sheet and spread out in a single layer. Bake 30 minutes. They will darken and may shrivel a bit; this is good. Remove from the oven and set aside.

In a large skillet, melt the butter with the remaining 2 tablespoons olive oil. Add the garlic and sauté until fragrant, about 1 minute.

Add the wine or broth and the coarse ground black pepper and bring to a simmer. Let the liquid reduce by half, about 2 minutes.

Add the roasted mushrooms and sauté until heated through, about 2 minutes. Stir in the parsley and season with salt to taste. Serve with crusty bread for soaking up the sauce.

Southwestern Polenta Crispy Fries
with Cilantro Lime Aioli

Golden brown and crispy on the outside and tender and delicious on the inside, these savory and generously spiced polenta fries are served with a tangy, citrusy sauce for dipping.

Ingredients for the Polenta

- 3 cups water
- 1 T non-dairy butter or margarine
- 1 tsp sea salt or kosher salt
- 1 cup yellow cornmeal
- chives or 2 T fresh
- 2 tsp onion powder
- 1 tsp garlic powder
- 1 tsp ancho (mild) chili powder
- ½ tsp dried oregano
- ½ tsp ground cumin
- ¼ tsp chipotle chili powder

Ingredients for the Aioli

- ½ cup No-Eggy Mayo (page 263) or commercial vegan equivalent
- 2 T fresh chopped cilantro
- 2 tsp fresh lime juice, or to taste
- sea salt and fresh ground black pepper, to taste

Preparation

Lightly oil a 9×5-inch loaf pan; set aside. In a medium saucepan, bring the water, butter or margarine and salt to a boil.

In large measuring cup, mix together the cornmeal and remaining ingredients.

When the water comes to a boil, reduce the heat to medium-low. While vigorously whisking, slowly pour the cornmeal mixture into the simmering water. Slow addition of the cornmeal with vigorous stirring ensures that the corn meal does not form solid lumps. If lumps form, keep whisking until they break apart.

Cook, stirring frequently, until the mixture is thick and begins to pull away from sides of saucepan. The mixture will cook quickly.

Spoon the cornmeal mixture into the loaf pan and smooth the top with the back of a spoon or rubber spatula. Let the mixture cool for about 15 minutes and then place plastic wrap directly in contact with the surface; refrigerate for 6 to 8 hours or until firm.

In the meantime, prepare the aioli by mixing together the ingredients in a small bowl. Cover and refrigerate until ready to serve.

Once the polenta has chilled and firmed, turn the cake onto a work surface. Cut the cake in half and then cut each half into "fries" or wedges (or any shape you desire). Deep fry the polenta in hot oil until golden brown and crispy. The polenta will take longer to brown than potato fries. Drain on a plate lined with several paper towels. Serve hot with the aioli.

Sicilian Panelle

Panelle, also known as Panella di Ceci, are Sicilian fritters made from chickpea flour and seasonings and are similar to fried polenta. They are a popular street food in Palermo and are often eaten between slices of bread or on a roll, like a sandwich. Panelle are believed to be of Arabic origin. The panelle can be cut into various shapes and sizes before frying.

Ingredients for the Panelle

- 1 cup chickpea flour
- 2 T dried parsley flakes
- 1 tsp onion powder
- 1 tsp dried basil
- ½ tsp garlic powder
- 2 cups water
- 2 T olive oil
- 1 tsp sea salt or kosher salt
- high-temp cooking oil for frying

Ingredients for the Relish (optional)

Mix together in a bowl:

- 3 Campari or Roma tomatoes, seeded and diced
- 3 T finely diced onion
- 3 T finely chopped flat leaf parsley
- 2 tsp olive oil
- 2 tsp fresh lemon juice
- sea salt or kosher salt and fresh ground black pepper to taste

Preparation

Oil and 8"x8" baking dish or line with parchment paper. Set aside.

Combine the chickpea flour, parsley, onion powder, basil and garlic powder in a bowl.

In a medium saucepan, bring the water, oil and salt to a boil. Reduce the heat to a vigorous simmer and sprinkle in a small portion of the flour mixture while whisking vigorously to avoid lumps. Continue to incorporate the flour mixture in increments. Cook the mixture until it begins to pull away a bit from the sides of the saucepan. It will be very thick.

Transfer the mixture to the baking dish and spread evenly. Let cool a bit and then cover with foil or plastic wrap and refrigerate for several hours or until completely chilled and firm set.

Cut the panelle into any desired shape and fry until golden brown in hot cooking oil. They take a little time to brown, so be patient. Transfer to a plate lined with paper towels to blot excess oil. Serve warm.

Pâté Champignon
with Cognac and Truffle Oil

An elegant, earthy and rich mushroom pâté flavored with cognac and truffle oil. This pâté has a strong mushroom flavor; for a milder pâté, reduce or omit the truffle oil.

Ingredients

- 5 oz/142 g **pressed** extra-firm tofu (not silken tofu)
- 1 to 2 tsp white or black truffle oil
  (according to intensity of flavor desired)
- 1 tsp fine sea salt or kosher salt
- 2 T non-dairy butter or margarine
- ½ 1b (8 oz) cremini mushrooms (baby portabellas), sliced
- ½ cup chopped shallots or onion
- ½ cup cognac, brandy or dry white wine (i.e., Pinot Grigio; Sauvignon Blanc)
- ¼ cup chopped flat-leaf parsley, lightly packed
- 6 cloves garlic, chopped
- 1 and ½ tsp fresh thyme leaves or ½ tsp dried thyme
- 1 tsp dried porcini or portabella mushroom powder, optional
- 2 T **refined** coconut oil, melted (not virgin coconut oil)
- ½ to 1 tsp cracked black pepper, or to taste

Preparation

For this recipe, it is important that the tofu be pressed as dry as possible.

Line a 2-cup minimum plastic, metal or ceramic container with plastic wrap. The container will serve as the mold to shape the pâté.

Crumble the tofu into a food processor. Add the truffle oil and salt and set aside.

In a skillet over medium heat, melt the butter or margarine. Add the shallots/onions and mushrooms and sauté until the vegetables are nicely browned. Add the cognac, parsley, garlic, thyme and optional mushroom powder and sauté until the liquid has completely evaporated. Transfer the contents of the skillet to the food processor.

Add the melted refined coconut oil to the food processor. The coconut oil is used to firm the pâté when chilled.

Process the mixture until smooth. Add the pepper and pulse a few times to combine. Taste and add additional salt or pepper as desired.

Transfer the mixture to the container, smooth the surface, cover with additional plastic wrap and refrigerate for several hours until firm. When firm, lift the pâté from the container and invert onto a serving plate. Peel away the plastic wrap. Spread on hors-d'oeuvre toast or savory crackers.

Curry Zucchini Corn Fritters

Shredded zucchini, sliced onion and corn kernels are seasoned with curry and fried until crisp and golden brown. This recipe yields about 1 dozen fritters.

Ingredients

- 2 average-size zucchinis (about 7 to 8 inches long)
- 1 can (about 15 oz or 1 and ½ cup) organic corn kernels, drained very well
- ½ of a medium onion, sliced very thin and then coarsely chopped
- ½ cup garbanzo bean (chickpea) flour plus more if needed
- 1 tsp curry powder
- ¾ tsp sea salt or kosher salt (plus 1 tsp for salting the zucchini)
- ½ tsp coarse ground black pepper

Preparation

Shred the zucchini with a standard vegetable grater or using the shredding blade on a food processor. Transfer the shreds to a large mixing bowl, add 1 teaspoon salt, stir well and set aside for 15 minutes. The salt will help draw out the moisture from the zucchini.

Pour off any excess liquid and place the shreds in a clean, lint-free kitchen towel or several layers of cheesecloth. Gather up the edges at the top and twist securely closed. Twist and squeeze the bundle into the sink to remove as much liquid as possible. Transfer the shreds back to the mixing bowl and set aside.

Add the well-drained corn kernels to a food processor fitted with a standard chopping blade and pulse the contents 4 times. The goal is to break up the majority of the corn, releasing the starch while still leaving some kernels intact. Do not over-process! Transfer the corn to the mixing bowl.

Add the onions, ½ cup garbanzo bean flour, curry, ¾ tsp salt and the black pepper. Stir thoroughly until a thick batter is created. If the mixture seems too loose, add 2 tablespoons additional flour. Set the mixture aside.

In a wok or deep skillet, heat ½-inch oil over medium-high heat. When the oil begins to shimmer, test the batter by carefully placing 1 heaping tablespoon of the batter carefully into the hot oil. After 1 minute, gently press down on the fritter with the back of a spoon to flatten it.

Continue to fry for a few minutes unto golden brown on both sides. Use 2 large spoons to help turn the fritter; this will prevent splashing of the hot oil. If the fritter holds together, repeat the process, working in batches to avoid overcrowding the skillet. If the fritter falls apart, use a slotted spoon to remove it from the oil and add a little bit more flour to the mixture to help it hold together.

Transfer the fritters to a plate lined with paper towels to absorb any excess oil. If necessary, reheat the fritters in a 350°F/175°C oven until hot. Serve immediately.

Falafel

Falafel are small, deep-fried patties made from ground chickpeas and a blend of herbs and spices. Falafel are a traditional Arabic food, usually served in a pita, which acts as a pocket, or wrapped in a flatbread and topped with various sauces and vegetable garnishes For my own recipe, I also incorporate ground split peas (which is optional) and season with my own blend of spices. This recipe yields about 16 falafel patties.

Ingredients for the Falafel

- ¾ cup dried chickpeas and ¼ cup dried yellow or green split peas (or 1 cup dried chickpeas)
- ¼ cup diced onion
- 4 cloves garlic, chopped
- 1 and ¼ tsp sea salt or kosher salt
- 1 tsp minced fresh rosemary or ¼ tsp dried powdered rosemary
- 1 tsp ground cumin
- 1 tsp ground coriander
- ¼ tsp red pepper flakes
- 6 T garbanzo bean (chickpea) flour or soy flour
- 2 T olive oil
- ½ tsp coarse ground black pepper
- ¼ cup chopped fresh parsley, loosely packed

Other Ingredients

- cooking oil for frying
- pita or flat bread
- Greek Tzatziki (page 197), Tahini Sauce (page 106) and/or hummus (several hummus recipes can be found in this cookbook)
- thinly sliced onion
- sliced cucumbers
- chopped tomatoes

Preparation

Place the dried chickpeas and split peas (or chickpeas alone) in a large bowl and add enough cold water to cover them by at least 2 inches. Let them soak for 24 hours, then drain thoroughly. Do not use canned chickpeas.

Place the drained, soaked chickpeas and split peas, onion, garlic, salt, rosemary, cumin, coriander and red pepper flakes in the bowl of a food processor fitted with a chopping blade. Process the mixture until all the peas are coarsely ground. Remove the lid and scrape down the peas as necessary to incorporate them into the mixture. Do not purée! It is important to retain a "grainy" texture".

Sprinkle in the garbanzo bean (chickpea) flour, olive oil, black pepper and parsley and pulse the mixture several times to combine. Turn the mixture into a bowl and refrigerate, covered, for a minimum of 30 minutes.

Form the chickpea mixture into balls about the size of walnuts and then gently press to flatten into small patties. The mixture will be moist and some will stick to your fingers, so keep a moist towel on hand while you work. Place the patties on a plate or cutting board.

In a deep skillet or wok, heat ½-inch of oil to 375°F/190°C, or for a full 5 minutes on medium-high heat. Fry the patties in batches for about 1 to 2 minutes on each side, or until golden brown. Drain on paper towels.

Stuff half a pita with 3 falafel patties or serve on a plate. Garnish with fresh produce and condiment(s) of your choice. Store any remaining falafel in a covered container or food storage bag and refrigerate.

To reheat, wrap the falafel securely in foil and place in a 350°F/175°C oven for 15 minutes; or briefly reheat in the microwave.

Toasted Moroccan-Spiced Chickpeas

A crunchy, zesty and healthy North African treat.

Ingredients

- 1 (15 oz) garbanzo beans (chickpeas), rinsed and drained well
- 1 T olive oil

Seasoning Blend Ingredients

- ½ tsp sea salt or kosher salt
- ½ tsp ground cumin
- ½ tsp ground coriander
- ½ tsp onion powder
- ½ tsp garlic powder
- ¼ tsp ground ginger
- ¼ tsp smoked paprika
- ¼ tsp ground cayenne or red pepper

Preparation

Combine the seasoning blend in a small dish. Set aside.

Preheat the oven to 400°F/200°C. Line a baking sheet with parchment paper.

Pat the chickpeas dry between paper towels then place on the baking sheet. Drizzle with the olive oil then place the baking sheet on the middle rack of the oven. Toss the chickpeas every 15 minutes, and continue to bake until deeply golden, dry and crunchy, about 40 to 45 minutes.

Immediately transfer the chickpeas to a mixing bowl and toss with the spice blend. Serve warm or at room temperature.

Fried Oyster Mushrooms
with Fire-Roasted Jalapeno Lime Tartar Sauce

Fried oyster mushrooms are a plant-based version of fried oysters. For this recipe, organic cornflake cereal crumbs are used for the breading because the light cereal sweetness mimics the sweetness of fried oysters. Regular fine breadcrumbs will work too.

Fresh oyster mushrooms are sometimes difficult to locate. However, canned oyster mushrooms can be purchased from your local Asian market and are very inexpensive. They also have the perfect texture for this recipe. If you cannot locate canned or fresh oyster mushrooms, other mushrooms of your choice, such as shiitake, chanterelles and even button mushrooms, can always be substituted. Serve with vegan tartar sauce or cocktail sauce. Here I've served them with a vegan fire-roasted jalapeno and lime tartar sauce (recipe included).

Ingredients

- 2 cans (about 7.5 oz drained weight) oyster mushrooms
  or 10 oz fresh oyster mushrooms, quartered
- ¼ cup all-purpose flour
- ¼ cup non-dairy milk
- 2 T No-Eggy Mayo (page 263) or commercial vegan mayonnaise
- ¾ cup cornflake crumbs or fine breadcrumbs, or more as needed
- 1 tsp Gentle Bay Seasoning (page 150) or commercial Old Bay™ seasoning
- 1 tsp kelp powder (optional)
- cooking oil for frying

Preparation

If using canned mushrooms, drain the water. Remove any tough portion of the canned or fresh mushroom stems. Slice any large mushrooms into quarters; medium mushrooms in half; and small mushrooms leave whole.

In a small bowl, whisk together the milk, flour and mayo until smooth and pour into a sealable food storage bag. Add a few pinches of salt, seal the bag and shake until the mushrooms are coated.

Add the cornflake crumbs/breadcrumbs, bay seasoning and kelp powder to a bowl and dredge the mushroom quarters in the crumbs until well-coated. Set the strips aside on a plate to dry while the oil heats.

In a deep wok or skillet, heat about ½-inch of oil over medium-high heat until the oil begins to shimmer. Fry the mushrooms until golden; they cook quickly, about 30 to 45 seconds, so watch them carefully. Remove with a slotted spoon and drain on a plate lined with paper towels. Serve hot with the condiment of your choice for dipping.

Fire Roasted Jalapeno and Lime Tartar Sauce

Ingredients

- 1 large jalapeno pepper
- ½ cup No-Eggy Mayo (page 263) or commercial vegan mayonnaise
- 2 T minced fresh onion

- 1 tsp fresh grated lime zest and a squeeze of fresh lime juice
- sea salt or kosher salt to taste

Preparation

Place the jalapeno directly on the stove burner over medium heat. Turn frequently with tongs until the pepper is blistered and blackened. Place the pepper in small food storage or paper bag and seal to hold in the steam. Let cool. The skin should slip off easily. Cut off the stem end, split the jalapeno lengthwise and remove the seeds. Finely mince and add to a small bowl.

Add the mayo, onion, the lime zest and a squeeze of lime juice. Mix well and season with salt to taste. Refrigerate to blend flavors and until ready to serve.

Roman Artichokes

A very simple yet elegant way to serve canned artichoke hearts as an appetizer.

Ingredients

- 1 can (14 oz before draining) artichoke hearts, rinsed well, drained and halved
- 2 T Better Butter (from my cookbook) or commercial vegan margarine
- 2 T olive oil
- 4 tsp minced garlic (4 cloves)
- 1 tsp dried oregano
- ½ tsp cornstarch or unmodified potato starch
- ½ cup dry white wine (e.g., Chardonnay, Sauvignon Blanc)
- ¼ teaspoon red-pepper flakes, or to taste
- pinch sea salt or kosher salt
- 1 T chopped fresh flat-leaf parsley

Preparation

In a small saucepan over medium heat, warm the olive oil. Add the butter or margarine and stir until melted. Add the garlic and oregano and sauté for 1 minute.

Whisk in the starch until smooth and then whisk in the wine. Add the red pepper flakes and salt. Bring to a simmer, stirring frequently, for about 2 minutes, and then remove from the heat.

In a small heatproof chafing dish or skillet, arrange the halved artichoke hearts. Pour the sauce over and place under the broiler to heat through, about 5 to 6 minutes. Garnish with chopped parsley and additional red pepper flakes if desired.

Serve with a crusty Italian bread to soak up the extra sauce.

Accompaniments

Green Beans
with Sweet Onion and Savory, Sweet and Smoky Almonds

Tender crisp green beans are tossed with sautéed sweet onion and toasted savory, sweet and smoky sliced almonds. This simple but classic and elegant dish yields about 6 servings.

Ingredients

- ½ cup sliced almonds
- 1 T tamari, soy sauce or Bragg Liquid Aminos™
- 1 and ½ tsp dark brown sugar
- 1 tsp liquid smoke
- 1 tsp Worcestershire Sauce (page 27) or commercial vegan equivalent
- 1 and ½ lbs fresh green beans, trimmed
- 1 large sweet yellow onion, diced
- ¼ cup non-dairy butter or margarine
- sea salt or kosher salt and coarse ground black pepper, to taste

Preparation

In a bowl, whisk together the tamari, brown sugar, liquid smoke and Worcestershire until the sugar is dissolved. Add the sliced almonds and toss well to evenly distribute the mixture. Cover and refrigerate for a minimum of several hours, and better overnight, to allow the almonds to absorb the liquid seasoning.

Preheat the oven to 350°F/175°C.

Line a baking sheet with parchment paper or a silicone baking mat and distribute the almonds in a single layer. Place the baking sheet in the oven on a middle rack and set a timer for 8 minutes.

Remove from the oven and stir the almonds, again redistributing them in a single layer. Place them back in the oven and bake for about 8 minutes or until the almonds are lightly crisp. Remove from the oven and let cool.

While the almonds are toasting, bring a large pot of water to a boil. Add the green beans and cook about 10 to 15 minutes or until just tender. Drain thoroughly.

Add the butter to a large skillet and place over medium heat to melt. Add the onion and sauté until golden. Add the green beans and almonds and toss thoroughly together. Continue to cook until heated through; season with salt and pepper taste. Transfer to a serving dish and serve immediately.

German Spätzle

Spätzle, which literally translates as "little sparrows", are noodle-like German dumplings. This recipe requires my Gentle Chef Vegan Eggz Essentials as a replacement for eggs, which in turn produces very light and tender dumplings. Gentle Chef Vegan Eggs Essentials is my own product available exclusively through ModernistPantry.com. If you cannot access my product, replace the Essentials with 2 teaspoons commercial egg replacer powder, such as Ener-G™ egg replacer, although results may differ.

To form the Spätzle, you can use a traditional Spätzle maker or a Spätzle press. If you don't have either device, a food mill or a standard colander with holes (not slots) will work too. This recipe yields 2 generous servings to 4 side servings.

Dry Ingredient

- 1 cup all-purpose flour

Liquid Ingredients

- 1 cup plain unsweetened soymilk or almond milk
- 2 tsp nutritional yeast flakes
- 1 and ½ tsp Vegan Eggz Essentials A
- ½ tsp Vegan Eggz Essentials B
- ½ tsp fine sea salt or kosher salt
- ¼ tsp ground nutmeg
- ⅛ tsp ground white pepper

Finishing Ingredients

- 1 to 2 T non-dairy butter or margarine
- sea salt or kosher salt and coarse ground black pepper to taste
- 2 T optional garnish, such as chopped green onion or minced chives, fresh chopped parsley and/or chopped fresh dill

Preparation

Bring about 3 quarts of water to a rolling boil in a large pot. Add two teaspoons of salt.

Spray the Spätzle maker or press on both sides, including the little basket with cooking oil spray. If using a colander, spray the interior and exterior bottom of the basket. Set aside.

While the water is coming to a boil, add the flour to a mixing bowl. Process the liquid ingredients in a blender for 20 seconds. Add the liquid mixture to the flour and whisk until a smooth and thick batter consistency is achieved. To thin the batter if desired, add small amounts of additional milk.

If using a Spätzle maker, rest it over the pot of boiling water. Spoon the batter into the basket and slide the basket back and forth to drop bits of batter into the water.

If using a press, add the mixture to the basket and gently press the batter, in increments, into the water. If using a colander, hold the basket handle with an oven mitt to protect from steam burns and press and scrape the batter through the holes in the bottom of the basket with a flexible spatula.

Cook the dumplings about 2 minutes. Use a slotted spoon or Chinese spider skimmer to collect the dumplings and place them in a bowl.

Transfer the dumplings to a colander in the sink and give them a light rinse; drain well.

In a large skillet over medium heat, melt 1 to 2 tablespoons non-dairy butter or margarine. Add the Spätzle to the skillet and toss thoroughly until heated through. Season with salt and black pepper to taste, transfer to a serving bowl and garnish as desired; serve immediately. Also try folding in Golden Cheese Melt (page 220) and garnishing with chopped scallions.

Charred Brussels Sprout Slaw
with Shallots and Toasted Pine Nuts

This dish is very easy to prepare and may just win over dinner guests who never cared much for Brussels sprouts before. Any cold leftovers make a unique and delicious Spring roll filling.

Ingredients

- fresh Brussels sprouts, about 1 lb.
- ¼ cup pine nuts
- 2 T non-dairy butter, margarine or mild olive oil (plus more as desired)
- 2 shallots, thinly sliced
- 3 cloves garlic, minced
- sea salt or kosher salt and coarse ground black pepper, to taste

Preparation

Remove the tough stems from the Brussels sprouts and discard. Remove any outer leaves that are damaged or wilted. Shred the sprouts using the shredding blade in a food processor. Set aside.

In a small dry skillet, toast the pine nuts over medium heat. Stir the nuts frequently to evenly toast and prevent scorching. Set aside.

In a large skillet or wok, melt the butter or margarine (or heat the oil) over medium-low heat. Add the shallots and garlic and a pinch or two of salt. Sweat the shallots and garlic, about 10 minutes. You should hear a faint sizzle – if the sizzle is loud, reduce the heat a bit. The goal is to draw out flavor without browning the shallots or garlic.

Add the slaw and a pinch or two of salt. Increase the heat to medium-high. Stir the mixture occasionally. The goal is to slightly char the vegetables just a bit. If the vegetables seem dry, add another tablespoon or two of non-dairy butter, margarine or olive oil, if desired. Cook until the slaw is tender crisp. Season the slaw with black pepper to taste and add additional salt as desired. Sprinkle with the toasted pine nuts and serve immediately.

Irish Colcannon

Colcannon is a traditional Irish dish consisting of creamy, buttery mashed potatoes and cooked cabbage seasoned with green onions, salt, pepper and parsley. Here, I've replaced the cabbage with kale, for the bright green contrast. If you prefer, replace the kale with tender cooked cabbage.

Ingredients

- 3 pounds russet potatoes (about 4 large)
- ½ cup non-dairy butter or margarine,
  plus 1 to 2 T additional melted butter or margarine for garnish
- 1 cup plain unsweetened soymilk or almond milk, warmed until hot
- 1 T olive oil
- 6 oz baby kale; or mature kale with tough ribs removed and then chopped
- 3 green onions, white and green parts, finely chopped
- sea salt or kosher salt, to taste
- coarse ground black pepper, to taste
- 2 T chopped parsley for garnish

Preparation

Peel and cut the potatoes into large chunks. Immediately immerse the cut potatoes in 4 quarts of water. Add 1 tablespoon of salt and bring to a boil. Cook until fork tender, about 8 to 10 minutes.

While the potatoes are cooking, flash sauté the kale and green onions with the olive oil in a large skillet until the kale is wilted and tender. Transfer to a bowl and set aside.

Drain the potatoes in a colander and then transfer to a large mixing bowl or back to the cooking pot. Mash the potatoes with the butter and hot milk. Add salt and pepper to taste. Stir in the sautéed kale and green onions.

Transfer the colcannon to a serving dish and garnish with the parsley. Make a well in the center of the colcannon and garnish with a tablespoon or two of melted butter or margarine. Serve immediately.

Potato, Leek and Fennel Gratin

Sliced gold potatoes, fennel bulb and chopped leeks are bathed in a rich non-dairy Gruyère cheese sauce and baked until browned and bubbly.

Ingredients

- 2 T non-dairy butter or margarine, plus 1 T for greasing the baking dish
- 2 and ½ lbs Yukon gold potatoes
- 2 large leeks, white and light green parts only,
  split lengthwise, rinsed well and chopped into half "moons"
- 1 large fennel bulb, cored and sliced very thin
- 2 cloves garlic, minced
- ½ tsp dried thyme leaves
- coarse ground black pepper, to taste
- 2 cups Gruyère Cheese Sauce (see following recipe)

Gratin Preparation

Grease the interior of a shallow, rectangular baking dish with 1 tablespoon butter or margarine and set aside.

Peel the potatoes and slice them ⅛-inch thick. A mandoline makes the job much easier and creates more uniform slices – but watch your fingers! Place the slices immediately into a large pot of water to prevent the slices from oxidizing (turning brown). Add 2 teaspoons of salt. Bring to a boil and cook for exactly 1 minute. Remove from the heat and drain the slices thoroughly in a colander. Set aside.

Add the remaining butter or margarine to a skillet and place over medium heat. Add the leeks and fennel and sauté until tender and golden. Add the garlic, thyme and a dash of black pepper and sauté an additional minute. Remove from the heat and set aside.

Preheat the oven to 375°F/190°C.

Prepare the Gruyère cheese sauce; set aside over low heat to keep warm.

Layer ⅓ of the potatoes in the bottom of the baking dish and top with half of the leek and fennel mixture. Pour half of the cheese sauce over the layers. Repeat layering with another ⅓ of the potatoes, the remaining leek and fennel mixture and finish with a layer of potatoes. Cover with the remaining sauce and season with additional ground black pepper.

Bake uncovered for 45 minutes or until browned nicely. Remove from the oven and serve.

Gruyère Cheese Sauce

Dairy Gruyère is a slightly salty, ripened Swiss cheese. While its texture and complex flavor is difficult to reproduce in non-dairy form, this cheese sauce captures the flavor of Gruyère fairly well, while retaining its own unique character.

Ingredients

- 1 cup Cultured Yogurt (page 194)*
- ¾ cup plain unsweetened soymilk or almond milk
- ¼ cup neutral vegetable oil
- ¼ cup tapioca starch
- 2 T nutritional yeast flakes
- 2 T mellow white miso paste
- 2 T extra-dry vermouth or dry white wine (optional)**
- ¾ tsp fine sea salt or kosher salt, or more to taste
- ¼ tsp dry ground mustard
- ¼ tsp ground coriander

*The yogurt can be replaced with plain unsweetened soymilk or almond milk and ¾ tsp lactic acid powder if necessary, although the finished flavor profile will differ.

**The vermouth or wine can be omitted for health or ethical reasons, although the finished flavor profile will differ.

Sauce Preparation

Process all ingredients in a blender until smooth. Transfer to a medium saucepan. Cook the mixture over medium-low heat, stirring slowly and continually with a flexible spatula.

As the mixture thickens and curdles (forms lumps), begin stirring vigorously until the curds disappear and the sauce becomes thickened, smooth and glossy. Season with salt to taste (Gruyère should be somewhat salty). Keep warm over low heat, stirring occasionally, until ready to use.

Holiday Green Bean Casserole

A classic holiday favorite consisting of tender green beans baked in an onion and mushroom sauce and topped with crispy fried onions.

Ingredients

- 1 and ½ lbs fresh green beans trimmed into bite-size pieces
- 2 T flour all-purpose flour or rice flour
- 1 tsp garlic powder
- 1 tsp onion powder
- 1 and ½ cups plain unsweetened soymilk or almond milk
- 2 T tamari, soy sauce or Bragg Liquid Aminos™
- 1 tsp Worcestershire Sauce (page 27) or commercial vegan equivalent
- 2 T olive oil
- 2 T non-dairy butter or margarine plus additional for "buttering" the casserole dish
- 1 and ½ cups finely chopped white or cremini mushrooms
- sea salt or kosher salt and ground black pepper to taste
- 1 and ⅓ cup crispy French-fried onions (recipe follows) or commercial equivalent

Preparation

Boil the green beans until just tender, about 10 to 15 minutes. Drain thoroughly and set aside in a large mixing bowl. Preheat the oven to 350°F/175°C. Lightly butter a casserole dish with the butter or margarine and set aside.

In a small dish, measure the flour, onion powder and garlic powder; set aside. In a measuring cup, measure the non-dairy milk and add the tamari and Worcestershire sauce; set aside.

Add the olive oil to a medium saucepan. Add the mushrooms and sauté until the excess liquid has evaporated from the mushrooms. Transfer the mushrooms to the mixing bowl with the green beans and set aside.

In the same saucepan, melt the 2 tablespoons of butter or margarine over medium-low heat and whisk in the flour mixture. Continue to stir for about a minute. The mixture will be very thick and pasty. Don't be concerned if the flour sticks to the bottom of the saucepan as it will loosen when the milk mixture is added.

Slowly whisk in the milk mixture until smooth, add a pinch or two of black pepper and bring to the mixture to a boil, stirring constantly. Reduce heat and simmer an additional 2 to 3 minutes. The mixture will have a somewhat thin consistency; this is desirable as it will thicken when the casserole is baked. Taste and add salt to your liking and additional black pepper, if desired. Remove from the heat.

Gently toss together the cream mixture with the green beans, mushrooms and ⅔ cup French-fried onions in the mixing bowl. Transfer to the casserole dish.

Bake uncovered for 25 minutes or until the bean mixture is hot and bubbling around the edges. Gently stir and top with the remaining ⅔ cup onions. Bake for an additional 5 minutes or until the onions are golden brown.

Crispy French-Fried Onions

Crispy French-fried onions make a superb topping for cooked vegetables, casseroles, meatless burgers and sandwiches.

Ingredients

- 2 large sweet yellow onions, peeled
- plain unsweetened soymilk or almond milk for soaking the onions
- 1 and ½ cups all-purpose flour
- 1 and ½ tsp sea salt or kosher salt
- 1 tsp coarse ground black pepper
- ¼ tsp cayenne pepper
- cooking oil for frying

Preparation

Mix the flour, salt, and ground pepper in a large bowl. Slice the onions and separate into rings. Soak the onions in the milk.

Heat about 1-inch of oil in a large skillet over medium-high heat until it begins to shimmer.

Dredge the onions in the seasoned flour. Give them a good coating of flour. Place the onions into the hot oil in the skillet. Don't try to do all the onions at one; just one batch at a time.

When the onions begin to brown around the edges, turn them over and cook an additional minute or so (they cook very quickly!) Remove the rings and lay them on a paper bag or paper towels to cool/drain. Serve immediately or store in an air-tight container for topping your casseroles.

Sage Dressing
with Mushrooms and Water Chestnuts

This is a traditional sage bread dressing or stuffing enhanced with sautéed mushrooms and crunchy water chestnuts. Begin this recipe a day ahead of time to allow the bread to sufficiently dry.

Ingredients

- 1 loaf (about 16 oz) white or whole grain bread
- 2 T neutral vegetable oil
- 1 medium onion, diced
- 2 ribs celery, diced
- 1 can (8 oz with liquid) whole water chestnuts, drained and cut in half
- 2 cloves garlic, crushed and finely minced
- 1 T dry rubbed sage
- 1 tsp dried thyme
- ½ tsp sea salt or kosher salt
- ½ tsp coarse ground black pepper
- ¼ cup non-dairy butter or margarine
- 12 oz white or cremini mushrooms or a blend of exotic mushrooms of your choice, cut into quarters or bite-size pieces
- ¼ cup chopped parsley
- 1 cup turky simmering broth (page 71) or vegetable broth

Preparation

Preheat the oven to 200°F/95°C. Cut the bread into ½-inch cubes and place in a single layer on 1 or 2 baking sheets. Place in the oven for 1 to 1 and ½ hours or until the bread is dry to the touch; a very slight degree of moistness is okay. Transfer to a large mixing bowl and let sit out overnight.

When ready to prepare the dressing, preheat the oven to 375°F/190°C. Grease a large, shallow baking dish with butter or margarine and set aside.

In a large skillet, add the oil and place over medium heat. Add the onions and celery and sauté until the onions are translucent. Add the water chestnuts, garlic, sage, thyme, salt and pepper and continue to sauté an additional minute. Transfer to the mixing bowl.

In the same skillet, melt 2 tablespoons of the butter or margarine over medium heat. Add the mushrooms and sauté until golden. Add the remaining 2 tablespoons butter or margarine and stir just until melted. Transfer to the mixing bowl, add the parsley and toss all of the ingredients together thoroughly.

Drizzle in half of the broth and toss thoroughly. Drizzle in the remaining half and toss until the dressing is evenly moistened. Transfer to the baking dish and bake uncovered for 45 minutes or until a nice golden crust forms on top. Serve warm.

Potatoes Dauphinoise

In the culinary arts, the French word "Dauphinoise" refers to a recipe in which potatoes are sliced, layered in a baking dish and then baked au gratin with garlic, butter, heavy cream, cheese (traditionally Gruyère or Swiss Emmental) and a hint of ground nutmeg.

The name Dauphinoise comes from the Dauphiné region of France, where the recipe is said to have originated. Although the names are similar, Potatoes Dauphinoise is not the same recipe as Dauphine potatoes, which are balls of puréed potatoes mixed with choux pastry and then deep-fried until light and crispy.

For the non-dairy version of this dish, Sauce Fromage Blanc was chosen for its flavor, as well as its simplicity in preparation. The combination of the cheesy sauce with the moisture from the boiled potato slices creates a superb heavy cream and melted cheese texture.

Ingredients

- 2 cloves garlic
- 2 and ½ lbs Yukon gold potatoes or russet potatoes
- 2 cups Sauce Fromage Blanc (recipe follows)
- ½ tsp ground white pepper
- 1 T non-dairy butter or margarine
- ground nutmeg

Preparation

Cut the garlic cloves in half and rub the interior of a shallow casserole dish. Set the dish aside and save the garlic.

Peel the potatoes and slice them ⅛-inch thick. A mandoline makes the job much easier and creates more uniform slices - but watch your fingers! Place the slices immediately into a large pot of water to prevent the slices from oxidizing (turning brown). Add 2 teaspoons of salt and add the cut garlic. Bring to a boil and cook for exactly 3 minutes.

Remove from the heat and drain the slices in a colander. Do not rinse with cold water and do not pat the potatoes dry with paper towels! The potatoes will continue to cook slightly as they cool in the colander. Discard the garlic.

Preheat the oven to 400°F/200°C.

In the meantime, prepare the Sauce Fromage Blanc according to the recipe and stir in the white pepper. Taste and season with additional salt as desired; set aside over low heat to keep warm.

Grease the interior of the baking dish with the butter. Place a layer of potatoes in the bottom of the baking dish and pour some of the cheese sauce over the layer. Repeat layering with the potatoes and the sauce. Be sure to leave enough sauce to cover the top of the potatoes.

Very lightly dust the top of the potatoes with ground nutmeg. Bake uncovered for 45 minutes. If the top has not sufficiently browned, set the oven on "broil" and cook an additional 1 to 2 minutes. Watch carefully so the potatoes do not burn. Remove from the oven and serve.

Sauce Fromage Blanc

This smooth, mild and creamy white cheese sauce is an ingredient in Potatoes Dauphinoise (see preceding recipe) and is also superb for pouring over pasta, potatoes, vegetables or savory filled crêpes. This recipe yields about 2 cups of sauce.

Ingredients

- 1 and ¾ cup plain unsweetened nondairy milk or almond milk
- ¼ cup neutral vegetable oil
- 3 T tapioca starch
- 2 T dry sherry or dry white wine
- 2 T nutritional yeast flakes
- 1 T mellow white miso paste
- 1 T sesame tahini
- ½ tsp fine sea salt or kosher salt, or more to taste
- ¼ tsp ground coriander

*The sherry or wine can be omitted for health or ethical reasons, but this will alter the flavor profile.

Preparation

Whisk the ingredients together in a small saucepan until smooth.

Place over medium-low heat and stir slowly and continually with a flexible spatula until the mixture becomes bubbly, thickened, smooth and glossy.

Taste and add salt as desired and/or additional soymilk to lighten the consistency to your preference.

Reduce the heat to low to keep warm until ready to serve, stirring occasionally.

Jellied Port Wine Cranberry Sauce

A whole-fruit jellied cranberry sauce made with organic sugar (commercial jellied sauce is typically made with corn syrup) and flavored with Port wine or pomegranate juice; or try fresh orange juice for a citrus flavor.

Ingredients

- 1 bag (12 oz) whole fresh cranberries
- 1 cup organic sugar
- ½ cup (120 ml) water
- ½ cup (120 ml) Port wine or pomegranate juice or fresh orange juice
- 1 and ¼ tsp agar powder

Special Supplies

- flexible silicone mold that will hold 2 cups liquid (such as used in non-dairy cheese making)
- blender

Preparation

Place the silicone mold on a small plate.

Examine the cranberries and remove any stray stems. Rinse them and place in a medium saucepan (reserve a few cranberries for garnish if desired). Sprinkle the sugar over the cranberries and the agar powder over the sugar.

Add the wine (or juice) and water. Bring to a boil and then reduce to a simmer for 10 minutes, stirring occasionally. You may hear the berries audibly pop as they cook. Watch the cooking pot so the mixture doesn't boil over.

Transfer the hot mixture to a blender. Cover and begin blending on low speed gradually increasing to high for 1 minute. If your blender doesn't have variable speed settings, cover and hold the lid with a kitchen towel to prevent hot liquid from explosively erupting from the blender.

Transfer the mixture to the mold and let cool. Cover with plastic wrap and refrigerate for several hours or until thoroughly chilled and set.

Remove the plastic wrap and run a dull table knife around the perimeter to loosen the jellied sauce (be careful not to damage the mold). Invert a serving plate over the mold and then flip the two plates over to release the jellied sauce. Garnish with the fresh cranberries and a sprig of fresh mint if desired. Serve cold.

Butter-Browned Brussels Sprouts
with Cauliflower Cashew Cream

Brussels sprouts are cooked until tender, skillet-browned in non-dairy butter until golden and topped with a luscious cream made from cashews and cauliflower.

Ingredients

- fresh Brussels sprouts, about 1 lb
- 2 T non-dairy butter or margarine
- ½ small head cauliflower, separated into florets
- ¾ cup water
- 2 T raw cashews (pre-soaking unnecessary)
- ¼ tsp dried thyme leaves
- sea salt or kosher salt and coarse ground black pepper, to taste

Preparation

Remove the tough stems from the Brussels sprouts and discard. Remove any outer leaves that are damaged or wilted. Cut the sprouts in half. Steam the sprouts over boiling water for 5 minutes. Set aside in a bowl.

Steam the cauliflower florets over boiling water until just tender, about 4 minutes. While the florets are steaming, add the cashews and water to a blender and process for 1 full minute. Add the steamed cauliflower, thyme and ¼ tsp salt to the cashew mixture and process the contents for 1 full minute.

Transfer to a small saucepan and place over low heat to cook gently until heated through, stirring occasionally. Season the cream with pepper and additional salt to taste.

In a large skillet or wok, melt the butter or margarine over medium-high heat. Add the Brussels sprouts and a pinch or two of salt and sauté until golden brown. Transfer to a serving platter or bowl and garnish with the cauliflower cashew cream. Serve immediately.

Creamed Baby Peas and Pearl Onions

Tender peas and pearl onions are bathed in a lightly-seasoned non-dairy cream.

Ingredients

- 12 oz pearl onions, from frozen, thawed and drained well
- 16 oz baby peas from frozen, thawed and drained well
- 4 T mild olive oil, divided in half
- 2 cups plain unsweetened non-dairy milk
- 1.5 oz/43 grams (about ⅓ cup) raw cashews (pre-soaking unnecessary)
- 1 T nutritional yeast flakes
- 1 and ½ tsp onion powder
- 1 tsp fine sea salt or kosher salt, or more to taste
- ½ tsp garlic powder
- ¼ tsp ground white pepper

Preparation

Add 2 tablespoons olive oil to a skillet and place over medium heat. Sauté the onions until lightly browned in a few spots. Transfer to a bowl and set aside.

In a blender, add the remaining 2 tablespoons olive oil, non-dairy milk, cashews, yeast flakes and seasonings. Process the contents on high speed for 2 full minutes and then transfer to a large saucepan.

Bring the mixture to a gentle simmer and cook until slightly thickened, stirring frequently. Stir in the onions and peas and continue to gently simmer, about 10 minutes. Transfer to a serving dish and serve immediately.

Hasselback Potatoes

Named after the Stockholm restaurant that first introduced them, Hasselback potatoes have been adopted widely by other European cuisines. The potatoes are kept whole but thinly sliced partially through which gives them a beautiful fan-like appearance. They're baked in a very hot oven which gives them a crispy exterior but tender interior.

Ingredients

- large Yukon gold or russet potatoes, unpeeled
- 1 T non-dairy butter or margarine for each potato
- optional: 1 clove of garlic, thinly sliced for each potato
- coarse sea salt or kosher salt, to taste
- coarse ground black pepper, to taste

Optional garnish

- finely chopped parsley or minced chives

Preparation

Preheat the oven to 450°F/230°C.

Place 2 chopsticks on your cutting surface parallel to each other and place a potato in between them. The chopsticks will be used as a cutting guide to prevent the knife from cutting all the way through the potatoes when slicing. If you don't have chopsticks on hand, use the handle side of 2 table knives. Using a sharp chef's knife, begin making ⅛-inch slices throughout the entire length of each potato.

In a small saucepan, melt the butter over low heat; alternately this can be done in the microwave. Place the potatoes on a baking sheet lined with parchment paper, and with a pastry brush, brush the melted butter into the gaps of every potato. Use your fingers to gently separate the layers if necessary. Make sure that every potato gets a generous amount of the melted butter. Generously season the potatoes with salt and pepper to taste. If using the optional garlic, insert the garlic slices randomly between the potato slices.

Place the potatoes in the preheated oven on a middle rack and cook for 1 hour and 15 minutes until crispy on the outside and tender on the inside. Garnish with fresh chopped Italian parsley or minced chives if desired.

Cheesy Broccoli Cauliflower Rice Casserole

A comforting family favorite!

Ingredients

- 1 T non-dairy butter or margarine
- 1 cup uncooked rice of your choice
- chikun simmering broth (page 41), vegetable broth or water*
- ½ medium onion, diced
- 2 cups mix of chopped broccoli and cauliflower
- Golden Cheese Melt (page 220)
- additional plain unsweetened soymilk or almond milk to adjust consistency as needed
- sea salt or kosher salt and coarse ground black pepper, to taste

The amount of broth or water required will depend upon the rice you are using; use the appropriate amount according to the directions on the package. For this dish, I use white basmati rice and 1 cup uncooked basmati rice requires 2 cups of broth or water.

Preparation

In a large saucepan, bring the broth or water to a boil. Add the butter or margarine, rice and onion. Stir well, cover, reduce heat to a simmer and cook for the amount of time suggested on the rice package.

Meanwhile, while the rice is cooking, prepare your cheese melt and set aside. Preheat the oven to 350°F/175°C.

During the last 10 minutes of cooking time for the rice, add the vegetables on top of the rice and replace the lid. Do not stir! The vegetables will steam while the rice completes cooking.

Stir the cheese melt into the rice/vegetable mixture and season with salt and pepper to taste. If the mixture seems a bit dry, stir in small amounts of soymilk in increments until the desired consistency is reached.

Transfer the mixture to a lightly oiled casserole dish, cover and bake for 30 minutes.

Uncover the casserole dish, set the oven on broil and lightly brown the top of the cheesy rice mixture under the broiler, about 5 minutes. Serve immediately.

Bhindi Masala
(Indian-Spiced Okra)

Bhindi masala is a very popular Indian dish consisting of spiced okra, onions and tomatoes. Okra is a powerhouse of nutrition due to its high soluble fiber, vitamin C, and folate content. It's also high in antioxidants and a good source of calcium and potassium. Okra contains a large amount of mucilage: a slimy substance which is responsible for its high soluble fiber content. This gooey mucilage is very evident when okra begins cooking but dissolves when thoroughly cooked and mixed with the acidity of the tomatoes.

Ingredients

- ¼ cup olive oil, divided in half
- 1 tsp cumin seeds
- 1 large onion, chopped
- 1 medium green chili, finely diced (mild or hot, your choice)
- 1 lb fresh okra (bhindi) cut into ½-inch pieces
  or a 1 lb bag of frozen cut okra, thawed
- 1 tsp sea salt or kosher salt
- 4 tsp coriander powder
- ½ tsp turmeric
- ½ tsp dry ground mustard
- ¼ tsp chili powder (mild or hot, your choice)
- large tomatoes, peeled and chopped * or 1 can (15 oz.) diced tomatoes

*To peel fresh tomatoes, drop them in boiling water for 1 minute and then immediately transfer to an ice water bath; the skins will slip off easily.

Preparation

Heat 2 tablespoons of the oil in a large skillet over medium-high heat. When hot, add the cumin seeds and cook for about 30 seconds.

Add the remaining 2 tablespoons of oil and the onion and green chili. Sauté until the onions are translucent. Add the okra and salt and cook, stirring frequently, until the vegetables begin to lightly brown, about 15 minutes. The okra will be very slimy – this is normal.

Now, stir in the masala (coriander, turmeric, mustard powder and chili powder) and cook for 5 minutes.

Add the chopped tomatoes, mix well and continue to cook until the tomatoes are cooked through and any excess moisture has been evaporated, about 15 to 20 minutes; the mixture should resemble a thick stew.

Add additional salt to taste and serve hot.

Jicama Slaw

Jicama (pronounced hik-uh-mah) is a large, bulbous root vegetable, weighing one to two pounds. Jicama has a rough brown skin which needs to be peeled before eating. The flesh is white, wet and crunchy, similar to a raw potato but with a slightly sweet and nutty flavor. This refreshing slaw is ideal for cooling the heat of spicy Mexican, Indian or Thai cuisine or simply as a side dish on a hot Summer day.

Ingredients

- 1 large jicama, peeled and shredded
- ½ red onion, shaved thin
- 2 carrots, shredded
- ¼ cup finely chopped cilantro leaves

Dressing ingredients

- ½ cup neutral vegetable oil
- ⅓ cup unseasoned rice vinegar
- 2 T organic sugar or brown rice syrup
- 2 T fresh squeezed lime juice
- 1 tsp ancho chili powder (or another mild chili powder)
- 1 tsp ground cumin
- 1 tsp sea salt or kosher salt
- ½ tsp coarse ground black pepper

Preparation

In a bowl, whisk together the dressing ingredients; set aside. Place the shredded jicama, red onion and shredded carrots in a large bowl. Pour the dressing over the jicama mixture and toss to coat well (you may not need all of the dressing; just add enough to thoroughly coat the mixture). Fold in the cilantro. Refrigerate until thoroughly chilled, allowing the flavors to merge together.

Mediterranean Cauliflower Couscous

This light and fluffy couscous contains no grain. It is comprised entirely of cauliflower with a Mediterranean blend of herbs and spices. The dish can also be served raw; simply omit roasting. You will need a food processor to achieve the proper couscous texture from the cauliflower.

Ingredients

- 1 head of cauliflower, cut into florets
- 2 T olive oil
- 2 T fresh lemon juice
- 4 T chopped fresh parsley (¼ cup) or 4 tsp dried parsley
- 2 to 3 cloves garlic, finely minced
- 1 tsp ground cumin
- ½ tsp ground coriander
- ½ tsp sea salt or kosher salt, or more to taste
- ½ tsp coarse ground black pepper, or more to taste

Preparation

Preheat the oven to 425°F/220°C.

Place about ¼ of the cauliflower florets into the food processor. Pulse until the florets are reduced to a grainy texture. Transfer the cauliflower "grain" to a large oven-proof skillet or a roasting pan. Repeat with the additional florets.

Add the remaining ingredients to the cauliflower and mix well to combine. Add additional salt and pepper to taste.

Place the skillet or roasting pan in the oven and roast for 25 to 30 minutes. After 10 minutes of cooking time, remove the skillet or pan and stir the mixture. Place back in the oven and continue to roast. Repeat stirring at the "20 minute" mark.

After roasting, fluff the couscous with a fork and transfer to a serving dish. Serve immediately.

Roasted Acorn Squash
With Cumin-Scented Couscous Stuffing

Roasted acorn squash is stuffed with a cumin-scented couscous, caramelized carrots, leeks, shallots, raisins and walnuts or almonds. This dish is very filling and is actually more appropriate when served as an entrée rather than a side dish. This recipe serves 4.

Ingredients

- 2 large acorn squash
- 2 T olive oil
- 1 large carrot, peeled and small diced
- 1 large shallot, diced
- 1 medium leek, split lengthwise, rinsed to remove grit and then chopped
- ¼ cup chopped walnuts or slivered almonds
- 1 clove garlic, minced
- ½ tsp ground cumin
- pinch cayenne or ground red pepper
- ½ cup chicken simmering broth (page 41) or vegetable broth
- ½ cup dry couscous
- 2 T dark raisins

Preparation

Preheat the oven to 350°F/175°C.

Using a cleaver or sharp, sturdy knife carefully split the squash from stem end to tip. The squash will tend to rock on the cutting board so exercise great caution when cutting and keep your fingers out of the way! Use a spoon to scoop out the seeds and stringy pulp. Brush or mist the flesh with cooking oil, season with a pinch or two of salt and place cut side down on a baking sheet lined with foil or parchment paper. Bake for 1 hour or until the rind of the squash can be pierced with a fork.

While the squash is baking, add the oil to a skillet and place over medium heat. Add the carrots and a pinch of salt and sauté until the carrots begin to caramelize a bit. Add the shallots and leeks and continue to sauté until golden.

Add the walnuts or almonds, garlic, cumin and red pepper and sauté for 1 minute. Remove from the heat and set aside.

In a small saucepan, bring the stock or broth to a brief boil and add the raisins. Remove the saucepan from the heat and stir in the dry couscous. Mix well and cover. Let rest for 10 minutes. Mix the couscous with the sautéed vegetables in the skillet; season with salt as needed.

Spoon the couscous mixture in the squash cavity. If reheating is necessary, place the stuffed squash in a baking dish, cover with foil and heat in a 350°F/175°C oven for 20 to 30 minutes. Serve immediately.

Creamy Parmesan Polenta

Polenta is coarsely or finely ground yellow or white cornmeal boiled with water, milk or broth into a smooth porridge. Try this creamy and flavorful polenta recipe as an alternative to mashed potatoes or rice when you plan your next dinner menu; makes 3 to 4 servings.

Ingredients

- 1 cup plain non-dairy milk, plus additional for adjusting consistency
- 1 cup chikun simmering broth (page 41), vegetable broth, or commercial vegan equivalent
- 2 T non-dairy butter or margarine
- ¼ tsp fine sea salt or kosher salt, or more to taste
- ½ cup yellow cornmeal (not corn flour)
- ¼ tsp coarse ground black pepper, or more to taste
- ¼ cup grated Hard Parmesano (page 208), or commercial vegan equivalent

Preparation

In a medium saucepan over medium-high heat, bring the milk, broth, butter or margarine and salt to a brief boil (keep an eye on the mixture so it does not boil over).

Immediately reduce the heat to medium-low and gradually and vigorously whisk in the corn meal. Reduce the heat to low, cover and cook for 20 minutes, lifting the lid and stirring every 3 or 4 minutes to prevent sticking.

Towards the last 5 minutes of cooking time, whisk in additional milk as needed to adjust the consistency. The polenta should be thick and creamy but never stiff.

Stir in the pepper and parmesan. Check the seasoning and add additional salt and pepper to taste. If necessary, adjust the consistency again by adding more milk.

The polenta may be made up to 20 minutes ahead of time and kept covered until ready to serve. Garnish if desired and serve.

Whipped Potato and Parsnip Gratin

A fluffy and creamy gratin of whipped potatoes and parsnips blended with non-dairy butter, tangy non-dairy sour cream and gooey, melted non-dairy Jarlsberg cheese.

Ingredients

- 6 medium russet potatoes
- 4 medium parsnips
- ¼ cup non-dairy butter or margarine
- ½ tsp fine sea salt or kosher salt
- ¼ tsp ground white pepper
- ⅛ tsp ground nutmeg
- 1 cup Instant Sour Cream (page 176) or Cultured Sour Cream (page 177) or commercial non-dairy equivalent
- 1 cup Jarlsberg Cheese Melt (page 219)

Preparation

Peel and cut the potatoes into large chunks. Place the potatoes immediately into a large cooking pot with plenty of water to cover. This will prevent oxidation of the potatoes (turning brown) while the parsnips are peeled and sliced.

Peel and slice the parsnips. Add them to the pot with 1 tablespoon of salt. Bring the water to a boil and cook until the vegetables are fork tender, about 15 minutes. Avoid overcooking.

While the water is coming to a boil and the vegetables are cooking, prepare the Jarlsberg Melt and set aside to cool.

Preheat the oven to 350°F/175°F. "Butter" a large baking or casserole dish and set aside.

When the potatoes and parsnips are done cooking, drain them thoroughly in a colander for a few minutes and then transfer to a large mixing bowl. Add the butter, salt, white pepper and nutmeg and mash thoroughly using a potato ricer or masher.

Add the sour cream and whip the mashed vegetables with an electric rotary mixer (if you have one). Otherwise continue to mash by hand until the mixture is smooth and fluffy.

Note: Never use a blender or food processor to mash potatoes as this will damage the cell structure of the potatoes and cause them to fall flat or become gooey. When potatoes are boiled, their starch granules swell. If those granules are broken too vigorously, the cells release large quantities of starch, resulting in potatoes with a pasty consistency.

Transfer the mixture to the baking dish and top with the Jarlsberg Melt. Bake uncovered for 30 minutes and then place under the broiler for 1 to 2 minutes to achieve a bubbly and browned cheese crust on top. Serve immediately.

Hari Chutney
(Cilantro Mint)

This bright green, tangy and refreshing Indian chutney is my absolute favorite condiment. Enjoy it with all plant-based Indian cuisine and as a spread or dip for samosa (deep-fried or baked pastry with savory filling), pakoras (Indian vegetable fritters), naan, papadum, roti and any and all other flatbreads and crackers. If you have a timid palate, start with ½ of the green chili and increase according to taste.

Try mixing the chutney with plain non-dairy yogurt for a uniquely different salad dressing. It also adds wonderful flavor to non-dairy cultured yogurt, sour cream and even vegan mayonnaise. The chutney will last about 1 week stored in the refrigerator; simply freeze any unused portion (try freezing in silicone molds or ice cube trays for easy use). This recipe yields about 1 and ¾ cup.

Chef's note: Cilantro is the predominant ingredient in this chutney and is essential to the flavor. If you're not a fan of cilantro, it's best to avoid this condiment since parsley or other herbs are not suitable substitutes for this particular recipe.

Ingredients

- 2 large bunches of cilantro (aka coriander leaves; excess stems at bottom removed)
- 1 large handful of mint leaves (stems removed)
- 1 medium yellow onion, peeled and chopped
- 1 small green chili, seeded and chopped (or a large chili if you can take the heat)
- 1 clove garlic, peeled
- 2 T fresh lemon juice
- 1 tsp cumin seeds
- ¾ tsp sea salt or kosher salt, or more to taste

Preparation

Process all ingredients in a blender until smooth; season with additional salt to taste. Store the chutney in an airtight container in the refrigerator for up to 1 week.

Onion Chutney

This is my own variation of the classic Indian restaurant-style condiment. It's delightful as a topping for Indian naan, papadum, roti and any and all other flatbreads and crackers.

Ingredients

- 1 T cooking oil
- 1 tsp whole cumin seeds
- 1 large sweet yellow onion, peeled and medium diced
- 3 T water
- 1 T tomato paste
- 1 tsp apple cider vinegar
- ½ tsp sea salt or kosher salt
- ½ tsp organic sugar
- ½ tsp ground turmeric
- ½ tsp ground coriander
- ½ tsp ground fenugreek
- ¼ tsp ground cayenne pepper, or more for a spicier chutney
- optional garnish: chopped cilantro

Preparation

In a small bowl, stir together the water, tomato paste, vinegar, salt, sugar and ground seasonings. Set aside.

Heat the cooking oil in a medium skillet over medium-high heat. When hot, add the whole cumin seeds and fry about 20 seconds. Do not let them burn. Immediately add the onions and stir. Reduce the heat to low and sweat the onions, stirring frequently, about 5 minutes.

Add the seasoned tomato mixture and stir well to combine. Season with additional salt to taste, as desired. Bring to a brief simmer and then remove from the heat to cool. The onions should still retain a crunch. Transfer to a storage container and chill until ready to serve.

Gourmet Refrigerator Pickles

These easy-to-make pickles are fresh, crisp, tangy and nicely seasoned. The amount of brine is sufficient for preparing 2 quarts of pickles.

Ingredients

- 1 dozen pickling cucumbers
- 1 large onion, thinly sliced
- 3 cups filtered water
- ½ cup champagne vinegar or white vinegar
- 3 T sea salt or kosher salt
- 1 T organic sugar
- 2 T minced garlic (6 cloves)
- 2 T fresh chopped dill
- 1 tsp whole coriander seeds
- 1 tsp whole peppercorns or ½ tsp red pepper flakes
- 4 whole allspice berries
- 2 bay leaves

Preparation

In a bowl or large measuring cup, dissolve the salt and sugar in the vinegar and water to create the brine. Divide the remaining ingredients among the 2 jars. If using a large container, simply add them to the bottom of the container.

Leaving the peel intact, slice the cucumbers in half or quarter lengthwise.

Stand the spears upright in the 2 jars. If using a large container, lay the spears on their side or layer the slices.

Pour the brine over the cucumbers, submerging them completely. Cover tightly. Refrigerate for a minimum of 72 hours, but the longer they "pickle", the better. Enjoy!

Giardiniera - Gentle Chef House Recipe

Giardiniera (pronounced jar-dih-nair-ah) is an Italian-American condiment of pickled vegetables. Commercial giardiniera is a bit too "vinegary" for my taste, so I created my own blend which is nicely pickled and seasoned but not over-powering. The vegetables are wonderful served "as is" or they can be drizzled with olive oil just before serving. Allow a minimum of 1 week for sufficient pickling before serving.

Brine Ingredients

- 2 bay leaves
- 6 cloves garlic, chopped and divided in half
- 1 tsp dried oregano, divided in half
- 1 tsp red pepper flakes, divided in half
- 3 cups filtered/purified water
- ½ cup white vinegar
- 3 T sea salt or kosher salt
- 1 T organic sugar

Fresh Ingredients

- 1 small head cauliflower, cut into florets
- 2 large carrots, peeled and thickly sliced
- 2 large ribs celery, thickly sliced
- 1 red bell pepper, seeded and sliced lengthwise into spears
- 1 medium onion, halved and sliced
- 12 whole pickled Greek pepperoncini (from a jar)
- optional: pimento stuffed green olives

Supplies Needed

- 2 large mason jars (home canning jars) with lids and lid rings (or other suitable glass containers with lids)

Preparation

Place 1 bay leaf, 3 cloves chopped garlic, ½ teaspoon dried oregano and ½ teaspoon red pepper flakes in the bottom of each jar. Set aside.

Prepare the brine by mixing the water, vinegar, salt and sugar in a non-metal container. Stir with a plastic or wooden spoon until the salt and sugar dissolves. Set aside.

Bring 4 cups of water to a boil in a pot and blanch the carrots and cauliflower for 1 minute. Drain in a colander.

Divide the vegetables in half (approximately) and begin layering and gently packing them into the 2 jars. Pour in the brine to the top of each jar and seal with the lids. Refrigerate for a minimum of 1 week (the longer, the better), turning the jars over occasionally to distribute the seasonings. Serve with a drizzle of olive oil and coarse ground black pepper, if desired.

Raw Live Sauerkraut

Sauerkraut is German for "sour cabbage," but is originally a Chinese invention made with rice wine. Sauerkraut is made from finely cut cabbage that has been fermented by various lactic acid bacteria which propagate naturally during the fermentation process. It has a long shelf-life and a distinctively sour flavor, both of which result from the lactic acid that forms when the bacteria ferment the sugars in the cabbage.

Every chef has their own recipe for preparing sauerkraut and this is my personal formula and technique that works for me every time, with no undesirable mold blooms to skim from the surface of the brine during fermentation. I've modified my original recipe in order to produce plenty of sauerkraut juice (which I consider a special treat). Sauerkraut takes roughly 5 to 6 weeks from start to finish, so plan ahead and be patient - the results are worth waiting for.

Ingredients

- 2 large heads green or red cabbage
- ¼ cup sea salt or kosher salt
- 5 cups filtered/purified water
- 1 T dried juniper berries (optional)
- 2 tsp caraway seeds (optional)

Supplies Needed

- 1 gallon wide-mouthed clear glass jar
- cheesecloth
- 2 one-quart food storage bags
- plastic wrap

Preparation

Before beginning, make sure the jar has been washed thoroughly with hot, soapy water and rinsed well; or run through the heated cycle in a dishwasher.

In a large saucepan, bring the water and salt to a brief boil and then remove from the heat, cover and then let cool until lukewarm.

Remove any loose and damaged leaves from the heads of cabbage and either discard the leaves, save for preparing stock or compost. Split the heads of cabbage lengthwise (from the crown to the core). Cut a "V" shape to remove the tough core from each half.

Place a half head, cut side down, on a clean work surface and using a very sharp knife, begin to slice or "shave" the cabbage as thinly as possible to create very thin, long ribbons. You can also use a special shredder which is specifically designed for shredding cabbage (they can be ordered online). I have one that was made in Poland and it works beautifully.

Repeat with the remaining cabbage. Take your time slicing the cabbage, as very fine shreds will yield the best texture in the finished sauerkraut (personally, I use only the long, thin ribbons for the sauerkraut and save any pieces that are too large or too small for vegetable stock).

If using the juniper berries and/or caraway seeds, sprinkle half in the bottom of the jar. Place half of the shredded cabbage into the jar and add half of the cooled salted water. Using a potato masher or similar object, pack down the cabbage as firmly as possible. Sprinkle the remaining juniper berries and caraway over the cabbage.

Add the remaining shredded cabbage and salted water and firmly pack down again. Fold a double layer of cheesecloth in half and cut to fit into the jar with some excess for tucking. Place on top of the cabbage shreds and using a dull table knife, tuck the cheesecloth snugly around the inner circumference of the jar. This will hold the shreds in place and keep them from floating upwards in the brine. Pour the cooled salted water over the cheesecloth.

Fill a food storage bag about two-thirds-full of water and seal. Tuck the bag into the second food storage bag and seal. The second bag will ensure that no leaks of water occur from the water-filled bag.

Place the water-filled bag into the jar on top of the cheesecloth. The weight of the bag will keep the mass of cabbage completely submerged in the brine during fermentation. If the cabbage is submerged completely, no undesirable mold blooms will occur. Seal the top of the jar with plastic wrap to prevent evaporation of the brine.

Place the jar in a cool place (a basement or cool pantry being ideal). A room temperature of 68 to 72 degrees is best for fermenting cabbage. Formation of gas bubbles after a few days indicates fermentation is taking place. Mark your calendar for 5 to 6 weeks.

Once a week, check the jar. The formation of gas bubbles will sometimes cause the packed shreds to rise in the jar, which can potentially expose the surface to air, thus encouraging undesirable mold blooms. Simply remove the plastic film and re-tuck and push the cheesecloth down around the inner circumference with the edge of a spoon. There's no need to remove the bag of water; simply work around it (but be careful not to puncture the bag!). Re-seal the top of the jar with plastic wrap.

When fermentation is complete, pack individual mason jars with the sauerkraut and add enough brine to keep the shreds covered with the liquid, while leaving ½-inch of headspace in the jar. Fully fermented sauerkraut can be kept tightly covered in the refrigerator for a few months. The sauerkraut can be eaten raw, which promotes a healthy intestinal flora; or it can be cooked and used in your favorite recipe.

Sweets and Treats

Lemon Meringue Pie

Tangy and refreshing lemon curd is poured into a pre-baked pie crust and then chilled until set. The pie is then topped with billowy clouds of eggless meringue and lightly baked to perfection.

About the meringue: The recipe and technique for the eggless meringue is an adaptation of a recipe and technique created by Goose Wohlt, who coined the term "aquafaba" and who was the first to use aquafaba in a meringue application (as far as I know).

For the meringue you will need a stand mixer with a balloon whip attachment or a handheld electric rotary mixer with a whip attachment or 2 beaters.

Pie Crust

- 1 nine-inch basic vegan pie crust or graham cracker pie crust

Pie Filling Ingredients

- 12 oz/340 grams extra-firm **silken** tofu, drained
- 1 and ¼ cup organic sugar
- 1 cup water
- ¾ cup fresh lemon juice
- 5 T cornstarch or unmodified potato starch
- 1 T fresh grated lemon zest
- ¼ tsp fine sea salt

Meringue Ingredients

- ½ cup organic sugar*
- 1 can (15 oz) cooked white beans** (Great Northern, cannellini or white navy) or garbanzo beans (chickpeas), **with no added salt**
- ¼ tsp guar gum, xanthan gum or sodium alginate (food gum stabilizes the meringue and discourages deflation when baked)
- ½ tsp real vanilla extract

In this recipe, the powdered sugar is created from scratch using organic sugar. If you wish to skip this step, simply substitute the organic sugar with commercial organic powdered sugar.

**In my opinion, white bean liquid possesses a milder flavor and a larger amount of natural mucilage than chickpea liquid, which makes it ideal for this application.*

Preparation

In a dry blender process the meringue sugar (½ cup) until finely powdered. Set the powdered sugar aside in a small bowl. This will be used for preparing the meringue and is not added to the pie filling mixture.

Preheat the oven to 375°F/190°C. Bake the pie crust for 12 to 15 minutes or until lightly browned around the edges. Remove and set aside to cool.

In the same blender, process the pie filling ingredients until smooth. Pour the blender contents into a large saucepan and cook over medium heat, stirring frequently with a flexible spatula. The mixture will be foamy and milky in appearance. Stir constantly as the mixture begins to thicken. Keep stirring until the mixture begins to bubble and the milky and foamy appearance transforms into a thick and gelatinous lemon curd.

Pour the filling into the pie crust, smooth the top gently with a rubber/silicone spatula or t he back of a spoon and place in the refrigerator uncovered for a minimum of 2 hours until the top of the pie is firmly set.

After the pie has chilled for a minimum of 2 hours, preheat the oven to 200°F/90°C while preparing the meringue.

Preparing the Meringue

Strain the liquid from the can of beans into a large mixing bowl or the bowl of a stand mixer (reserve the beans for other uses). Sprinkle in the food gum or alginate and begin whipping on high speed for 3 full minutes.

Gradually begin to incorporate the powdered sugar, in increments, while whipping. Continue to whip the mixture until soft peaks begin to form. Add the vanilla and continue to whip the mixture until it is voluminous and stiff peaks begin to form. This will take several more minutes.

Spoon and spread the meringue onto the surface of the pie, avoiding the edges by ½-inch. Create soft peaks in the meringue using the back of a spoon. Bake in the oven for 30 minutes.

To lightly brown the meringue after baking, set the oven on "Broil" and position the pie on an oven rack close to the flame source. Keep the oven door open while doing this and watch the meringue carefully - it will brown quickly and can burn easily. Rotate the pie as needed until the peaks are evenly browned. The peaks of the meringue can also be browned using a butane kitchen torch.

Remove to cool for about 5 minutes and then place the pie in the refrigerator uncovered to chill thoroughly for several hours until completely set before serving. Keep any leftover pie refrigerated but do not cover or the meringue will turn into a gooey liquid.

For Mini Lemon Meringue Tarts

Prepare the pie filling according to the recipe. Fill individual frozen mini filo cups with the filling and refrigerate as recommended. Then top with a small dollop of meringue and bake according to the directions. Refrigerate until chilled and serve.

Key Lime Pie

A graham cracker pie shell is filled with a citrusy and refreshing key lime curd. The pie can be topped with non-dairy whipped cream if desired; or simply garnish with additional lime wedges or zest.

Pie Crust

- 1 nine-inch basic vegan pie crust or graham cracker pie crust

Pie Filling Ingredients

- 12 oz/340 grams extra-firm **silken** tofu, drained
- 1 and ¼ cup organic sugar
- 1 cup (240 ml) water
- ¾ cup fresh key lime or regular lime juice
- 5 T cornstarch or unmodified potato starch
- 1 T fresh grated key lime zest
- ¼ tsp sea salt

Preparation

Preheat the oven to 375°F/190°C. Bake the pie shell for 12 minutes. Remove and set aside to cool.

In a blender, process the pie filling ingredients until smooth. Pour the blender contents into a large saucepan and cook over medium heat, stirring frequently with a rubber or silicone spatula and scraping the sides of the saucepan as you stir. The mixture will be foamy and milky in appearance. Stir constantly as the mixture begins to thicken. Keep stirring until the mixture begins to bubble and the milky and foamy appearance transforms into a thick and gelatinous lime curd.

Pour the filling into the pie crust, smooth the top gently with a rubber/silicone spatula or the back of a spoon and place in the refrigerator uncovered for 2 hours until the top of the pie is firmly set. After 2 hours, cover with plastic wrap. Garnish with non-dairy whipped topping and/or lime wedges or zest, if desired, before serving.

Bananas Foster Chimichangas

Ripe bananas cooked in a sweet butter rum sauce are rolled in a flour tortilla, fried until crisp and golden brown and served hot with a scoop of non-dairy vanilla ice cream and dusting of cinnamon. This recipe yields 2 large dessert portions or 4 smaller portions.

Ingredients

- 3 ripe but firm bananas
- ¼ cup non-dairy butter or margarine
- ½ cup light brown sugar
- 2 T dark rum
- 2 ten-inch flour tortillas
- Vanilla Bean Ice Cream (recipe follows) or commercial non-dairy vanilla ice cream
- ground cinnamon for dusting
- cooking oil for frying
- 2 toothpicks for securing rolled tortilla

Preparation

Peel and slice the bananas. Melt the butter or margarine in a medium skillet over medium-high heat. Stir in the brown sugar. Add the bananas and toss to coat with the butter and sugar mixture. Remove the pan from the heat and add the rum. Place back over the heat and cook until the bananas have softened and the butter mixture has thickened slightly. Remove from the heat.

Spoon ¼ of the bananas onto a tortilla and roll up like a burrito, tucking in the ends. Secure with a toothpick. Repeat with the remaining tortilla. Reserve the remaining banana and rum sauce mixture for topping the chimichangas after frying.

Add a thin but complete layer of cooking oil to another skillet and place over medium-high heat. Fry the chimichangas until golden brown, turning with tongs to brown them evenly. They will brown quickly. Transfer to a plate lined with a paper towel to drain.

Cut each chimichanga in half and transfer to a dessert plate. Top with a scoop of ice cream, then the banana and sauce mixture and garnish with a dusting of cinnamon. Serve immediately.

Vanilla Bean (or Chocolate) Ice Cream

The sugar content in homemade ice cream is balanced with the cream content which acts as an anti-freeze to prevent it from freezing solid. An assortment of other ingredients, such as chopped nuts, chopped dried fruit, and bits of dark chocolate, etc. can be added as desired. The ice cream mixture is typically cooked to dissolve the sugar but the blender works well for this purpose - no cooking required. However, an ice cream maker is required for this recipe.

Ingredients

- 3 and ½ cups soymilk or almond milk*, room temperature
- 1 and ¼ cup organic sugar
- 2 tsp real vanilla extract
- caviar (pulp) scraped from 1 split vanilla bean
- ½ tsp guar gum, sodium alginate or xanthan gum
- ½ cup refined or virgin coconut oil, melted

For chocolate ice cream: Omit the vanilla bean and add ⅓ cup unsweetened cocoa or carob powder.

Preparation

Begin processing all ingredients, except for the coconut oil, in a blender. With the blender running, add the coconut oil in a slow but steady stream. Continue to process about 20 seconds and then transfer to a sealable container and refrigerate until very cold. When well chilled, pour the cream mixture into your ice cream maker. Process the mixture according to your ice cream maker's instructions and then freeze to firm. To serve, thaw briefly until it reaches the desired texture for scooping.

Fresh Fruit Ice Cream
(Cashew Cream Base)

Heavy cashew cream and puréed fruit form the base for this delightful frozen treat. An ice cream maker is required for this recipe.

Ingredients

- 1 cup (5 oz/142 grams) raw cashews
- 2 cups non-dairy milk of your choice
- ¾ cup organic sugar
- ½ tsp guar gum
- 2 cups chilled fruit purée, smooth or semi-chunky

Preparation

Place the cashews and milk into a container with a lid, seal and place in the refrigerator to soak for a minimum of 8 hours. After soaking, place the ingredients in a high-powered blender and process on high speed for 2 full minutes.

The cream will now need to be strained to remove the solids. To do this, pour the cream into the nut milk bag over a large bowl or pitcher.

While holding the top of the bag with one hand, gently knead the bag to help the cream pass through the ultra-fine mesh – avoid forcing the cream through. Discard or compost the solids in the bag.

Optionally, the cream can be poured (in increments) into a strainer lined with 4 layers of cheesecloth. Stir the cream gently with a spoon to help it pass through the cheesecloth.

Pour the heavy cream into a blender and add the sugar and guar gum; process until smooth. Pour the mixture into a container and refrigerate until very cold (or place in the freezer for about 30 minutes).

When well chilled, pour the cream mixture into your ice cream maker and add the chilled fruit purée. Process the mixture according to your ice cream maker's instructions.

Milk Chocolate Pudding

Rich, creamy and deliciously non-dairy. This recipe yields about 3 cups or six ½ cup servings.

Ingredients

- ½ cup (2.5 oz/71 grams) raw cashews (pre-soaking unnecessary)
- 2 and ½ cups (600 ml) non-dairy milk
- 2 T cornstarch or unmodified potato starch
- 1 cup organic sugar
- ⅓ cup unsweetened cocoa powder
- 2 tsp real vanilla extract
- ¼ tsp sea salt or kosher salt

Preparation

Place a medium mesh strainer over a large glass bowl or BPA-free plastic storage container and set aside.

Add all ingredients to a blender and process on high speed for 2 full minutes. Stop to scrape down the sides of the blender as necessary.

Pour the mixture into a large saucepan and place over medium heat. Stir slowly and continually with a whisk. Whisk vigorously as the mixture begins to thicken (vigorous whisking will help to prevent lumps from forming). Continue whisking until the mixture begins to bubble.

Pour the mixture into the strainer over the container and stir with the whisk to press the mixture through the mesh. Cover the container with a lid or plastic wrap and let cool for about 15 minutes and then refrigerate for several hours until well-chilled.

To serve, stir the mixture thoroughly and spoon into individual dessert cups. Garnish the individual cups with non-dairy whipped cream, if desired.

Chocolate Mousse Torte

This sinfully rich and decadent chocolate mousse torte is the real deal: Semisweet chocolate ganache is folded into fluffy non-dairy whipped cream and chilled on a chocolate cookie crust, topped with more whipped cream and garnished with shaved chocolate. If you're looking for a low-calorie, low fat, healthy dessert, this recipe is not for you.

Ingredients

- 2 cups soymilk, room temperature plus an additional ⅔ cup for the ganache (sorry, no substitutes)
- 2 cups refined or virgin coconut oil, melted
- ½ tsp guar gum or xanthan gum
- ⅔ cup organic powdered sugar
- 1 tsp real vanilla extract
- 8 oz non-dairy semi-sweet baker's chocolate
- 16 non-dairy chocolate sandwich cookies (e.g., Newman-O's™; Oreos™)

Supplies Needed

- 8-inch springform pan
- parchment paper
- cooking oil spray
- stand mixer with whip attachment or handheld electric mixer with rotary beaters or whisk attachment
- food processor
- pastry bag with decorative tip for piping the whipped cream

Advance Preparation

Prepare the whipping cream (this is best done the day before preparation of the torte). Add the 2 cups of soymilk to a blender with the food gum and begin processing on high speed. Incorporate the melted coconut oil in a slow but steady stream while processing. Transfer the cream to a sealable container and refrigerate until thoroughly chilled, a minimum of 12 hours. The cream must be very cold or it will not whip properly.

Preparation

Place a large mixing bowl, along with the mixer attachments, in the refrigerator to chill.

Shave some of the chocolate with a vegetable peeler or paring knife and set aside to be used as a garnish for the torte before serving. This is optional but makes a lovely presentation. Break the remaining chocolate into pieces which will be melted for the ganache later.

Scoop the chilled, thickened cream into the chilled mixing bowl, add the vanilla, and begin whipping on high speed. Add the powdered sugar in increments while whipping and continue until the cream has stiff peaks. This will take a few minutes. Avoid overwhipping or the cream will eventually separate and turn into sweet butter. Place the bowl of whipped cream into the refrigerator to stay cold.

Line the bottom of the springform pan with parchment and mist the sides with cooking oil. Place the cookies into the food processor and process until finely ground. Press the cookie mixture into the bottom of the pan. Set aside.

In a small sauce pan, bring the remaining soymilk to a brief simmer. Remove from the heat and add the broken chocolate. Whisk until melted and smooth. Place in the refrigerator to cool about 20 minutes.

Transfer half of the whipped cream to another mixing bowl (the remaining whipped cream will be piped onto the chocolate mousse later, so keep it chilled until ready to use). Fold in the cooled chocolate ganache and continue to fold until no white streaks remain. Spoon into the springform pan and spread evenly even over the crust. Cover with wrap and chill for a few hours to set.

Remove the torte from the springform pan and transfer to a serving plate. Using the pastry bag with a decorative tip, pipe the remaining whipped cream onto the mousse. Garnish with shaved chocolate and serve.

'Nog Cheesecake
with Brandied Caramel Sauce

Not too fluffy and yet not too dense, this lusciously smooth non-dairy cheesecake captures the flavor of holiday eggnog without the eggs and without the dairy.

Premade non-dairy cream cheese is not required because the cheesecake filling is created in one easy step. However, the proper baking items are required for success, so please follow the recipe and technique as written.

The filling also requires two specialty ingredients, kappa carrageenan and lactic acid powder, which can be purchased from ModernistPantry.com and other online retailers such as Amazon.com. These ingredients are also commonly used in vegan cheese making.

Special Kitchen Items

- 8" springform pan
- 9" cake pan
- large pan for the bain-marie (water bath)
- large baking sheet to support the bain-marie (optional)
- large food storage container for chilling/storing the cheesecake
- parchment paper
- cooking oil spray
- blender
- food processor (optional)

Ingredients for the Crust

- 1 commercial vegan graham cracker crust

Ingredients for the Cheesecake Filling

- 2 cups (10 oz/284 grams) raw cashews (do not presoak in water)
- 3 cups homemade or commercial soymilk (sorry, no substitutes; this recipe relies on the curdling action of the soymilk when the lactic acid is introduced)
- ¾ cup organic sugar
- ¼ cup nutritional yeast flakes
- 3 T brandy or dark rum
- 4 tsp kappa carrageenan
- ½ tsp ground nutmeg plus ¼ tsp for garnish
- ¼ tsp sea salt
- 4 tsp lactic acid powder

Ingredients for the Brandied Caramel Sauce

- ½ cup packed light brown sugar
- 3 T non-dairy milk
- 2 T non-dairy butter or margarine
- 1 T brandy or dark rum (omit for plain caramel sauce)

Preparation

Trace the circumference of the bottom of the springform pan on parchment paper and cut. Assemble the springform pan and spray the interior generously with cooking oil. Line the bottom with the parchment paper and mist the paper with cooking oil.

Position an oven rack in the middle of the oven. Preheat the oven to 325°F/165°C.

Process the graham cracker crust in a food processor until finely ground. Alternately, crush the crust into crumbs in a large bowl. Add the crumbs to the oiled and lined springform pan and pack evenly on the bottom and halfway up the sides. The oiled pan will help the crumbs stick to the sides. Set aside.

Add the dry raw cashews to a blender with the soymilk and process on high speed for 2 full minutes. Add the remaining filling ingredients except for the lactic acid and process until thoroughly blended. With the blender running, add the lactic acid all at once. The mixture will immediately thicken and stop turning in the blades – turn the blender off.

Pour the filling into the springform pan and gently shake the pan side to side or tap the sides to release any air bubbles and help the filling settle.

Place the springform pan into the cake pan and set the cake pan into the bain-marie. Do not use aluminum foil as an alternative to the cake pan for preventing water from leaking into the springform pan. Water will condense inside the foil and ruin the cheesecake. Trust me on this one. If using an aluminum roasting pan for the bain-marie, place it on a large baking sheet for support and for ease transferring to and from the oven.

Pour very hot tap water into the bain-marie halfway up the sides of the cake pan. Be careful not to splash water into the cheesecake filling.

Transfer to the oven and bake for 2 hours.

Remove from the oven and carefully remove the cake pan from the water bath. Let the cheesecake cool to room temperature and then remove from the cake pan and release from the springform mold. Leave the cheesecake on the bottom of the springform mold and transfer to the storage container. Seal and refrigerate until thoroughly chilled.

About an hour before serving, prepare the sauce. Add the sauce ingredients to a small saucepan and bring to a brief boil while swirling the saucepan contents occasionally. Watch carefully or the sauce may boil over. Immediately reduce to a simmer and cook for exactly 4 minutes, again swirling the contents occasionally. Set aside to cool at room temperature.

To transfer the cheesecake to a serving plate, carefully slide a thin flexible spatula between the parchment paper and the crust and slide onto the plate. Moisten a knife with warm water to slice the cheesecake. Drizzle individual slices with the sauce. Store the cheesecake in the sealed container in the refrigerator.

Holiday Gingersnap Cheesecake

This lusciously smooth non-dairy and egg-free holiday cheesecake is flavored with molasses, ginger, cinnamon and clove and baked in a gingersnap crust. If desired, top with non-dairy whipped cream and a dusting of cinnamon before serving.

Premade non-dairy cream cheese is not required because the cheesecake filling is created in one easy step. However, the proper baking items are required for success, so please follow the recipe and technique as written.

The filling also requires two specialty ingredients, kappa carrageenan and lactic acid powder, which can be purchased from ModernistPantry.com and other online retailers such as Amazon.com. These ingredients are also commonly used in vegan cheese making.

Special Kitchen Items

- 8" springform pan
- 9" cake pan
- large pan for the bain-marie (water bath)
- large baking sheet to support the bain-marie (optional)
- large food storage container for chilling/storing the cheesecake
- parchment paper
- cooking oil spray
- blender
- food processor

Ingredients for the Crust

- 10 oz vegan gingersnap cookies
- ¼ cup non-dairy butter or margarine, softened

Ingredients for the Cheesecake Filling

- 2 cups (10 oz/284 grams) raw cashews (do not presoak in water)
- 3 cups plain soymilk (sorry, no substitutes; this recipe relies on the curdling action of the soymilk when the lactic acid is introduced)
- ¾ cup organic sugar
- 3 T unsulfured molasses
- 4 tsp kappa carrageenan
- 1 tsp ground ginger
- ½ tsp ground cinnamon
- ¼ tsp ground cloves
- ¼ tsp sea salt
- 4 tsp lactic acid powder

Preparation

Trace the circumference of the bottom of the springform pan on parchment paper and cut. Assemble the springform pan and spray the interior with cooking oil. Line the bottom with the parchment paper and mist the paper with cooking oil.

Position an oven rack in the middle of the oven. Preheat the oven to 325°F/165°C.

Process the gingersnap cookies and softened butter/margarine in a food processor until finely ground. Add the crumbs to the oiled and lined springform pan and pack evenly on the bottom and halfway up the sides. Set aside.

Add the dry raw cashews to a blender with the soymilk and process on high speed for 2 full minutes. Add the remaining filling ingredients except for the lactic acid and process until thoroughly blended. With the blender running, add the lactic acid all at once. The mixture will immediately thicken and stop turning in the blades – turn the blender off.

Pour the filling into the springform pan and gently shake the pan side to side or tap the sides to release any air bubbles and help the filling settle.

Place the springform pan into the cake pan and set the cake pan into the bain-marie. Do not use aluminum foil as an alternative to the cake pan for preventing water from leaking into the springform pan. Water will condense inside the foil and ruin the cheesecake. Trust me on this one. If using an aluminum roasting pan for the bain-marie, place it on a large baking sheet for support and for ease transferring to and from the oven.

Pour very hot tap water into the bain-marie halfway up the sides of the cake pan. Be careful not to splash water into the cheesecake filling.

Transfer to the oven and bake for 2 hours.

Remove from the oven and carefully remove the cake pan from the water bath. Let the cheesecake cool to room temperature and then remove from the cake pan and release from the springform mold. Leave the cheesecake on the bottom of the springform mold and transfer to the storage container. Seal and refrigerate until thoroughly chilled.

To transfer the cheesecake to a serving plate, carefully slide a thin flexible spatula between the parchment paper and the crust and slide onto the plate. Moisten a knife with warm water to slice the cheesecake. Top with non-dairy whipped cream and a dusting of cinnamon before serving, if desired. Store the cheesecake in the sealed container in the refrigerator.

Chocolate Lover's Cheesecake

A semi-sweet chocolate lover's dream without the eggs and without the dairy! Premade non-dairy cream cheese is not required because the cheesecake filling is created in one easy step. However, the proper baking items are required for success, so please follow the recipe and technique as written.

The filling also requires two specialty ingredients, kappa carrageenan and lactic acid powder, which can be purchased from ModernistPantry.com and other online retailers such as Amazon.com. These ingredients are also commonly used in vegan cheese making.

Special Kitchen Items

- 8" springform pan
- 9" cake pan
- large pan for the bain-marie (water bath)
- large baking sheet to support the bain-marie (optional)
- large food storage container for chilling/storing the cheesecake
- parchment paper
- cooking oil spray
- blender
- food processor

Ingredients for the Crust

- 16 non-dairy chocolate sandwich cookies (e.g., Newman-O's™; Oreos™)

Ingredients for the Cheesecake Filling

- 2 cups (10 oz/284 grams) raw cashews (do not presoak in water)
- 3 cups homemade or commercial soymilk (sorry, no substitutes; this recipe relies on the curdling action of the soymilk when the lactic acid is introduced)
- 8 oz non-dairy semi-sweet baker's chocolate
- ¾ cup organic sugar
- 1 and ½ tsp kappa carrageenan
- ¼ tsp sea salt
- 2 tsp real vanilla extract
- 4 tsp lactic acid powder

Preparation

Trace the circumference of the bottom of the springform pan on parchment paper and cut. Assemble the springform pan and spray the interior generously with cooking oil. Line the bottom with the parchment paper and mist the paper with cooking oil.

Shave a bit of the chocolate with a vegetable peeler or paring knife and set aside to be used as a garnish for the cheesecake before serving. This is optional but makes a lovely presentation. Break the remaining chocolate into pieces which will be melted for the ganache later.

Position an oven rack in the middle of the oven. Preheat the oven to 325°F/165°C.

Place the cookies into the food processor and process until finely ground. Add the crumbs to the oiled and lined springform pan and pack evenly on the bottom. Set aside.

In a small saucepan, bring 1 cup of the soymilk to a brief simmer. Remove from the heat and add the chocolate pieces (not the shaved pieces saved for garnish). Whisk the ganache until completely melted and smooth. Set aside.

Add the dry raw cashews to a blender with the remaining 2 cups of soymilk and process on high speed for 2 full minutes. Add the remaining filling ingredients except for the lactic acid and process until thoroughly blended. Add the melted chocolate mixture and blend until smooth.

With the blender running, add the lactic acid all at once. The mixture will immediately thicken and stop turning in the blades - turn the blender off.

Pour the filling into the springform pan and gently shake the pan side to side or tap the sides to release any air bubbles and help the filling settle.

Place the springform pan into the cake pan and set the cake pan into the bain-marie. Do not use aluminum foil as an alternative to the cake pan for preventing water from leaking into the springform pan. Water will condense inside the foil and ruin the cheesecake. Trust me on this one. If using an aluminum roasting pan for the bain-marie, place it on a large baking sheet for support and for ease transferring to and from the oven.

Pour very hot tap water into the bain-marie halfway up the sides of the cake pan. Be careful not to splash water into the cheesecake filling.

Transfer to the oven and bake for 2 hours.

Remove from the oven and carefully remove the cake pan from the water bath. Let the cheesecake cool to room temperature and then remove from the cake pan and release from the springform mold. Leave the cheesecake on the bottom of the springform mold and transfer to the storage container. Seal and refrigerate until thoroughly chilled.

To transfer the cheesecake to a serving plate, carefully slide a thin flexible spatula between the parchment paper and the crust and slide onto the plate. Moisten a knife with warm water to slice the cheesecake. Store the cheesecake in the sealed container in the refrigerator.

Classic Holiday Pumpkin Pie

A favorite Autumn and Winter treat and perfect for celebrating the holidays. Vegan pumpkin pies are often made with tofu as a replacement for the evaporated milk and eggs. Although I use tofu frequently and successfully in eggless egg recipes and desserts, I find its undertaste to be rather noticeable and distracting in pumpkin pie. Therefore, my goal was to create a pumpkin pie using a creamy cashew base which allows the flavor of the pumpkin and the warm spices to predominate.

Ingredients

- 1 nine-inch vegan graham cracker pie shell or basic pastry crust
- ½ cup (2.5 oz/71 grams) whole raw cashews
- 1 cup non-dairy milk
- ¾ cup light brown sugar packed
- 2 T cornstarch or unmodified potato starch
- 1 tsp ground cinnamon
- ½ tsp ground ginger
- ¼ tsp ground cloves
- ¼ tsp ground nutmeg
- ¼ tsp fine sea salt
- 1 can (15 oz) pumpkin purée

Preparation

Soak the cashews in water in the refrigerator for about 8 hours to soften and hydrate. To expedite the soaking process, pour boiling water over the cashews and let soak for 1 hour.

Preheat the oven to 425°F/220°C.

Drain the cashews and add them to a high-powered blender. Add the non-dairy milk and process for 2 full minutes.

Add the remaining ingredients and process until completely smooth. The mixture will be quite thick, so occasionally stop to scrape down the sides of the blender with a spatula and stir the contents back down into the blades as necessary. Use a tamper tool if provided with your blender.

Spoon the mixture into the pie shell and smooth the surface with a spatula or large spoon. Don't worry about a few swirl marks as they will minimize when the pie cools. Place the pie on the middle rack of the oven and bake for 15 minutes.

Reduce the heat to 350°F/175°C and continue to bake for an additional 50 to 55 minutes or until a toothpick inserted in the center of the pie comes out clean (do not exceed 60 minutes).

Remove the pie and cool completely on a wire rack (until the underside of the pie plate no longer feels warm). Loosely cover with plastic wrap and refrigerate until completely chilled and firm before slicing and serving. Try to avoid laying the plastic wrap in direct contact with the surface of the pie as moisture condensation will result. The pie can also be chilled in a large, sealable storage container. Top individual slices with a dollop of non-dairy whipped cream, if desired.

Note: The surface of the pie will appear dry after baking; this will resolve once cooled and chilled.

Panna Cotta

Panna cotta (Italian for "cooked cream") is an Italian dessert of thickened sweetened cream set in a mold. The cream may be classically flavored with vanilla, or with rum, coffee and other flavorings.

Ingredients

- 2 cups soymilk or almond milk, room temperature
- ½ cup organic sugar
- 1 and ½ tsp kappa carrageenan
- 2 tsp real vanilla extract
- 1 cup refined or virgin coconut oil, melted

Items Needed

- silicone mold(s) for shaping the panna cotta
- blender

Preparation

Add the soymilk or almond milk to a blender with the sugar, kappa and vanilla. Begin processing. With the blender running, incorporate the coconut oil in a slow but steady stream.

Transfer the mixture to a medium saucepan and cook over medium heat, stirring frequently, until the mixture comes to a simmer. Do not leave the pan unattended as the mixture can boil over. Divide the mixture between the molds. Let cool about 30 minutes and then refrigerate until completely chilled and set.

To serve, unmold onto a serving plate and top with your favorite fruits, sweet sauces, syrups, or garnishes as desired.

Eggless Egg Custard Pie

This egg-free and dairy-free custard pie is very easy to prepare. It has a sliceable but delicate, silky texture and can be used for custard pie as suggested or served on its own in individual dessert ramekins. This recipe yields enough custard for 1 nine-inch pie or 7 half-cup servings.

Ingredients

- 3 and ⅓ cups non-dairy milk
- 3 T cornstarch or unmodified potato starch
- ¾ cup organic sugar (for a sweeter custard increase by ¼ cup)
- 2 T nutritional yeast flakes
- 1 and ½ tsp agar powder
- 1 tsp real vanilla extract
- ⅛ tsp fine sea salt or kosher salt (a pinch)
- 2 T non-dairy butter or margarine
- fresh grated nutmeg for dusting (about ¼ tsp)
- 1 nine-inch unbaked pie shell of your choice

Preparation

Prebake the pie shell in advance for the time recommended for that particular crust.

Preheat the oven to 375°F/190°C. Although the custard is cooked in a saucepan, the oven is necessary for finishing and creating a golden "baked custard" surface.

To prepare the custard, pour the milk into a large saucepan and whisk in the starch until dissolved. Add the remaining ingredients except for the nutmeg and place over medium heat. Please note that the butter or margarine will melt and combine as the mixture heats. Cook until the mixture comes to a soft boil while stirring constantly with a flexible spatula to prevent scorching. Do not walk away from the mixture as it heats or it can quickly boil over. Remove the saucepan from the heat.

Pour the custard into the pre-baked pie shell and dust with the nutmeg. Place the pie on a baking sheet and bake for 10 minutes.

Let the custard cool until the bottom of the pie pan is lukewarm. Unlike traditional egg custard which cooks and sets in the oven, eggless custard sets as it cools. Transfer to the refrigerator and chill uncovered until completely set, about 1 hour. Once set, loosely cover with plastic wrap until ready to serve.

For Custard without a Pie Crust

Pour the custard mixture into 7 individual ramekins and dust with the nutmeg. Place the ramekins on a baking sheet and bake for 5 minutes. Remove from the oven to cool. Unlike traditional egg custard which cooks and sets in the oven, eggless custard sets as it cools. Let the custard cool until the bottoms of the individual ramekins are lukewarm. Transfer to the refrigerator and chill uncovered until completely set, about 1 hour. Once set, loosely cover with plastic wrap until ready to serve.

Chef's Favorite Chocolate Chip Cookies

Store the cookies in an airtight container or food storage bag as soon as they're cool to retain freshness. Serve with an ice-cold glass of non-dairy milk. Pure nirvana!

Ingredients

- ½ cup neutral vegetable oil
- 1 cup packed light brown sugar
- ¼ cup soymilk or almond milk
- ½ tsp baking soda
- 2 tsp real vanilla extract
- 1 and ¾ cup all-purpose flour (measure by scoop and level)
- 1 pkg (about 10 oz) semi-sweet chocolate chips (make sure they're vegan)
- optional: ½ cup chopped nuts of your choice

Preparation

Preheat the oven to 375°F/190°C.

Cream together the oil and the brown sugar.

Add the milk, baking soda and vanilla and mix well.

Add the flour and mix well. The dough will be stiff.

Fold the chocolate chips and optional nuts into the dough.

Drop by the large tablespoonful onto a non-stick cookie sheet (you will need to bake in two batches) and bake for approximately 13 to 15 minutes (until lightly kissed with golden-brown around the edges). Transfer to a plate to cool.

Whole Grain Bread Pudding
With Drunken Raisins and Salted Caramel Sauce

Ingredients for the Bread Pudding

- 12 standard slices day-old whole grain bread, cubed
- ½ cup raisins
- brandy, rum, whiskey or water (for rehydrating the raisins)
- 12 oz/340 grams extra-firm **silken** tofu, drained
- 1 and ¼ cup soymilk or almond milk
- ¾ cup organic sugar
- ¼ cup cornstarch or unmodified potato starch
- 2 T nutritional yeast flakes
- 2 T non-dairy butter or margarine, softened; plus, additional for greasing the baking dish
- 2 tsp real vanilla extract
- ½ tsp ground cinnamon, plus additional for sprinkling over pudding
- ¼ tsp ground nutmeg
- pinch fine sea salt

Ingredients for the Salted Caramel Sauce

- ¼ cup non-dairy butter or margarine
- ½ cup light brown sugar
- 2 T non-dairy milk
- ½ tsp fine sea salt

Preparation

Place the raisins in a small dish and add just enough liquor or water to cover. Let stand until the raisins have absorbed as much liquid as possible, about 1 hour. Drain and discard any excess liquid.

Grease an 8-inch baking dish with non-dairy butter or margarine; set aside. Preheat the oven to 375°F/190°C.

Place the cubed bread into large mixing bowl and set aside.

Add the remaining bread pudding ingredients to a blender and process until smooth. Pour the contents over the cubed bread and toss thoroughly until the mixture is absorbed into the bread. Add the raisins and toss to combine. Transfer the moistened bread to the baking dish and bake uncovered 1 hour. Remove from the oven to cool until warm or room temperature. Cooling is important as this will help set the pudding.

For the caramel sauce, add the butter and brown sugar to a small saucepan and place over medium-low heat. Cook, stirring frequently, until the sugar dissolves and the caramel mixture begins to bubble. Whisk in the non-dairy milk and stir until smooth. Add the salt and bring to a boil. Remove from the heat to cool and thicken for 5 minutes before serving. Plate the bread pudding and drizzle the warm caramel sauce on top. Serve immediately.

Alphabetical Recipe Index